# Storycrafting

## A Process Approach to Writing News

# Storycrafting

## A Process Approach to Writing News

### Kenneth L. Rosenauer

**Blackwell**
Publishing

**KENNETH L. ROSENAUER** is department chair and associate professor of journalism and English at Missouri Western State College in St. Joseph. He has worked at the *St. Joseph* (Missouri) *News-Press* and the *Savannah* (Missouri) *Reporter*. Dr. Rosenauer has been editor of *College Media Review*, the flagship journal of College Media Advisers. He also was editor of *CMA Newsletter*. He was inducted into the College Media Advisers Hall of Fame in 2003.

©2004 Blackwell Publishing

Blackwell Publishing Professional
2121 State Avenue, Ames, Iowa 50014, USA

| | |
|---|---|
| Orders: | 1-800-862-6657 |
| Office: | 1-515-292-0140 |
| Fax: | 1-515-292-3348 |
| Web site: | www.blackwellprofessional.com |

Blackwell Publishing Ltd
9600 Garsington Road, Oxford OX4 2DQ, UK
Tel.: +44 (0)1865 776868

Blackwell Publishing Asia
550 Swanston Street, Carlton, Victoria 3053, Australia
Tel.: +61 (0)3 8359 1011

Authorization to photocopy items for internal or personal use, or the internal or personal use of specific clients, is granted by Blackwell Publishing, provided that the base fee of $.10 per copy is paid directly to the Copyright Clearance Center, 222 Rosewood Drive, Danvers, MA 01923. For those organizations that have been granted a photocopy license by CCC, a separate system of payments has been arranged. The fee code for users of the Transactional Reporting Service is 0-8138-0946-0/2004 $.10.

Printed on acid-free paper in the United States of America

First edition, 2004


Library of Congress Cataloging-in-Publication Data

Rosenauer, Kenneth L. (Kenneth Lee), 1949-
   Storycrafting : a process approach to writing news / Kenneth L. Rosenauer.—1st ed.
       p. cm.
   Includes bibliographical references and indexes.
   ISBN 0-8138-0946-0 (alk. paper)
   1. Journalism—Authorship. I. Title.

   PN4781.R57 2004
   808'.06607—dc22
                                         2003028032


The last digit is the print number:  9  8  7  6  5  4  3  2  1

# Dedication

To Janet
Wife and Best Friend

# Contents

# Chapter 7.
# Content, 111

# Chapter 8.
# Evidence: Human
# Sources, 129

## Chapter 18.
## The First Amendment,
## Libel and Privacy, 317

## Chapter 19.
## Trends: Public Journalism
## and Convergence, 333

## Index, 351

# Preface

Welcome to "Storycrafting." This textbook is user-friendly. More importantly, it is user-helpful in leading you to hone your skills as a storyteller, particularly as a story-teller-journalist. This is not a simple task. Good writing seldom is. You will find that writing stories demands much, but this textbook can help you meet the challenge.

Most news writing textbooks focus on the product, news stories, and then leave you to your own devices to figure out how to write them—the "see this, now do this" school of writing. It is a lot like being shown a piece of chocolate cake—even encouraged to taste it—and then expected to go bake one just like it. A difficult if not impossible task.

"Storycrafting," however, shows you the "chocolate cake" and then gives you the recipe you can follow to bake your own. The recipe is the writing process, a term with which many of you already may be familiar. It recognizes that writing success is contingent upon three kinds of activity:

- Gathering the material for the story.
- Shaping it into a story form that works well for both the material and readers.
- Revising, polishing and proofreading the final story draft.

The "chocolate cake" largely is comprised of stories from the campus press—student journalists writing for college and university newspapers across the country. Their stories are much like your stories, written about similar experiences and for similar readers.

Another essential component of the process that "Storycrafting" encourages is regular, appropriate feedback, first from peers in your class and then from your teacher. Your peers respond to your drafts as interested readers, members of your campus community who happen to be dealing with the same issues as you—both inside the classroom and out. Your teacher is your coach, who serves many roles, including guide, adviser, investor, mechanic, cheerleader, director, reader and evaluator.

Finally, the "Storycrafting" process recognizes the value of community:

- The campus community of which you are an active member.
- The writers community with whom you work in the classroom.
- The readers community to whom you write.

Your campus is a place where many of you live. Certainly, it is a place where all of you work as students. It is a community very much like cities, towns and villages across the country, with governing bodies, business activities and social events. It is *your* community, and it is about this community that you will write your news stories.

Your writers community, as we noted earlier, provides feedback, modeling and support for your storytelling. Your classroom, in fact, will be your newsroom, where you and your peers will practice and work to perfect your storytelling skills.

Finally, your readers community initially will be your peer review partners and teacher. However, "Storycrafting" encourages your class to publish your work, using a class news sheet, a Web newspaper, your campus newspaper or your local community newspaper. Expanding your audience enhances the value of the stories you write.

Each of these communities gives you a sense of place and a sense of purpose as a storyteller-journalist.

Whether involving stories told around an ancient campfire or delivered lightning speed to a contemporary computer screen, storytelling always has been a vital activity in the community. With this textbook, with your peers and teacher and within your classroom, you begin your storytelling apprenticeship, and you join a tradition older than the act of writing that gives it life today.

Embrace the challenge and enjoy the journey.

## Using This Textbook

"Storycrafting" is organized into three parts:

- "The Process."
- "The Practice."
- "The Profession."

"The Process," comprising the first four chapters, takes you through the "Storycrafting" writing process and provides a firm foundation for *how* you will approach writing. Also, this section introduces you to various aspects of *what* you will write for your news stories. The goal is to allow you to begin working as a storyteller-journalist as soon as possible—gathering information for and writing real stories that you publish in your classroom newsroom for real audiences.

"The Practice" builds on the basics you cover in "The Process" and provides ample opportunity in Chapters 5 through 16 to practice while you become increasingly familiar with the particulars of news stories. We will review news, story content, evidence, interviewing, leads, structure, style and revision. In addition, the section ends with online publishing—information, explanation and recommendations for putting your stories online, where you can extend your audience beyond the campus to the world.

"The Profession" wraps up the textbook with three chapters that target additional aspects of the profession you someday may enter. Journalistic conduct, media law and current trends are the subjects you will cover in this section.

You should be comfortable reading most chapters at a single sitting and discussing each during two or three one-hour class periods, or comparable time. While chapter order necessarily is fixed here, your teacher will decide the actual order you will cover chapters to suit his or her particular approach.

No workbook is available with "Storycrafting." That is intentional. After all, the best way for you to learn to tell stories well is to regularly practice writing them, and the best stories to write are those for which you gather real information from observation and real sources.

Therefore, practice exercises throughout the textbook will keep you challenged and actively engaged in the "Storycrafting" process. Exercises avoid stale and routine approaches. Instead, you will practice and polish your storytelling skills with various journalistic activities and on real stories—mostly those you write yourself.

Finally, you are encouraged to go to the "Storycrafting" Web site at <www
.newsprof.com>, where you will find additional resources, textbook updates and a
link for you to e-mail the author with your questions, your comments, your suggestions and your complaints.

## *Acknowledgments*

Please indulge me a few personal lines here as I acknowledge the considerable contributions so many have made to "Storycrafting."

The premise for this textbook was my doctoral dissertation, completed during fall
1997 at the University of Missouri-Kansas City. Therefore, I am indebted to my dissertation committee, chaired by Dr. Cheryl Grossman and comprised of the following members: Dr. Susan Adler, Dr. Joan Dean, Dr. Dan Mahala, Dr. Anthony Manzo
and Dr. Randall Roorda.

I am appreciative, too, of my students, who usually managed to teach me at least
as much as I taught them during the past 27 years.

To all the student journalists and their campus newspapers whose stories
enlivened the pages of "Storycrafting" and gave meaning to my explanations, I am
most thankful.

Two people provided much-needed reading and response to drafts of the "Storycrafting" manuscript. David Swartzlander, on the journalism faculty at Doane College in Crete, Neb., offered many valuable suggestions for the first five chapters. Bill
Church, creative writer and editor of "The Mochila Review" at Missouri Western
State College in St. Joseph, was my "editor-in-residence" for the entire manuscript.
He read, questioned, challenged, encouraged and commented for the past 14
months. Most of his excellent advice I followed. Any weak spots or problems in the
textbook would be where I did not.

Finally, I owe considerable thanks to a professional colleague and dear friend for
the past 23 years, Dr. Lillian Lodge Kopenhaver, associate dean of the School of Journalism and Mass Communication at Florida International University in Miami. Her
longtime personal support and encouragement have been a lifeline. Just as importantly, she suggested that I submit manuscript chapters and a proposal for "Storycrafting" to publication representatives at the 2002 meeting of the Association for
Education in Journalism and Mass Communication in Miami. If she had not, this
textbook would still be stuck in my head waiting to be written.

October 25, 2003
At Saint Joseph, Missouri

# Part 1
# The Process

# Chapter 1
# Principles of Storycrafting

*O Reader! had you in your mind*
*Such stores as silent thought can bring,*
*O gentle Reader! you would find*
*A tale in everything.*

—William Wordsworth

## Chapter Contents

## *QuickView*

While storytelling generally has served to teach and preach, the modern storytelling of journalists primarily involves the traditional goals of news writing: to inform, to educate and to entertain.

Of particular value in this chapter is an overview of the writing process, an approach that stresses how writers write rather than what they write. The process is one that affirms solid principles you can apply in your writing, especially in the news stories you complete this semester.

Your instructor and peers will be partners in your storytelling as you rely on their feedback and encouragement and respond to them as your most immediate and real audience.

---

## *Storytelling*

It satisfies an elemental need, this storytelling, a longing to share experience with other people. We do not so much learn storytelling but rather grow into it. Like DNA it embodies who we were, who we are and who we will be.

### The Origins of Storytelling

Once upon a time, there were no stories because there was no language. Yet, early humans needed to share understandings and experiences beyond the moment. So, rudimentary gestures, grunts and sounds became representations of ideas. Over time, certain sounds took on consistent meaning, and oral language was born. This, in turn, enabled basic storytelling. Eventually, written symbols evolved that represented the sounds, and this system comprised written language.

Storytelling not only coincided with language development but also was one of the most powerful stimuli that encouraged its growth. The need to communicate complex ideas and ever-changing situations demanded expanding vocabularies.

Anne Pellowski, who has studied the history of storytelling, suggests that storytelling originated in play activities, with gifted but ordinary people entertaining members of their social groups. She offers a number of theories on the origins of storytelling, including that it:

- Grew out of the playful, self-entertainment needs of humans.
- Satisfied the need to explain the surrounding physical world.
- Came about because of an intrinsic religious need in humans to honor or propitiate the supernatural forces believed to exist in the world.
- Evolved from the human need to communicate experience to other humans.
- Fulfilled an aesthetic need for beauty, regularity and form through expressive language and music.
- Stemmed from the desire to record the actions or qualities of one's ancestors, in the hope that this would give them a kind of immortality.

Notice the consistent element in each of the theories above, that storytelling grew from need. Humans need to tell stories—and to hear them. Another storytelling authority, Robert Atkinson, says, "Even though professional storytellers don't all agree on what stories can and cannot do, the important point seems to be that storytelling *is* fulfilling some real needs in people: the need to use the imagination, the need for community, the need for sharing personal truth."

Novelist and creative writing professor Joyce Carol Oates writes, "The love of storytelling—to hear stories, and to tell them—is universal in our species. Those with an apparent talent for writing, which is to say a talent for using language as painters use paint, as musicians use their instruments, are not of a special breed but simply mirror the common human desire."

Whether called storytellers, bards, minstrels, gleemen, troubadours or jongleurs, some of their messages were termed *folktales,* repeated generation after generation. In time they became fixed elements of particular social groups. Other messages were more or less real accounts of meaningful moments in the life of the community.

A common goal of folktales was to educate children in correct behavior in an entertaining way, and such narratives were, and often still are, powerful tools. "The boy who cried wolf," for example, is an Aesop's Fable that offers both an intriguing and believable childhood experience—at least for children of Aesop's time.

### The boy who cried wolf

Retold by Heather Forest

There once was a shepherd boy who was bored as he sat on the hillside watching the village sheep. To amuse himself he took a great breath and sang out, "Wolf! Wolf! The Wolf is chasing the sheep!"

The villagers came running up the hill to help the boy drive the wolf away. But when they arrived at the top of the hill, they found no wolf. The boy laughed at the sight of their angry faces.

"Don't cry 'wolf', shepherd boy," said the villagers, "when there's no wolf!" They went grumbling back down the hill.

Later, the boy sang out again, "Wolf! Wolf! The wolf is chasing the sheep!" To his naughty delight, he watched the villagers run up the hill to help him drive the wolf away.

When the villagers saw no wolf they sternly said, "Save your frightened song for when there is really something wrong! Don't cry 'wolf' when there is NO wolf!" But the boy just grinned and watched them go grumbling down the hill once more.

Later, he saw a real wolf prowling about his flock. Alarmed, he leaped to his feet and sang out as loudly as he could, "Wolf! Wolf!"

But the villagers thought he was trying to fool them again, and so they didn't come.

At sunset, everyone wondered why the shepherd boy hadn't returned to the village with their sheep. They went up the hill to find the boy. They found him weeping.

"There really was a wolf here! The flock has scattered! I cried out, 'Wolf!' Why didn't you come?"

An old man tried to comfort the boy as they walked back to the village. "We'll help you look for the lost sheep in the morning," he said, putting his arm around the youth, "Nobody believes a liar . . . even when he is telling the truth!"

A familiar story to most of us, one that is even fun to hear repeated. More importantly, it delivered—and still delivers—a poignant lesson to listeners about honesty and responsibility.

Historical accounts, on the other hand, gave people a sense of their ancestry. These laid out a map of experiences, tracing paths to the important events that helped shape their sense of who they were. Of course, these accounts were not always altogether accurate, but they typically contained at least grains of truth. Davy Crockett, for instance, was a real American hero. Born in 1786, he died along with 139 others at the Battle of the Alamo in 1836. The following tall tale illustrates the high esteem with which Crockett was held.

### Frozen dawn

Retold by S. E. Schlosser

One winter, it was so cold that the dawn froze solid. The sun got caught between two ice blocks, and the earth iced up so much that it couldn't turn. The first rays of sunlight froze halfway over the mountain tops. They looked like yellow icicles dripping toward the ground.

Now Davy Crockett was headed home after a successful night hunting when the dawn froze up so solid. Being a smart man, he knew he had to do something quick or the earth was a goner. He had a freshly killed bear on his back, so he whipped it off, climbed right up on those rays of sunlight and began beating the hot bear carcass against the ice blocks which were squashing the sun. Soon a gush of hot oil burst out of the bear and it melted the ice. Davy gave the sun a good hard kick to get it started, and the sun's heat unfroze the earth and started it spinning again.

So Davy lit his pipe on the sun, shouldered the bear, slid himself down the sun rays before they melted and took a bit of sunrise home in his pocket.

Clearly, about the only truth in this tale is that Crockett was a real person and a real hunter, perhaps even a bear hunter. Yet, such highly exaggerated skills are understood clearly by listeners. The story expresses the kind of admiration we continue to give to our own modern superheroes.

Both of these kinds of stories served as a way to teach and preach, to connect one generation to the next, establishing common stories and a common history. In fact, some suggest it is these stories that establish a culture and mold a people. In a sense, we *are* the stories we tell and the stories we hear.

Stories help to make meaning of human existence, revealing who we are and how we behave. They are means by which we share our understanding of the world in which we live.

## Journalists: The Modern Storytellers

"Storycrafting" is based on the premise that all good writing is a form of storytelling. Whether it be a personal essay, a cover letter for a job application or a piece of short fiction, such good writing communicates a clear message of experience in a meaningful way to a select audience. Our particular concern, though, is the storytelling of journalists, especially those who write news for print or online media. They continue the tradition of making meaning of our world as they report about events, people and trends. This task is an exciting adventure.

Consider what it means to take up the challenge of recording and communicating the important and relevant news of your community. As a journalist, you are a member of a special group of storytellers—no longer positioned around a campfire telling the tribe its ancient tales. Instead, you are seated at a computer terminal typing the new tales of a modern community, using print and online media to convey your messages.

Most importantly, and this cannot be overemphasized, while most other storytellers deal with fiction, you work only with facts. You do not have license to invent characters or material. As a journalist, your concern with truth and accuracy must do more to shape your storytelling than your desire to spin a good yarn.

The following story is similar to earlier historical accounts, such as "Frozen dawn." It, too, gives readers a sense of their past and maps experiences that connect important events. It differs, though, in its authenticity and accuracy.

## Salvaged bell to ring again

### USS Arizona artifact will play central role in Sept. 11 ceremony

By Rachel Williamson

After being salvaged from a sunken battleship in Pearl Harbor, almost melted for raw material and hidden in the old UA clock tower, the now-visible USS Arizona bell will toll once again on Sept. 11.

The bell is one of two salvaged from the sunken USS Arizona battleship, which sank on Dec. 7, 1941, and it is now visible in the clock tower of the Student Union Memorial Center.

It will ring out during a Sept. 11 ceremony on the UA Mall.

But the bell almost met a much different end. In 1944, during World War II, the bell was scheduled to be melted for raw material needed at the time.

Bill Bowers, a 1927 UA graduate and a captain of the United States Army at the time, noticed the bell in a crate. He thought of his alma mater—UA.

"I just thought that there's only one place for this bell," Bowers said.

The bell was delivered to the university in 1946.

A few years later, the bell was placed in the clock tower of the Memorial Student Union. Although the bell could be heard after each UA sports victory against out-of-state teams, it was never seen.

Ninety-nine-year-old Bowers will be the first to ring the historical bell this year on Sept. 11.

"I'm deeply honored to ring it in the new tower," Bowers said. "I don't know how I could expect anything more in my life."

The bell will ring once for each UA alumni that died in the Sept. 11 attacks last year.

Six UA alumni have been confirmed as victims of the Sept. 11 attacks, said Veda Kowalski, associate dean of students. There may be as many as eight.

According to Bowers, Sept. 11 is an ideal time for the bell to ring.

In the future, on the third Wednesday of every month, the bell will ring seven times at 12:07 p.m., said Dan Adams, director of Arizona Student Unions.

The numbers 12 and seven represent Dec. 7, the day the USS Arizona battleship sunk at Pearl Harbor.

Instead of only ringing for sports victories, the bell will also honor special awards given to UA. Each month a list of everyone being commemorated will be posted in the union.

This tradition will probably not start until January, Adams said.

Arizona Daily Wildcat
University of Arizona

Journalists in small communities or large have unique opportunities today to tell stories that make a difference in people's lives. Their writing informs, educates and entertains. Unlike the folklore and tales of the earlier storyteller, journalistic writing strives to be authentic in its representation of the life of the community. It should be clear by now that all good storytelling is not journalism, as with "Frozen dawn," but good journalism always involves effective storytelling.

Basically, Oates says, "writers are individuals born with a love of language, for communicating—'telling.' The forms of telling are many, but the impulse is a simple one: the desire to bring into the world something that did not previously exist, stamped with the individual's perspective and personal style."

## For Practice

1-1. Pair off with one of your classmates. Then, do the following:

a) Spend a few minutes thinking of a story you can share from your experience.
b) Each of you should tell the other the story, making sure you provide sufficient detail for your partner to get a full sense of the experience.
c) After you have shared, discuss what was effective in the story and its telling and what was not. Offer suggestions that would improve the storytelling experience.

1-2. Write the same story you shared with your classmate, and follow the suggestions for improvement that you feel are appropriate. Feel free to make other changes that will provide a stronger story. In class break into groups of three and do a "round-robin," passing your stories along to one another until all have read everyone's story. Briefly discuss the stories and what you each found interesting and entertaining in them.

1-3. Photocopy or print a short, popular folktale or fairy tale from either a book in your library or an online site and bring it to class. Then, do the following:

a) Pair off with one of your classmates and read the tale to your partner.
b) Discuss the key points of each tale: who, what, when, where, why and how.
c) For the next class write the tale as a modern news story, making sure you include the key points near the beginning.
d) During the next class share the story with your partner and discuss how it compares with the original.

1-4. Find an interesting news story and bring a copy to class. Then, do the following:

a) Pair off with a classmate and swap stories.
b) Discuss the key points of each story: who, what, when, where, why and how.
c) For the next class use the key points of the news story to write a folktale or fairy tale.
d) During the next class share the tale with your partner and discuss how it compares with the original.

# *The Writing Process*

Writing tends to be a personal, individual, even solitary experience. And writers often develop their own methods for creating their stories. Nevertheless, most successful writers work through a number of steps as they write, and these comprise what is known as the writing process.

Some writing experts believe that writers need usually to pick wrong words or write awkward phrases to eventually find the right words and smooth phrases. In fact, language is the means by which discovery occurs as writers seek meaning in their experiences and communicate it. You must make the writing process your own, and "Storycrafting" provides a basis for considering approaches that will work effectively.

The steps in the writing process typically include the following:

- Generating ideas/gathering material.
- Organizing the material.
- Drafting.
- Revising.
- Publishing the work.

## Generating Ideas/Gathering Material

How you generate ideas is related to the kind of story you are writing. For example, personal essays—a mainstay of the college composition classroom—usually are a product of a your own ideas rather than the ideas of others. Also called *expressive writing*, the personal essay allows you to draw from your own experiences, feelings and perspectives. So, generating material may be as simple as thinking about things that you want to say and then saying them. At times, you can use a variety of devices to help you come up with material. These include freewriting, brainstorming, mapping, questioning, sketching or researching. Usually, the purpose of expressive writing is to inform and entertain.

On the other hand, some writing relies primarily on the ideas of others. You search sources for information on a subject you pick or are assigned. Your goal is to discover what others have said about the subject and to support what you want to say. You probably know this best as *research writing*, and it usually is used to inform.

A third type is *creative writing*, comprised of short stories, novels and poetry. As a creative writer you might use a combination of both expressive and research techniques to generate your material. Most often, creative writing entertains readers.

Journalistic or *news writing*, though, is the type of writing with which we are most concerned. It is closer to research writing than to the other two because the content of news writing is intended to be factual, with most of it gathered from sources outside the writer, including observations of events, interviews with other people and research of documents and online materials. Importantly, journalists bring to their information gathering an extensive background developed from years of specializing in covering certain areas and aspects of the community. Working as a journalist, you seek to inform, to educate and to entertain.

## Organizing the Material

Once you have gathered enough material to begin writing your story, the next step involves putting the details into an appropriate order. The kind of writing you are doing helps to determine what organization you will use.

For example, the personal essay tends to be packaged in a traditional introduction-body-conclusion order, with the body bearing the burden of supporting the point of the paper. If the intent of the essay is to share a personal experience that was profound and taught an important lesson, then narration—or chronology—might organize the details. On the other hand, if the goal is to compare and contrast two items, such as a Chevrolet Tahoe and a Ford Explorer, then one approach would present the criteria, or points, about the Tahoe followed by the same kind of criteria about the Explorer.

Other organizing patterns include description, process analysis, cause and effect, classification, illustration and definition.

The research paper also benefits from one or more of the patterns of organization above. At times, chronology may be the logical choice to present the research, or a least-to-most important order might benefit the writer's control and the readers' understanding of the material.

Generally, chronology is the pattern of choice for short stories and novels. On the other hand, poetry tends to be organized in specialized ways based upon the poet's purpose, the poem's message and the particular style of poetry being written.

The traditional organization for news stories has been the inverted pyramid, in which writers present material in most-to-least important order, beginning with the lead, which introduces the main point of the story. However, in recent years many journalists have shifted from the inverted pyramid and begun using narrative and creative techniques more frequently, making their stories more interesting and inviting.

Organizing material is a critical step if the story is to communicate successfully to readers. Your purpose, content and audience help determine your choices, which are tempered mostly by the kind of writing you are doing. As most of you already are quite aware—based on your previous writing experiences—the bulk of the organizing activity you do as you prepare to write is mental. Some of you might even go so far as to sketch on paper the order of presentation of your details. Occasionally, you might write a detailed outline that you hope to follow.

Regardless of your approach, planning how you *want* to present your material, as well as how it *needs* to be presented, is an activity that will make writing less daunting and more successful.

## Drafting

By the time you get to this point—actually putting pen to paper or fingers to keyboard—you are like the runner poised on the starting line of a 100-meter sprint. You have prepared, you have planned and now you need to carry through.

An important point to remember is this: Almost no one writes anything perfectly the first time. If you try to do so, you likely will set yourself up for disappointment. Instead, your early drafts should be attempts to package the material you have gathered in the order you planned—the content and order you *think* may work.

Writers take a couple of different approaches when they draft. Some prefer to write quickly to capture all of the ideas crowding their minds. Others write a bit, read what they have written and then tinker with their writing before moving on. Whichever approach works for you, it is not necessary to use *all* of your material. Instead, use only as much of your gathered material as necessary to make your point clear and complete to readers.

On the other hand, be open to adding new material to your story. You may find your drafting has generated the need for additional details. Either you find a hole in your content that you should fill or you discover an additional dimension you had not foreseen.

Your first draft should focus primarily on *what* you want to say. Do not be too concerned with *how* you want to say it. Later, once your content is firmed up, you can concentrate on conventions—spelling, word choice, punctuation, grammar and style.

Drafting is at the heart of good storytelling. The act of writing can be intensely demanding; it also can be intensely fulfilling. Do not spend *too little* time and effort on this step.

## Revising

Once you are satisfied with basic content, set the writing aside, even if only for a few minutes. Get up. Stretch your legs. Visit the fridge or soft drink machine. Take these few moments to gain both distance and a fresh perspective. When you return to your story to begin revising, or *re-seeing*, you need to consider it in a different way.

Of all the lessons you learn from "Storycrafting," one of the most important is that excellence in a story comes not from its writing but from its revision.

Too many inexperienced writers find revision tough to do. They give their stories one shot and call it quits. Admittedly, writing is hard work, and they tire of the task. Besides, they think, the story seems clear and complete to them.

First-draft stories often lack polish. They are not the best effort of the writers.

Even good suggestions for improvement may not encourage some writers to go beyond first drafts. Sadly, this situation may occur because of their sense that the story is "good enough."

Novice journalists have the mistaken notion that it is more important that they write *quickly* rather than *completely*. Of the two, the second criterion is the one on which you must concentrate, especially now. Quickness will come with practice and experience.

The culprit in many weak stories is a lack of information, explanation or illustration that speaks clearly and completely to readers. The material may seem sufficient for writers because of what is termed the *knowledge factor*. Writers allow their own knowledge of the topic to mask what readers need to know about it. In other words, fewer details and less explanation seem needed for what the writers already consider a familiar subject. The downside, of course, is that writers in this situation give short shrift to readers' needs.

Remember that you write for readers first, yourself second. Revision is most successful when you read as your readers will read. This role anticipates what readers already know and what they need to know to understand your story.

Among the tools you might employ for revision are the following:

• Reading the story aloud.
• Having another person read it aloud to you.
• Seeking peer review and response.

Reading your story aloud forces you to slow your reading, often allowing you to see what you have written versus what you *think* you have written.

Hearing it read by someone else offers similar benefits. In addition, it tends to increase the distance between you and your writing, encouraging you to be more objective. Peer review—that is, reading and response by other students—has the same advantages, plus the chance for real readers to consider and respond to your work-in-progress.

Keep an open mind as you revise. Value the responses from others who read your story, but weigh the merits of their suggestions carefully. If a suggestion seems wrongheaded, ask others their opinions on the issue. If they agree with the original suggestion, then it likely is valid, something on which you should act. Advice from your editor or teacher, meanwhile, is probably sound and deserves greater standing.

The goal during revision is to polish and improve your story—to make it the best it can be. Remember that revision is not an afterthought. It is integral to excellent writing.

## Publishing the Work

The final step in the writing process is publishing—making it available to an audience—which can take one of several forms. Submitting your story to your teacher for evaluation is the most common. Other methods include the following:

• Posting the story on a classroom bulletin board along with the other stories completed by your classmates.
• Laying out the stories on pages using design software, like Adobe PageMaker, Adobe InDesign or Quark Xpress, and then printing copies for everyone in class.
• Uploading the stories to a Web site accessible to students in the class.

The term *publishing* is carefully chosen to reflect the finished nature of the story. Working toward closure with each of your assignments tends to motivate you to do your best work on deadline and allows you to move on.

## Recursive Nature of the Process

While these steps are presented in a particular order here, writers tend *not* to follow these in sequence all of the time. Instead, they work through the steps *recursively*; that is, they move back and forth through the steps, dealing with the demands of their writing at that moment.

For example, generating ideas or gathering material necessarily must be a starting point for all writing. Once sufficient material is in place, writers may begin organizing it into a logical order, appropriate for the purpose, audience and content. However, this step often is embedded in the act of initial drafting, so it may be difficult to separate it.

At times writers may work through steps, generating material, organizing and planning, and drafting. Then, during revision, they may discover their stories need additional material, which sends them back to the first step. Consequently, the new material needs to be placed into the story, drafted and polished.

Other writers prefer to write in chunks, pausing to read, revise and polish before moving to the next chunk. What is important is not the sequence but that all the steps are completed in an order that works well for you and for the story.

## For Practice

1-5. Pair off with one of your classmates. Your task is to write a brief story about a single, interesting experience your partner has had. The following are the kinds of experience you are seeking:

- Kicking the winning field goal in a championship football game.
- Trying out for the varsity cheerleading squad.
- Being locked out of the house with no one else at home.
- Winning first place in a photography contest.
- Going fishing with an elderly relative or friend.

a) Interview one another to determine an appropriate experience. This is a lot like a "fishing expedition," where you know there are fish in the lake and it is your job to hook one. Likewise, you know your partner has had interesting experiences. You need to ask some general questions that will help you to narrow your focus to one that you think will work.

b) Once you have "hooked" one, begin writing more specific questions that satisfy your curiosity and likely will enable readers—your classmates—to understand and appreciate your partner's experience. Interview your partner, taking notes quickly and carefully.

c) Before the next class draft a story using as much of the information that you believe will cover your subject and satisfy your readers. Recall the steps in the writing process and be aware of how you follow them in your own writing.

d) At the next class meeting share your draft with your partner. Get his or her response about how accurately and effectively you have captured the moment.

e) Then, share the draft with two other classmates.

1-6. Pair off with one of your classmates. Your task is to write a minibiography of your partner.

a) Prepare questions that you think will generate the material you need.

b) Then, interview one another, taking notes quickly and carefully.

c) Before the next class draft a story using as much of the information that you believe will cover your subject and satisfy your readers. Recall the steps in the writing process and be aware of how you follow them.

d) At the next class meeting share your draft with your partner. Get his or her response about how accurately and effectively you have presented the minibiography.

e) Then, share the draft with two other classmates.

f) Submit the draft to your teacher.

## Ownership

An important tenet in effective storytelling is the sense of ownership you need to take in your stories. This concept suggests that what you write should grow from your own experience:

- *Your* observations.
- *Your* questions.
- *Your* notes and research.
- *Your* struggles to draft and make sense of this experience for readers.
- *Your* revising and polishing of the story to completion.

"Storycrafting" has neither fact sheets nor a supporting workbook. Instead, the stories you write will be real, created from material you gather on your own campus. Instead of "pretending" to write news stories, you will be writing as a real journalist from the outset, producing authentic stories. This engenders ownership, and ownership gives you a powerful and vested interest in the writing you do. Ownership also enables you to claim authority for the subjects you are writing about, and it motivates you to perform at your best.

However, ownership also carries with it responsibility. You bear the burden of ensuring that the information you gather and craft into a story is appropriate, complete and reader centered.

## Readership

Reader-centered writing tends to communicate best. When your story is tailored for your readers, it does the following:

- Respects what you think they know and anticipates what they need to know.
- Answers questions they will have and satisfies their curiosity.
- Presents the material in a way that is comfortable and appropriate for them.

In most instances your readers do not know everything you know about the subject. It is up to you to gauge your audience to grasp how much they know. This is important, since telling readers what they already know is a waste of time and might make them feel as if you are talking down to them. It also is important because it allows you to weigh your story material, giving special attention and position to that which is new to readers.

As you work to understand your readers, you should put yourself into their position, where you have a sense of their questions about your subject, particularly questions involving information unfamiliar to them. Then, you can determine how much material they need to satisfy their curiosity about the subject.

Importantly, when you are reader oriented, your stories will be written in ways that are familiar and readily understandable to readers. Word choice, sentence structure and tone are three of the more common concerns. When you align these with your readers, they will more readily understand the material and feel that the story speaks to them.

## *Peer Review*

When writing, you tend to follow rituals that allow you to engage the material in effective, appropriate ways. You may prefer to write in your music-filled room, a quiet spot in your backyard or a bustling computer lab. In addition, you might be more comfortable writing with pencil and a yellow legal pad, a trusty old manual typewriter or a laptop computer.

Of real concern, though, is that you do not become so absorbed in your work that you end up writing too much for yourself and not enough for others. While this may be acceptable for diaries, journals and some poetry, it can be disastrous for stories intended for others.

An excellent method for maintaining a connection to your audience is peer review. Essentially, you want a sounding board for your work, others whom you can ask the following:

- How am I doing?
- Is this story making sense?
- What is working? What is not?
- Is it interesting?
- Is it complete?
- Does it satisfy your curiosity?
- What else do you need to know about the subject?

"Storycrafting" encourages organized peer review within your journalism classroom. One of the major advantages of classroom peer groups is that you will be working with other students who are busy with the same kinds of activities as you. They, too, are journalists working through the demands of news writing. They are familiar with both this textbook and your campus community—two of the key influences on your story writing for this class.

You need not accept as gospel all the advice you get from your reviewers. Try to weigh their suggestions against your own judgment as a writer. At the same time, you must be open to constructive criticism and new ideas. By distancing yourself from your story, you likely will be less defensive and more objective. Otherwise, you disable one of the vital tools that can help your writing to improve.

You also will be serving as a reviewer of your classmates' stories—usually the same student or students who are reviewing your draft. If peer review is to be productive, you must trust one another and invest time in and attention to the stories you read. You must be honest in your responses, but you do not have to be unkind or tactless.

Outside your classroom likely are many others who can review your stories effectively. These include your parents, a trusted friend, the staff at writing centers on your campus, experienced reporters on your student newspaper or community-based journalists.

In fact, you might rely upon several of these readers of your story-in-progress to give you feedback that reinforces what you are doing well and offers advice about some things you might do better.

Remember that your primary goal with review should not be mere reinforcement of what you have written but rather encouragement for and advice about improving your story-in-progress.

## Coaching

One of the most important aspects of the "Storycrafting" writing process is coaching. For many years newspapers and magazines have employed writing coaches to work with reporters. Their goal is to assist writers in communicating more effectively with their audiences.

Writing coaches work much like their counterparts in athletics. There, as you know, coaches teach and train their athletes. They push and prod to get the players to give their best, reaching beyond their previous limits and successes to continue growing in their skills. Yet, for all that coaches say and do, when it comes to actually playing the game, they must remain on the sideline or in the dugout and allow their teams to perform.

In writing classes this role typically is filled by your teacher, who participates in the process of your story writing at various points in its development. Good coaches do not intrude excessively in the writing process. Respecting the principle of ownership, they allow writers to retain ultimate control of and decision making for their work.

Moreover, coaches are not proofreaders. At times, your teacher-coach may point out particularly troublesome problems with conventions in your writing and encourage you to correct them. However, it is not the teacher-coach's responsibility to locate weaknesses and errors in your stories or to correct them for you.

Coaches certainly should respond to your story content. They are knowledgeable, motivated and experienced readers, and they usually will try to see not only what you have written but also what you might write. This duality of vision is one of the strengths they bring to the process.

Coaching activities your teachers are likely to use include the following:

- Leading discussion of particular techniques that you and your classmates might try.
- Offering brief in-class tips to your peer group at work on stories.
- Arranging somewhat longer out-of-class conferences where you and your teacher consider your story one-on-one.

Most teacher-coaches invest the bulk of their time *after* peer review but *before* publication.

Some of you already may be familiar with the principles of storycrafting covered here and may use them in your writing. For others this material is fresh and new. Either way, you now can be confident moving to the next chapter, where we will cover basic story-writing tools and techniques.

## Crafting and Drafting

Both Exercise 1-7 and Exercise 1-8 put your powers of curiosity and observation to the test. Each exercise expects that you analyze what is worthwhile and decide what to include and what to ignore. Use *all* of your senses, not just sight. Consider the following tips as you work.

- Concentrate on the big parts and the small details as you gather information.
- Use exact terms and specific words.
- Write more notes than you think you will need.

## For Practice

1-7. Attend an event on your campus that likely will be covered by the campus newspaper. Then, do the following:

a) Take notes on what you believe are the important details and actions of the event.
b) After the event highlight those details that you think are most important and that should be included in a story.
c) Work your way through the list numbering from most important to least.
d) Submit a copy of your prioritized, highlighted list to your teacher *before* the campus newspaper publishes its story.
e) Compare your decisions about what was most important to decisions made by the newspaper after the story is published there.
f) Submit the comparison to your teacher.

1-8. Spend an hour in a busy building on your campus, such as the student union, administration building or recreation center. If you have spent time in the building previously, look for what may be new or different. If you are unfamiliar with the building and its activities, *everything* will seem new, so look for what is interesting. Be observant. Be curious. Then, do the following:

a) Write down at least three potential story topics.
b) Select your favorite from the list.
c) Write down all the details you observe about the topic.
d) Find three people who either are in charge or are participating and ask them questions about the topic, including who, what, when, where, why and how—the standard journalist's questions.
e) Type a rough draft of the story. Your main concern is content. Do not worry about the organization of material or possible surface errors involving spelling, punctuation, grammar or style.
f) Submit your three story topics and the draft of your selected topic to your teacher, who will consider its *potential* as an effective news story.

## Chapter 1 Bibliography

Atkinson, Robert. *The Gift of Stories: Practical and Spiritual Applications of Autobiography, Life Stories, and Personal Mythmaking*. Westport, Conn.: Bergen and Garvey, 1995.

Forest, Heather. "The Boy Who Cried Wolf." *Story Arts*. <http://www.storyarts.org/library/aesops/stories/boy.html>.

Oates, Joyce Carol. *Telling Stories: An Anthology for Writers*. New York: W.W. Norton and Co., 1998.

Pellowski, Anne. *The World of Storytelling*. New York: R.R. Bowker Co., 1977.

Schlosser, Sandra E. "Frozen Dawn." *American Folklore*. <http://www.americanfolklore.net/folktales/tn.html>.

Williamson, Rachel. "Salvaged Bell to Ring Again." *Arizona Daily Wildcat*. 29 August 2002. <http://wildcat.arizona.edu/papers/96/4/01_4.html>.

Wordsworth, William. *William Wordsworth Collection*. *The Columbia World of Quotations*. 1996. <http://www.bartleby.com/100/337.6.html>.

# Chapter 2
# Basic Story-Writing Tools and Techniques

*The press is a mill that grinds all that is put into its hopper. Fill the hopper with poisoned grain and it will grind it to meal, but there is death in the bread.*

—William C. Bryant

## Chapter Contents

## QuickView

Chapter 2 takes you into the nitty-gritty of news-writing basics, where telling your stories follows long-held traditions and effective practices. The tools and techniques presented here will equip you to make the transition into the storytelling that journalists do.

Among those are the five Ws and H, the basic news elements that comprise most stories you will write. Answering these for your readers will make your stories more complete. Added to them is a seventh basic element, "so what," which puts your stories into context, giving readers a sense of the consequence of the stories—for both them and others involved.

Interviewing and notetaking basics provide sound practices and tips that will assist you in one of your most demanding tasks, gathering your material. A crucial step in the writing process covered in Chapter 1, this gathering of your material has direct bearing on the success of your storytelling.

---

Sitting around campfires on chilly evenings, storytellers find their voices. They speak of tales tall and old. They reach deep into their imaginations to create real from unreal. With the crackling of fire, eyes widen and hair rises on the backs of necks as listeners react to storyteller magic.

That same magic you must seek. It is a magic that can bring life to life events. While traditional storytellers mine their messages from deep within their imaginations, storyteller-journalists harvest material from the world around them. The effect can be the same, whether fiction or fact. Listeners and readers must have their attention captured and must be moved—to empathy, to fear, to anger, to love, to action, to awareness or to understanding.

## "Aboutness"

Good storytellers write *about* something. Some of you may roll your eyes at that and respond, "Well, of course!" It seems so obvious that it does not need be mentioned, right?

Nevertheless, among the flaws most common in many stories is their lack of "aboutness"—a clear focus on a particular message for readers. This may happen for a couple of reasons: One is that storytellers sometimes have too little information before they begin writing. The result is a vague, poorly supported story with a weak emphasis. It does not seem to be *about* anything. Another is that storytellers have a wealth of information—so much that they have trouble knowing where to start and what to stress when they begin writing. The result in this instance is a content-cluttered story, also with weak emphasis. It seems to be *about* everything.

Aboutness is a balance and blend of the right amount of material focused on a specific, valid point. It demands that storytellers make choices, lots of choices.

Among those choices are the following, what we might term *aboutness factors*:

- Topic of concern.
- Kind of information to gather.
- Story focus.
- Amount of information to use for support.
- Order to present the supporting information.
- Relevance to readers.

## Topic of Concern

Effective storytellers understand that success with aboutness begins long before they reach their keyboards. As with most writing, that success starts as early as deciding which topic to cover. Some topic choices are better. While one readily could argue that all topics are newsworthy, it is unlikely that all are *equally* newsworthy. Some are more important, timely and interesting than others.

Make sure you judge your choice of topic based on all three of these criteria. Aboutness need not be forced when you know your story is important, timely and interesting. Storyteller magic grows more easily from such tales that want to be told. When you find those, you know it in your head. More importantly, you know it in your heart.

## Kind of Information

Storytellers know that the *kind* of information they gather has considerable bearing on aboutness. As a storyteller-journalist ask yourself the following questions:

*Am I getting all my material from a single source?*

The issue of single-source stories is your first concern. Say the story is rather simple and straightforward, such as a coming-events item on a book sale sponsored by the English majors club. Then, a single source is sufficient. At times only one source is able or available to provide information.

However, some editors and publications enforce policies that discourage use of single sources. In fact, most stories benefit from multiple sources because they tend to provide both depth and additional perspectives.

Finally, media history has numerous glaring examples of hoaxes pulled off because stories were based on single sources. Wisdom suggests that you locate more than one source whenever possible.

*Is my source only human or only document?*

When dealing with multiple sources, you also must be concerned with whether they are only human or document; that is, does your information come from people, printed or online materials or both? Again, you may not always have choices here; there may be only a single human source.

In most instances, human sources are better, since what they tell you tends to be authentic, credible and often colorful. Whenever possible, though, gather documents that support human sources. The more complex and compelling the story, the more likely document sources are available and the more likely your story will benefit from including them with your human sources.

Resist the urge to avoid using documents merely because locating them requires additional research and time.

*Is my source objective or subjective in relation to the topic?*

The next point concerning sources is whether yours is objective or subjective. In other words, are sources neutral in relation to the topic of your story, or do they have a stake in it? Are they biased?

Say, for example, that the campus Student Senate reporter, Mike, is covering a controversial funding request. He interviews the president of a new fraternity that is seeking funding from student government. Mike knows that the fraternity president's comments will be subjective because the president has a personal and financial interest in the story.

Mike also interviews a senator who regularly opposes funding for Greek organizations. He also is subjective, since he has an ax to grind. Pitting comments from both of these sources against one another provides conflict, which makes for a good story, but it also provides balance, limiting the effects of bias in the story.

A third source Mike uses is the Student Senate's bylaws, which he cites in the story and helps to interpret for readers.

The presentation of the bylaws involved in the controversy offers neutral input as well as depth.

The result is a well-rounded story that does a good job delivering the message to readers.

*Is my source credible?*

When you tell a story, you want readers to accept it as factual and true. You want the information to come from sources that readers believe.

Locating credible sources is not always easy, but it is vital. As we saw above, sources may be biased. By itself, that is not a problem. Most readers can identify this bias and filter the information accordingly. Yet, they still want and need sources they can *trust*. Credibility of sources is crucial to the success of stories. In fact, the sources *are* the story.

Ultimately, readers must believe sources if they are to believe the story.

*Is my material comprised of facts or opinions?*

Another aspect of the kind of information you gather is whether it is comprised of facts or opinions. While facts provide the basis for most effective stories, good storytellers seek opinions from their sources, particularly for complex stories.

Especially needed are those opinions that help to analyze and interpret the facts. Otherwise, readers may not be able to understand fully the consequences of the facts they read.

*Is my information technical and difficult to comprehend?*

Finally, the more technical and difficult your information is to understand, the more you must work to explain and interpret it rather than merely present it. When you know enough about your topic and the facts you have gathered, you can provide that clarification yourself.

However, reporters increasingly are challenged by the complexity of their stories and must rely on expert sources.

# For Practice

2-1. Get a copy of a recent issue of your campus newspaper. You will use the preceding questions to analyze the kind of information used in stories there.

a) Select three stories that you find interesting.
b) Ask the following questions about each story:
   1) Did all of the material in the story seem to come from a single source? Identify the source(s).
   2) Were the sources only human or only document? Or both? Explain.
   3) Did the source(s) seem subjective or objective in relation to the subject? Give examples and explanations to support your assessment.
   4) Do sources seem credible? Why?
   5) Was the material comprised of facts or opinions? Give examples.
   6) Was the material technical and difficult to comprehend? Give examples.

## Story Focus

From the first word of their tales good storytellers know exactly where they are taking their audiences. They have a sharp sense of story focus, which likely is one of the most critical factors in aboutness. As early as possible in reporting your story, you must capture a sense of what your story will cover. This will allow you to make wiser choices in the questions you ask and the information you gather.

Be careful, though, that you do not narrow your topic too much too soon. Hold off until you are nearly finished interviewing and researching before nailing down the story focus, which allows your mind to remain more open to possibilities. You also can more easily retain your own objectivity.

Actually, it is only *after* gathering sufficient information that you can reliably narrow story focus. It is only then that you know enough to know. Remain flexible, ready to shift gears to find the right focus if you discover the story is not following the original focus.

On the other hand, resist the urge to avoid limiting your topic at all. This is an inviting trap, especially when you have a wealth of gathered material. Just remember: The narrower the topic, the more specific the support, the clearer the message and the stronger the story.

## Amount of Information

At many family get-togethers, members often bring too much food—typically more than twice as much as they possibly could eat. Happily, everyone has a variety of dishes from which to choose, no one ever leaves the table hungry and what is not eaten usually makes fine leftovers for another meal.

Follow the same principle in how much material to gather for a story: Always get much more than you think you will need.

Aboutness improves when storytellers avoid writing beyond their understanding. In other words, they know more than they are sharing. As a result, what they share with readers tends to be richer and stronger.

## Order of Information

Another concern with aboutness is the order in which you present your information. As we will discover in Chapter 3 and in Chapter 13, you have a variety of options to organize your stories. Just as one-sized clothing seldom fits everyone well, a single organizing format does not fit all stories.

Traditional structure for news stories is the inverted pyramid. This pattern opens with a summary lead followed by supporting and explanatory details in decreasing order of importance. Today, though, this structure often is replaced by others, especially chronological or narrative order—the standard for storytellers outside journalism. Other structures worth considering are description, Wall Street Journal and advance.

## Relevance to Readers

Effective storytellers watch members of their audience. They seek clues to how they respond to the story. If attention lags, storytellers may pick up the pace, increase the gestures or raise the pitch. They understand that audiences vary. What works well for one group may not have the same effect on the next, so they need to adjust their telling. Sometimes it is not enough to change their delivery. Instead, storytellers need to change their material to something of more interest. In these ways storytellers work to make their tales relevant to their audience.

As a storyteller-journalist you must make stories relevant to your readers. This aspect of aboutness deals exclusively with readers—their wants, needs and interests. How to acquire that understanding can be difficult.

The easiest way to begin is to *ask them*. Talk with other students and ask what they are interested in and curious about. In addition to one-on-one encounters, reader surveys and reader focus groups can provide feedback. Articles in professional journalism periodicals discuss the shifting nature of reader interests as well. Answers from enough readers using these different techniques eventually will give you a pretty good sense of what is relevant to them.

## *Story Elements*

When storyteller-journalists write, they rely on traditional elements called the five Ws and H, as well as the less traditional SW, all of which are linked to a series of questions:

- *What:* What is the main concern of the storyteller? What is the most important thing happening?
- *Who:* Who is primarily involved? Who is doing something? To whom is something being done?
- *When:* When is it happening?
- *Where:* Where is it happening?

- *Why:* Why is it happening?
- *How:* How is it happening?
- *So what:* So what about these elements? Why should readers care?

These seven elements comprise material for many story leads, which will be covered later in this chapter. Posing these questions and then using the answers to build your leads helps you to center the story for readers.

## What

You may notice that all questions key on the *what*, suggesting its importance among the elements. Your careful selection of the right *what*, therefore, is essential to the success of your story.

You may ask, "What do you mean, the right what?"

While it is obvious what some stories should be about, most stories could emphasize one of several things. Consider the following examples and "what happened" in each:

### Single What—fired

Fired:

Western University President James F. Kelley fired his top aide Friday.

### Multiple Whats

Voted to deny, request for funding, heated debate:

The Student Senate Friday voted to deny a request for funding by a new fraternity following a heated debate.

As above, the main *what* in stories typically rests in the verb (fired and voted to deny) around which the lead sentence is structured. Such choices are not set in concrete. While there is little question about the appropriateness of the *what* chosen in the first example, check the following versions of the Student Senate lead:

Heated debate punctuated the Student Senate session Friday as two sides argued the merits of a request for funding by a new fraternity.

A new fraternity lost its bid for funding Friday following heated debate at the Student Senate meeting.

When the votes were cast and tempers cooled, the fraternity had lost.

When more than a single *what* presents itself, the issue becomes which to use to key your lead. Sometimes that choice is a no-brainer. At other times, though, it is a storyteller's judgment call, which must be based on analysis of what is most important for this story. When faced with a tricky call, you would be wise to write versions that stress each of the choices, examine each and then decide which best carries the message of the story to readers.

## Who

Choice of *who* tends to be less troublesome. The simplest way to choose is to ask, "Who did what?" or "To whom was what done?" Yet, judgment usually plays a role here as well.

In the single-*what* example, President James F. Kelley answers the question of who did what, while his top aide answers the question of to whom what was done. Choosing Kelley over the aide to lead the story is correct because Kelley is president of the university. The aide is a subordinate. Also, Kelley was the one who acted by firing the aide.

When several important things are happening, the various versions of the lead might focus on different events that happen and involve different subjects. The first of the multiple-*whats* examples above stressed the vote to deny, and the Student Senate is the main *who*. In the other two versions the fraternity is the *who* of choice.

How you settle such matters falls to your judgment. Listen to your storyteller's voice. The goal, of course, is picking the *who* that best fits the *what*.

## When

The time element in stories is important, yet here you have choices, too.

The first is how specific to make the time element. For example, in an advance story readers who wished to attend the Student Senate meeting on the funding request would want to know what time and day it is scheduled. On the other hand, in the follow story the next issue, readers probably would not need or want to know exactly what time the Senate met. The day and whether it was morning (a.m.) or afternoon/evening (p.m.) would be sufficient.

Time elements in other stories might be even less specific, given as next week or last week, the actual name of a month or even the actual year.

In cases where the *when* is either inconsequential or unknown, references such as recently, some time ago, soon or in the near future may be sufficient.

The position of *when* in a sentence is another choice. Whenever possible put the time element next to the main verb. If it does not sound right there, move it to a spot where it does sound right.

## Where

The *where* tells readers the location of what happened. An advance story on the Student Senate meeting that is to review the funding request certainly would include *where* so that readers would be able to attend if they wished. The follow story, though, would have limited need for the location of the meeting, unless it were out of the ordinary.

For that reason the *where* may not be required, but including it probably is wise.

Yet, if your story is covering the high crime rate in a particular area of campus or a pizzeria that gives students a 25 percent discount, make sure you present the specific *where*.

## Why

The importance of the *why* should not be underestimated. Usually, it provides explanation and analysis that is vital to reader understanding. Writers seldom play it high in the lead because it tends to be wordier than the other elements. This slows reading and comprehension and clutters a lead. The follow story on the denial of the funding request would be much weaker if it failed to include *why*—mostly, why it was denied, but also why there was heated debate and why the fraternity sought the funding. Failure to include *why* in the story can frustrate and irritate readers more than most other omissions.

If you are writing a story about a professor who dies after falling from a four-story building on campus, your *why* is not about why he died but about why he fell. Also, for a story about the student who won the student government presidency, *why* she won, given the obvious vote count in her favor, is not the emphasis but rather why she ran for office or why voters elected her.

## How

*How* something happened often is excluded in stories. If you sought to give how the funding request was denied, you also would deal with the obvious: that the Student Senate voted, their method of voting, their authority to vote and so on. How particular senators voted, though, is worthwhile.

On the other hand, there are occasions when the *how* is important enough to include, even placed early in the lead. Examples of those would be how someone was killed or how someone survived a deadly situation.

## So What

The final element, *so what*, is a reader-dedicated concern. It presupposes the question from the reader and answers it, often getting at explanations that the other elements may miss. It tells the impact on readers.

If *so what* were considered for the funding denial, particularly as it impacts the fraternity, the writer might let readers know that failure of this funding to pass means failure of the fraternity to establish itself.

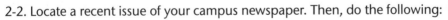

## *For Practice*

2-2. Locate a recent issue of your campus newspaper. Then, do the following:

a) Select five news stories.
b) Identify the story elements in each on a sheet of paper.
c) Determine if any of the seven elements are missing. If any are, is it a serious omission? Why or why not?
d) Decide if the element that launches the lead is the best choice.
e) Revise each lead to begin with a different element than the original and write your version on a separate sheet.
f) Submit a copy of the five stories and your answers to this exercise to your teacher.

# *Backgrounding*

Effective storytellers wisely set the stages for their tales, providing much more than the *where*. Backgrounding is both a planning and writing activity. During planning you background by researching and interviewing to learn what is behind the topic of your story as well as what has been written previously. You know you need to do backgrounding when you are confused by or unfamiliar with the topic and realize that you cannot answer questions readers may have.

In the funding-denial example, you may recall that Mike used the Senate bylaws as a third source for his preview story. In fact, before he even left the newsroom, he read though the bylaws and photocopied the pertinent sections that had bearing on the fraternity's request.

In addition, he reviewed the procedures for requesting and granting funding. When he had a question about the requirements for requests, he phoned the Senate vice president. Mike also learned in that conversation that only full-time, currently enrolled students would be allowed to address the Senate during discussion.

By informing himself, Mike avoided the problem of writing on a topic about which he knew too little. In the increasing complexity of 21st century life, journalists must respond more frequently and appropriately to this demand. With this background Mike better understood the Senate bylaws that applied, so he was able to ask the right questions of his human sources.

As a writing activity backgrounding gives readers supplementary details that provide context for the current story and help to explain some of the more unfamiliar issues. In this instance, Mike was able to include specific and relevant details that went beyond merely presenting the issue and allowed him to explain and interpret it for readers.

## Interviewing

Interviewing is the most important newsgathering tool at your disposal. Your ability to meet people, establish rapport, ask relevant questions and get specific answers will have direct bearing on your success as a storyteller-journalist.

## Meeting People

By now you know that documents are a rich source of material. However, they are static and unchanging. They cannot respond to your questions, and they cannot interact with the dynamics and immediacy of breaking news events.

People, on the other hand, provide details that can make your stories sing. Human sources are alive; they often are residents of communities where readers live and work. They relate and respond to the moment, particularly to your questions. Human sources are indispensable.

For those reasons you must be able to meet people of every age, social group, income level, ethnic background, religious belief and political persuasion. Some of you naturally look forward to such opportunities. Others of you who are less gregarious and outgoing will find meeting people troublesome. If you hope to be an effective storyteller, though, you must overcome inhibitions and connect with people.

## Establishing Rapport

First, you establish rapport by making connections. You and your source may find that you have things in common. For example, you both may enjoy rooting for the same football team. The two of you may share an appreciation for a good book. Each of you may have attended the same high school. You may each have a quick wit and good sense of humor. Most importantly, both of you want to get the facts of an issue to an interested audience.

The way you find that rapport is by communicating with your source in a friendly, reassuring manner. As you arrive at an interview, do not immediately whip out your notebook and begin firing questions.

Instead, dedicate the first few minutes of nearly every interview to breaking the ice and just "visiting." Observe your surroundings. Does your source have football memorabilia displayed? What books are on her shelves? Perhaps a photograph of a boat is hanging on the wall. These and other items are clues to interests that you may share. Ask about them, and provide similar information in return.

However, do not overdo it. You are meeting with this person to get information, not necessarily to form a lifelong friendship. Be sensitive to body language and other cues that suggest your source is short on time and anxious to move along. Cut the small talk at that point, pull out your notebook and get to work.

Be cordial, but professional.

Above all, be courteous. Your source is doing you a favor in granting time to be interviewed. No one is required to talk to journalists. Also, be respectful. That means you treat your source as a person of value. That also means you show up for the interview on time and appropriately dressed. Certainly, that means that you prepare for your interview.

## Asking Relevant Questions

What to ask in an interview is paramount. To make the most of this newsgathering opportunity, you must prepare for it.

The first step is to do some backgrounding. You cannot ask relevant questions if you have no idea what the topic involves, and it is not your source's job to fill you in on *everything* you need to know.

So, do some research. Start with your newspaper's morgue, searching for previous stories on the topic. After that, check library databases or go online. As you recall from before, backgrounding has the double benefit of helping you to prepare for your interview as well as providing you additional material to support your story. The people you interview will know if you have done your homework and will appreciate your taking the time to research the topic.

Once you have finished backgrounding, write down questions to ask your source. This prepares you to go into the interview and concentrate on your source's answers. Two questions that must start every interview, no matter the subject, are the following:

- How do you spell your name?
- What is your title?

Next, decide which questions have priority. If you run out of time in the interview, you do not want to leave with key questions unasked. Target the concerns that make this story newsworthy right now, and keep the subject narrow rather than global.

Remain flexible, though, with the questions and their order. Do not march through your list of questions without paying attention to what your source is telling you. You are conducting a conversation. Listen and respond to what the source says by asking questions related to the source's answers. As you listen to the answers, your source may cover answers for questions you had planned. Also, your source's answers may call for new questions you could not have anticipated.

Mostly, be curious. Some of your best questions and some of your best stories will come because you saw or heard something that made you curious.

Develop questions that draw from the source both facts and feelings, both of which are valuable material for your story. While it certainly is unacceptable for you as the storyteller to share *your* feelings about a topic, it is both legitimate and desirable for your source to do so. Besides, the subjective responses you get from your sources provide the human element that cold facts from documents cannot.

Certainly, part of the pleasure of interviewing is your interaction with another person. Good interviews are effective conversations between two people. However, remember why you are there—to get information from the source. If you do too much talking, you defeat your purpose.

When you finish the interview, always do four things:

- Ask if the source has anything to add.
- Ask if you may contact the source if you have any additional questions.
- Ask if the source can recommend others whom you might interview on this topic.
- Thank the person.

All of these show your respect for the source and help to firm the rapport you already may have established.

## Getting Specific Answers

While asking the right questions is crucial, they are meaningless if they do not garner specific answers.

At times, you will get vague answers because your questions are not phrased carefully enough to narrow the topic. Correct that flaw by rephrasing questions to get at exactly what you want to know. Sometimes, you will need to split a complex question into several questions that target parts of the issue. Keep in mind that an interview is a dialogue, where the two of you are involved in a conversation.

Of course, occasionally you will get vague answers because your source chooses to be vague. When that happens, ask the question again, perhaps in somewhat different words. Another approach is to ask follow-up questions that concentrate on the source's answers.

For example, you ask your source, "What is the cost of the employee benefits package you are proposing?"

He responds, "Oh, it's quite economical."

His response is subjective—something you certainly might use in the story. Unfortunately, it also is vague. Follow up with another question: "Could you put that cost into dollars?"

# Notetaking

Few of you have the skills of a professional stenographer, yet your notes must be clear and reasonably complete. While strong notes cannot guarantee an excellent story, it is a sure bet that weak notes will not generate strong stories. All of you already have frequent opportunity to practice effective notetaking in the other college classes you are taking. Many of the same good habits you employ there will make it easier to interview sources.

Among the tools that you may use are the following:

- Good listening habits.
- A personal shorthand.
- The right materials.

## Good Listening Habits

Most people take listening pretty much for granted. It is not usually something at which they work. Or need to. However, listening during an interview cannot be a casual activity if you want to gather material that is accurate and usable. More than any other storytelling, news stories must be accurate. Also, it does little good for you or the source to waste time gathering material that is not usable.

Remember that there is a clear distinction between hearing and listening. Hearing is a passive experience, requiring little more than your awareness of sounds. Your goal while interviewing is active listening, which involves concentration.

Interviewing is a complex activity. You might liken it to juggling three balls and talking with an audience at the same time. While taking notes in an interview, you must ask a question, listen to the answer, write down *relevant* material in appropriate form, be responsive to your source and be ready to ask another question. Typically, you are constantly writing as you listen and sort through the material.

Of major concern here is what you select to write and the form you use to write it. Few reporters can transcribe exactly *all* that a source says. Fortunately, you do not need to. Instead, your notes should be a blend of facts, key words and phrases and a healthy dose of exact quotes. Yet, you must be sure that your material accurately reflects what your source is telling you. This is particularly true for what you note and later use as the speaker's exact words.

Your focused listening should enable you to note the most "quoteworthy" of the source's comments and transcribe them exactly. There is no leeway in journalism for "close enough." It must be right on the money. All that separates you from a rumormonger is your accuracy with material and your credibility with readers.

Finally, your writing must be legible enough so that at least *you* can read it.

## Personal Shorthand

First, understand that you should never use a sentence when a phrase will do or a phrase when a word will do. A particularly valuable tool to assist you in that regard is a personal shorthand.

Begin with the following suggestions:

- w/: with.
- w/o: without.
- &: and.
- %: percent, percentage.
- < >: less than, greater than.
- @: at.
- i.e.: that is.
- e.g.: for example.
- #: number.
- ex: example.
- vs.: versus.
- b/g: background.

Use "shortcut" abbreviations that cut off the ends of common words. Examples: admin., univ., pres., subj., max., min., chem., biol.

Drop vowels and keep the consonants that carry most of the sound. Examples: rdg., wrtg., stu. gvt., chkg. acct., stu. hsng., prkg.

Use numbers instead of writing them out.

## The Right Materials

Good Scouts know that they need to be prepared. Good reporters do, too.

Reporter's notebooks are standard issue among professional journalists. These narrow spiral tablets with wide-lined paper are conveniently sized to fit into many pockets and purses. The stiff cardboard covers provide a firm enough surface on which to write, whether you are standing or sitting. Yet, some reporters opt for legal pads, preferring the larger page size to the convenience of slipping them into pockets.

Prefer pen to pencil, and always keep more than one pen handy.

Tape recorders, no matter how small and inconspicuous, generally are not necessary and, in fact, can be a distraction for sources who find them intimidating.

## For Practice

2-3. Select a course in which you are enrolled where the professor relies mostly on lecture to conduct the class and for which you usually take notes. Then, do the following:

a) Take careful notes, practicing your personal shorthand as effectively as you can. Make a special effort to answer the five Ws, H and SW.

b) Listen carefully for quoteworthy comments the professor makes, and write those down exactly.

c) After the class ask the professor for additional explanation on any points that are unclear. Ask any of the journalist's questions left unanswered.

d) Draft a "story" on the lecture, with a lead you believe summarizes its focus and supporting details that expand and explain.

e) Submit to your teacher.

## Composing at the Keyboard

Composing your stories at a computer keyboard will not make you a better writer, but it will make the writing you do easier and more efficient. The keyboard is a tool, and like any other tool it works best in the hands of someone familiar with its use. To that end you will be more successful composing at the keyboard if you are comfortable with keyboarding, knowledgeable of the word processing software you are using and willing to incorporate both effectively into your writing process.

### Keyboarding

All of you come to this class and this textbook with varying degrees of typing or keyboarding skill. Just as a professional photographer must be able to handle a camera with such ease as to work with it effortlessly, so too writers must be able to handle a keyboard. Hunt and peck might be enough to get you by the occasional report or project. Of course, you might even be able to corral someone else into typing those for you. But as a storyteller, particularly a storyteller-journalist, you must type regularly and with reasonable skill. Your goal is to type accurately with moderate speed.

If you are able to enroll in a short course in keyboarding, try that. Alternatively, typing tutor software is widely available, with many accessible online as either freeware or shareware. Ultimately, though, your typing success will be determined by practice, practice, practice.

### Word Processing Software

While keys on a typewriter are pretty much all there is to that tool, the keyboard on a computer is merely the mechanical access; software comprises the intelligent part of that tool.

It is up to you to be proficient in software use. If available and you consider yourself a severe computer neophyte, take a course in word processing. Otherwise, boot the software and begin working with it. Explore the pulldown menus. See what features are available and practice using them. Talk to peers who have a good handle on the software and pick their brains. Learn whatever you can from whomever you can. If all else fails, open a manual or digital help menu.

Most important, use the special features available. For example, all good word processing software has spell check, yet some students never use it. Same goes for grammar check. While none of these checks are perfect, they encourage users to think through questions about common spelling and grammatical errors and weaknesses. If your software figures readability level, use it regularly to get a sense that your writing offers easy flow and clear meaning.

For example, the chapter you are reading is 8.3 using the Flesch-Kincaid Grade Level score. This rates text on a U.S. grade-school level. So, the score of 8.3 means that an eighth-grader should be able to understand the document. Aim for similar levels for most of the stories you tell.

## Writing Process

The cornerstone of "Storycrafting" is your use of writing process in your stories. Composing at the keyboard fits the process well, since it invites you to revisit your writing and easily make appropriate improvements. As long as you do not perceive a typed story as a finished story but rather as one still open to changes, word processing will serve you well.

## Crafting and Drafting

Stories from the campus dining hall can be fun to write and run the gamut of possibilities. This also is the first opportunity for your peer partners to review your work. Follow the tips below for each writer to make the experience a good one for all involved.

- One writer should read *aloud* his or her story draft for the following Exercise 2-4. Hold comments until the writer has finished.
- Take brief notes while the writer is reading so that you can comment on specific parts of the essay when you talk to the writer.
- Pay special attention to the revealing and informative details the writer provides.
- Speak directly to the writer and take responsibility for your opinions. Work at giving tactful responses, both positive and negative, but be firm and fair rather than nice.
- Begin with supportive, positive comments about the strengths of the story to constructive criticism of weaknesses and to suggestions for improvement. Be specific about what is working and what is not.
- Ask the writer for comments on your responses to his or her story. Find out which responses were most helpful and which were least helpful.
- Go to the next writer and repeat these steps.
- Remember that peer review is a vital part of the writing process. Your role as reviewer is as an interested reader.

## For Practice

2-4. Go to the campus dining hall to interview people there about the meal being served. Then, do the following:

a) Decide beforehand whether you want to emphasize those preparing the meal or those eating it. Try to imagine what point you want to make in the story.
b) Regardless of whom you emphasize, interview representatives of both sides for balance. Carefully record their names, appropriate identifications and contact information.

c) Keep appropriate notes of what your sources say. Include in your notes details of setting—sensory details that take the reader to the location, as well as details of action—those relevant, interesting things that are happening in the dining hall.

d) Listen carefully for quoteworthy comments from your sources and write them down exactly.

e) Draft a story on the meal, with a lead you believe summarizes its focus and supporting details that expand and explain.

f) Swap stories with a peer review partner or group and give written reader feedback. Submit the draft and peer feedback to your teacher.

g) After your teacher has reviewed your draft and peer feedback and has offered suggestions, check back with your sources, if necessary. Revise as required.

h) Submit a final draft to your teacher.

## Chapter 2 Bibliography

Bryant, William C. *Quotations for Creative Thinking.* <http://creativequotations.com/one/609a.htm>.

# Chapter 3
# Basic Story-Writing Forms

*Good writing is a kind of skating which
carries off the performer where he would
not go.*

—Ralph Waldo Emerson

## Chapter Contents

## *QuickView*

This chapter focuses on what you do with the material you gather. News stories follow various patterns that respond to needs of both content and audience, with traditional or creative openers, or leads, and body developments that deliver the details in appropriate ways.

We also will examine the variety of stories you may write, categorized by the content and purpose of each.

Finally, we will cover the basics of personal style, journalistic style and AP style.

Call me Ishmael. Some years ago—never mind how long precisely—having little or no money in my purse, and nothing particular to interest me on shore, I thought I would sail about a little and see the watery part of the world.

*Moby Dick*
—Herman Melville

It was the best of times, it was the worst of times, it was the age of wisdom, it was the age of foolishness, it was the epoch of belief, it was the epoch of incredulity, it was the season of Light, it was the season of Darkness, it was the spring of hope, it was the winter of despair . . .

*A Tale of Two Cities*
Charles Dickens

The cold passed reluctantly from the earth, and the retiring fogs revealed an army stretched out on the hills, resting. As the landscape changed from brown to green, the army awakened, and began to tremble with eagerness at the noise of rumors.

*The Red Badge of Courage*
Stephen Crane

# Leads

Among the most important tools storytellers use to share their stories are the openers. They know it is imperative to capture their audience's attention quickly and completely.

The same is true for storyteller-journalists and their openers, or leads, which grow directly from material they gather during research and interviews. Leads powerfully direct both story development for the writer and story understanding for the reader. Some journalists begin crafting their leads during the interview or on the trip back to the newsroom. Other journalists use lead writing as a means of planning how their stories will unfold. Some journalists even write leads last, preferring to write the body of their stories first.

Regardless of approach, leads fashion a focus that makes stories work with gathered materials.

## Summary Leads

Journalists traditionally have relied on the summary lead, or lede as it was spelled to avoid confusion with the lead that is a metal and pronounced differently. This brought together all of the five Ws and H, usually in a single sentence. As a result, the summary lead has been called a *clothesline lead,* because all of the elements are hung out in it, like clothing that was hung to dry on washday. Also, it has been termed the *AP lead,* because it was commonplace among stories distributed by the Associated Press.

Consider the following example of the summary lead, which presents the who, when, how, what and why (with the where implied):

The Western University board of regents Monday passed a 26 percent tuition hike for fall 2004 to offset $3 million in state budget cuts.

Summary leads work quite well when you want to present a good deal of material quickly. Moreover, newspaper readers are accustomed to this pattern and grasp key elements easily. Such leads continue to open straightforward stories and are useful today for readers who want to know quickly what happened.

While summary leads are still commonplace, many journalists today modify the format. They expand the summary into several paragraphs to present story elements instead of packing them all into the first paragraph. This alternative offers several benefits:

- It opens up the top of the story.
- It tends to be more flexible.
- It still allows writers to cover all the important story elements early in the story.

See how the summary lead example above might be presented in this modified format, which still includes the original elements:

Western University students will face a 26 percent tuition hike next fall.

The increase comes as the university works to offset state budget cuts that have cost the university $3 million.

The university board of regents passed the tuition increase Monday evening at its regular monthly meeting.

As you prepare to draft a traditional or modified summary lead, review the story elements and select the one that works best to begin the opening sentence. As noted previously, the most common choices are either the *what* or the *who did what*.

## Creative Leads

Journalists during the last quarter of the 20th century began to spurn summary leads in favor of creative, or feature, leads that capitalize on creative techniques rather than emphasize news elements. There are three main reasons for this:

- Growing competition from magazine, broadcast and online media—all of which prefer creative approaches.
- The invention of the computer. Since stories could be edited easily with the computer, different story structures beyond the inverted pyramid could be used, invoking different leads.
- The preference of many modern readers for softer, more inviting story approaches versus the hard-edged, direct summary lead.

See how this example of a creative lead opens the tuition increase story above:

Western University students are going to have to dig deeper, borrow more or work longer to pay their tuition next fall.

And they have no real choice in the matter.

The 26 percent tuition increase, which was approved Monday by the university board of regents, comes on the heels of $3 million in state budget cuts.

Draft your creative lead by:

- Capturing an appealing image or highlighting an unusual point.
- Showing rather than telling.
- Using language that is carefully selected for its richness and clarity.
- Making it imaginative, making it interesting.

Yet, do not use creative leads for all your stories. Traditional forms still do a better job telling many stories.

Also, some readers do not wish to wade through three or four paragraphs to get to the heart of the story. They want to know at first glance what happened—and whether they wish to continue reading about it.

Finally, too much of a good thing usually is bad. Variety demands you mix lead formats. You can read more about the following creative leads in Chapter 11:

- Anecdotal leads.
- Scene-setter leads.
- Descriptive leads.
- Direct address leads.
- Question leads.
- Direct quote leads.

## Lead Lengths

Short. That is what most leads need to be.

The traditional journalistic lead carries the heavy burden of presenting the central idea, but it must be read quickly and easily.

This is especially true of summary leads, which should average about 19 words. Leads of 30 or more words are too long. While creative leads may run three or four paragraphs, writers compromise by keeping paragraphs short, with many comprising of a single sentence.

## For Practice

3-1. Review one or more issues of your campus newspaper. Then, do the following:

a) Clip or photocopy three stories with summary leads and two stories with creative leads.
b) Using a highlighter, mark each of the leads and label them appropriately.
c) Count the number of words in each lead and write that next to the lead.
d) Share your examples with two other students in your class and see if they agree.
e) Submit the marked stories.

# *Story Development*

As observed earlier, a well-written lead makes crafting the rest of the story much easier since it can serve as a road map. Your choice of format is based on the material with which you are working, as you seek to provide the best vehicle to deliver it to readers. Common story structures include the following:

- Inverted pyramid.
- Chronology.
- Description.
- Wall Street Journal.
- Advance.

## Inverted Pyramid

Inverted pyramid is the traditional pattern for news stories. Usually opened with a summary lead, the content is presented most to least important. It typically has no conclusion, ending with the last paragraph that carries the least-important details. The easiest way to determine if your material actually follows the inverted pyramid order is to read through the story. As you do, ask if anything you are reading is more important than anything above it. If yes, move the detail up.

See how the following story illustrates the inverted pyramid.

### Festival unites community

By Jay Kirby

Tiger spirit invaded downtown Columbia last night when, for the third year, Twilight Festival took a twist to become the Tiger Twilight Festival.

"It's like a huge pep rally," said Carrie Gartner, executive director of the Downtown Columbia Associations. "Marching Mizzou comes out, they march up Eighth Street, column to column. The Golden Girls come out, and people hand out beads."

Marching Mizzou, the Golden Girls, Mizzou Tigers for Tigers, an organization focused on saving Bengal tigers, University Bookstore and the athletic department had displays at the festival.

Andrew Grinch, assistant director of marketing for the athletics department, said the festival helps involve the athletes in the community.

"There's a sense that the athletes and cheerleaders are untouchable," Grinch said, "so we have them out here visible where people can see them or have their picture taken with them or talk to them for a while."

The festival is a good chance for MU to promote fall sports such as football, soccer and volleyball, Grinch said. In addition to the band and cheerleaders, he said, members of the soccer and gymnastics teams promoted their sports.

"We walked around, handed out brochures about games and tried to get people to buy season passes," cheerleader and junior Jenny Weeks said.

Gartner said the idea for the Tiger Twilight Festival started as a way for downtown merchants to associate with students during the football season.

"This is just focused on the community and trying to have a good town-gown relationship," Gilbert said. "Town-gown" refers to the relationship between [campus and community].

Thursday night was the last Twilight Festival of 2002. The festival takes place every Thursday evening in June and September.

"We will go out with a bang with this one," Gartner said.

The Maneater
University of Missouri

## Chronology

Another format is chronology, or narrative order. It works best with action accounts. Chronology tends to be the simplest because it demands only that you present details of an event in the order they happened. It also is the most natural order for the same reason.

Yet, be selective in your use of chronology to structure stories. It works best with shorter news stories that finish with a punch—a payoff for readers who have stayed until the end. It should not become an easy alternative to one of the other more effective and appropriate formats.

The following story shows how simple chronology, beginning in the third paragraph, can present the circumstances involving a vicious dog.

### Case of vicious dog still under investigation

By Amy Preston

Owners of a rottweiler dog could face charges after their pet held grade school children at bay Tuesday morning, Riley County law enforcement officials said.

While no filing of the case has occurred, Terry Holdren, assistant county attorney, said it is under review.

Police were called to Tuttle Cove Street at about 8:19 a.m. Tuesday for the report of a vicious rottweiler dog. The call came from USD 383 bus driver Roni Ortiz, who approached three grade school children in the road, trying to avoid the dog, said Lt. Kurt Moldrup, of the Riley County Police Department.

Ortiz positioned her bus between the dog and children, loaded the children in her bus, and then immediately notified the police department.

"The bus driver clearly saved those kids from any harm," Moldrup said. "She did outstanding. She protected those kids."

When RCPD officials arrived to the scene, Moldrup said the dog went up to one officer's car and tried to attack the vehicle. An animal warden sprayed the dog with pepper spray; however, Moldrup said it had no effect.

Moldrup said officers attempted to make contact with dog owners Bryan and Marie Smith, 4437 Tuttle Cove Road, at this time, but there was no luck.

"The dog remained vicious and they couldn't just leave," Moldrup said.

As a result, officials used three tranquilizer darts, but the dog continued to get upset, Moldrup said.

Don Ross, senior animal control officer, said there could have been a number of reasons as to why the tranquilizer darts failed on the dog.

"Sometimes it just depends on the dog," Ross said. "When it's really adrenaline-pushed and excited for a period of time, that could have an effect on it. There's a lot of factors there."

Ross said that the breed of the dog did not matter.

"It just depends on how it is," he said. "If it's an aggressive dog, it's an aggressive dog—it doesn't really matter what breed it is."

[A tranquilizer dart], Ross said, goes to the extremities of the animals and is supposed to put them out without killing the animal.

"The main goal is to capture without killing," Ross said. "Killing is the absolute last [resort]."

After the dog did not subdue, police officers then shot the dog with shotgun-propelled bean bags—yet it didn't phase the pet, Moldrup said.

As a result, police officers used lethal force, shooting the dog a total of four times, Moldrup said.

"They did everything in their power to take this dog [without lethal] force, but it escalated and lethal force was necessary," Moldrup said.

The owners were notified of the incident when they returned home.

Moldrup said the dog had previous history with violence after it had bitten an officer this summer.

The Kansas State Collegian
Kansas State University

## Description

Another format to consider is description, or space order. It relies on the ability of the storyteller to craft a vibrant word picture. Description can bring to life coverage that otherwise might be routine. What is important here is to set a scene and then to transport readers to the scene and the moment.

The key to this format, and other creative patterns, is use of the nut graf, which does two things:

- It provides the summary focus following the anecdote.
- It serves as transition from the anecdotal material to the large issue.

A nut graf situated early in the story will ensure that readers know where the story is going.

The following story excerpt is among the most effective using this approach. Note how the nut graf is tucked unobtrusively into the third paragraph.

### The wine is fine off the Shawnee vine

By Evan Rau

Driving through the beautiful Shawnee Forest of Southern Illinois, one comes to an oasis on Route 127 just north of Alto Pass.

There has been little else beside forest and orchard for miles, but here, cars are lined up several rows deep on both sides of the two-lane blacktop.

Everywhere, people are sweating and smiling, glasses are tipped, and some Southern Illinoisans are tipsy. Not one of the 1,500 visitors feels disappointed upon leaving the Shawnee Hills Wine Trail Festival at the Alto Vineyards Saturday and Sunday.

Friends at the fest are busy visiting each of the wine booths. Alto Vineyards, the Owl Creek Vineyard, the Pomona Winery, the Von Jakob Vineyard and Winghill Vineyard and Winery all present their selections, which have won nearly 90 awards in the 2002 Illinois Wine Judging Competition.

From the sweet, wood-aged Porto Di Guido to the crisp Jonathan, the vast range of wines was enough to impress the most experienced connoisseur.

Folks did not limit themselves to crowding into booths for tastes of wines.

Jeremy Griffith sat at a shaded picnic table peacefully with his two perky Chihuahuas, Wilson and Tela, both named after songs performed by Phish. He listened to the mellow beat sounds of Blue Afternoon swirling around the winery as he waited for his wife, Lauren, to return.

"Nice atmosphere, nice place," said the SIU glass student, noting that he has come to the fest for the past four years.

People are found everywhere, but most are taking refuge from the sun under the large broadleaf trees near the house. They get a great view of the band, every wine tasting stand and the rolling terrain that serves as a backdrop to the whole party.

Some are spread out on blankets, nodding their heads to the beat of the music, lounging with their dogs and friends. Others are set up with beach umbrellas, folding chairs and wicker picnic baskets, resting their wine glasses in special glass-holding stakes set in the ground.

Attire ranges from cut-offs to khakis, and from tie-dye to polo shirts. No one judges anything but the wine here.

In the welcome cold of the bottling room, owner Paul Renzaglia stops to discuss wine but winds up conducting an entire tour of his winery.

His father, Guy, founded Alto Vineyards 13 years ago and it has remained a family run business since then.

As a visitor departs for a while from the festivities and wine booths, he or she walks through the vineyards surrounding the winery, which proves to calm the soul even more.

The conga beats and smooth guitar of Blue Afternoon muffle and distance themselves, overtaken by the sound of crickets and grasshoppers. The turbulent hum of the crowd melts into an airy decrescendo, with only an occasional howl of excitement leaping above the vineyard and arcing into the hills

\* \* \* \* \* \* \* \* \* \*

The Daily Egyptian
Southern Illinois University Carbondale

## Wall Street Journal

Unique among these story development formats is the Wall Street Journal. Popularized by the newspaper of the same name, it is especially useful for issue stories.

It opens with a captivating anecdote, a feature angle targeting an individual who serves as a representative of a larger group or class of people. This may comprise one-fourth to one-third of the story. The piece then expands at the nut graf to deal with the large issue, which fills most of the rest of the story. It wraps up with a short reference back to the original person, using a technique referred to as a "hook," or "circle kicker," because it circles back to the lead.

Properly handled, the Wall Street Journal pattern is valuable in its ability to personalize an issue that might otherwise be distant or removed from readers' experience.

This format, with the nut graf in the fifth and sixth paragraphs, is well illustrated in the following excerpt.

### New technology making bridal registry easier, more efficient

#### Computerized system allows guests to access registries at other stores

By Dan Smith

Jamie Gfeller wasn't looking forward to registering for her Jan. 4 wedding.

Gfeller, senior in family studies and human services, said picking out items to last a lifetime seemed like a daunting task at first.

But when it came time for her and fiance Tyler Breeden, senior in agricultural economics, to make their list, they were surprised.

"At first, I was really dreading it, but now it's gotten so much easier," Gfeller said. "It's not like you have to write down everything you want."

Thanks to special scanning guns now in use at most department and specialty stores, Gfeller and Breeden had a good experience registering at Pier 1 Imports, Target and Dillard's, she said.

The new technology is a welcome addition for couples and their wedding guests, said Jenni King, Dillard's bridal sales associate and junior in accounting.

"You choose your gifts," she said. "You choose what you want in your home, whereas it used to be that people would buy what they think you need. You'd get 20 toasters, how many sets of CorningWare and whatnot.

"Now, you can come in, choose what goes with your taste, design your own living or dining room, and it makes it so much easier on people shopping."

\* \* \* \* \* \* \* \* \* \*

But small stores don't necessarily mean wedding couples have to miss out on anything on their wish lists, Beth Franklin, J.C. Penney catalog supervisor, said.

"Our store is more on the lower level of registering," she said.

"If you go to the bigger stores like the Topeka J.C. Penney, where they carry the whole line, they actually can scan what they want there. Then, we can get a list through any J.C. Penney store in the country. If they're registered here, their guests can go ahead and pull them up at any other store."

That kind of convenience has Gfeller looking forward to her special day.

"It helps because it's so simple that I don't mind doing it," she said. "Registering can take a lot of time, and by making it so simple, it doesn't seem like a burden."

The Kansas State Collegian
Kansas State University

## Advance

Advance stories are among the most frequent you will write. Usually short and simple, these preview an event of interest to readers. Summary leads, which usually open these stories, stress points of interest to readers who may wish to attend the events. Standard event leads stress *what* and *who*. If the event is a speech, the lead should include speaker, topic and audience. Also, time, day and place—the *when* and *where*—are essential for all advances.

Supporting and explanatory material, usually presented in inverted pyramid order, comprises the body of an advance. The purpose is to inform about the event and encourage attendance.

The following advance is similar to many you will encounter.

### Salsa hits 7th Street

By Isaac Thomas

Members of the Center for Student Life and Cozumel Mexican restaurant will hold a Fall Fiesta on Philadelphia and North Seventh streets from 6 to 10 p.m. Friday.

The streets will be decorated with authentic Mexican regalia, and salsa band Ritmo Caribeno will perform and give informal salsa dance lessons to the public.

The sponsor of this event, the Downtown Indiana Association, hopes it will surpass last year's Ox Roast, which yielded an attendance of approximately 100 people. This year they worked to bring in the talented 12-piece band from Cozumel's Pittsburgh location in Shadyside.

"They are very talented musicians. . . . They pull quite a turn-out," said Downtown director Jennifer Luzier. Ritmo Caribeno will be playing later Friday night at Cozumel restaurant, and a cover charge will be applied.

Those involved hope this multicultural event will fulfill the Downtown mission statement of "striving to bring together the IUP community and the residents of Indiana."

The association has already surpassed last year's total by selling more than 200 tickets.

Tickets are $10 and can be purchased at Cozumel's, the Downtown office, the Student Life office in 102 Pratt Hall or at the event itself.

After 8 p.m., those who wish not to divulge in the delectable comidas de Mexicas can purchase tickets solely for the salsa show for $5.

The Penn
Indiana University of Pennsylvania

## *Follow Stories*

If advances are among the stories you will write most frequently, follow stories on those events are similarly commonplace. However, not all advances demand follows; do those for events of consequence, where readers gain from finding out what happened. Although advances tend to be simple and routine, their follow counterparts often can be quite complex and powerful.

Information presented in advances, such as speaker/topic or event, day, place and audience, is repeated in follow stories but always in different form. While those details typically hold important positions in advance leads, follow story leads are more likely to focus on *what* the speaker said or *what happened*.

Other types of follow stories emphasize aspects of the story that grow from the event.

See how the following two stories—the first an advance and the second a follow—spin from one side of the event to the other.

**Advance**

### Candidates clash at UH tonight

Cougar News Staff

One of the city's most heated political races will come to campus tonight when the candidates for District 25 of the House of Representatives debate in the University Hilton.

"Education: that's what this is all about," said junior political science major Monica Granger, the president of the College Libertarians at UH, which is co-sponsoring the debate with the College Republicans.

"I think the students deserve a chance to make a choice by themselves, and the mass media isn't providing that chance," she said.

The candidates debating will be Democrat Chris Bell, Libertarian Guy McLendon, Republican Tom Reiser and the Green Party's George Reiter.

College Republicans President Philip Poe, a senior communication major, said the candidates for the 25th District were asked to debate at UH for many reasons.

"The 25th District is the most heated race and the most important race in the city right now," he said. "There's no incumbent, so it's a wide-open race."

Other reasons were that Reiter is a physics professor at UH; many UH students live in the 25th District and since redistricting took place, UH partly falls in the 25th District (the rest is in the 18th District, where the campus used to be). The debate will start at 7:30 p.m. in the University Hilton's Shamrock Room. Granger said it is free, and the audience members will be let in on a first-come, first-served basis.

\* \* \* \* \* \* \* \* \* \*

The Daily Cougar
The University of Houston

**Follow Story**

### Candidates trade barbs in debate

By Ray Hafner

Congressional candidates for District 25 lined up along the political spectrum to debate Tuesday night, with Democratic candidate Chris Bell's accusation that Republican Tom Reiser is an "extremist" characterizing the night's exchanges.

That exchange was part of several attacks on Reiser as Bell stepped out of his normally easygoing attitude. Bell attempted to paint himself as a reasonable reformer who is capable of creating "common-sense solutions."

Reiser stressed his fiscal background as a businessman, saying that, if elected to the House of Representatives, his goal would be to serve on the appropriations committee.

"My goal as a congressman will be to make life better for small-business people," he said, noting that 99 percent of all businesses are considered small businesses.

Filling out the slate were two third-party candidates, George Reiter from the Green Party and Guy McLendon from the Libertarian Party.

UH physics professor Reiter is running on an anti-war platform, and while having no delusions about actually winning, he called his candidacy a referendum on the Iraq war issue.

"A vote for me is a way to express your opposition to the war," he said.

Reiter hopes that if he takes 5 to 10 percent of the vote, Congress will take note.

McLendon, a die-hard constitutionalist, actually held a copy of the U.S. Constitution throughout the debate, saying that its ideas had been "gutted by faulty definitions of a few key words" over the years.

McLendon supports abolishing the Federal Department of Education, privatization of Social Security and even allowing concealed handguns on college campuses.

It was Bell's sometimes oblique but most often frank barbs at Reiser, however, that stood out in the debate.

\* \* \* \* \* \* \* \* \* \*

The Daily Cougar
The University of Houston

## *Updates*

Updates include stories that continue for both short and longer periods. For example, a severe parking crunch on campus might see coverage in several successive issues of your newspaper. On the other hand, racial unrest that may flare up from time to time also fits the characteristics of updates, as does the investigation into a dormitory fire.

In these instances you should carry key elements of the previous stories into the next. Importantly, though, repeated details should be revised slightly and should drop lower in successive stories written about the continuing focus.

See how the following excerpts take readers through the ongoing investigation of a local murder. Note how the focus of each successive story is on something different than the original story.

**Original Story**

### Chicago man killed in Carbondale

By Greg Cima

A 24-year-old Chicago man was shot to death in the 500 block of South Lake Heights at about 2:40 a.m. Saturday.

Rodney E. Jones of 12154 Justine St., Chicago, died from a gunshot wound to the chest at Memorial Hospital of Carbondale at 3:35 a.m., according to the Jackson County Coroner's office.

Mark S. Crymes, 23, of 1404 N. Wall St. was arrested in connection with the shooting. Crymes is charged with murder, armed violence, aggravated discharge of a firearm and trespass, according to police. Crymes was taken to the Jackson County Jail.

Elizabeth Crim, who has lived in the Lake Heights neighborhood for four years, said she woke up because of the gunfire and saw people in her front yard lifting Jones into the car that transported him to the hospital. She said Jones, who went by the nickname of "Boo," was in the neighborhood on occasion with friends.

* * * * * * * * * *

The Daily Egyptian
University of Southern Illinois Carbondale

**First Update**

## Chicago man killed after altercation, police say

By Greg Cima

Witnesses in the early Saturday death of a 24-year-old Chicago man said he had been in an altercation with the shooter, police said.

Rodney E. Jones, 24, of 12154 Justine St., Chicago, died after being shot twice during the early morning hours Saturday. Police said Jones died after being shot in his back and arm, contrary to earlier reports that he had been shot in the chest. Jones was pronounced dead at 3:35 a.m. Saturday, according to the Jackson County Coroner's office.

Mark S. Crymes, 1404 N. Wall St., was arrested shortly after the shooting in a nearby residence. Crymes was charged with murder, armed violence, aggravated discharge of a firearm and trespass, according to police. Crymes was taken to the Jackson County Jail.

* * * * * * * * * *

The Daily Egyptian
University of Southern Illinois Carbondale

**Second Update**

## Police seeking second suspect in Saturday killing

By Greg Cima

Police are seeking a Carbondale man in connection with the shooting death of a Chicago man early Saturday.

Reginald L. Cavitt, 21, is sought for his connection to Mark S. Crymes, 23, of 1404 N. Wall St., who was arrested and charged with murder, armed violence, aggravated discharge of a firearm and trespass shortly after the shooting death of Rodney E. Jones, 24, early Saturday morning.

Jones, of 12154 Justine St., Chicago, died at 3:35 a.m. Saturday after being shot in the arm and back, police said. Jones was shot at about 2:40 a.m. Saturday in the 500 block of South Lake Heights and was driven to Memorial Hospital of Carbondale by individuals at the scene. X-rays determined Jones was shot with a small-caliber handgun but no weapon has been recovered.

Cavitt is wanted on two charges of murder, aggravated discharge of a firearm, unlawful use of weapons and possession of weapons by a felon in connection with the shooting. Cavitt had a previous conviction of robbery in 1998.

\* \* \* \* \* \* \* \* \* \*

The Daily Egyptian
Southern Illinois University Carbondale

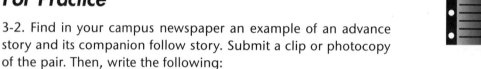

## For Practice

3-2. Find in your campus newspaper an example of an advance story and its companion follow story. Submit a clip or photocopy of the pair. Then, write the following:

a) Read the advance to see if it includes all the necessary details that will encourage readers to attend, including the *when* and *where*.
b) For the advance identify the speaker, topic and audience *or* event as well as the time, day and place.
c) For the companion follow story identify what the speaker said or what happened at the event.

3-3. Find in your campus newspaper an example of an update. Include the original, which presented primary information, and the update. Submit a clip or photocopy of the pair. Then, write the following:

a) What details presented in the first story are repeated in the second? How are they revised for the second? Where in the story are the repeated details given?
b) What new details are presented in the update? Are these important enough to warrant the update, or does it seem the newspaper is "treading water" in keeping a story alive?

## Using Others' Words

Journalists rely on the material they gather from others to do their storytelling. As opposed to personal columns or editorials, in which journalists express their own ideas and opinions, news stories present the ideas and opinions of others. On the surface, at least, journalists and news stories are conduits through which flows the material.

However, as should be clear by now, the filtering and shaping journalists do are essential. They are the difference between a mere list of events, ideas, facts and opinions and an inviting, carefully crafted story.

While your excellent description of a house fire or a three-car pileup can make your story come to life for readers, comments from your sources usually are what give the story meaning.

You have three ways to use others' words; see how each is illustrated in the passages below:

**Direct Quotation**

These are the speaker's exact words:

The president knew the university history, he knew its potential and he put together a strategic plan that could take us there," regent Phil North said.

**Paraphrase**

Note in the following example how the reporter's words express the source's ideas:

Regent Phil North said Kelley understood where the university was and where it could be as he developed the strategic plan for the future.

**Summary**

This passage moves to a level more general and further removed from the direct quote and paraphrase:

Regents had high praise for university President John J. Kelley.

Because you must become deft at handling all three ways to use others' words, let us spend time reviewing each.

## Direct Quotation

The most careful representation of others' ideas and opinions is direct quotation. These are the *exact* words of your source, not just an approximation of the ideas. Two criteria guide use of direct quotation:

- It deals with material that is important to the story and integral to reader understanding.
- It is so well spoken by your source, so powerfully stated, that paraphrase will not do it justice.

If the material does not meet both of these criteria, paraphrase it.

However, resist the urge to overdo direct quotations. Novice journalists rely on direct quotations as crutches to avoid having to write what sources meant as opposed to what sources said. Therefore, the general rule is this: The fewer direct quotes, the better.

Of course, as we saw earlier, your notetaking will help determine which method you use to share others' words. Essentially, you cannot generate a direct quotation from notes that only summarized or paraphrased a source's comments. If something is quoteworthy, you must capture it when your source says it.

## Paraphrase

Paraphrase is your rendition of others' key ideas and opinions, presented in a new form. Paraphrase changes the wording of your sources' comments without changing the meaning.

Paraphrase rather than directly quote information from an undistinguished passage. This lets you share sources' ideas and opinions more concisely and, at times, more clearly. The mental process required for effective paraphrase also helps you to better grasp the meaning of the original.

Paraphrase is the most common form that others' words will appear in your stories. Rely on it for nearly all the material from sources in your stories.

### Summary

A close companion of paraphrase, summary is the most general use of your source's comments. While paraphrase is a specific restatement in your own words of supporting details, summary is a brief, more general restatement in your words of the main points or facts.

Yet, summary can be quite difficult for inexperienced storytellers to craft. It demands that you have crystal clear understanding of the original material as you pack a lot of meaning into condensed form. Summary looks at the big picture. It provides overview that makes it easier for readers to understand how the other material comes together.

You will use summaries for many of your news story leads and to help organize parts of your stories.

---

## *For Practice*

3-4. Review one or more issues of your campus newspaper. Then, do the following:

a) Photocopy or clip *three* stories.
b) For each identify and label the type of development used: inverted pyramid, chronology, description, Wall Street Journal, advance or other.
c) Using a highlighter, mark the summarized material on the *first* story.
d) Using a highlighter, mark the paraphrased material on the *second* story.
e) Using a highlighter, mark the direct quotes on the *third* story.
f) Share your results with two other students in class and see if they agree with your decisions.
g) Submit the marked stories.

---

## *Story Style*

Traditional storytellers often develop reputations for their style. Perhaps they clothe themselves in period dress. They may use language befitting the settings and periods of their stories. Their delivery may be calm and deliberate or fiery and intense. All of these elements of storyteller style relate directly to the success of storytellers, making their tales come alive.

Style within the context of "Storycrafting" refers to three things:

- A writer's personal style.
- Traditional journalistic style.
- Associated Press style.

## Personal Style

Personal style is a distinctive, sometimes unique, delivery that writers give their stories. It typically deals with writing issues that involve choices. For example, the exact word you use when several are available is a matter of style. So is your use of shorter sentences versus longer. Style may involve a flair for figurative language or peppery sentence structures or flowing, artistic passages. Like fingerprints or signatures, personal style belongs to the person and is not changed without effort.

By now, most of you have developed elements of personal style. Hold on to those that are effective, but get rid of those that detract from your writing. Like any habit acquired through repetition over time, changing your personal style is not simple, yet if you hope to be a good storyteller, you cannot allow weak personal style to become an obstacle.

For example, a reflection of the colloquialisms among many Americans today is incorrect use of the participle *seen*. It is proper to say, "He <u>was</u> <u>seen</u> walking along the canal." It is *not* proper to say, "I <u>seen</u> him walking along the canal." The correct usage, of course, is "I <u>saw</u> him walking along the canal." While most people are willing to forgive common spoken errors, they are less likely to overlook those same errors in writing.

For in-depth assistance beyond "Storycrafting," consider one of the following resources:

- "The Elements of Style," William Strunk Jr. et al.
- "Lapsing into a Comma: A Curmudgeon's Guide to the Many Things that Can Go Wrong in Print—and How To Avoid Them," Bill Walsh.
- "On Writing Well," William K. Zinnser.
- "Style: Ten Lessons in Clarity and Grace," Joseph M. Williams.
- "Working with Style: Conversations on the Art of Writing," John R. Trimble.
- A good English handbook covering usage and conventions.

## Traditional Journalistic Style

Since the first U.S. newspaper, Publick Occurrences, Both Foreign and Domestick, was published in Boston in 1690, journalists have developed a unique style. This style likely differs from that you use to write short stories, essays, research papers or e-mail to your friends. It stresses clarity, brevity and conciseness.

Roy Peter Clark of the Poynter Institute explains the characteristics of journalistic style in the following list:

- The language of journalism is concrete and specific, especially when it comes to dogs and the names of dogs.
- The language of journalism is active.
- The language of journalism . . . is front-heavy.
- The language of journalism is democratic, and, if I may say so, American.

- The language of journalism is different from speech, but more like speech than most other forms of prose.
- The language of journalism is plain.
- The most valued quality of the language of journalism is clarity, and its most desired effect is to be understood.

He suggests that these qualities are the measure by which a journalistic piece can be called a story versus an article.

In addition to language are a handful of other features that characterize journalistic style. We will review those in later chapters.

### Associated Press Style

Layered upon your personal style and traditional journalistic style is Associated Press style. For the most part, this style already relates to and supports traditional journalistic style, but it takes you well beyond the general provisions noted above and gives specific usage across the board.

The primary resource for AP style, of course, is The Associated Press Stylebook and Briefing Manual on Media Law, which is organized like a dictionary and updated regularly.

Just as no one expects that you read and memorize a dictionary, your use of the AP Stylebook is for reference. Consult it whenever you have more than one way to say or present something.

## Crafting and Drafting

You and your peer review partners should be moving past that awkward, get-acquainted stage by now. As you review drafts for either Exercise 3-5 or Exercise 3-6, concentrate on answering the following questions as part of your discussion.

- What seems to be the main idea of the story? Is it clearly stated in the lead?
- What words or phrases in the story stand out to you?
- What headline would you give to this story?
- What one thing did you like best? Why?
- What one thing did you like least? Why?
- What one idea would you like the writer to add?
- What one idea do you think could be cut (if any)?

## For Practice

3-5. Pick a speech, presentation or event that will take place on your campus and that has not been covered yet with an advance by your campus newspaper. Then, do the following:

a) Find sources who can provide you necessary information for the story.
b) Interview each and take careful notes, practicing your personal shorthand as effectively as you can.
c) Listen carefully for quoteworthy comments the sources make, and write those down exactly.
d) Draft an advance with a lead you believe summarizes the focus and with supporting details that expand and explain.
e) Swap stories with a peer review partner or group and give written reader feedback. Submit the draft and peer feedback to your teacher.
f) After your teacher has reviewed your draft and peer feedback and has offered suggestions, revise as required. If necessary, go back to sources for more information.
g) Submit a final draft.

3-6. Find a news story for which no update has been written but for which one might be appropriate. Clip or photocopy the original story. Then, do the following:

a) Find sources who can provide you new information for the story, particularly key sources from the original story.
b) Interview each and take careful notes, practicing your personal shorthand as effectively as you can.
c) Listen carefully for quoteworthy comments the sources make, and write those down exactly.
d) Draft an update with a lead you believe summarizes the focus and with supporting details that expand and explain. Stress new information, but include necessary key details from the original story that enable readers to understand the update.
e) Swap stories and original clips with a peer review partner or group and give written reader feedback. Submit the draft and peer feedback to your teacher.
f) After your teacher has reviewed your draft—along with its accompanying original story—and peer feedback and has offered suggestions, check back with your sources, if necessary. Revise as required.
g) Submit a final draft.

---

# Chapter 3 Bibliography

"Candidates Clash at UH Tonight." *The Daily Cougar.* 22 October 2002. <http://www.stp.uh.edu/vol68/41/news/news2.html>.

Cima, Greg. "Chicago Man Killed After Altercation, Police Say." *The Daily Egyptian.* 1 October 2002. <http://newshound.de.siu.edu/fall02/stories/storyReader$755>.

Cima, Greg. "Chicago Man Killed in Carbondale." *The Daily Egyptian.* 30 September 2002. <http://newshound.de.siu.edu/fall02/stories/storyReader$732>.

Cima, Greg. "Police Seeking Second Suspect in Saturday Killing." *The Daily Egyptian.* 3 October 2002. <http://newshound.de.siu.edu/fall02/stories/storyReader$791>.

Clark, Roy Peter. *The American Conversation and the Language of Journalism.* St. Petersburg, Fla.: Poynter Institute for Media Studies, 1994.

Crane, Stephen. *The Red Badge of Courage*. (1895). In *Online Literature Library*. 8 January 2002. <http://www.literature.org/authors/crane-stephen/the-red-badge-of-courage/chapter-01.html>.

Dickens, Charles. *A Tale of Two Cities*. (1859). In *Online Literature Library*. 8 January 2002. <http://www.literature.org/authors/dickens-charles/two-cities/book-01/chapter-01.html>.

Emerson, Ralph Waldo. *Quotations for Creative Thinking*. <http://creativequotations.com/>.

Hafner, Ray. "Candidates Trade Barbs in Debate." *The Daily Cougar*. 23 October 2002. <http://www.stp.uh.edu/vol68/42/news/news1.html>.

Kirby, Jay. "Festival Unites Community." *The Maneater*. 27 September 2002. <http://www.themaneater.com/story.cgi?id=14161>.

Melville, Herman. *Moby Dick*. (1851). In *The Life and Works of Herman Melville*. 25 July 2000. <http://www.melville.org/hmmoby.htm#Excerpts>.

Preston, Amy. "Case of Vicious Dog Still Under Investigation." *Kansas State Collegian*. 16 October 2003. <http://kstatecollegian.com/stories/101603/new_puppy.shtml>.

Rau, Evan. "The Wine Is Fine off the Shawnee Vine." *The Daily Egyptian*. 6 September 2002. <http://newshound.de.siu.edu/fall02/stories/storyReader$287>.

Smith, Dan. "New Technology Making Bridal Registry Easier, More Efficient: Computerized System Allows Guests to Access Registries at Other Stores." *The Kansas State Collegian*. 4 October 2002. <http://www.kstatecollegian.com/stories/100402/new_tech.shtml>.

Thomas, Isaac. "Salsa Hits 7th Street." *The Penn*. 2 October 2002. <http://www.thepenn.org/vnews/display.v/ART/2002/10/02/3d9b628fca429>.

# Chapter 4
# Setting Up the Newsroom

*A newspaper is not just for reporting the news as it is, but to make people mad enough to do something about it.*

—Mark Twain

## Chapter Contents

**The Campus Community**
Government
Business Activities
Social Events
Meetings and Speeches
Accidents
Crime

Education
Technology
For Practice
**Story Beats**
Scenario for a City Hall Beat
Sample Campus Beats

For Practice
Covering Your Beat
**Story Deadlines**
Crafting and Drafting
For Practice

## QuickView

The main concern of Chapter 4 is to offer you a foundation and framework for your classroom newsroom, from which you will work with your instructor and peers in gathering and writing your stories. With your classroom as your newsroom, it follows naturally that your community for coverage should be your college campus—a place that you know or soon will know.

Your method of covering your campus community is the beat, either a geographical or a topical way to ensure that you and your peers do a thorough job of telling stories covering a wide array of areas, activities and voices.

Finally, you will learn the importance of meeting deadlines, which will make you and your classmates an effective storytelling team.

Storytellers come to their telling moments with a clear knowledge of their task. They bring with them a storyteller's perspective: an awareness of who they are, who they are speaking to, the time and place of their stories and a particular goal in telling them.

Storyteller-journalists need to acquire the same perspective.

Writers tend to write best about what they know best. Moreover, writing tends to improve when writers take ownership of their writing. These two principles provide the basis for setting up the classroom newsroom.

Recall one of your previous writing experiences. Perhaps you wrote an essay about the motorcycle accident that broke your leg, a painful but important life experience. Your writing was familiar, realistic and natural. No doubt you were comfortable and successful with that essay because you wrote about an experience that was your own.

This is true because it is *easier* to write about the familiar. Moreover, writers are more effective when they have all the details of the experience readily available. In such instances, writers take ownership of their writing.

## *The Campus Community*

You may recall from Chapter 1 that ownership involves not only writing stories from your own perspective but also gathering the material for those stories. As a result, your story assignments for "Storycrafting" will be based on information you gather about the events, people and trends from somewhere you know, or soon will know, quite well—your own campus.

Your classroom will become the newsroom from which you and your classmates will cover your campus community. While few of you will become fully familiar with *all* areas of your campus, each of you should become very familiar with *some* areas.

A college campus is like any other community. As a result, writing about—and to—that community parallels the work that professional journalists do every day. The stories below from college newspapers across the country illustrate the same wide range of coverage as you will find in any off-campus city or town.

### Government

Both a college governance board as well as student government likely operate on your campus. Its members discuss and debate issues that determine much of the operation of the campus community. Therefore, the government beat should be an important area for news.

This certainly is the case in this story from Colorado, where a delay in student government elections has drawn criticism from several student groups.

#### Students react to elections

##### Delay will hurt groups' funding, they say

By Jessica Fruchter

While student government elections remain in an apparent tailspin, there is one thing that almost all parties involved can agree upon—UCSU's appellate court's decision to postpone elections will only make things worse.

The ruling to delay voting by a week prompted a coalition of student groups to speak out Monday at a press conference on the CU-Boulder's campus.

Students said they fear the delay will worsen an already visible problem of voter apathy on CU's campus.

"(The delay) will really hurt referendum groups," said Stephanie Tidwell, a member of CU's Rainforest Action Group. "We (student groups) need to get an entire 10 percent of the student body to vote for us in order to receive student funding."

"We've been working really hard to get the word out," Tidwell added. "Now students are going to be told they can't vote. They're going to think this is a mess and why did they bother."

"Personally I feel totally disenfranchised by this entire court procedure," she said.

The Rainforest Action Group was one of several student groups, including Ecopledge, Sinapu, Student Outreach Retention Center for Equity, and the Student Environmental Action Coalition represented during Monday's press conference.

"By delaying this election, the appellate court has actually punished all the referendum groups, the candidates, UCSU proper and the students who depend on a reliable election at CU," CU Sinapu co-director Joshua Ruschhaupt said in a statement Monday.

Calling this year's elections a "huge fiasco," Tidwell said all referendum groups seeking funding during this year's election face a potential loss because of the delay.

"They've really done the referendum groups a huge disservice. We're going to have to work twice as hard and twice as long to pull this off," she said. "We'll do everything we can do to keep campaigning. This really calls into question the state of student government."

Referendum organizers say the elections should proceed as planned.

"We want the court to redress this," Tidwell said. "We'd like for the elections to go on and for the results to remain confidential until the appeal is resolved."

Referendum groups are not alone in their concern.

Members of the election commission requested over the weekend that the court amend its decision to suspend elections and instead freeze results pending the appeal.

"(We would) prefer every candidate remain on the ballot and for the election not to be disrupted," said Kirk Hamm, UCSU law school senator and member of the election commission.

"(The postponement of elections) will kill voter turnout," he said. "I have great sympathy (for the referendum groups)."

Hamm said as of Monday afternoon he was still unsure if the court had accepted the amendment.

Representatives from UCSU's appellate court did not return calls by press time.

The Colorado Daily<br>The University of Colorado-Boulder

## Business Activities

Whether your college is public or private, it runs like any other business. The college operates on income, or revenue, from various sources, and spends those funds on whatever is deemed necessary to conduct well the business of education. Business topics can be dry and dull, yet business stories are classic hard news and demand excellent writing to inform readers of how business activities will impact them.

The following library-renovation story from Pennsylvania details a handful of business decisions, beginning with a concept study in 2000 and culminating in the go-ahead for the $15 million project.

### Linderman Library to undergo $15 million in renovations

By Lauren Eisner

The recently approved Linderman Library revitalization project will cost an estimated $15 million and will transform Linderman into an updated intellectual center.

There will be numerous renovations to restructure Linderman. These include a new classroom and group seminar space, along with a commons and café space. Handicapped access will be added to the building for easier navigation. New heating and air conditioning systems will be installed for the preservation of collections and for the comfort of all visitors to the library.

President Greg Farrington recently gave the go-ahead for the project to continue. "Being given 'a go' on the Linderman Library project is a testament to the hard work done by a large number of people including both LTS staff and Lehigh faculty," said Bruce Taggart, Vice Provost for Library and Technology Services. "It is also a recognition of the centrality of both libraries and humanities at Lehigh."

"This academic year marks the 125th anniversary of Linderman Library (the early rotunda section) and there will be some special celebrations in the coming months for the whole campus to enjoy," said Sue Cady, Director for Administrative and Planning Services for Library and Technology Services.

The plans for the Linderman renovations began approximately three years ago and have passed through many necessary stages. There was a "concept study" in 2000 to discuss the role of the library. Many meetings have been held, including meetings with faculty, staff and student senate.

"There was thinking about how Linderman might fit into the 20-year campus and facilities plan that was being developed with the assistance of Sasaki Associates at the time," said Cady.

Fund raising will be vital to the completion of the project goals. Jean Farrington has taken on the job of fund-raising project manager for the Linderman project.

"The goal is to raise the estimated Linderman revitalization project cost of $15 million and we will seek support from Lehigh alumni, friends, corporations and foundations for the project," said Farrington. "The fund-raising plans are being developed this semester."

The time frame for the construction and completion of the renovations is currently unknown. There are many aspects, including fund raising for the project, that must be completed before Lehigh can "break ground."

The selection of an architect to design the needed renovations for the project is currently being worked on. "Once a firm has been recommended to the trustees and then approved, approximately a year of design work will follow. The design process will be overseen by Tony Corallo and Facilities Services," said Taggart.

The conclusion of the project is expected to have a very positive impact on all of the Lehigh community.

"I think the revitalization will be wonderful—taking a building that is already physically "central" to the campus and enhancing its "central" role within the academic mission," said Cady. "It's very exciting to think about Linderman being preserved as a beautiful historic building and at the same time upgraded and updated to serve as a humanities library and program building on into the future."

The Brown and White
Lehigh University

## Social Events

Throughout your school year are many campuswide and student-oriented events. Coverage of these is valuable and can be a pleasure to write. While follow stories are worthwhile for some events, most are written as advances.

The following Malaysian cultural night is an advance that focuses on both entertainment and educational aspects of this annual event.

### Cultural night to bring Malaysian traditions to campus

By Andrew Mabe

Many races and traditions combine to make one country—the United States isn't the only nation that can be described in this way.

The opportunity to experience sights, sounds and cuisines of Malaysia will be offered to the public during Malaysian Cultural Night at 5 p.m. Sunday in the Great Hall of the Memorial Union.

Malaysia is a democratic country in Southeast Asia populated by 25 million people.

Chinese, Indian and Malay are the predominant races that make up the country.

The Malaysian Students' Association will share the country's traditions with the people of Ames.

"Our purpose is to introduce and educate the community about Malaysian culture and customs, as well as our food and performances," said Nurhidayah Azmy, senior in construction engineering.

Following a cultural display in the Memorial Union hotel lobby, a Malay wedding ceremony will be re-enacted.

This involves a blessing offered to the "bride and groom" by the guests of honor, including some who traveled a great distance.

"What's special about our event this year is the Malaysian ambassador from Washington, D.C. will be coming for the first time ever," Azmy said.

The ambassador, Dato Sheikh Abdul Khalid Ghazzali, and ISU President Gregory Geoffroy will be among those attending the celebration.

In addition to witnessing a wedding portrayal, there will be five traditional dance performances.

"The first one will be a Chinese line dance," Azmy said.

"Then a Malay dance, which is an interpretation dance."

The traditional Malay dance tells the tale of a sick person who is healed by a fairy, Azmy said.

The cultural performances throughout the night will serve to entertain and build attendees' appetites for dinner, Azmy said.

"Since we have so many races, Malaysian food is influenced by Malay, Chinese and Indian food," Azmy says.

The menu for the evening features roti canai, a popular flat bread that is fried and eaten with curry chicken.

A rice dish, known as nasi lemak, will also be served, along with two other Malaysian dishes and a dessert.

The Malaysian Cultural Night also serves as a philanthropic event.

"Every time we do the Malaysian Cultural Night, there is a beneficiary," said Royson Chong, senior in computer engineering.

In past years, the event has raised money for organizations, such as the Red Cross.

This year, the United Way of Story County will receive the proceeds.

"[The United Way] funds specific programs directly, rather than letting the money go through administrative costs first," Chong said.

Tickets for the event are $7 for students and $10 for the general public.

Iowa State Daily
Iowa State University

## Meetings and Speeches

It is likely that different groups and individuals regularly meet and present speeches on your campus. Both advances and follows are helpful, with the former bringing out interested crowds and the latter informing readers who could not attend.

This story from Kansas previews the visit of "Hairspray" filmmaker John Waters, offering readers ample reason to make plans to attend.

### Filmmaker and author to speak at KU campus

By Michael Vennard

The Student Union Activities office announced last week filmmaker and author John Waters would visit the University of Kansas next Tuesday for a lecture and book signing.

SUA Forums Coordinator Quinn Gorges, Wichita senior, said the "John Waters: Cinematic Immunity" presentation would include a lecture by Waters, questions from the audience and a screening of the 1988 Waters film "Hairspray." The lecture at Woodruff Auditorium in the Kansas Union will begin at 8 p.m.

Tickets for the event will cost $6 with a KU ID or $10 for the general public. Tickets are for sale at the SUA box office in the Kansas Union as well as the Lied Center and Murphy Hall box offices.

Gorges said Waters would sign books and DVDs at the Oread Bookshop in the Kansas Union from 4 p.m. to 5 p.m. on the same day. Before that, Waters will briefly address KU film students at 3 p.m. at Oldfather Studios.

"It's really exciting to have someone like Waters come to Lawrence," Gorges said yesterday.

Film student Patrick Rea said he looked forward to seeing Waters speak next week.

"I want to ask him how he started out and find out how he got to where he is now. I think a lot of graduating film students would like to hear his advice," Rea, Schuyler, Nebraska, senior, said.

In preparation for the filmmaker's visit to Lawrence, Liberty Hall, 642 Massachusetts, will screen Waters' 1972 cult film "Pink Flamingos" this Friday and Saturday night.

David Nickol, Liberty Hall's video store manager, said tickets for the 11:30 p.m. screenings would cost $4 in advance and $5 the day of the movie.

"I've seen his movies for years and years and the opportunity to see him speak, I'm excited about it. From what I hear he's a very good public speaker," Nickol said.

> University Daily Kansan
> The University of Kansas

## Accidents

Anyplace you find people, you will find the potential for accidents. Some may seem routine, but all are important as hard-news coverage that readers want and need to know.

Injuries to two pedestrians near campus are the topic of an accident story from Florida.

### Traffic stalled, two women hurt in Archer Road wreck

By Tracy Swartz

Two pedestrians were injured Thursday morning after police say a catering truck hit them in front of Shands at UF.

Joan Kelley was in serious condition Thursday evening, while Betty Britt was deemed fair, said Shands spokeswoman Jennifer Porter.

The two women were crossing the street when they were hit by Jillian Williams, driver of the Tubby's Mobile Catering truck, said Gainesville Police spokesman Keith Kameg.

He said that witnesses reported there was a large vehicle in the left turn lane that concealed the women. The light turned green and the women crossed the street into Williams' lane.

"The driver continued at about 30 mph at the same time the two women walked in front of the [large] vehicle and the driver couldn't stop," Kameg said.

Kameg said he didn't know the final destination of Britt, an Orange Springs resident, and Kelly, a Gainesville woman who works in the human resources department at the Veterans Affairs Medical Center.

But the two pedestrians were transported immediately to Shands.

Williams declined comment.

Traffic was tied up on Archer Road for slightly more than an hour, Kameg estimated.

He doesn't anticipate any charges will be filed.

> The Independent Florida Alligator
> The University of Florida

## Crime

Similarly, anywhere you find people you also will find the potential for crime. Regardless of the type of crime, its coverage is vital to a campus audience.

With vandalism among top crimes plaguing most campuses, it is not surprising that officials are trying to curb the trend with installation of surveillance cameras, as covered in this story from Pennsylvania.

### HUB cameras hope to deter vandalism

By Allison Czapp

The HUB will be under surveillance by the end of this week, according to Co-op director Dennis Hulings.

Security cameras were installed throughout the HUB, the Co-op Store and outside of the HUB in an effort to promote a safe environment, Hulings said.

Cameras will be monitored by several directors in the HUB from a "secure place" in the building, but monitoring can also be done over the Co-op network. The Co-op Store has is own monitoring system inside the store.

These security measures cost about $81,000, Hulings said, which was figured into the original plans of HUB expansion.

"It seems like a lot of money, but . . . I think it will end up being a good investment," he said.

The "good investment" is in preventing vandalism and other crimes to the HUB. Hulings said when the new HUB first opened in January, two windows were broken.

During spring break more windows were broken and "potato gunned."

Other incidences include torn-down fences and smashed cigarette urns.

"Plus," Hulings said, "there have also been some thefts that if we had cameras in place we'd be able to help out."

During the summer, a student was robbed outside of the HUB at the MAC machine. Hulings said the bank's exterior camera, however, was re-directed before the robbery took place so nothing was recorded.

"Hopefully if that were to happen again we would have other cameras in position that would have assisted," Hulings said.

Some cameras are already in operation, but Hulings said he didn't know the exact number of cameras installed. The cameras were installed in places like the computer lab, the lobby to the student offices, The Penn office, commuter lounge, fitness center and others. Notices will be placed around the HUB to alert people they are under surveillance.

Security was first used in the HUB during the mid-'90s when students attending late-night events had to pass through metal detectors to enter the HUB.

"The whole idea and the whole intent here is one of safety," Hulings said. "We want (people) to feel comfortable when they come here."

The Penn
Indiana University of Pennsylvania

## Education

Education, after all, is the purpose for your college to begin with. It also is the reason you and others are there. Relevant coverage of education, particularly local issues, affects everyone in your audience.

This story from North Carolina predicts an increase in the number of engineering students on campus because of additional faculty and facilities.

### Engineering enrollment could rise

By Whitney Beckett

Although the University is still only considering a plan to add 200 students to the undergraduate student body, officials believe most of the additional students would likely enter as engineers.

The Pratt School of Engineering's recent increased investments in faculty and facilities—foremost among them the $97 million Center for Interdisciplinary Engineering Medicine and Applied Sciences under construction—created a natural inclination to increase the engineering student body, a plan that has been hinted at in recent years, Provost Peter Lange said.

However, the potential distribution of new students between Pratt and Trinity College is yet to be determined, and the Board of Trustees—who will ultimately approve the decision—will not officially consider the issue this weekend during their meeting.

"There really isn't any 'pressure' to grow the student body," Pratt Dean Kristina Johnson and Pratt Senior Associate Dean of Education Phil Jones wrote in a joint e-mail. "With the addition of 20 or so faculty and the new facility, it is only logical to look at the feasibility of increasing the undergraduate enrollment in Pratt."

Last month, Dean of the Faculty of Arts and Sciences William Chafe announced the proposed increase as a means of offsetting rising costs. The added tuition would generate an additional $2 million to $4 million.

Lange agreed that the change would increase revenues, but argued that growth in Pratt would be the real motivation. "It's only natural that an institution that is making that kind of investment would increase in size," Lange said. "Increasing enrollment would not be [intended] to make more money, but that will be an effect."

Pratt could handle a maximum boost of 50 students per year for four years—increasing its undergraduate enrollment from approximately 900 now to about 1,100, Johnson and Jones said. Half of Pratt students' tuition, and all of Trinity students', feeds into the Arts and Sciences budget.

Before any new students could be added, however, campus facilities would have to catch up with the growth. Additional students would require a new dormitory on East Campus, a revised plan for upperclassmen on West Campus and perhaps increased dining amenities, Executive Vice President Tallman Trask said. This would delay any growth until at least fall 2005.

To increase the class size by 50, the University would need to accept 100 more applicants, Director of Admissions Christoph Guttentag said. Officials agreed that they would not increase the size of the student body to the detriment of its quality and selectivity. Last year, the school accepted 22.5 percent of its applicants, down from 24.5 percent the year before, but is still less selective than its peer institutions.

"There might be slight changes, but I doubt that they would be particularly notice-able, either in the classroom or in the Duke community," Guttentag wrote in an e-mail. "Both the Trinity and Pratt applicant pools are large enough and strong enough to handle an increase of this magnitude without significantly affecting the quality of the student body."

Trinity Dean Robert Thompson said that although Pratt's increased facilities would allow it to absorb additional students easily, the real determining factor of which school would get the newcomers would be on who applies.

"Everything depends on the strength of the applicant pool," he said.

Thompson added that any increase would require changes to class offerings, like adding more first-year Writing 20 sections.

The presence of additional students would enrich the engineering school's cur-riculum, its deans said.

"Having more students would allow for adding more student-driven activities, as well as strengthening existing programs and projects," Johnson and Jones wrote. "Also, a larger faculty and student body will make it feasible to broaden course offerings, particularly at the advanced levels, and enhance research opportunities for undergraduates."

The Chronicle
Duke University

## Technology

Since our society is fully involved with and invested in technology, you can expect your college to be similarly impacted. Your readers, therefore, will want full details in technology stories that concentrate on explaining, as opposed to just presenting facts and figures.

With instant messaging services all the rage, this story from Texas explains its impact on students and faculty.

### Instant Messenger sweeps campus

By Kelsey Guy

Walk down almost any floor of a residence hall and your ears are bombarded with the sound of electronic doors opening and closing and the tones of messages sent and received.

Students all over campus use instant messaging services such as AOL Instant Mes-senger, Yahoo! Messenger, ICQ and Microsoft Messenger to communicate to each other and to friends at other universities.

For students far from home, online instant messaging is a quick and convenient way to catch up with old friends. "IMing" is also an easy way to talk to multiple peo-ple at once and plan group events without multiple phone calls.

"I mainly use it to talk to friends that aren't easy to get ahold of," first-year Car-rie Ince said over the sound of typing. "I mean I'm not going to just talk to people on campus, but it is a lot easier to find out what nine people are doing by IMing them instead of calling them."

Some students also use messaging to help them study. It's easy to ask a classmate a quick question about an assignment or upcoming project. But for many students, IMing quickly becomes a distraction. Busy students looking to stay signed on without the constant distraction of instant messages resort to using an away message to inform friends they are busy.

"You can leave it on with an away message and you can still get stuff done," first-year student Shannon Clark said. "It's a lot easier (than other modes of communication) and it's free, but I do think people aren't communicating as much in person because of it."

Unfortunately, the anonymity of instant messaging often results in poor etiquette.

"Instant messaging is almost like a cop-out," Ince said. "If you're having a fight with a friend or something, then you don't have to deal with it in person. I guess it just makes things easier on people when they don't have to look at the other person."

Around campus, messaging use differs between students and staff. Instant messaging is very common for students but can only be found in small pockets of the faculty and staff. Instead, e-mail is the communication of choice among the faculty.

"Most [staff] here use electronic mail, Yahoo! or AOL," said Allen Gwinn, senior director of technology for SMU. "Webmail is by far the biggest Web-based service used on campus. The second is people reading the news and things like that."

Bruce Meikle, manager of network services, said that faculty use Webmail to drop quick questions about things they are working on but not much else.

"We've been looking into tools to recommend (instant messaging), but as of yet, we have found nothing," said Abby Kinney of ITS User Services in the Bradfield Computing Center. "But here, the help desk uses it to communicate with the consultants."

Regardless of who uses such services now, upcoming changes might encourage more people to choose a provider. Not only does it help the sales of computer accessories and products, but companies such as Logitech have come up with ways to incorporate live video feed with normal text boxes, which is something that homesick students will be happy to use.

Logitech is marketing its product to companies like AOL and while there are no plans yet, AOL is looking into the product. As instant messaging becomes more user-friendly, its popularity will only continue to rise on campus, in both residence halls and academic departments.

The Daily Campus
Southern Methodist University

## For Practice

4-1. Pick up a current copy of your campus newspaper. Then, do the following:

a) Locate all of the news stories (but not more than 10) and then label each using one or more of the categories above to identify their *main* focus.

b) Split into peer groups of three or four and discuss your answers.
c) Does everyone agree on the main focus for each?
d) Is there a good spread across the categories, or are most clustered around just a few?
e) What are the consequences of a spread or a cluster?

4-2. Break into peer groups and review the categories above. Jot down any specific news story ideas that you and your classmates should cover on your campus.

## Story Beats

One of the most effective means by which many journalists cover their communities is the beat. A beat is a standard area of coverage, either geographical or topical. It gives reporters a particular focus for their stories; it also helps ensure that a community is thoroughly covered.

A significant advantage of beats is that reporters are able to become familiar with them—the people, or sources, who typically populate the beats as well as the events and trends that happen there.

Geographical beats are centered on places. For example, a reporter might be assigned to the City Hall beat, and anything happening at that location would be his or her responsibility. On the other hand, a beat that is topical is subject-oriented, like those listed earlier. For example, a reporter on the government beat will deal with those stories involving government, regardless of where they might take place.

Traditionally, geographical beats have been more commonplace because they positioned reporters physically in the locations where their news responsibilities were strongest.

Topical beats, though, tend to be more popular today among most media, mostly because these beats are less restrictive and allow reporters to go where necessary to fulfill their news responsibilities. Moreover, new technology enables and encourages topical beats, given the ease by which reporters can use cellular phones, laptop computers and digital transmission of data.

Some media, though, might use a *combination* of geographical and topical beats.

### Scenario for a City Hall Beat

Typically, a city government reporter for a morning daily newspaper will work a rather flexible schedule, based on when sources are available and when events take place. Influencing these factors is the daily deadline by which the reporter must complete stories for the next publication or major broadcast.

Let us say, for example, that it is Monday, and a retirement ceremony for a long-time city employee is scheduled for 11 a.m. The mayor will sign and present a proclamation honoring the man, who worked 28 years as a city engineer.

The previous Wednesday, Lynn, the city government reporter, learned of the event from the mayor's public relations director, who had sent her a news release attached to an e-mail message. From the release she gathered the basic background on the employee and highlights of his years of service to the city. Then, she wrote the

PR director an e-mail message in which she asked him to clarify some points from the news release.

Later that afternoon while running her beat at City Hall, Lynn visited the retiring city engineer and questioned him about his work for the city. She asked how things had changed during his tenure, his thoughts upon leaving city service and about any plans he might have following retirement.

On Thursday Lynn stopped by City Hall for an appointment with the mayor, which she had scheduled a week earlier. She interviewed him for an hour about the capital improvement tax that the city hoped to put before voters. After she gathered information for the tax piece, she asked the mayor questions about the retiring city engineer, whom, she learned, had worked with the mayor's father 20 years earlier. Both had been involved with the restoration and redevelopment of the city's river-front park. For the Friday edition of the newspaper, Lynn prepared a brief advance story on the proclamation and retirement ceremony.

On Monday she arrived 30 minutes before the event to check in with the PR director for any updates on the ceremony. Since there were none, she went to the Council chambers, where the event was scheduled. The ceremony went off without a hitch. Lynn took note of how many people attended, paying particular attention to any well-known members of the audience. Afterward, she picked up a copy of the proclamation from the PR director. After stopping for lunch, she headed back to the newsroom to begin writing her story.

She gathered the information from the news release, the additional comments from the PR director, the notes from her interview with the mayor, her written observations from the ceremony and the copy of the proclamation. For her opener Lynn zeroed in on the connection between the mayor's father and the city engineer, linking it to the ceremony that day. Then, she began working in relevant details from the different sources. At one point, she phoned the PR director to check on the spelling of a couple of names and some other details.

An hour later she finished the story and moved an electronic copy of it along to the news editor. She made a few phone calls. Then she checked the newspaper morgue for stories dealing with the city's last capital improvements tax campaign. After printing out copies of several of the stories, Lynn drove to City Hall to run her beat before the 4:30 p.m. City Council meeting.

## Sample Campus Beats

As your class prepares to set up beats for campus coverage, consider the following geographic list as a starting point, modifying the coverage as required for local conditions. Alternatively, set up topical beats for your campus beginning with appropriate subjects in the earlier campus community section.

- Academic departments (one or more reporters, as needed).
- Administration (one or more reporters, as needed).
- Alumni office.
- Athletics (one or more reporters, as needed): intercollegiate, intramural.
- Bookstore.
- Business office.
- Campus security.

- College relations office.
- Computer/technology services.
- Food services.
- Fraternities and sororities (one or more reporters, as needed).
- Governance groups: college, faculty, student.
- Maintenance.
- Residence halls.
- Student clubs and organizations (one or more reporters, as needed).

## For Practice

4-3. Split into peer groups. Then, do the following:

a) Draw up a list of beats that you believe your class should cover on your campus.
b) Once all of the peer groups have completed their lists, your teacher will ask for input to develop a single list.
c) Make sure you discuss why a certain beat should be covered. Or why not.

4-4. Working in peer groups, review a beat listing for your campus. Then, do the following:

a) If the number of beats does not match the number of students in your class, split up beats to accommodate more than one reporter *or* modify beats so that all are covered by available students.
b) Come together as a class and compare results. Try to reach a consensus.

4-5. Your teacher ultimately may decide how beats will be covered for stories you write this term. A quick method is to assign students to beats. Alternatively, students might bid for beats in which they are most interested, with the teacher making final decisions.

### Covering Your Beat

Once your teacher has assigned your beat, where likely you will work for some time if not for the remainder of the semester, you should consult college directories and other resources to gather the names, titles and contact information (building/room number, phone, e-mail address) of key people there.

Then, visit your beat. Introduce yourself to the people and further acquaint yourself with operations and activities there. You also should explain that you are covering your beat to gather information for class assignments.

Explain that the stories will be used for a class print publication, a class Web site or one of the existing campus student publications—an issue that you and your teacher will review and determine in discussions in Chapter 5. In addition, leave your own name and contact information with the people on your beat in the event that they should want to contact you.

## Story Deadlines

Journalists live by deadlines. And whether they are working for a daily, weekly, monthly or annual publication, those deadlines are vital to the smooth operation of the medium. Those deadlines also can be troublesome for reporters who choose not to abide by them.

The secret behind meeting deadlines is self-discipline.

Some students already are self-disciplined, and deadlines will be of limited concern to them. However, others will need to acquire an appreciation for deadlines and diligently work to meet them. One way to work toward this self-discipline is to begin by establishing and meeting mini-deadlines for the story assignments in this class.

As you may recall from Chapter 1 and Chapter 2, effective writing is a process that involves several steps. Generally, these include gathering material, writing the rough draft(s) and editing and polishing the final draft. Remember that effective writing tends to be recursive as opposed to linear; that is, there is movement back and forth among the steps rather than completion of the steps in a single direct line.

Setting mini-deadlines for each of these steps will help to simplify them, pace your work more efficiently and allow you to meet final deadline more easily. Moreover, mini-deadlines will give your peers a chance to review and respond to your work.

In addition, you may be working on more than one story at a time, with each at different stages of completion. We saw an example of a professional reporter who had several stories-in-progress with Lynn, the City Hall reporter mentioned earlier in this chapter. You would be wise this semester to have two or more stories in progress at any point, which will allow you to select the best to finish when a final deadline draws near.

Remember that meeting deadlines requires self-discipline. Given the right focus and motivation, you should find meeting deadlines a reasonable task.

---

## Crafting and Drafting

Role-playing can be a valuable addition to your peer review activities. As you respond to Exercise 4-7, consider playing the part of one of your peer partner's story sources or story subjects. Use a little imagination, but try to be faithful to the role. Make sure you address the following:

- As source or subject of the story, what story content do you appreciate? Why?
- What story content bothers you? Why?
- As source or subject what else might the writer add to the story? Why?
- What might the writer cut? Why?
- Has the writer presented quoteworthy comments you made?
- As source or subject how do you *feel* about what the writer has reported?

## For Practice

4-6. Visit each office on your assigned beat and introduce yourself to the key people, following the advice given above. During your introductory visits try to discover story opportunities and jot them down for future reference. Then, do the following:

a) Select one that has the most merit and is most timely. Begin gathering material for a story by picking up any printed supporting materials, checking the campus newspaper morgue for previous coverage and conducting some basic research, as appropriate.

b) Write what you think the central idea for the story may be. Submit your list of story opportunities as well as the supporting materials, notes and main point of your selected story to your teacher for review and feedback.

4-7. After your teacher has returned the reviewed materials, you should do the following:

a) Do additional backgrounding, as required.

b) Interview each source and take careful notes, practicing your personal shorthand as effectively as you can.

c) Listen carefully for quoteworthy comments the sources make, and write those down exactly.

d) Draft a story with a lead that effectively opens and best fits the story. Keep in mind the central idea you earlier developed.

e) Swap stories with a peer review partner or group and give written reader feedback. Submit the draft and peer feedback to your teacher.

f) After your teacher has reviewed your draft and peer feedback and has offered additional suggestions, revise as required.

g) Submit a final draft.

## Chapter 4 Bibliography

Beckett, Whitney. "Engineering Enrollment Could Rise." *The Chronicle.* 4 October 2002. <http://www.chronicle.duke.edu/vnews/display.v/ART/2002/10/04/3d9d835d119d7>.

Czapp, Allison. "HUB Cameras Hope to Deter Vandalism." *The Penn.* 2 October 2002. <http://www.thepenn.org/vnews/display.v/ART/2002/10/02/3d9b58d7db9dc>.

Eisner, Lauren. "Linderman Library to Undergo $15 Million in Renovations." *The Brown and White.* 29 September 2002. <http://www.bw.lehigh.edu/story.asp?ID=15585>.

Fruchter, Jessica. "Students React to Elections: Delay Will Hurt Groups' Funding, They Say." *The Colorado Daily.* 9 April 2002. <http://www.coloradodaily.com/articles/2002/04/09/export2430.txt>.

Guy, Kelsey. "Instant Messenger Sweeps Campus." *The Daily Campus.* 27 August 2002. <http://www.smudailycampus.com/vnews/display.v/ART/2002/08/27/3d6afb5c797ab?in_archive=1>.

Mabe, Andrew. "Cultural Night to Bring Malaysian Traditions to Campus." *Iowa State Daily*. 6 November 2003. <http://www.iowastatedaily.com/vnews/display.v/ART/2003/11/06/3fa9bd4aee94f?in_archive=1>.

Swartz, Tracy. "Traffic Stalled, Two Women Hurt in Archer Road Wreck." *The Independent Florida Alligator*. <http://www.alligator.org/edit/news/issues/02-fall/current/b03shands4.html>.

Twain, Mark. *Quotations for Creative Thinking*. <http://creativequotations.com/>.

Vennard, Michael. "Filmmaker and Author to Speak at KU Campus." *The University Daily Kansan*. <http://www.kansan.com/stories.asp?id=200210020008>.

# Part 2
# The Practice

# Chapter 5
# Getting to Work

*He presents me with what is always
an acceptable gift who brings me
news of a great thought before
unknown. He enriches me without
impoverishing himself.*

—Ralph Waldo Emerson

## Chapter Contents

## *QuickView*

Good stories will just about tell themselves. Do not get in their way.
You are a storyteller on the verge of joining a community of story-tellers. Your work will have the potential to inform, to educate, to entertain and to excite. Whether you are telling tales at the campfire or the keyboard, invest yourself in the experience. You are more than messen-

ger; you are molder, shaper and framer of stories. Respecting the limits of your genre, you give substance and meaning to the material you gather. Now you can begin working as a storyteller.

---

Storytellers constantly are looking for new material. They listen. They observe. They ask questions. They remember. They never know when a squib of information may spin a good tale.

## Material Gathering

As you begin to work at storytelling, you cannot let the excitement of sharing the story take control. You serve several allegiances as a journalist, which transcend the storytelling moment. These involve responsibilities to the following:

- To your publication, its editors and even the discipline of journalism at large to present your best work.
- To your sources to report what they tell you fairly, accurately and appropriately.
- Most importantly, to your readers to give them what they need and want to know.

In fact, service to your readers must direct most of what you do, and "Storycrafting" consistently stresses that premise, in this chapter and throughout the textbook.

### Developing Story Ideas

Before you run your beat, spend time developing some story ideas. What do readers know already, and what do they need to know to understand your area of campus?

Check the campus calendar of events to see if any relate to your beat. Go online to your campus Web site and see what events involve your beat. In offices on your beat look for standard handouts, like fliers, brochures and other published materials. Pick those up and build a reference folder.

In addition, visit with peers and others about your beat, the people there and what they do. Especially valuable is information from students who may have covered your beat previously. They might have a treasure trove of material that never made it into the stories they wrote.

A rich resource is your campus newspaper morgue or archives, where previous issues are maintained. Scan issues of the paper, concentrating on headlines that include key words linking to the people, activities and themes from your beat. When one grabs your attention, read down into the story. Make paper or mental notes, but the best advice is to write rather than recall. Develop story ideas using follow-ups, trends and annual activities.

For example, say your beat includes campus security. You find a story from last November covering the purchase of new computers and software. These will help security provide more accurate reporting of crime statistics, as required by the Jeanne

Cleary Disclosure of Campus Security Policy and Campus Crime Statistics Act. The system has been in place for almost a year now.

### Story Possibility #1

Do a story on how well the computers and software have worked. See if the security office has had any glitches with the system and how they have overcome them. Go online and get additional background on the federal law and its requirements, which are the impetus for campus security to report these statistics.

Also, find out where students and others can access the information—then do so yourself, and see what it includes.

### Story Possibility #2

You should be able to develop a trends story on campus crime; perhaps burglaries at campus residence halls show an uptrend—or downtrend. Either has potential for a story that is important to many of your readers. Jot down the numbers. Check the crime-reporting statistics from other colleges and universities in your region or state. How do they compare in the same category of residence hall burglaries? Whether they reveal the same trends, you have comparable material to use with the story about your campus.

### Story Possibility #3

A third angle could be checking on the annual activities. Crime reporting likely is completed by a certain deadline each year. Once you know when last year's report was filed, you can anticipate this year's report and plan to cover it. At that point, obviously, you can compare this year's numbers with last year's, resulting in a story that not only reports the new numbers but also explains to readers their impact.

## Learning What Readers Care About

Talk with members of your campus community, particularly students, who are potential readers of your stories, about what they want to know concerning your beat. For example, one of them might tell you about a broken emergency call box located in a dark area of campus. The student claims it has been out of service for the past six weeks, and she is concerned because she must walk through that area each Monday for a night class.

First, check the call box to confirm it is broken. If it is, contact the appropriate person in the security office and ask about it. Is the office aware it is not working? What is wrong with it? What is being done to repair it? What is the cost of repair, and when is it likely to be fixed? Have there been similar problems previously? If yes, check the morgue for possible coverage. All this information likely will provide most of what you need for a basic story.

However, consider developing a related story, often termed a *sidebar,* about the campus emergency call box system. How many units are there? Where are they located? Prepare a map pinpointing these locations, or ask someone else to do so. How often in the past year have students and others made calls using the boxes? Have any of those been false alarms or crank calls? What kinds of calls have been made? With enough related details, you can prepare a table or chart, also called an *infograph,* which will help readers quickly sort through and better understand information.

Of course, for the main story and sidebar, interview security sources and students for their perspectives—including facts, figures and feelings.

The result can be solid coverage that focuses on a problem and helps to alleviate it. In such instances you can derive a good deal of satisfaction in knowing you were instrumental in making your campus a safer place.

In general as you cover your beat, plan and keep your own schedule for interviews and material gathering so that you can be timely in coverage. Such self-discipline can help you to avoid missing a story opportunity. You also will do a better job serving your readers.

## Hitting the Beat

First, get to know your beat. Be sure you follow recommendations concerning development of your beat from Chapter 4. Your first visits likely will be tedious, especially if you do not know the people there or understand exactly what they do. Learning this takes time; however, you can move along more quickly if you actively apply yourself to getting to know your sources and their responsibilities in the campus community. Make it a point to visit people on your beat frequently. You need not run beats like clockwork, but at least visit often enough that you can cover stories in timely fashion.

Get to know your sources and let them get to know you; you are building trust as well as acquiring information. Learn the job titles and responsibilities of the people on your beat. Especially get to know secretaries and office clerks on your beat. They are a wealth of background and information, and they often are more accessible to you than many of their bosses. After you are familiar with your beat, you can reduce frequency of visits.

So, what do you do when you visit your beat? Be curious. Be observant. Ask questions. Among the questions you might consider are the following: What is new here? What is different? Then, find out more about the *what* you have targeted and ask questions related to the remaining story elements: Who? When? Where? Why? How? So what? Whenever possible, ask for copies of paper documents that not only save you the need to write but also provide accurate detail, depth and background. You also should pick up copies of the calendar of events and activities for your beat.

News on any beat is as plentiful as pebbles on a beach. Yet, it is not just a matter of getting material for *any* story; it is more important to locate and tell the most provocative stories, the ones that will have the most impact on the most readers.

## Taking Notes during Interviews

Remember the notetaking checklist from Chapter 2:

- Look for major themes and central ideas in what your source says.
- Ignore distractions.
- Be alert to signal words that cue content.
- Anticipate direction of comments.

- Consider how facts support ideas.
- Summarize and repackage into key words.
- Listen between the lines to tone and voice.
- Put to good use the lag between speed of speech and speed of thought.

Ask your source to repeat or explain material you do not understand.

During interviews take notes quickly and accurately. Plan not to write everything. As suggested in Chapter 2, use shorthand, write key words, prefer phrases to sentences. However, be alert to quoteworthy comments, and write those exactly. If necessary, ask your source to repeat a comment.

Make sure you invite your source to spell all names, as well as unfamiliar words. Moreover, you should ask for definitions, explanations or examples of important terms. All of this special effort helps ensure your story is accurate and complete.

You must know enough to understand the subject of your story. If you do not understand it, you cannot explain it to readers. If your first source does not give you sufficient information, ask for suggestions about others you might interview on the topic. It usually is easier to gather information from these follow-up sources. After all, you already should have most of what you need, and letting the additional sources know what you know allows them to fill in holes and supplement perspectives.

## *For Practice*

5-1. Go to your campus newspaper and review issues for the previous 12 months, scanning headlines for any key words that may connect to your beat. Then, do the following:

a) Photocopy stories, if possible. Otherwise, take notes on key details.
b) Do not forget to include the publication date of the newspapers in case you need to return to them for more information.
c) Make note of important stories that do not seem to have been followed up.
d) Submit your materials to your teacher for review and response.
e) After your teacher returns your materials, check the response and recommendations. Put these materials into a tickler file for reference and future stories.

5-2. Pick the most interesting and timely story from your tickler file for an update story. Then, do the following:

a) Locate additional background, as required.
b) Interview previous sources and new sources, if appropriate, and take careful notes. Practice your personal shorthand as effectively as you can.
c) Listen carefully for sources' quoteworthy comments, and write those down exactly.
d) Draft a story with a lead that effectively opens and best fits the story. Keep in mind the earlier story. Include the previous details but not too high in the story.

## Story Drafting

Ideally, you have gathered more information than you will need to tell a good story. Now, begin writing.

Whenever possible, draft your lead first. It is worth spending extra time to write the lead. Make it a grabber—something that will force readers to stop scanning, set their bottled water aside and pay close attention. At the same time, though, the lead must accomplish an equally daunting task—it must make clear to readers the focus of your story. Do not raise questions. Answer them. What is this story going to be about? Where is this story going? Why is this story important? These and other questions you should anticipate and cover.

See how the following lead is both grabber and focus for what follows below:

### Pudding wrestling adds flavor to Homecoming week

By Jayson Merkley

From traditional Greco-Roman roots to the glitz and glamour of modern sports entertainment, wrestling has seen many evolutionary incarnations. But of all such attempts to reach the grappling ideal, perhaps the newest and closest version was ISU Homecoming week pudding wrestling.

The Bengal
Idaho State University

As you recall from Chapter 2, writing the lead first offers a major benefit: It gives direction for the story to both you and your readers. Draft several versions unless you are convinced that your first effort is best. Move from big choices, like which element you will use to begin your lead, to smaller choices, like whether to use one word or another.

When you cannot get a handle on a lead, begin writing the body of the story. You can return to the lead later and write something that works.

Drafting the rest of your story is a matter of cashing in on the hard work of your interview. The payoff, of course, is that you have plenty of material from which to draw. With a working lead in place, review your notes and begin prioritizing the material. A scratch outline may be helpful, and keying it to your notes can make retrieval simple and complete.

Write about what is important, what is interesting. Find the order of development that works best for your material, for your chosen angle, for your audience. Inverted pyramid is always an option, in which you cover the story elements from most to least important. That accomplished, flesh out the story by adding specific details that explain and expand earlier information. However, while inverted pyramid may be an easy option, it may not be the best option. Consider also the creative forms of development discussed in Chapter 3.

Write until you run out of *important* material and have covered your subject sufficiently to satisfy readers. Do not write until you have exhausted your notes. You want always to write within the limits of your understanding, not beyond them. If you run out of material before fully covering your subject, you likely will need to return to your sources for more material. Better that than to try to slip by an incomplete story.

You cannot make up for a weak, incomplete story by writing a better one on the same subject for the next assignment or issue.

Keep your words, sentences and paragraphs short, on average, but vary their lengths to avoid tedium. Set off the well-spoken direct quotations of your sources by giving them their own stage in a paragraph of their own. Follow direct quotes with supporting details that illustrate and explain the content of the quotes. But do not merely repeat content of direct quotes.

After completing the first draft, many writers take at least a brief break and let their stories rest. Some writers, though, stop working and submit their stories.

Big mistake.

Resting briefly and returning to revise is good. Even if only for a few minutes, writers can come back to their drafts and give them fresh looks. Those looks should start with a slow and careful reading of the text.

Reading it aloud is best. Listen to your writing, but do not fall in love with it. Your writing is alive and malleable, open to reshaping until it finally is published. Do not become fixed on a single draft unless you are sure it is your best effort.

In the following example you can see how the lead from the pudding-wrestling story is developed:

The pudding wrestling event, sponsored by the Program Board, saw some of ISU's fiercest competitors face off in a battle for control of pudding-filled kiddy pools. A large circle of curious students quickly gathered on the quad, surrounding the perilous pudding pit just outside the vanilla and butterscotch splash radius.

Evoking the image of a young Rick Flair, junior Brad Cole intimidated foe and crowd alike with an explosive belly-flop into the creamy white pudding puddle. He made short work of his opponent, employing a DDT-like finishing maneuver he calls the Culminator.

"Mental victory is the key to success," Cole said about his in-ring strategy. "I like to take things from other wrestlers and incorporate them into my own style." Cole said Stone Cold Steve Austin has been one of his wrestling inspirations.

The competition in the women's division was even more intense. The female pudding wrestlers showed the crowd a new definition of aggression and ruthlessness. But in the end, everyone walked away as friends.

"I never feared for my life, just for my hair," said cosmetology-student-turned-pudding-wrestler Rebecca Bybee. She described the experience as fun overall, but added, "I got my trash kicked. It tasted sick and it was freezing cold."

ISU senior Kavina Wienhoff was in great wrestling form throughout the afternoon, establishing herself as a dominant force in the short but colorful history of ISU pudding wrestling. Opponent after opponent found herself pinned and at Wienhoff's mercy. Fittingly, Wienhoff was crowned the undisputed women's pudding wrestling champion.

* * * * * * * * * *

"I think pudding wrestling attracts a bigger crowd than some of the past Homecoming activities, and it's good to get more people involved," said pudding wrestling master of ceremonies Amanda Anson. "People have seen mud wrestling and Jell-O wrestling, but pudding wrestling is something new that people want to see."

The Bengal
Idaho State University

## *Peer Review*

Whether called peer groups, editing teams or readers' circles, those classmates who read and respond to your stories-in-progress are excellent resources. They are members of your storytelling community, and they are your first audience—one that actually can respond to your story. Ideally, three or four students comprise a peer group, small enough to allow all to respond to one another's writing within a typical class period but large enough to get an effective sampling of responses.

### Benefits of Peer Review

Peer review is not intended to replace feedback from your teacher, who also will coach you as part of the writing process. Instead, it offers many additional advantages in its own right. Peer review does the following:

- It provides you with comments and suggestions from an interested, engaged audience—your peers.
- It allows you to see your classmates' writing. When their work is good, it can be a model for you to follow. When it is bad, it can be a model to avoid. Also, reading classmates' stories helps you to position your own writing within your storytelling community.
- It gives you opportunity to spot weaknesses in others' writing that you may then identify more readily in your own.

You and your peer groups will have regular opportunities to share drafts of your stories. Before you release your story for review, though, make sure you have given it your best effort and that it is reasonably free of surface errors—those involving punctuation, grammar, spelling and usage. Peer review is *not* designed for your peers to write the story but to improve the draft of a work-in-progress.

### Peer Review Tips

When you are reading a classmate's story, your primary concern is with content, what the writer says, followed by how the writer says it. As you peer-edit, keep the following tips in mind:

#### General Points

Do not skim but read the story quickly one time—no pencil in hand.
On the second, more careful reading, grab your pencil and make notes.
You often can phrase your responses as directive questions and comments: "Did

you consider this possibility?" "Keep this material; it is working well." "Consider cutting this; it confuses me." "Can you come up with any specific examples?"

Do not forget positive comments, too: "Your lead really pulled me into the story." "That second direct quote is great." "Your story has excellent details that really help me to understand the situation."

### Story Opener, Lead

Look for the main idea. Does the opener present it or lead effectively into it? Remember the role of the nut graf from Chapter 3.

Is the opener a grabber? Does it encourage you to read on?

### Story Body, Development

Is the rest of the story presented in a suitable order? If yes, say so. If not, ask questions, such as "Did you consider organizing your story using something besides inverted pyramid?"

Is there more information than you want to know? Material that does not support or advance the main idea is irrelevant. Ask if the writer might consider cutting it.

Is there too little information to clearly support and explain the main idea? Ask the writer to consider adding material where you find it would be helpful.

Is all information except common knowledge attributed to a source?

Are both indirect and direct quotes used, with preference given to the former? Are direct quotes well chosen for being powerful, provocative, snappy?

Does the writer avoid inserting his or her own opinion into the story? If no, suggest it be cut and perhaps replaced by comments from an outside source.

### Proofreading

Do not assume that it is your responsibility to locate all surface errors in stories you read; however, when you find them, circle them, as opposed to correcting them. In addition, you may note in the margin that the error involves a particular problem, like spelling or punctuation.

If you are suspicious about punctuation, grammar, spelling and usage but unsure what exactly the problem and solution are, you may want to cast your responses in terms of questions: "Have you checked spelling, especially the spelling of names?" "Should this be a comma or a semicolon?" "Is this subject singular or plural?"

## Responding to Peers

Our discussion has stressed what reviewers should consider saying to writers. Yet, peer review is most fulfilling when it is a dialogue, two people talking and responding to one another in real time. At this point, we will consider how reviewers might engage writers following their review and how writers might respond to suggestions, praise or criticism.

### From the Reviewer's Perspective

The written notes from peer editing are only the beginning of this part of the process. Peer review should be a dialogue if it is to be fully effective. The comments should open a door to discussion between two or more people in a peer group. When you have finished reviewing a peer's story, you should not walk away and trust that the writer will understand all your comments. Now is the time to talk with one another. Be ready to explain what may be unclear in your comments.

For particular passages that are problematic, avoid telling the writer exactly how you would write it or how he or she might write it. Instead, pose questions, particularly the "what if" variety and others from the lists earlier. The goal is to encourage improvements you need as a reader without taking control from the writer.

Your role as a peer reviewer is supportive and cooperative, not competitive. You are a reader responding, and that gives you a position of privilege that the writer should respect and that you should not abuse.

## From the Writer's Perspective

Respond aloud to questions and comments posed by a reviewer. Let all those in your peer group know how you might deal with the issues raised. In some cases you might be unsure of an appropriate answer, or you might even be confused by the question. Discussion among the peers in your group may lead to brainstorming or suggestions to help you resolve the problem.

Remember that peer review relies on both respect for and trust in one another. Be tactful and polite in all you say, especially if suggestions seem critical. Some of you might have a difficult time handling criticism, especially if the comments are not phrased tactfully or constructively.

First, resist the urge to either attack or totally ignore reviewers. Criticism is part of the writing process and may be quite valuable, since it can:

- Tell you how you might improve performance.
- Identify weaknesses in your writing.
- Show you how others see your work.

You should know that criticism is either valid, invalid or a reasonable difference of opinion.

If valid, realize how fortunate you are to have the opportunity to improve a weakness, solve a problem or correct an error.

If invalid, you have several options. Certainly, you can acknowledge whatever truth there might be in the criticism. You also might grin and bear it or politely disagree with it. Importantly, you might ask the reviewer for clarification: "Would you give me some specific evidence?" "Can you explain what is wrong in different words?" With this you have invited the peer reviewer to participate in finding solutions.

If a difference of opinion, ask questions of the reviewer to make sure you clearly understand what he or she means. Work together to see if your dialogue might encourage one or the other of you to shift positions. Of course, ultimately you and the critic might just recognize your differences of opinion and leave it at that.

When you are finished with peer discussion, take time to thank all your peer reviewers for giving you the chance to improve or correct your work. This shows you can be objective and professional.

Of course, what you do following peer review is crucial. You no longer have to wonder what readers will think of your story or how they will respond to your story. You now have that feedback from interested readers. In some instances, what they tell you may push you back to earlier stages of the writing process, perhaps because they encouraged you to gather more material to support key ideas in your story. That accomplished, you will need to continue negotiating the demands of evaluating the new material, its place in the story-in-progress and exactly how you will express it. Note here the recursive nature of the writing process at work.

## For Practice

5-3. Take the story draft you completed for Exercise 5-2. Then, do the following:

a) Swap stories with a peer review partner or group and follow the recommendations and tips just listed.
b) Make sure you give each other written reader feedback.
c) Hold on to the draft and written feedback.

## Teacher as Coach

Teachers are key members of your storytelling community. Just as the writing process lays out clear opportunities and responsibilities for you as a storyteller-journalist, so it identifies teachers as coaches during the development and drafting stages of your writing.

The role of coach is varied, often encompassing many of the following jobs as well: instructor, assessor, friend, mentor, facilitator, demonstrator, adviser, supporter, fact finder, motivator, counselor, organizer and planner.

You likely are familiar with the role of coaches in various settings, but most commonly related to sports. There, coaches assist players in numerous ways, including:

- Teaching players the basic techniques, strategies and rules of the sport.
- Leading players in regular opportunities for practice.
- Motivating players to spot their own strengths and weaknesses and to capitalize on the former while working to eliminate the latter.
- Guiding players in their growth toward mastery of the sport.

Writing coaches complete these same kinds of activities when they work with student journalists. Good coaches, whether working with sports or writing, help their charges to achieve levels of performance that would have been less likely without their assistance. They create conditions that encourage learning to happen and find ways to motivate their students to work beyond their current accomplishments.

Work closely with your teacher-coach, who can intervene in the writing process at any point, either at your request or on his or her own initiative. You could be having a hard time generating story ideas on your beat. Perhaps you are having problems locating a source to give you key information for a story-in-progress. Maybe you do not understand a certain procedure that takes place on your beat. It even might be that your peer-editing group has given you several good suggestions, and you are unsure which, if any, is best to follow. Your teacher-coach is an excellent resource in all these instances.

Be advised, though, that many teacher-coaches will not necessarily give you direct answers or tell you what to do. They may prefer to help you to understand your options and the consequences of each and then let you make your own choices. You remain in control of your writing and, ultimately, your own success—a basic tenet of the writing process.

## Conferences

Nowhere is the role of your teacher-coach more evident than in the regular writing conferences you may share—a cornerstone in the coaching component of the writing process.

Typically, conferences are scheduled later in the writing process—after you have made your best effort to write your story. Most teacher-coaches want to see a draft of your story before conferences so they will have time to read and reflect on your work.

Much of the success in conferencing comes from the ability of teacher-coaches to examine your text and imagine it differently; in other words, they cannot read a student's story without also simultaneously (and unconsciously) reading several other versions of the story as well. Their goal is to go beyond the current presentation of the news story to try to draw out possibilities, to imagine what the story might be trying to become.

When the current draft is very good, those possibilities are not strong enough to replace it. However, as is sometimes the case, when the possibilities imagined by teacher-coaches are more effective than the draft, teacher-coaches will find ways to encourage movement in that direction.

Conferences offer numerous benefits. They:

- Provide continued opportunities for students to learn about the writing process.
- Focus attention on a work-in-progress from a new and fresh perspective.
- Help to generate and clarify ideas and audiences.
- Offer support for specific editing needs.
- Identify areas of writing that can and need to be developed.

The coaching metaphor comes into full play here, as teacher-coaches work alongside writers in a supportive and directive role. At this point more than any other, teacher-coaches are vital. They encourage writers on a specific level to improve their works-in-progress and on a more general level to grow as storytellers.

Some teacher-coaches prefer question-based approaches, where they ask related and leading questions to allow writers to take active roles in the conference and ultimately in their revisions. Other teacher-coaches seek a more direct route, recommending such things as alternate story lead possibilities, additional sources or a different story structure. Good teacher-coaches, though, emphasize that all choices in your writing are yours; you retain control of the content and presentation.

As with your peer reviews you will gain most from those conferences where you and your teacher-coach are engaged in dialogue.

## Responding to the Teacher-Coach

Dialogue during conferences presents opportunities to answer questions from teacher-coaches and to clarify what teacher-coaches may be telling you. Therefore, feel free to ask questions as well.

Once the conference is over, the work of writing continues. Do not rush to finish. As noted earlier in the chapter, you have a responsibility to the journalistic profession, to your sources, to your readers, to your story, to your teacher-coach and even to yourself to make the most of this stage of the writing process.

Of all those to whom you owe responsibility, none holds more sway in your responses than teacher-coaches. After all, they are most knowledgeable of the profession and of storytelling in their classrooms, and they are the ones who eventually will evaluate and grade your stories.

Yet, the aim is not to hand over the control and responsibility of your story to the teacher-coach in an attitude that says, "Just tell me what to do, and I'll do it." The two of you are participating in a cooperative effort from which all stand to benefit.

On the other hand, in your zeal to retain control of your writing, do not ignore your teacher-coach's good advice. Your teacher is the pro in this situation—as well as the one evaluating your final draft.

If you have concerns about suggestions from your teacher-coach, you might well consider trying some of the same techniques recommended earlier in the section on responding to peers.

## Revising: Editing and Proofreading

Revising is comprised of editing and proofreading, two similar but distinctively separate steps in the writing process. The first is a review of content—what the story says; the second is a review of form—how the story says it.

Many writers tend to work at both late in the process—after they have drafted their stories and following both peer review and teacher conferencing. As noted in Chapter 1, some writers revise as they draft. Whichever method you prefer, you must both edit and proofread to make your story the best it can be.

As you revise, remember to whom you are writing, what they know and what they need to know.

### Editing

Editing involves focusing your attention on the following:

- Lead.
- Content.
- Structure.
- Clarity.
- Style.

Your lead is the most important component of your story. It must effectively grab readers' attention and present or direct them to the central idea of the story. Is the lead interesting? Does it stress the best elements? Is it appropriate for the story? Spend whatever time is necessary to make sure you have a lead that works. Remember that many readers may not venture past a weak lead to find an important, interesting story.

Content is the next concern in editing. Consider first the content suggestions given you by your peers and teacher-coach. Which are necessary to implement? What other content issues might you address? Have you provided sufficient support to make clear the point of your story? Is all the material in the story relevant to the lead? Are each of the five Ws, H and SW sufficiently explained? Do you have a good mix of direct to indirect quotes, with preference given to the latter?

As you review the structure of your story, recall that you have a handful of options, including inverted pyramid, narrative, description and Wall Street Journal. Which to choose? Of course, consider the old standby, inverted pyramid, wherein material is presented most to least important. Narrative serves content that is action oriented, taking readers through time. Description is valuable to organize stories that move readers through space. Finally, the Wall Street Journal pattern is specialized, excellent for stories that evolve from a specific example or two to the larger issue—and back.

Somewhat subtle but still of concern is clarity. Do *you* understand all the terms you have used in the story? If not, readers also may not understand them. Check with knowledgeable sources for definitions and examples. Then, use common alternatives or define the unclear terms. Both will benefit from pertinent, revealing examples. Is the meaning of each sentence clear? Are pronouns used effectively so that they help to avoid unnecessary noun repetition? Are pronoun references clear to readers?

The last editing matter is style, which involves personal style, traditional journalistic style and Associated Press style—all of which we covered in Chapter 3. Personal style is the way you like to write, the preferences you have for certain vocabulary, sentence structures and presentation.

Recall the following points of traditional journalistic style and use them in your storytelling:

- Write short paragraphs.
- Write short sentences, but vary them occasionally with a longer sentence.
- Prefer short, simple words that are easily and quickly understood.
- Prefer active voice, which presents material in subject-verb-object order.
- Prefer concrete nouns.
- Prefer active verbs, which enliven and sparkle.
- Stress what happened versus what did *not* happen.
- Use third person.
- Use last names only after first reference where the full name was given.
- Avoid editorializing—giving your opinion or using loaded terms.
- Cut clichés and trite language.
- Cut unnecessary words.

- Avoid empty wording, such as there is or there are and many uses of who, that, which.

Associated Press style requires you to apply particular ways of writing to your story. It takes time and patience but mostly a willingness to refer frequently to the AP Stylebook to comply with this style. Use it as you do a dictionary. The main categories are as follow:

- Capitalization.
- Abbreviation.
- Spelling.
- Numerals.
- Usage.
- Punctuation.
- Sports guidelines.
- Business guidelines.
- Internet guidelines.

## Proofreading

Once you are finished editing, some of your more painstaking review begins with proofreading. Being nitpicky at this point is a plus.

Jack Hart, Oregonian senior editor for writing and staff development, writes about grammar, punctuation and usage errors: "In the grand scheme of things, mechanical errors aren't what really matter. As Don Murray, the Pulitzer Prize-winning writing coach, has said, 'Our newspapers are filled with poorly written stories in which no grammatical rule is bent and no word misspelled.' Unfortunately, Murray's observation has a corollary that's especially true around here. Readers often fail to notice the quality of a well-written and well-reported story because it's marred by trivial mechanical errors."

Some handy proofreading tips are the following:

- Proofread from a printed copy of your story rather than on the computer screen. Many writers find it easier to read ink on paper. Also, some studies show that reading from a computer screen takes 25 percent longer than reading from a printout.
- Proofread for only one kind of error at a time. If you concentrate first on spelling, ignoring other kinds of errors, this singleness of purpose likely will help you to concentrate.
- Read slowly and read aloud. The two work together, resulting in a greater chance of your seeing what is actually there rather than what you think is there.
- Circle every punctuation mark. Then, review each to make sure you can justify its use. Too often, writers insert punctuation by habit rather than by rule.
- Read the story backwards. This is helpful to check spelling, encouraging you to look at each word.

As you might gather, a key to successful proofreading is forcing yourself to slow your reading and look at exactly what you wrote. Attention to detail pays off as you proofread for the following:

- Spelling.
- Grammar.
- Punctuation.

Your first line of defense against spelling errors is the spell checker on your computer. Failure to use it is an invitation to error. On the other hand, do not rely *only* on the spell checker. Most have a limited dictionary; words not in it will show up as misspelled. In addition, some words will not appear misspelled if they are another correctly spelled word, such as "there" for "their" or "to" for "too" or "your" for "you're." The best guardian against misspelling is still the standard dictionary or English handbook, which you must use for every word of which you are unsure.

Grammar can be more troublesome. Grammar checkers, available with most word processing software, encourage you to closely examine your writing for proper use of conventions. These include capitalization, commonly confused or misused words, passive voice, possessives, punctuation, sentence structure, subject-verb agreement and the like. However, realize that grammar checkers are fallible, missing some errors and citing errors where none exist.

## For Practice

5-4. Gather your draft and peer responses from Exercise 5-3. Then, do the following:

a) Submit the draft and peer feedback to your teacher.
b) After your teacher has reviewed your draft and peer feedback and has offered additional suggestions—either in writing or in conference or both, revise as required.
c) Make sure you follow advice on revising given above.
d) Submit a final draft.

## Story Publishing

Once you have finished revising your story, you do what all storytellers do: You give it to an audience to read. This is an important movement toward closure, which is especially valuable for you. The goal of revision—to improve the story—makes it difficult for some writers to finish drafting. They continue seeking improvements to achieve the "perfect" story. Yet, most stories must be published in a timely manner, and perfection is a goal likely beyond the grasp of any writer. Publishing allows you to let go of the story and move on.

You have several avenues for publication of your story:

- Your teacher.
- A classroom news sheet.
- A class-developed Web newspaper.
- Your campus newspaper.
- A community newspaper.

## Your Teacher

Of course, within the context of your class, your first audience for the final draft of your story must be your teacher. Most stories you likely will submit for final evaluation and grading. This is not only a standard step in the educational process but also an important opportunity for feedback from a professional in your audience.

## Classroom News Sheet

Producing a classroom news sheet is similar to publishing your own class newspaper. Since your stories have been written using word processing software, they already are digitized and can be organized easily into an appropriate design using pagination software, such as Adobe PageMaker, Adobe InDesign or Quark Xpress.

Use of larger format photocopying with at least 11 × 14-inch paper will make designs easier and more effective. You can print enough copies of each "issue" to accommodate your class, plus a few extra for those you wish to include in your audience

## Class-Developed Web Newspaper

To reach a larger audience beyond your classroom, you might consider developing a Web site on which to publish your stories. Again, because they already are digitized, putting them online is a relatively easy matter—so long as you have access to the Internet and a basic understanding of either HTML or Web-design software.

A flashy design is unnecessary, though at least a simple, attractive presentation makes your story forum more inviting. In fact, you may choose to go totally no-frills. Post stories to a clickable index page that opens the word processed stories.

The Web site has the advantage of being free to low cost but with the potential of reaching larger audiences. The only limitation to readership is who has knowledge of the site's URL, or Web address. In addition, a Web newspaper allows you to use color as well as photographs, art and graphics, if you wish.

We will cover Web newspapers in Chapter 16.

## Campus Newspaper

A prime outlet for publication is your campus newspaper. Since your stories focus on the campus community and cover a campus beat, they should have the same basic audience as that of the campus newspaper. Moreover, your story likely conforms to most of the same content and style expectations as stories in the campus newspaper.

Your teacher may be willing to work with student editors to coordinate submission of the stories you and your classmates write. Alternatively, you may submit your stories on your own. Your goal, of course, is to get a wide and appropriate audience.

## Community Newspaper

The last resource for publication is your local community newspaper. Its readership likely overlaps that of the campus newspaper, and many stories of interest on campus will have interest off campus. The additional benefit of publishing off campus is the increased credibility and stature that community newspapers can claim. That may not always be the case, of course, given the significant growth in the campus press, some of which may have larger circulations than off-campus counterparts.

## Teacher as Evaluator

Earlier your teacher served as coach, working alongside you as you developed and drafted your story. That relationship is an important one. At some point in most classroom situations, however, the teacher's relationship with you must shift from coach to evaluator. This change is difficult for some students to accept. In fact, it is sometimes difficult for teachers to make the transition.

Nevertheless, when this time comes, your teacher must evaluate your story based on its success at meeting various criteria. Those may include some or all of the following:

• Story opener/lead.
• Content.
• Structure.
• Quotations.
• Creativity.
• AP style.
• Conventions.

The feedback that may accompany your story evaluation also is essential to your continuing growth as a storyteller-journalist. Quality is typically preferred to quantity in this department. Take advantage of every opportunity to hone skills and achieve success.

---

## Crafting and Drafting

Exercise 5-5 will give many of you your first chance to have your writing "published." You already have shared your work with your peer review partners and your teacher. Likely, that has not been too much of a concern. However, extending your audience to the entire class, the entire campus or beyond is exciting. And a little scary. The larger audience means a lot more people will be reading your story. Some of you even may experience the writer's version of "stage fright."

Do not let the experience unnerve you. Instead, use the tension to increase your motivation to do your best. Before long the anxiety will ease. For most writers, though, the excitement of being published stays with them.

## *For Practice*

5-5. Gather both paper and digital copies of the final draft of your story from Exercise 5-4 to publish in a classroom news sheet, a class-developed Web newspaper, your campus newspaper or a community newspaper. Then, do the following:

a) Work with your peer group or with the entire class, as directed by your teacher.
b) Decide which method of publication you will use for your stories. Your teacher will have the final say for this.
c) Based on the method of publication, organize peer groups or the entire class to work effectively to publish the stories.
d) If you choose the news sheet or Web newspaper, try to make your publication available to others outside your class, if possible.

## *Chapter 5 Bibliography*

Emerson, Ralph Waldo. *Quotations for Creative Thinking.* <http://creativequotations.com/>.

Hart, Jack. "Prevent Punctuation and Grammar Errors That Hurt Credibility." *Jobs Page: Your link to newspaper careers.* 1998. <http://www.freep.com/jobspage/academy/hart.htm>.

Merkley, Jayson. "Pudding Wrestling Adds Flavor to Homecoming Week." *The ISU Bengal.* <http://www.isubengal.com/news/298314.html?mkey=529567>.

# Chapter 6
# News

*[News is] anything that*
*makes the reader say*
*"Gee whiz!"*

—Dr. Ink

## Chapter Contents

## *QuickView*

All of you have a sense of what news is, yet if pressed, how clearly could you define it? Therefore, we open this chapter with the challenging task of trying to do just that, define news. We will examine dictionary, traditional and contemporary definitions for a clearer understanding of the meaning of news.

How journalists decide what is newsworthy—particularly what stories are *more* newsworthy than others—is our next concern. We will use traditional news values, also called triggers, to explore how to make such judgments.

We will find that journalists today are changing story content to suit audience interest, mindful that the special qualities of story serve well the complex demands of delivering news.

Finally, our review of the components of effective news stories—experience and audience—will guide us to fine-tune choices we face as storyteller-journalists.

---

Storytelling has been the dominant topic in "Storycrafting" thus far, as we seek to understand better this vehicle by which journalists deliver news. On the other hand, while we have referred frequently to news, we have done little to explain it.

Like the proverbial elephant in the living room, news is a term we can no longer ignore.

# Definitions of News

News. Exactly what is it? For much of journalistic history folks have been trying to figure that out. It has not been simple or easy. Yet, like some prosecutors' definitions of pornography, experienced journalists know news when they see it.

Michael Schudson explains news in this way: "A news story is an account of the 'real world,' just as a rumor is another kind of accounting of the real world, and a historical novel another sort of account of the real world. It is not reality itself (as if any sequence of words and sentences could be) but a transcription, and any transcription is a transformation, a simplification, and a reduction."

Most of the stories journalists tell fall into the general category of news. The remaining content includes features, sports, opinion and miscellaneous information elements. Occasionally, a story will cross over; that is, it will fall into two categories, such as when your college's football team wins its conference title.

Unfortunately, many inexperienced student journalists overlook the richness of news opportunities that surround them. Given a beat to cover and a deadline to meet, they too often return empty handed, moaning, "There's nothing going on."

Ignoring an obvious reason for a few students' failure to locate something newsworthy to report—that they do not make a sincere effort to do so—some students just do not have a clear sense of the news that is there. To acquire that sense, we will begin at the beginning, with a sampling of some of the best old and new takes on the meaning of news.

## Dictionary Definitions of News

Dictionaries tend to be consistent in their definitions of news.

Webster's New World Dictionary says that our word news comes from the Middle English newes, meaning "novelties," which was derived from Old French noveles or Medieval Latin nova, both of which referred to "what is new."

The dictionary entry reads: "1 new information about anything; information previously unknown. 2 a) reports, collectively, of recent happenings, esp. those broadcast over radio or TV, printed in a newspaper, etc. b) any person or thing thought to merit special attention in such reports . . ."

The Merriam-Webster Dictionary, which dates the origin of the term as the 15th century, is quite similar: "1 a: a report of recent events b: previously unknown information . . . 2 a: material reported in a newspaper or news periodical or on a newscast b: matter that is newsworthy."

The American Heritage Dictionary of the English Language offers this entry: "1a. Information about recent events or happenings, especially as reported by newspapers, periodicals, radio, or television. b. A presentation of such information, as in a newspaper or on a newscast. 2. New information of any kind . . . 3. Newsworthy material."

## Traditional Definitions of News

More colorful and certainly more varied than dictionary definitions are some traditional interpretations of news offered by journalists and others, including the following examples.

* To a philosopher all news, as it is called, is gossip, and they who edit it and read it are old women over their tea.

  —Henry David Thoreau, author and naturalist
* Journalism is literature in a hurry.

  —Matthew Arnold, poet and critic
* When a dog bites a man, that is not news, because it happens so often. But if a man bites a dog, that is news.

  —John B. Bogart, Editor of the New York Sun
* News is the first rough draft of history.

  —Philip L. Graham, U.S. newspaper publisher
* Surprise, the stuff news is made of.

  —William E. Giles, journalist
* News is history shot on the wing. The huntsmen from the Fourth Estate seek to bag only the peacock or the eagle of the swifting day.

  —Gene Fowler, editor

## Contemporary Definitions of News

While journalists and others regularly have defined news, those definitions keep changing. Actually, the meaning of news evolves in response to shifts in current events, audience interests, economics and technology.

Some examples of recent definitions include the following:

* The conflict between the men who make and the men who report the news is as old as time. News may be true, but it is not truth, and reporters and officials seldom see it the same way. . . . In the old days, the reporters or couriers of bad news were often put to the gallows; now they are given the Pulitzer Prize, but the conflict goes on.

  —James Reston, U.S. journalist
* It's all storytelling, you know. That's what journalism is all about.

  —Tom Brokaw, NBC News

- News is anything of significance that happens to a community or that affects a community—from government activity to commerce, crime and social trends. It's something new—that people probably don't know about. Something novel, unusual, or counter intuitive. Something that has wide impact and importance, that transcends the immediate event.

  —Jeannine A. Guttman, executive editor

- When I first heard the question "What is news?" in journalism school, I was a bit shocked by the arrogance of the answer. "News is what I say it is." That's the way it was in the old school. The old pros who said it meant it. News is what we say it is.

  —Tom Bettag, TV producer

- Basically information that enables citizens to be actors in their society.

  —Jesse Hirsh, activist and media analyst

## Nose for News

This combination of dictionary, traditional and contemporary definitions initially may be confusing and unsettling. Many of you seek simple, clear explanations of what news is. If that were available, the task of storyteller-journalists might be much easier.

Yet, take heart. You are in good company; the best journalistic minds have not simplified the meaning of news, as certainly should be clear by the varied definitions above. What is important for you to know about these different definitions of news is that, rather than exact meaning, you need a *sense* of news, what some have termed a *nose for news*.

This will give you greater flexibility identifying and gathering news in varied situations. It also will help you to focus on the kinds of stories you need to tell.

In the remainder of the chapter we will concentrate on refining your nose for news.

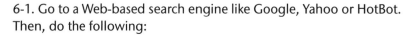

## For Practice

6-1. Go to a Web-based search engine like Google, Yahoo or HotBot. Then, do the following:

a) Locate three traditional or contemporary definitions of news *not* listed above.
b) Type each along with its URL. Print copies for your peer group.
c) Discuss your definitions with members of your peer group.
d) The group then should pick the best three definitions from all they located.
e) Each of the peer groups should discuss its top three with the entire class.
f) Submit your definitions to your teacher.

## Triggers

*Triggers,* or *news values* as they are more traditionally known, offer the best way to help you decide what is newsworthy. The standard list includes the following seven:

- Novelty.
- Audience.
- Proximity.
- Prominence.
- Timeliness.
- Impact.
- Conflict.

We term these triggers because of their power to draw coverage by storytellers and interest from readers. While much of the triggering is a no-brainer—triggers naturally demand attention—reasonable judgment on your part will make these tools more efficient and improve your nose for news.

The more triggers you can apply to any given topic or the greater intensity of a single trigger, the more newsworthy it is and, just as important, the greater its appeal to readers. Interpret triggers wisely and you will more frequently match coverage to interest. Ignore them, and you will write stories of little value.

As you follow the discussion below, try to imagine the kinds of stories on your campus triggered by each news value.

## Novelty

If it is new or unusual, it triggers attention, and if it triggers attention, it should trigger coverage.

Novelty can involve serious matters, but usually topics are lighthearted, even oddball. Do not allow novelty-based stories to descend to the level of supermarket tabloid.

Instead, when you locate a story possibility with novelty, handle it carefully. Such stories do not need to be hammered to work. In fact, underplaying a novel topic usually is more effective. Just the right touch, the particular angle, can make it a delight to write and to read.

## Audience

This measure is one that forces you to consider the demographics typical of your readers. Is the majority older? Younger? Is their median income at $30,000 or below? $50,000 or above? Are most blue collar? White collar? Do most live in older urban neighborhoods or in low-density subdivisions? What is the ethnic breakdown? Religious? Political? What is the literacy rate of your readers?

These and other factors help you to identify audience and derive additional understanding about what may interest them and trigger coverage. You cannot know too much about your audience.

## Proximity

The closer to home the topic, the stronger the trigger for coverage and interest.

This value is geographical and, working alone, may not make topics newsworthy or interesting. However, in concert with other values, proximity enhances and raises the potential of stories that you should tell.

## Prominence

The more important the people in a story, the stronger its newsworthiness.

Thus, something that happens may not be of much value *unless* it happens to an important person. Then, prominence triggers coverage.

## Timeliness

Old news is no news is an adage that fits this trigger. The closer in time that coverage follows a topic, the timelier it is. In addition, a story has timeliness if it is published when appropriate for both topic and readers.

In many communities served by more than one medium, competition traditionally has pushed each to be first to tell a story. However, particularly in recent years, this haste has resulted in inaccurate information being published or broadcast.

Speed may win the race to be first with coverage, but inaccuracy and incompleteness can cost dearly—in terms of loss of credibility and eventually declining readership. Be timely and be first to break a story, if possible, but never at the expense of accuracy and completeness.

## Impact

Key to impact as a news value is judging how much a particular topic is likely to affect your readers, in terms of both how many and how deeply they might be affected. A small impact on many people is probably just as meaningful as a great impact on only a few.

This is a particularly potent trigger, since alone it often is sufficient to warrant newsworthiness.

## Conflict

Of all the triggers that influence coverage, conflict is the most powerful. Whether involving man against nature or man against man, conflict is an elemental force. It feeds human hunger for tales that recount the responses of two opposing forces—the victories and losses between worthy foes. The more unequal the foes, the greater the conflict and the better the story. The most dynamic conflicts are those that find man, especially a single man, victorious against overwhelming forces.

Frequently, the only difference between either the David-and-Goliath story or Homer's "Odyssey" and modern stories are the particulars of who, where and how. Conflict is timeless, and most conflicts recur repeatedly. Building on its role in storytelling, master narratives and fiction, conflict is what makes stories stories.

---

## For Practice

6-2. Select five news stories from the most recent issue of your campus newspaper. Identify the news values in each. Then, do the following:

a) Explain each news value in relation to each of the stories.
b) Decide the order of importance of the triggers within each story.
c) Offer arguments for the order you chose.
d) Discuss with members of your peer group the choices you made.
e) Try to find consensus in your group about the triggers and their order, and pencil those onto your sheet.
f) Submit your answers to your teacher.

6-3. Find and photocopy examples of stories that emphasize each of the seven triggers just listed.

a) Include written explanation of each trigger in relation to each of the stories.
b) Submit the stories and your explanations to your teacher.

## *Shifting News Story Content*

News by most people's definitions is timely, important and interesting. However, the form of the news that is reported, as well as the news that goes unreported, are both of concern to today's media audiences. Karen Allen says, "The problem is, the news that is reported doesn't interest everybody, and the news that isn't reported may still interest many." Population growth and commercialization, Allen continues, have made news a product or commodity that must appeal to the widest audience possible.

This demand for "general interest," therefore, means that much of what media report may be of little or no interest to a particular individual. As a result, a large segment of the population feels disconnected from traditional media, and many turn to the wealth of more individually tailored content online.

### Online Competition

Online competition has been a major influence in changing the news content of newspapers. Historically, when a new medium joins the mix—whether radio or television or the Internet, all media feel the impact and change their content. Thus, we now are experiencing that impact with the continuing growth and development of the World Wide Web.

In addition, according to a survey by the Project for Excellence in Journalism, the shift in news content of newspapers has been away from straight news: "Twenty years ago, coverage was dominated by straight news accounts of events—what happened yesterday. Today, the news tends to have a more mediated or thematic approach to stories. In 1977, more than half of all stories (52%) were basically straight news accounts of what had happened. By 1997, that figure had fallen to less than one in three stories (32%), a 40% drop."

Joe Friday of television's "Dragnet" used to remind witnesses that he wanted "just the facts"—the meat and potatoes of straight news. Readers today, though, want more than just the facts. Don Fry and Roy Peter Clark identify six things readers want from newspapers:

- News about themselves and their communities.
- Information they can find easily and understand.
- Explanation of the world they have to cope with.
- News about real people they can identify with.
- Interpretations of events that help give them meaning.
- Interesting stories to read.

## Frames

To accommodate these reader demands, newspaper journalists have widened and diversified the range of storytelling devices or approaches they use to compose stories. These are called frames. Another Project for Excellence in Journalism study found the 13 most common frames in newspapers:

- Straight news account: Presents the five Ws and H.
- Conflict story: Stresses conflict that is inherent to the situation or is growing among participants.
- Consensus story: Focuses primarily on the points of agreement in an issue or event.
- Conjecture story: Concentrates on conjecture or speculation of what is to come.
- Process story: Develops how to do something, how something is done or how something works.
- Historical outlook: Places current event or situation into historical perspective.
- Horse race: Tells who is winning and who is losing.
- Trend story: Explains how the current news item fits an ongoing trend.
- Policy explored: Presents policy and its impact.
- Reaction story: Stresses the reaction or response from one or more of key figures.
- Reality check: Examines closely the truthfulness of a statement or information.
- Wrongdoing exposed: Uncovers injustice or criminal acts.
- Personality profile: Profiles the key news figure.

We will discuss additional aspects of frames in Chapter 13.

## For Practice

6-4. Find and photocopy examples of the six kinds of stories above that Fry and Clark say readers want today. Then, do the following:

a) Provide clear written explanation showing how each fits the category you claim.
b) Indicate the frame each seems to use.
c) Discuss your examples and answers with members of your peer group.
d) Submit your materials to your teacher.

## Weighing the Importance of News

Modern civilization is enriched by an abundance of information from traditional and new media. You and your readers have access to more news from more sources than ever. This largess, though, means readers must sift through large amounts of material for information they want and need.

While a sizable number of people prefer this freedom, many still want newspapers to continue gatekeeping—making decisions about what is most important and presenting it. Triggers help journalists to complete this task, but other factors also influence story importance.

## The Influence of Triggers

We saw above that triggers help you determine what topics are newsworthy. They also serve an additional role in helping journalists to gauge which stories are more important than others. This is helpful for at least two reasons.

First, newspaper editors need to be able to rank order the available stories—nearly always more than will fit an issue. Contrary to popular notion, newspapers determine how many pages they will publish based primarily on how much advertising they have sold, not on how much news is available. Space limitations mean that all stories cannot run. As a result, even newsworthy stories may be cut—a necessary byproduct of gatekeeping.

Second, editors need to know how to play the stories that make the cut. While all stories in this group may be newsworthy, not every story is *equally* newsworthy. Those with a greater number of triggers or those with fewer but more powerful triggers will head the list. The most important likely will run front page above the fold—the privileged position of lead story. The rest run lower or on inside pages.

## The Influence of Other Factors

Editors also judge importance on how well a story meets the goals of journalism—to inform, to educate and to entertain. The order of these goals is pertinent. It reflects the relative value of each, at least from the traditional viewpoint, with the chief task of journalism to inform. Thus, these criteria privilege news stories that primarily inform over those that primarily entertain. However, news stories that do all three pack a powerful punch.

Roy Peter Clark cites Jay Rosen in amplifying and updating journalistic goals:

- To improve the nature of public discussion on issues.
- To define problems.
- To sharpen arguments.
- To seek common ground.

We will explore these concerns more fully in later chapters, particularly Chapter 19, where we will see how the public journalism movement responds specifically to Clark and Rosen's goals.

Another measure used in weighing story importance is quite practical—whether or not a staff reporter wrote a story. It is logical and economical to give more weight to stories written by paid staff versus those from syndicates or wire services. Moreover, the majority of staff stories have another edge: They are local.

Of course, this edge has its limits, as strong enough triggers can make non-staff stories more important than locally produced material.

Weighing the importance of news is more art than science; clearly, your choices remain subjective, influenced by individual perspectives and preferences. Use all available measures and contexts if you hope to keep sharp your nose for news.

## Components of Effective News Stories

A good yarn is a thing of beauty to storytellers—something they can use to string an audience along the rises and falls, ins and outs of experience. What is especially beautiful about an effective story is that it combines the right experience with the right audience.

And when these components come together, storytellers sing.

### Experience

As systems of communication developed and became increasingly sophisticated, the information, or message, being transmitted could be increasingly complex. This meant that humans could communicate beyond simple ideas—the basic needs of the moment—and share abstract concepts and experience.

You may recall from Chapter 1 that this ability to communicate abstracts allowed humans to become storytellers. Unable to deliver real experience beyond its moment, experience became story. And it is this need to share experience that drives both storytellers and journalists.

So, which experiences are the "right experiences" for storyteller-journalists? Importantly, few are "wrong."

Some are just better than others.

Use the triggers and journalistic goals discussed previously in deciding which experiences to report. Reading the stories that others are reporting also helps to keep you aware of different perspectives. Finally, knowing what appeals to your readers is invaluable as well.

A safe bet: If a story interests you, it likely will interest fellow students who are your readers.

### Audience

The other element that clinches successful storytelling, audience, is one that storyteller-journalists sometimes misunderstand, downplay or even ignore. Yet, it is essential that you have a clear and accurate sense of who is reading your stories.

Good storytellers understand that they must suit their tales to their audiences. For a live group presentation, of course, this task is less daunting—the audience is present and visible. Their reactions and responses become part of the storytelling moment, guiding the storyteller.

As a storyteller-journalist, though, you cannot see your audience. In fact, what you know of your audience may be limited or wrongheaded. When this happens, you are in trouble.

As we learned from the study discussed earlier, journalists are disconnected from their audiences, and audiences are not happy about it. As a result, newspapers have lost credibility, respect and ultimately many of their readers.

In response, many newspapers are using demographics to get a better idea of who their audiences are. In addition, surveys, polls and focus groups are revealing what audiences know and what they want to know. And newspapers are tailoring content to be more audience-friendly.

You should anticipate and respect what your audience knows and determine what they need to know; you should answer questions they will have and satisfy their curiosity; and you should present material in a way that is comfortable and appropriate for them.

In other words, strive to match experience to audience.

## News as Story

Recall from Chapter 1 that "Storycrafting" considers all good writing as storytelling. The magic of story presents news to an audience in effective, appropriate and user-friendly ways.

Jack Lule considers storytelling "an essential part of what makes us human. We understand our lives and our world through story. Perhaps stories are so much a part of us because human life itself has the structure of story. Each of us has a central character. Each of us knows, better than we know anything, that life has a beginning, middle, and end. We *need* stories because we *are* stories."

The most exciting experience put into words does not guarantee a successful piece of writing—though, admittedly, it helps to have powerful content. Nor does the use of narrative a good story make—though most readers tend to find narrative appealing.

Rather, story is a mindset that writers bring to the writing moment. It disdains preconceived notions, expected content and forced forms. Instead, this sense of story privileges a tempered creativity that directs content and format.

Content must be complete but concise, like the porridge Goldilocks found most tasty and gobbled up—it was not too hot or too cold; it was *just right*. As we discussed earlier in this chapter, story also must be presented in a format or frame that is *just right* for content and for readers. Clark of the Poynter Institute for Media Studies says that this is the difference between writing a story and just writing an article.

He suggests that much of what journalists write today is the latter—articles packed with information but otherwise dull and lifeless. When he wants to share experience with people, he writes the former, a story. He says that people do not read "Hamlet" for information—to learn how to dig graves or how to travel to Elsinore. They read Shakespeare's tragic masterpiece "because it is an experience. A virtual reality. It seeks not to inform us, but to form us." He adds that "stories can brighten information, and . . . information can enrich stories." News and story do not exist apart but rather in harmony.

As most of us have come to realize, fiction seldom is more powerful or dramatic than real experiences that fill our world each day, whether they happen in the halls of power at the White House in Washington or the halls of poverty at a flophouse in Los Angeles.

As journalists, especially print journalists, we are charged with making those experiences come to life for an audience. We are, in fact, charged with telling stories. When you work a beat, your first goal is to discover and uncover the newsworthy experience. Then, you should gather more details than you need, enough to satisfy your curiosity first and your readers' next. Finally, you craft your story using the format that suits the experience and your readers.

If you are successful, experience runs full circle—from its happening to its rehappening.

## Crafting and Drafting

As you draft and revise your story for Exercise 6-5, ask yourself the following reader-focused questions:

- What is the most important thing I want my readers to know? Do I include that in the story's lead?
- Have I given my readers enough explanation and examples to understand clearly the point of the story?
- Do I give my readers enough background or context to interpret the current story?
- What impact will this story have on my readers? Which readers?
- Why should my readers care about this story? Does my story make that "so what" clear?

## For Practice

6-5. Run your regular beat, and locate one or more story possibilities. You should *prefer* those that fit Fry and Clark's six kinds of stories that readers want. Then, do the following:

a) Interview each source and take careful notes.
b) Listen carefully for quoteworthy comments the sources make, and write those down exactly.
c) Draft a story with a lead that effectively opens and best fits the story.
d) Keep in mind the seven news values as you draft.
e) Swap stories with a peer review partner or group and give written reader feedback. Submit the draft and peer feedback to your teacher.
f) After your teacher has reviewed your draft and peer feedback and has offered additional suggestions, revise as required.
g) Submit a final draft.

# *Chapter 6 Bibliography*

Allen, Karen. "The History of Modern Journalism." *It's News to Me: Journalism in the Internet Age.* 1999. <http://www.carleton.ca/jmc/cujo/showcase/allnews/history.htm>.

Allen, Karen. "Some Thoughts on 'What Is News.'" *It's News to Me: Journalism in the Internet Age.* 1999. <http://www.carleton.ca/jmc/cujo/showcase/allnews/podium1.htm>.

*The American Heritage Dictionary of the English Language.* 4th ed. Boston: Houghton Mifflin, 2000. <http://www.bartleby.com/61/>.

Arnold, Matthew. "What Is News." *Poynteronline.* 8 April 2002. <http://www.poynter.org/content/content_view.asp?id=2831>.

Bettag, Tom. "Evolving Definitions of News." *Journal of Press/Politics.* 1 June 2000.

Bogart, John B. "Classic Quotes." *The Quotations Page.* 2003. <http://www.quotationspage.com/search.php3?Search=news&Author=&C=mgm&C=motivate&C=classic&C=coles&C=lindsly&C=poorc&page=3>.

Brokaw, Tom. *Northwestern University Byline* (Spring '82). *The Columbia World of Quotations.* Ed. Robert Andrews, Mary Biggs, and Michael Seidel. New York: Columbia University Press, 1996. <http://www.bartleby.com/66/>.

Clark, Roy Peter. *The American Conversation and the Language of Journalism.* St. Petersburg, Fla.: Poynter Institute for Media Studies, 1994.

Dr. Ink. "What Is News." *Poynteronline.* 8 April 2002. <http://www.poynter.org/content/content_view.asp?id=2831>.

Fowler, Gene. *Skyline.* (Viking, 1961). *Simpson's Contemporary Quotations.* Ed. James B. Simpson. New York: Houghton Mifflin, 1988. <http://www.bartleby.com/63/9/8009.html>.

Fry, Don, and Roy Peter Clark. "Return of the Narrative." *Quill 182: 4* (1994).

Giles, William E. *National Observer* (19 October 1964). *Simpson's Contemporary Quotations.* Ed. James B. Simpson. New York: Houghton Mifflin, 1988.

Graham, Philip L. *The Columbia World of Quotations.* Ed. Robert Andrews, Mary Biggs, and Michael Seidel. New York: Columbia University Press, 1996. <http://www.bartleby.com/66/>.

Guttman, Jeannine A. "What Is News? Broadening the Definition." *Civic Catalyst Newsletter.* 22 April 1991. <http://www.pewcenter.org/doingcj/civiccat/displayCivcat.php?id=95>.

Hirsch, Jesse. In Karen Allen, "Some Thoughts on 'What Is News.'" *It's News to Me: Journalism in the Internet Age.* 1999. <http://www.carleton.ca/jmc/cujo/showcase/allnews/podium1.htm>.

Lule, Jack. *Daily News, Eternal Stories: The Mythological Role of Journalism.* New York: Guilford Press, 2001.

*Merriam-Webster Online.* <http://www.m-w.com/>.

Neufeldt, Victoria, ed. *Webster's New World Dictionary of American English.* 3d college ed. New York: Prentice Hall, 1991.

Project for Excellence in Journalism. "Changing Definitions of News." *Journalism.org.* 6 March 1998. <http://www.journalism.org/resources/research/reports/definitions/default.asp>.

Project for Excellence in Journalism. "Framing the News: The Triggers, Frames, and Messages in Newspaper Coverage." *Journalism.org.* <http://www.journalism.org/resources/research/reports/framing/frame.asp>.

Reston, James. "The Tug of History." *The Artillery of the Press* (1966). *The Columbia World of Quotations.* Ed. Robert Andrews, Mary Biggs, and Michael Seidel. New York: Columbia University Press, 1996. <http://www.bartleby.com/66/>.

Schudson, Michael. *The Power of News.* Cambridge, Mass.: Harvard University Press, 1995.

Thoreau, Henry David. "Where I Lived, and What I Lived For," *Walden* (1854). *The Columbia World of Quotations.* Ed. Robert Andrews, Mary Biggs, and Michael Seidel. New York: Columbia University Press, 1996. <http://www.bartleby.com/66/>.

"Two Ways To Read, Three Ways To Write." *Poynteronline.* 1 January 1998. <http://www.poynter.org/content/content_view.asp?id=5363>.

# Chapter 7
# Content

*Looking back, I imagine I was always
writing. Twaddle it was too. But
better far write twaddle or anything,
anything, than nothing at all.*

—Katherine Mansfield

## Chapter Contents

## QuickView

We begin our discussion of content with an in-depth review of the journalist's questions, the five Ws, H and SW. We will discover how these few, simple questions can generate interesting and complete content.

We also will consider again both "aboutness" and audience needs—two topics that deserve additional explanation and illustration. Understanding each concept is critical if you expect your stories to be successful.

Next, hard news and soft news are traditional labels for categories into which all news stories fit. We will learn how to distinguish one from the other and the value of each.

We will close the chapter covering previews, follows, updates and sidebars—all stories with certain content that serves readers.

You are sitting in the hall outside your classroom on Monday morning. A classmate walks in the door. A broad white bandage covers her forehead, and fresh bruises show purple on her left cheek. She is limping, favoring her left leg.

"What happened to you?" you ask.

"Oh, I was in a car accident."

"Gee, how did it happen? Did somebody run into you?"

"Nah. I was driving too fast coming around the curve on Old County Road and just lost it."

"Oh, that must have been awful. Are you hurt badly?"

"No, I was lucky. I ended up with just a few bumps and bruises. Thank God for my seatbelt."

"Goodness, yes. When did it happen?"

"Well, I was coming home from the ballgame Saturday night. I guess it was about 10:30."

"Are you going to be OK?"

"Yeah, I think so, but I'm sure gonna be more careful driving at night on dark, curvy roads."

## Five Ws, H and SW

The exchange above may be fictional, but the pattern is all too real, reflecting the natural curiosity of the inquiring student. Embedded in that pattern are many of the workhorse questions of the reporter, the five Ws and H—what, who, when, where, why and how. Also, you may recall from Chapter 2 that in addition to those six questions is a seventh, so what.

These questions feed our inquisitive nature. They also comprise baseline questions that storyteller-journalists use to launch the gathering of details for their stories. Like water poured into a pump head to prime it and make it possible to draw new water from the well, the journalists questions are quick, easy and important starters in any interview.

Chapter 2 also noted that the journalist's questions tend to spin around the main *what*, and each can move in several directions. We revisit those questions along with a few additional:

- *What:* What is the main concern of the storyteller? What is the most important thing happening? Are there other *whats* that the story covers?
- *Who:* Who is primarily involved? Who is primarily doing something? Are there valuable roles that other people play in the story?
- *When:* When is it happening? Are there other time elements in the story that are of value to readers?
- *Where:* Where is it happening? Are other places significant in the story?
- *Why:* Why is it happening?
- *How:* How is it happening?
- *So what:* So what about these elements? Why should readers care?

Do not allow the simplicity of these questions to belie their value nor their true depth. Let us examine more closely how each is developed in a story from the

Georgetown Voice. You will see how these questions reveal the multiple layers of detail that are typical of a fully developed story.

## Look at the fish, Daddy!

By Debbie Hwang

A 5-year-old boy runs around the small pond, pointing excitedly into the water. "Look at the fish, Daddy!" he says, while standing precariously on the rocks lining the pond. Lying discreetly beside him, almost hidden by the grass, is a brass plaque dedicating the water memorial to a Georgetown student from his friends and family. In February 2000, David Shick (MSB '01) died after suffering from injuries in an alcohol-related brawl that took place in the parking lot behind Lauinger Library. Shick had been walking home from Champions bar when he became involved in the fight and was sent to the hospital after receiving serious wounds to his head.

Three years later, most people's memories—if they have any at all—rest on the memorial that was erected next to White Gravenor in memory of Shick's death. Most students at the University now never knew Shick and most do not know of the details surrounding his death.

Three years later, has Georgetown learned anything from the death of Dave Shick?

This semester, Georgetown students have an opportunity to take advantage of free access to a personalized Internet assessment of high-risk drinking behavior called MyStudentBody.com—a website created with the support of the National Institute on Alcohol Abuse and Alcoholism.

Upon logging onto the website, each person is prompted to create a personal profile based on age, gender, race, year in school and level of alcohol consumption. With this confidential profile, each user can track his or her own alcohol consumption level per week and compare it to national averages.

Other tools available on the website include a blood alcohol calculator, a calorie calculator, a budget calculator, a profile of alcohol laws by state and "Anatomy 101," which describes the effects that alcohol has on different parts of the body. The website is a great resource for students. And to top it off, it's not preachy.

Since Shick's death, several University-sponsored groups have been created to focus on campus drinking culture. One such group, sponsored by Health Education Services, was created this semester with the goal of showing Georgetown students the positive social norms that the Georgetown community has around health issues, particularly alcohol. The group recently took a survey that found that an estimated 97 percent of Georgetown students would walk a friend home if they knew that he or she was inebriated.

So, perhaps students have learned after all. If they haven't, the Advisory Neighborhood Commission will make sure that they do. In the past year, the majority of bars in the surrounding Georgetown area have limited their customers to the over-21 crowd at all times. Although a flash of a fake ID and a bat of the eyelashes used to be all that was needed to get into a bar three years ago, there is now an Intellicheck ID-scanning machine.

Angry neighbors used Shick's death as the ultimate excuse for putting the heat on area bars to more heavily monitor their crowds for underage drinking. The pressure has also been put on the Metropolitan Police Department to perform bar sweeps more regularly and to patrol areas of high student concentration. Since Shick's death, the infamous Block Party has also been cancelled—most likely never to be revived again.

Until neighbors stop hearing about drunken fights on campus, and until they stop being woken up by students screaming on their way home from parties, they will not stop taking efforts to crack down on underage drinking.

The majority of Georgetown students are responsible when they drink. Now all they have to do is prove it.

The Georgetown Voice
Georgetown University

## What

Let us examine the various *whats* that the story covers.

- A father-son visit to a small pond.
- A brass plaque dedicating the water memorial.
- David Shick's death.
- Alcohol-related brawl.
- Champions bar.
- Most people's memories.
- A personalized Internet assessment of high-risk drinking behavior called MyStudentBody.com.
- Several university-sponsored groups created to focus on campus drinking culture.
- Flash of a fake ID.
- A bat of the eyelashes.
- Intellicheck ID-scanning machine.
- Heat on area bars.
- Bar sweeps.
- The infamous Block Party.
- Drunken fights.
- Underage drinking.

Since most stories tend to revolve around *what*, it should not be surprising that the list of *whats* in this story is the longest at 16. Note how the *whats* establish concrete detail and firm up a sense of reality necessary for readers to feel like they are reading about actual places and events. *Whats* help readers to situate themselves in relation to the story.

*Now ask yourself:* Which of the *whats* above is the most important? Why? Is it played up in a lead or nut graf? Compare your answers with members of your peer review group.

## Who

Next, let us see how many relevant *whos* are presented in the story.

- Five-year-old boy.
- David Shick.
- Most students.
- Georgetown students.
- Each person.
- The group.
- The Advisory Neighborhood Commission.
- Health Education Services.
- Georgetown community.
- Angry neighbors.
- Metropolitan Police Department.

At 11 the number of *whos* is a distant second to the *whats*. Naturally, "who did what" pairs these news elements but clearly show that, in this story at least, not all *whats* have a *who* attached.

*Now ask yourself:* Why is that? Compare your answers with members of your peer review group.

## When

Several *whens* relate to the *whats* in the story.

- February 2000.
- Three years later.
- This semester.
- Since Shick's death.
- Recently.
- In the past year.

Readers want and need time elements to understand sequencing of events, to see how some *whats* relate in time to other *whats* and to relate all events to the readers' own here and now. A glance at the six *whens* above gives us a clear sense of time movement in the story.

*Now ask yourself:* Why are there no exact *whens* in the story, such as Thursday or Feb. 19, 2000? Compare your answers with members of your peer review group.

## Where

A careful examination of the story shows eight *wheres* that provide locations in the story.

- Around the small pond.
- In the parking lot behind Lauinger Library.
- Next to White Gravenor.
- At the university.
- Surrounding Georgetown area.
- Into a bar.
- Areas of high student concentration.
- On their way home.

*Wheres* are similar to *whens* in how they fix events—but in place rather than time—so that readers can mentally map out key spots. Whether all readers actually understand where all these locations are is less important than the fact that the writer has provided them to enhance the story's reality. Even if you have never been to Georgetown, you appreciate the *wheres* that position you in the story.

*Now ask yourself:* Why are some *wheres* in the story more specific than others? Compare your answers with members of your peer review group.

## Why

*Why* is a journalist's question that may be obvious, implied or unknown. Yet, increasingly readers are expecting journalists to provide clearer and more complete explanations of *why*. In the story above we can see that most of the *whys* are spelled out.

• Why the brass plaque is there: It commemorates Shick's death.
• Why students can log on to MyStudentBody.com: They can track their own alcohol consumption level per week and compare it to national averages.
• Why several university-sponsored groups were created: To focus on campus drinking culture.
• Why a particular group was created this semester: To show Georgetown students the positive social norms that the Georgetown community has around health issues, particularly alcohol.
• Why bars are now more heavily pressured to monitor crowds for underage drinking: Neighbors are angry over Shick's death.

All five of these *whys* respond to what readers need to know to understand some other detail in the story. Yet, stories often leave some *whys* unanswered. For example, why did Shick get involved in the fight?

*Now ask yourself:* Discuss the unanswered *why* above. What other *whys* are not answered in the story? Should they have been? Compare your answers with members of your peer review group.

## How

*How* is even trickier in most stories. It often is a question that does not need answering because the answer is obvious.

• How Shick was injured: In an alcohol-related brawl.
• How Shick died: He suffered head injuries.
• How the university has worked to prevent another alcohol-related death: It has created several groups that focus on drinking.
• How neighbors have worked to prevent another alcohol-related death: They put pressure on both bars and local police.

The limited number of *hows* in this story is typical of most. Yet, even though *how* is less common, you cannot ignore it for certain aspects of stories. Certainly, readers often are able to guess at how something happened, but good storyteller-journalists do not force much guessing on their audiences. If not answering a *how* may leave readers hanging, go ahead and explain it.

*Now ask yourself:* Are there other *hows* not answered in the story? Are you left hanging because of that? Compare your answers with members of your peer review group.

## So What

*So what* defines the meaning of the story and focuses on consequences. Three passages deal with this in the story.

- "Three years later, has Georgetown learned anything from the death of Dave Shick?"
- "The group recently took a survey that found that an estimated 97 percent of Georgetown students would walk a friend home if they knew that he or she was inebriated. So, perhaps students have learned after all."
- "The majority of Georgetown students are responsible when they drink. Now all they have to do is prove it."

This news element draws the fewest hits, as expected. Moreover, the answers to *so what* often are not given in the text; instead, storytellers and their audiences rely on embedded understandings. Such is the case in the story above. We ask *so what* of the death of Shick, of the group survey and of the claim that students now drink responsibly.

*Now ask yourself:* What does the story tell you of these three *so whats*? How much must you assume or take for granted? Compare your answers with members of your peer review group.

---

## *For Practice*

7-1. Select three stories from your campus newspaper and locate *all* of the five Ws, H and SW. Then, do the following:

a) Mark each with a highlighter.
b) Type the lists of each.
c) Swap the highlighted stories and your typewritten lists with a peer review partner.
d) Read through the stories. If five Ws, H and SW were not marked, do so and add to the list.
e) Discuss each other's results.
f) Submit the stories and lists.

---

## *"Aboutness"*

We first discussed *aboutness* in Chapter 2, where we found that the term refers to a variety of concerns for storytellers and their audiences. Essentially, aboutness is a balance and blend of the right amount of material focused on a specific, valid point.

In the storytelling you have completed up to this point—regardless of how much or how little that might be—your success often has hinged on how well you have dealt with aboutness. The simplistic approach asks, "What is the story about?" You will do fine so long as you are willing to stretch that single question out like the fellow pulling taffy on the Boardwalk in Atlantic City, making it cover a multitude of concerns.

However, give your arms a rest from the taffy and instead parse the concept as we did in Chapter 2 with the following "aboutness factors":

- Topic of concern.
- Kind of information to gather.
- Story focus.
- Amount of information to use for support.
- Order to present the supporting information.
- Relevance to readers.

As you approach and develop storytelling moments, your sense of aboutness will grow from these elements. Don Fry writes, "To paraphrase the late James Reston, journalists write letters to friends they don't know, about interesting things their friends didn't have time to find out about. And the best ones use storytelling as their vehicle."

Your goal is to get at the heart of the story that you want to write and, in a sense, the story that *needs to be written* for your particular audience at this particular time.

## Audience Needs

What exactly does your audience want and need to know? That is a key question good storytellers ask of themselves, and it is one that you must answer as you gather information, draft your story and revise it for publication.

Let us review the top of the following story to see what we might surmise about audience.

### Parking policy change gives impound authority

By Sally Villarreal

The Faculty Senate voted in favor of a new parking policy for chronic offenders at its meeting Wednesday with an 8-1 vote.

The new policy defines chronic offenders as people who have five or more tickets in a 12-month period. Those parked illegally would have their cars impounded and be subject to a $150 chronic offender fee.

Disciplinary action would be taken against chronic offenders who receive 10 or more tickets in a 12-month period with the new policy. Students will be referred to Student Justice and faculty and staff will be referred to their superiors.

However, the Senate revised the policy taking out a provision that would allow students to be suspended and faculty and staff to be fired if they continue to abuse policies and get more than 10 parking tickets in a 12-month period.

The current policy prohibits chronic offenders, people who have had five or more parking tickets in a semester or 10 or more in a 12-month period, from parking on campus.

\* \* \* \* \* \* \* \* \* \*

The Daily University Star
Southwest Texas State University

Several factors in an audience assessment help to determine how this question of what an audience wants and needs to know was handled:

- The particular topic being covered: A new parking policy aimed at chronic offenders.
- The likely audience who will read the story: Students, faculty and staff at Southwest Texas State University—especially those who have received lots of parking tickets.
- What the audience already may know about the topic: While this may be difficult to answer, a search of the online archives of The Daily University Star showed that parking problems were the topic of more than 200 stories since 1995, suggesting that regular readers have been given a healthy dose of coverage of the issue.
- What may be happening in the audience's lives right now: Again, tough to pin down, but we might assume that the decision to implement a stricter policy is due to growing numbers of scofflaws and parking problems.
- The medium for which the story is being written: The original story appeared in the print edition of The Daily University Star; this version came from its online edition.

A second story excerpt focuses on cutting a master's program due to budget reductions. Notice the opening focus on a single student, a pattern reminiscent of the Wall Street Journal format.

### Museum studies may be under the ax

By Melissa Lee

Jacqueline Shalberg has just one question:
Why her?
She always thought her major was safe. She never expected her program—rated among the top five in the nation—to fall under the budget ax.
But that's just where the University of Nebraska-Lincoln first-year graduate student in museum studies finds herself.
On Monday, Chancellor Harvey Perlman announced his proposals for $7.5 million in reductions at UNL. Among the cuts was the master's degree program in museum studies, which would save about $25,000.
It is the first academic program to be proposed for elimination during Nebraska's recent budget problems.
But in the days following Perlman's announcement, those tied to museum studies have rallied in support of the program. And on Thursday evening they gathered in Nebraska Hall to discuss how to fight the possible cut.

About 40 students, alumni and professors enjoyed sandwiches and brownies while they tossed out reasons to save the museum studies program.

\* \* \* \* \* \* \* \* \* \*

The Daily Nebraskan
The University of Nebraska-Lincoln

Let us review the same factors as before for an audience assessment of readers at the University of Nebraska-Lincoln and what they may want and need to know:

- The particular topic being covered: The proposed cut of a master's program in museum studies.
- The likely audience who will read the story: Students, faculty and staff involved with the museum studies program, as well as others who may fear future cuts in their programs.
- What the audience already may know about the topic: A search of The Daily Nebraskan online archives suggests that the news of the program cut first came to light only three days earlier, in a story covering the general announcement of proposed budget cuts. In fact, an upbeat story published just four months earlier suggested that the museum studies program, established in 1990, was part of a growing national trend that boasted more than 200 universities with programs similar to that at UNL.
- What may be happening in the audience's lives right now: The opening focus on the museum studies graduate student personalizes the impact of the proposed cut. Yet, an archives search suggests that budget cuts have been a hot topic, with more than 100 stories published during the previous 12 months. Thus, regular readers of The Daily Nebraskan have had opportunity to learn plenty about cuts.
- The medium for which the story is being written: The original story appeared in the print edition of The Daily Nebraskan; this version came from its online edition.

Determining story topic and content that will suit audience interest is essential if your stories are to have relevance. Be aware of what is happening on your campus that may impact your audience. Strive to anticipate and be sensitive to their concerns. Serve them well, because it is unlikely anyone else can step in and more effectively do that job.

## *For Practice*

7-2. Select three stories from your campus newspaper and identify the following "aboutness factors" in each. Submit to your teacher copies of the stories and your answers.

a) Topic of concern.
b) Kind of information gathered.
c) Story focus.

d) Amount of information used for support.
e) Order of the supporting information.
f) Likely relevance to readers.

---

# Hard News and Soft News

*Hard* and *soft* are terms often applied to news; as you might suspect, the usual and expected meanings of hard and soft actually do fit. This is especially true if you think of hard as sharp edged, driving, solid and soft as rounded, easier going, cushioned.

## Hard News

Hard news traditionally has been the mainstay of journalists. It includes spot news and breaking news—the important events of a community. Hard news is immediate, or at least timely, and seeks to clarify the impact of news on people's lives in an accessible, simple, matter-of-fact way. Examples might include a rash of vandalism targeting student cars parked in dormitory lots, a proposed tuition hike, the election of a student government president or the firing of a popular professor.

Hard news can deal with nearly any topic and relies on objective reporting of the facts. It traditionally expects that journalists maintain distance. Content should be clear and strong enough to speak for itself and enable readers to respond as they wish.

Let us look at excerpts of two hard-news stories.

### Feds target campuses

By Jessika Fruchter

Keeping their promise to leave "no stone unturned," government investigators looking for terrorists have expanded their scope to include university campuses, including at CU-Boulder.

According to the American Association of Collegiate Registrars and Admissions Officers, federal investigators have contacted administrators from over 200 university campuses since Sept. 11 to interview certain international students. The University of Colorado at Boulder was among those universities.

Lt. Tim McGraw, spokesman for CU-Boulder police, confirmed that the FBI has had continued contact with University officials since Sept. 11.

\* \* \* \* \* \* \* \* \* \*

The Colorado Daily
The University of Colorado-Boulder

### Robbery, drug violations increase

#### New campus crime statistics show lowered alcohol infractions

By Whitney Beckett

Reported robberies and drug violations increased last year, while liquor law violations were down, according to 2001 campus crime statistics released this week.

Robbery showed the largest increase, more than doubling from four to 10. Drug-related arrests increased from 16 to 19 and drug violation referrals jumped from eight to 21. Aggravated assault, burglary, motor vehicle theft and alcohol violations all decreased between 2000 and 2001.

"We're doing a good job, but we're not happy with any level of crime," said Maj. Robert Dean of the Duke University Police Department.

\* \* \* \* \* \* \* \* \* \*

The Chronicle
Duke University

## Soft News

Soft news historically has approached storytelling more creatively. Topics of traditional soft-news stories tend to be less serious or at least less dynamic in their impact on people's lives. Sometimes, less important hard news is presented in a lighthearted way, emphasizing some humorous or odd element. Essentially, while soft news may be interesting and desirable, it tends *not* to be the news that shapes people's lives and impacts the community in meaningful ways.

Examples of soft news might be an upcoming greased-pig contest, the problems caused by the regular morning visits of a woodpecker, the announcement of a new night class in candy making or a student who protests planned dormitory fee increases by wearing a barrel and little else around campus.

Excerpts from two soft-news stories should help to clarify appropriate topics and how these are presented.

### Mice seek shelter in Adams House

By Ebonie D. Hazle

Two formidable foes were awaiting Adams House residents when they returned from their winter breaks: reading period and mice. Many students living in entryways A and B of the House found that the creatures were indeed stirring, in their hallways and under their beds.

In an e-mail to residents on Saturday, Adams House Masters Sean and Judith Palfrey said they are "distressed" that students have had to deal with the infestation and offered the reassurance that it "will all be over soon."

\* \* \* \* \* \* \* \* \* \*

The Crimson
Harvard University

### Special athletes ready for medals

By Jessica Reese

Twelve-year-old Sara Burton of Coralville has nine Special Olympics gold medals to her name, but the gymnast whose specialty is twirling a 10-foot rainbow-colored ribbon is mainly in it for the fun.

This weekend, Sara will don her sparkly, black-and-red leotard in the 15th annual Midwinter Special Olympics Tournament at the UI Field House, where more than

700 athletes from across the state will compete in gymnastics, basketball, power weightlifting and cheerleading events.

What's Sara's winning strategy that garnered her three gold medals last year? "Definitely, no mistakes," she said.

\* \* \* \* \* \* \* \* \* \*

The Daily Iowan
The University of Iowa

## Previews and Follows

Coverage that spins around events and situations falls into two general categories, previews and follows.

Previews alert readers to opportunities. An informed public can be an involved public, and it is important for the media to keep readers informed.

Follows, as you might suspect, look back at events and let readers know what happened. This is especially valuable for those readers unable to attend.

### Previews

Specialized previews like advance stories, which we discussed in Chapter 3, use a standard formula to give readers details of particular events. The main goal of most advances is to provide notice. They are simple and straightforward. Depth of detail is neither required nor expected. Name of the event, day, date, place and some basic explanation are usually all you need.

For example, an advance story focusing on an election might tell readers what the ballot covers and offer when and where they can vote. Other advances can run the range of possibilities: registration for fall semester classes at the university, a Saturday morning gathering of Audubon Society members and others at a nearby wildlife refuge, a one-night performance of "The Words of Albert Schweizer and the Music of Bach" or a young hunter training session presented by the state Department of Conservation.

The typical advance markets some event in hopes that readers will respond by attending.

Some previews, however, develop a context or background for situations that are upcoming and unfolding. Previews of this type do more than provide notice; they offer explanation. Depth is necessary on those points readers need to understand to make decisions about what the situation means to them and how they might relate it to their own lives.

An election preview would spell out the issue in detail, with the background for the proposal, pros and cons of its passage, what exactly its passage or failure would mean for readers and what margin it will take for approval. Other examples of previews might include the closing of a busy thoroughfare to construct two additional lanes for traffic, a school board meeting at which $2.9 million in cuts were being reviewed, changes in the annual Apple Blossom Parade and Festival or the trial of a 15-year-old boy accused of murdering a classmate.

While some preview stories may encourage readers to respond by attending and participating—just as advance stories do—their main purpose is to inform and educate the public. See how this is handled in the following excerpt of an election preview.

### DSG candidates face off today

By Kevin Lees

In preparation for the Duke Student Government presidential runoff election today, the two remaining candidates focused their positions as each made a final push for votes. Today's runoff will pit juniors Taylor Collison and Matthew Slovik against each other for the DSG presidency. In the first vote March 4, Slovik received 32.5 percent of the vote to Collison's 26 percent.

Both candidates spent Monday campaigning. Slovik said he was trying to buoy current supporters and reach out to other possible supporters, while Collison said he met with groups and talked to freshmen at the Marketplace on East Campus Monday night.

Collison seemed to have sharpened his rhetoric as the outside candidate more able to make the changes he said were necessary for the student government.

"I still feel I'm the best candidate for the position, the only candidate right now who will go into DSG and not be bound by the problems that have kept DSG inactive," he said.

Collison said he would focus on attracting the votes of the over 40 percent who did not vote in the first election—57.4 percent of the student body voted March 4, a record-high turnout.

"You see a lot of people who think DSG hasn't represented them since they've been here," he said.

Both candidates stressed that they hoped their original supporters would return to vote for them as well.

Slovik remained confident about today's vote and hoped he would end up on top again in the runoff.

"I couldn't feel any better about my position heading into the runoff," Slovik said. "[I hope to] continue to show all the people who voted for me that I am the most experienced candidate and that I will help make the biggest difference for the student body."

DSG Attorney General Will Fagan said the online voting window would be open longer today, from 9 a.m. until 11 p.m., but that DSG would not operate any physical polling stations.

Christina Hsu, Asian Student Association president, said that although the body has not endorsed anyone since the first election, ASA was very complimentary to Collison in its first endorsement of junior Shaomeng Wang for president. Wang, who received 15.8 percent of the vote, has endorsed Slovik. In the closing days of the campaign, Wang had accused Collison supporters of tearing down his signs, a charge that DSG officials decided was unfounded.

* * * * * * * * * *

The Chronicle
Duke University

## Follows

Follow stories do just what is suggested: They follow events and situations. They provide the results.

Follows are not always written about events for which advances were published. Readers do not need or want to know how many pancakes were served at the Lions Club Pancake Breakfast, *unless* that number is exceptional or surprising. Likewise, journalists may not write a follow for a dramatic event, such as how well it was performed or how many attended—*unless* something about the event was unusual.

Instead, follows are standard coverage for any event or situation of *consequence*. Although a preview may have gotten reader attention and even reader response—thinking about its impact, perhaps discussing it with others or even participating in an event—a follow provides a record of what happened and, increasingly, an explanation of what it means.

For readers who did not attend the event, a follow is essential if they are to remain informed. For those readers who attended, follows may help them to better understand the event or situation. Well-written follows include enough background to make clear what the new material means. Story background is old or previously published information that fills in for those who did not read the preview or that jogs the memory of those who did.

Follows are vital for events where new information was presented or decisions were made, such as the school board meeting considering budget cuts or the murder trial of the 15 year old. What the school board *decided* at its meeting will have impact on many people in the community, so readers will want to know results to determine the impact on their lives. On the other hand, many readers will be interested in the murder trial, not only for its drama but also because they are concerned with such crimes. They want to know what evidence may be presented each day and how the prosecutor or defense attorney is presenting each side of the case. Certainly, they will want to know the outcome.

Here is an excerpt of the follow story for the election preview at Duke University that we read earlier.

### Slovik wins DSG runoff

By Molly Nicholson

Matthew Slovik is set to become the next president of Duke Student Government after defeating Taylor Collison by a 10.3 percent margin in Tuesday's runoff election.

Slovik, a junior, received 55.15 percent of the vote, compared to Collison's 44.85 percent. In the March 4 executive elections, Slovik led Collison by 6.49 percent, short of the 10 percent required for a presidential candidate to win.

Candidates have until 11 p.m. Wednesday, when the results are official, to file any complaints.

"I'm ecstatic, and I'm really looking forward to working with the new executive committee," Slovik said. "I want to say 'thank you' to everyone who supported me and voted. The campuswide support means so much to me. I went into (the runoff) knowing that whatever happened, the student body would be in good shape."

As for next year, Slovik said, "My plans are to shape a DSG that's going to be more about the students and that's going to stand up for what it believes in, that's going to make life better for the student body."

Despite his loss, Collison, who is also a junior, remained positive and looked to the future. "Thanks to everyone that was behind me," he said. "Just because you're not DSG president doesn't mean you can't make a huge impact on this campus."

*  *  *  *  *  *  *  *  *  *

The Chronicle
Duke University

## For Practice

7-3. Find and photocopy three examples of hard news and three examples of soft-news stories from your campus newspaper. Write brief explanations of how each fits the selected categories.

7-4. Find and photocopy three examples of previews and their companion follows from your campus newspaper. Describe what details from the preview are repeated in the follow for each pair.

## Updates and Sidebars

Similar to follow stories are updates. Both are written *after* events, but follows are written as soon as possible, typically for the next issue, while updates may be written at any time afterward. Updates are generated whenever new information or a new development is available. Like follows, updates must contain background that supports the new material.

The amount of background is based on several factors:

• How complicated the event or situation is.
• How unclear the new material might be without the old material.
• How long it has been since the original follow was published.

Do not assume that readers read the earlier stories. Moreover, readers' memories typically are short and limited. You are wiser to give too much background than too little, but try to maintain some sense of appropriateness.

Sidebars are specialized stories that accompany main stories, especially those of major consequence that may be quite complex and lengthy. They are not designed to stand alone but rather to run near the main coverage. Usually, sidebars provide carefully selected supporting details that otherwise might clutter or bog down the main story.

This is in deference to modern readers who are more inclined to read stories and story packages that do not *appear* lengthy.

## Crafting and Drafting

We will concentrate in Exercise 7-5 and Exercise 7-6 on the facts you gather and use in your stories.

Steve Buttry, writing coach for the Omaha World-Herald, suggests that just because stories demand *strong detail* does not mean they need *lots of details*. For each detail you use in the story, ask the following questions:

- Does it add to the story? If it just adds a fact you had in your notebook, do not use it.
- Does it help readers develop a mental image?
- Does it make characters seem more human and real?
- Does it present irony or humor?
- Does it help place readers at the scene?
- Does any fact repeat something already said? Cut it.
- Can a direct quote be said better in a paraphrase?
- Have you double-checked all facts?

## For Practice

7-5. Run your regular beat and locate an event for which you can do a preview story and a follow story, the first right away and the second after the event. Then, do the following for the preview:

a) Interview appropriate sources and take careful notes.
b) Listen carefully for quoteworthy comments the sources make, and write those down exactly.
c) Draft a story with a lead that effectively opens and best fits the story.
d) Swap preview stories with a peer review partner or group and give written reader feedback. Submit the draft and peer feedback to your teacher.
e) After your teacher has reviewed your draft and peer feedback and has offered additional suggestions, revise as required.
f) Submit a final draft.

7-6. Cover the event for which you did a preview in Exercise 7-5. Then, do the following for a follow story:

a) Repeat steps a through c in Exercise 7-5 for the follow story.
b) Make sure you repeat appropriate background details from the preview in the follow story, but do not present them too high in the story.
c) Swap follow stories with a peer review partner or group and give written reader feedback. Submit the draft and peer feedback to your teacher.
d) After your teacher has reviewed your draft and peer feedback and has offered additional suggestions, revise as required.
e) Submit a final draft.

## *Chapter 7 Bibliography*

Beckett, Whitney. "Robbery, Drug Violations Increase: New Campus Crime Statistics Show Lowered Alcohol Infractions." *The Chronicle.* 3 October 2002. <http://www.chronicle.duke.edu/vnews/display.v/ART/2002/10/03/3d9c3378c5e53>.

Buttry, Steve. "Becoming a Storyteller, Not Just a Reporter." *No Train, No Gain: Training for Newspaper Journalists.* <http://www.notrain-nogain.org/Train/Res/WriteARC/teller.asp>.

Fruchter, Jessica. "Feds Target Campuses." *The Colorado Daily.* <http://www.coloradodaily.com/articles/2001/11/16/export1356.txt>.

Fry, Don. "Foreword." Alice M. Klement and Carolyn B. Matalene, eds. *Telling Stories: Taking Risks.* Belmont, Calif.: Wadsworth Publishing Co., 1998.

Hazle, Ebonie D. "Mice Seek Shelter in Adams House." *The Harvard Crimson.* 13 January 2003. <http://www.thecrimson.com/article.aspx?ref=256074>.

Hwang, Debbie. "Look at the Fish, Daddy!" *The Georgetown Voice.* <http://www.georgetownvoice.com/news/299183.html?mkey=529547>.

Lee, Melissa. "Museum Studies May Be under the Ax." *The Daily Nebraskan.* 14 March 2003. <http://www.dailynebraskan.com/vnews/display.v/ART/2003/03/14/3e715d473312e>.

Lees, Kevin. "DSG Candidates Face Off Today." *The Chronicle.* 18 March 2003. <http://www.chronicle.duke.edu/vnews/display.v/ART/2003/03/18/3e7718eed6b21?in_archive=1>.

Mansfield, Katherine. *Quotations for Creative Thinking.* <http://creativequotations.com/>.

Nicholson, Molly. "Slovik Wins DSG Runoff." *The Chronicle.* 19 March 2003. <http://www.chronicle.duke.edu/vnews/display.v/ART/2003/03/19/3e78766fa8dfc?in_archive=1>.

Reese, Jessica. "Special Athletes Ready for Medals." *The Daily Iowan.* <http://www.dailyiowan.com/news/392863.html>.

Villarreal, Sally. "Parking Policy Change Gives Impound Authority." *The Daily University* Star. 6 March 2003. <http://www.universitystar.com/03/03/06/news4.html>.

# Chapter 8
# Evidence: Human Sources

*I cannot tell how the truth may be;*
*I say the tale as 't was said to me.*

—Katherine Mansfield

## Chapter Contents

## *QuickView*

Evidence from human sources is the subject of this chapter. We will open with a review of curiosity and observation, discussing also how critical thinking plays a role in helping you to make valid judgments.

We will find that supporting details in our stories is evidence, essential to make the point and prove the claim of the story. Backgrounding is an additional element of many stories that need such information to establish a context for the current focus.

We will finish our review of evidence by detailing effective relationships with human sources, the pitfalls associated with anonymous sources and the conventions you should follow in citing sources.

An article in "Workbench: The Bulletin of the National Writers' Workshop" suggests that journalists must be vitally curious:

> The more you expose yourself to different people, places, and things, the easier curiosity becomes. Journalists must push themselves to see the unseen, hear the unheard, touch the untouchable. They do these things because, in a way, journalists are the eyes and ears of the public. Journalists have access to places other people don't. They get to talk to people the general public never even gets close to. They get exposed to things other people wouldn't even dream of seeing or hearing.

## Curiosity and Critical Thinking

Curiosity is a close companion of storytellers. It encourages them to wonder about the characters they see or envision and the characters' experiences. It makes them ask "What?" as well as "What if?"

Curiosity also is a key aspect of critical thinking. Scientists, inventors, problem solvers, journalists and others must use it constantly. And critical thinking likely is an activity you do more often than you imagine. Whenever you apply focused wondering on a question or problem, you are critically thinking.

This morning as you stood in the cafeteria or kitchen considering your breakfast options, you used critical thinking to determine what you would eat. Perhaps the breakfast buffet offered the standard weekday morning fare: french toast, pancakes, bacon, sausage, ham, scrambled eggs, omelets, hot oatmeal, grits, four cold cereals, two kinds of bagels, three kinds of pastries, orange and apple juices, milk and coffee. Either you chose them all, which is unlikely, or you had to pick several items that suited your appetite and your interest. Even if cold pizza from your refrigerator was the only available choice, you had to decide whether to eat it or forgo breakfast altogether. Feast or near famine, you used critical thinking to pick.

You also relied on critical thinking when you stopped by the library to find materials for your history research report. Say you were given the choice of writing about any aspect of the American Civil War. Since you are from Missouri, you decided to research its role in the war. You used critical thinking to narrow your broad choices and decide *what* your report would cover, but you were nowhere close to being done.

Next, you needed to locate as much information as you could about the role of Missouri and Missourians in the Civil War. So, did you start with the encyclopedia? Did you hunt for a reference book on the Civil War? Did you check the computerized catalog for books on Missouri that might be in your library's holdings? Or did you go right to the CD-ROM databases and search for magazine and journal articles? Eventually, you may have done all four. What should be clear by now is that even deciding *how* to locate material involves critical thinking.

Curiosity may have killed the cat, according to the adage, but it is one of the most important characteristics of effective storyteller-journalists. When they look around, they wonder. Their minds fill with questions. They do not just shrug, ignore what they see and go about their business. Instead, they use critical thinking to seek answers to questions like these concerning state budget cuts just announced:

- How much is the state cutting from the university budget?
- How does this cut compare to cuts at other state universities? Other state agencies?
- Why is the state cutting university funding?
- What is the university planning to do to make up for budget cuts?
- Why is the university covering the shortfall in this way?
- How will the university's response to the cuts affect programs? Students?
- Will faculty and staff be laid off?
- Will tuition and fees increase?
- Are there alternatives to the planned cuts? To the planned increases?
- What do administrators, faculty, staff and students think of the cuts?

Effective storyteller-journalists are not satisfied with the obvious—the simple, easy answers to their questions, those just asked as well as others generated by the five Ws, H and SW. They want to understand. They begin by observing. Then, they mine material from human sources and documents. Their goal is evidence or proof.

## Observation

Take time to look. Take time to listen. Even before you begin asking questions, looking and listening will make you a better storyteller, a better reporter.

Most people today admit that they are too busy, that they are too rushed. They hurry through their days, hopping from one activity or meeting to another. And hurried days lead to hurried lives, with little time spent on observation. It is not necessarily important that you take time to smell the roses, as the saying goes, but you should at least *notice* the roses.

### Intentional Observation

Observation is not passive and laid back. To be worthwhile, observation should be intentional and should use all your senses. Seeing and hearing are the most important, but do not discount the opportunities afforded by smelling, tasting and feeling. What about the rumble of traffic that keeps dormitory students awake at night? Or the smell of alcohol on a football coach's breath after Saturday's game? What is causing the acrid smell coming from a chemistry lab in the science building?

Intentional observation gathers all the sensory details, and using critical thinking, you sort through those to decide what seems curious, what may be of interest or value.

When you are walking or driving on campus, be aware of what is going on around you. What is different? New? Unusual? Unchanging? Why? What story there is waiting to be told? Be intentional in your observation.

### Observation at Work

Say you are in the administration building to interview the vice president for academic affairs. While waiting, you chat with his secretary, who mentions she has been working long hours in the past two weeks on a sizable grant proposal. You had not heard about that. Would that make a good story?

Later, in the vice president's office, you look around. What catches your eye? Plaques and awards are clustered in one corner. Photographs of family sit on his desk.

A pair of old boxing gloves hangs on the wall. On an easel is an artist's rendition of a proposed new residence hall, which you recall the college board of regents is supposed to discuss next month. A table next to his desk is stacked with folders and books, several open next to a legal pad of notes. A glance at some titles reveals that these deal with genomes. Besides opportunities for breaking the ice and establishing rapport, which of these may open the way for a story that you had not expected?

You go to the student union to grab a bite to eat. On the walls you see several flyers inviting students to come to an organizational meeting a week from Friday for a new student theater group. You do not recall reading anything in the campus paper on that. Is it newsworthy?

Service in the food court is slower than usual. Few people seem to be working the food line. A glance back into the kitchen area reveals fewer people working there than you recall previously. You wonder why. Is a story there?

You sit down to eat and overhear a couple of students talking about theft in their residence hall. At another table students are chuckling about a streaker who has been showing more than his face at various residence halls during the past week. A couple of students walk by and clearly are angry over the lack of heat in their rooms last night. Are any—or all—of these worth considering for a story?

Do not assume someone else already may know about and will follow up on these leads. Relevant and newsworthy stories regularly are missed because no journalists stopped to ask questions and pursue answers. Maybe you do not have time or opportunity to do so. At least take a moment to ask potential sources for their names and contact information and share these with fellow reporters or campus newspaper editors.

In all these cases your observation should draw your curiosity, and your curiosity should lead you to ask questions. Finally, you need to gather evidence.

## For Practice

8-1. Go to the student union or other busy building on campus and spend up to an hour observing what is going on. Then, do the following:

a) As you observe, be curious about what you see.
b) Take notes on everything of interest. Be sensitive to the small details as well as the large.
c) As you write, try to zero in on one or two activities.
d) Expand your observations by interviewing appropriate sources who are either participating or observing the activity.
e) Draft a lead and brief account that establishes what was appealing about the activity.
f) Submit to your teacher.

## Evidence

Sources give you information that you use to develop stories. However, if you recall the connection made earlier between curiosity and critical thinking, you would be wise to shift your perspective and understanding of that information. It is not just a collection of details. It is *evidence*.

## Proving a Point

Seeing information as evidence increases its value to both you and your readers. It is not only details about something. It is organized and focused for purpose—to prove a point. And even the simplest story needs to make clear a purpose, to prove a point to readers. Critical thinking involves problem solving, and as you work your way through awareness of a problem and sort out what information will help to lead to a solution, your identification of appropriate and convincing information as evidence makes your task easier and more effective.

Evidence, of course, is a term we expect to find used in either a court of law or a scientific lab. There the term's traditional meaning for an attorney or a scientist is clear. Evidence is proof. Journalists who do not consider the details of their stories as evidence are at a clear disadvantage. They concentrate on presenting instead of convincing.

The objective role of the traditional journalist seems to encourage the apparently neutral perspective of presenting—and then letting readers decide for themselves what the details mean. Modern journalists, however, understand that the complexity of much of what they report demands that they go beyond presenting, that they move to explaining and convincing.

Wherever you find evidence, whether it be courtroom, lab or newsroom, it is the same: It is predominately facts. Once in possession of these facts, attorneys, scientists and journalists must be determined to explain their meaning and to prove their consequence. At that point expert witnesses often are brought in to provide reliable opinions. In each instance a claim is made, and the evidence is used to prove the claim.

For example, consider the following claims:

- The defendant is guilty of embezzling $123,000.
- The virus infecting these people is a strain of H1N2 flu.
- The $5.8 million school bond issue will provide numerous benefits to the community.

What kinds of evidence likely would be needed to prove these claims?

Just because something is evidence does not mean it must be handled with kid gloves or treated religiously, like something that is sacred. Evidence merely is comprised of facts, figures and responses from sources that journalists organize and focus for purpose; to prove a point; to make stories clear, complete, understandable and convincing.

The journalist, just like the attorney and the scientist, must be willing to run evidence through the rigors of testing and questioning to make sure it is valid. This examination of evidence, therefore, benefits all involved by assuring that it is what it seems to be and that it ultimately leads to the conclusions to which it seems to lead.

## Amount of Evidence

How much evidence is necessary to be convincing varies. Sometimes even limited evidence is sufficient to prove a claim. However, attorneys, scientists and journalists learn quickly that they should gather as much evidence as they can. During an investigation they know it is foolhardy to assume limited evidence is enough. Instead, they search, investigate, question, comb for minutiae, dig and probe. The weaker each piece of evidence, the more evidence is needed.

Similarly, the more serious, complex and consequential the claim, the more evidence is expected. Ideally, they end up with a wealth of information, perhaps more than they will need to prove their cases. They also curb the impulse to finalize their claims until the gathering is done—though they are always open to hypotheses, or educated guesses that can help to further guide their evidence gathering—and the examination is complete.

## Kinds of Evidence

Another variable of evidence is the type of information of which it is comprised. Cold, hard facts tend to be stronger evidence than opinions of even expert witnesses. That is, what something actually *is* tends to be more reliable than what someone *thinks* or *believes*.

However, attorneys, scientists and journalists expect that a good deal of both types of evidence is necessary to prove their claims. This is especially true when neither type is sufficient for proof; to be convincing, each type must support the other. In those cases attorneys, scientists and journalists work to weave facts with human recollection, comments and opinions, resulting in carefully tailored products that carry their claims to their audiences.

As much as each of these professionals might be convinced of the validity and truth of his or her claims, it is not for the professionals ultimately to decide their merits. That is left to the juries, the scientific community and the readers.

Review the evidence, marked by underlining, explaining just what a piece of legislation will change in the following story.

### Name change legislation filed again

By Danny Stooksbury

A lot more than just its name might change for Missouri Western if Bill 767 is passed by Missouri Legislation.

On Dec. 1 Missouri State Representatives Rob Schaaf and Ed Wildberger sponsored a bill that would mark Missouri Western's third effort to gain university status. The bill will be submitted to state legislation at the beginning of the 2004 session.

"I think the name would only be reflective of what we've been doing for some time," Martin Johnson, dean of liberal arts and sciences, said in a September interview.

If the bill is passed Missouri Western would assume university status as of Aug. 2004 and would then be authorized to offer master's level degree programs in accounting, subject to the approval of the Coordinating Board for Higher Education. In addition, any new master's degree programs would require approval.

Bill 767 does not stop there, however. In addition to the name change there would be other significant changes at Western. It is proposed that in the summer of 2007 Missouri Western State University would have to submit all associate degree programs to the Coordinating Board for Higher Education.

Western would then be allowed to retain any current and future associate degree programs; however, any programs not approved would then be discontinued as of July 1, 2011. The Western criminal justice, engineering and nursing departments could potentially be the hardest hit if all current programs are not retained.

This could also be potentially harmful to Missouri Western's A-Plus program. This program grants scholarships to students entering college with a limited economic background who are pursuing a two-year degree.

The board of regents might also see a change if legislation approves of the bill. It is proposed that any public institution of higher education shall be governed by a board of governors.

The board of governors would be composed of seven voting members and one nonvoting member appointed by the governor of Missouri with the advice and consent of the senate.

The current members of the board of regents would make up the initial board of governors on the effective date.

The last attempt at a name change was defeated May 2. Western then attempted to attach its name to a bill that gave Missouri Southern State College its change in name.

Southern received the name change in August, while Missouri Western was not included on the bill.

The Griffon News
Missouri Western State College

The evidence in this story appears primarily objective, detailing the changes that would come if the Legislature passed the name-change bill. Since the reporter gives no sources for most of his information, readers would have to assume it came from public record.

The single attributed source, the college dean of liberal arts and sciences, offers the only subjective evidence, an opinion suggesting that the bill would merely reflect what the college already has been doing.

The story seems reasonably complete and objective, following traditional journalistic guidelines. Because the story does not offer pros and cons concerning the changes, another story certainly might be warranted to consider those. As we will learn in future chapters—particularly Chapter 19—journalists could choose to work with all the stakeholders to find a *solution* to what some may see as a problem in making the college a university.

---

## For Practice

8-2. Clip or photocopy three solid news stories from your campus newspaper. Then, do the following:

a) Read each carefully, searching for key evidence that proves the point or claim of the story. Make sure you distinguish between facts and opinion.

b) Using a highlighter, mark those pieces of evidence.

c) Type an argument for each story explaining how the evidence you have selected clearly supports and proves the point or claim of the story.
d) Finally, note any holes in the evidence that should have been filled.
e) Submit to your teacher.

## *Backgrounding*

While much of the best evidence bears directly on the claims that attorneys, scientists and journalists make, each also must find evidence that lays the groundwork for the circumstances surrounding the case. Journalists call this backgrounding.

Storytellers understand the value of establishing setting in their tales. In fact, some of the best storytellers are masters of creating a real or realistic context within which their stories take place. While their plots carry listeners and readers through the action and allow for development of character, their settings put the actions and characters into imaginable places where their audiences may never have ventured.

The backgrounds in journalists' stories are comprised of these same kinds of details. Their readers also must sense the contexts for stories if they are to fully understand and appreciate them. Unfortunately, background details too often are overlooked or underplayed by inexperienced journalists. They *assume* readers already know the background; moreover, they *assume* readers know exactly the same background as the journalists know. Such assumptions are dangerous.

Instead, it is wiser to assume that readers do *not* know the background. Then, journalists will be compelled to lay their groundwork. They will cull from the newspaper morgue any previous related stories and offer details and summary that leads to the current incident or situation. They will ask their sources for information that helps to show what was happening, both leading up to and surrounding the incident or situation. And they will draw upon their own sense of how the focus of their stories fits within the world of the reader.

Care, too, must be taken not to overdo the background. For many stories journalists may have access to large amounts of material from previous stories. Certainly, they cannot repeat all of this. Instead, they must selectively cull the most pertinent details to provide groundwork for their current stories.

The result should be effective summary of previous material. And all of this must be tightly written to avoid overwhelming the details of the current story and confusing readers as to the story focus.

The following two excerpts show how each writer blends background into the current stories.

In the first story three paragraphs give details that enable readers to understand the zoning decision on which the story is focused. However, most of the second story actually is background, which gives a roundup to readers of a running debate between the university administration and faculty. The background is underlined in each.

### Neighborhood defeated in zoning battle

By Gil Song

With its shady, oak-lined avenues and 19th century homes, the residents of the Heritage area in Austin are protective of their neighborhood.

The area has been involved in an ongoing zoning battle for four one-bedroom cottages that occupy the northeast corner of Washington Square and 31st Street. The structures were commissioned by former UT Athletic Director L. Theo Bellmont, who began renting the properties to athletes and other residents in 1936.

The fate of the cottages was decided last week when a City Council commission unanimously voted 7-0 to deny the association's request for historic zoning status.

Historic status would have prevented Larry Paul Manley, the former executive director of the Texas Department of Housing and Community Affairs, from building a luxury apartment complex on the site.

"We went down in flames at City Council," said Lindsey Crow, a member of the Heritage Neighborhood Association who lives a block away from the cottages. "[Washington Square] is the most wonderful street in our neighborhood. It's such a unique street, worthy of landmark district status. The only hope we had was the historic designation."

The Historic Land Commission used a 13-point criteria to determine the historical significance of the homes. And although city ordinance states only one of the criteria has to be met in order to qualify for historic zoning status, the decision ultimately was up to the commission to decide how well it met all the criteria, said Mark Walters, a senior planner for the city of Austin.

"We took into consideration both sides of the case," said Steve Sedowsky, the city's historic preservation officer. "But the unanimous decision was that they are not landmarks."

Although the homes met eight of the 13 criteria for historic landmark status, neighborhood residents say they will not fight the decision in the courts.

The Heritage neighborhood's confines run from Guadalupe Street and Lamar Avenue between 29th and 38th streets. One of the wider streets in the neighborhood, Washington Square is only one of two without an apartment complex, Crow said. However, Manley's plans for a seven-unit apartment complex will leave Grandview Avenue as the sole apartment-less street.

\* \* \* \* \* \* \* \* \* \*

The Daily Texan
University of Texas at Austin

## Smith to deliver State of the University

By Ray Hafner

President Arthur K. Smith will address the Faculty Senate today for his annual State of the University speech and perhaps attempt to calm faculty angry over what many deem an authoritative and unilateralist method of conducting faculty affairs.

The faculty's displeasure with the administration came in to focus at the last Faculty Senate meeting Sept. 18 when the 2002 Faculty Climate Survey found the administration "seriously deficient" in several areas.

The survey also gave a 73 percent disapproval rate of Edward Sheridan, the provost and senior vice president for academic affairs. Smith was given a 44 percent disapproval rate, with 43 percent approving.

A debate over how to confront the administration has been playing itself out in the opinion pages of the Houston Chronicle and The Daily Cougar in recent weeks.

"The present UH administration is clearly not the best. In fact, it is quite substandard," wrote engineering professor Michael Economides in the Oct. 8 Chronicle.

"The hardball tactics of disingenuous leaders, whose pride takes precedence over the well-being of the enterprise, are simply not acceptable," wrote art professor Angi Patton on Monday in the Cougar. The piece was a thinly veiled satire of the UH administration's performance.

In Saturday's Chronicle, Board of Regents Chairman Gene McDavid also wrote a column in defense of Smith and his administration: "He continues to prepare the university and the UH System to succeed in today's rapidly changing educational and economic environments."

He went on to call the recent publicity a disservice to the regents and "an undeserved insult to Smith."

Also backing the administration, finance Professor R. Richardson Pettit wrote in Monday's Chronicle, "each faculty member has an agenda closely tied to his or her own research and teaching. Because of those efforts and because of the strengths of the emotion and affection each has for those scholarly efforts, faculty are almost always at odds with those who have an affect on the allocation of scarce resources.

"The UH administration under Arthur Smith has been relatively even handed, effective and successful at bringing in world-class faculty, at improving student services and in developing relationships with the larger Texas community," he continued.

Joseph Eichberg, Faculty Senate president, said many of the issues will likely be addressed today.

At the last meeting, senators voted to meet with Smith and Sheridan to discuss the faculty climate.

Eichberg said those meetings have since taken place, and he will present those results before the Senate today.

The Daily Cougar
The University of Houston

---

## For Practice

8-3. Clip or photocopy three solid news stories from your campus newspaper. Then, do the following:

a) Read each carefully, searching for background that provides context for the story.
b) Using a highlighter, mark the background.
c) Type an explanation for each story explaining how the background offers context to understand the current story.
d) Finally, note any holes in background that should have been filled.
e) Submit to your teacher.

---

## Human Sources

Our discussion of observation offers many storytelling moments, and the people in the examples are potential sources of information. Regardless of how many or how few details each might provide, these sources provide you something with which to begin. And that is the key.

For example, if the students who complained about lack of heat in their rooms cannot tell you why, they at least can tell you how low the temperature in their room dropped, how they felt, when the problem occurred, if it has happened before and what officials are telling them about it.

Armed with those details, you can locate and interview additional students about the situation and its impact on them. You can go to Leaverton Hall and find it is cold indeed. In the hall you run into Don Ellsworth, the assistant housing director, and ask him questions. For those he cannot answer, you ask who might be able to tell you. He suggests you ask Housing Director Eleanor Martin, and you interview her. And then another and so on. Your goal, of course, is to locate enough of the right college officials and other sources who should be able to tell the cause of the problem, what is being done to resolve it, how much it might cost and when it might be taken care of.

The resulting story may not be a Pulitzer Prize winner. It is, however, a newsworthy story that should be told. It gives voice to people who need access to a public forum, and it helps readers make sense of the world around them.

All stories benefit from human sources. Readers like to hear what other people say about topics of interest, and human sources can personalize stories and lend credibility to story content. Equally true is that some stories cannot be told without human sources. Moreover, well-chosen quotes from them can make memorable even the most routine stories.

The following criteria will help you to decide which sources may help you to tell your stories best. Those sources should be:

- Knowledgeable.
- Accessible.
- Trustworthy.
- Credible.

## Knowledgeable

It is true that each of us is knowledgeable about many things; it is equally true that there are topics about which we may know little, even nothing. Your task is to find sources who are *knowledgeable about the topic you are covering*, who can add to the information you already have and who can increase your understanding of the topic. Sometimes this is a no-brainer. With the cold dorm room example, the first and most logical sources are the students directly affected. Next is the assistant housing administrator—a college official with responsibility for the residence halls and whom you happened to meet in the hall.

Once you learned all you could about the topic from him, you had one final question, a question you must *never* fail to ask a source: "Who else can give me additional details about this?"

It is worthwhile to restate that point: Never leave an interview without asking the source who else you might interview for the story.

Inexperienced journalists either do not know or forget to ask that question. As a result, their jobs usually become harder. They may struggle to locate others who are knowledgeable. They may give up and try to write their stories with incomplete details, leaving many questions from their readers unanswered. That is most unfortunate, since all it takes is to remember to ask that key final question at every interview.

Most people are naturally helpful. So long as sources do not feel threatened by you or the story you are developing, they likely will work with you to find the information you need. If they know you have relevant questions that they cannot answer, most sources will go out of their way to help you to get information.

Who to begin interviewing for information often is straightforward. However, this is not always the case, especially for sensitive issues that some people would rather not see covered. In such cases your hunt is more difficult but not necessarily impossible.

Even when secrets extend to the White House, there may be knowledgeable sources willing to get information out to the media.

Bob Woodward and Carl Bernstein of The Washington Post had "Deep Throat," an anonymous source who gave them just enough details to allow them to dig deeper and in different places on their own. Eventually, they uncovered wrongdoings that included top presidential staffers, and their coverage broke the Watergate scandal. As a result, President Richard M. Nixon resigned.

All because Woodward and Bernstein had at least one knowledgeable source.

## Accessible

The next desirable trait of sources is that they are accessible to you. If you cannot ask someone questions, that source is useless to you.

Recall that no one *has* to agree to be interviewed by journalists. Granting access is a courtesy, even for politicians and other movers and shakers who need exposure in the media to share their expertise and keep their jobs. Yet, some of your most knowledgeable and reliable sources are busy. Their time is valuable and limited, and they cannot drop everything to visit with you.

For sources who are on your regular beat, you would be wise to set up a standard time to meet. Such scheduling allows them to arrange their days efficiently and gives you regular access. If you do not have a fixed time, then at least calling in advance will let your sources know you need to meet and will allow you to find a time suitable for both of you. In addition, you should let your sources know how much time you think you will need for your interview—five minutes versus 90 makes a big difference in the schedules of busy people. Calling ahead also may save you a wasted visit in the event sources cannot take time to meet or may not even be in their offices.

The nature of the story you are writing certainly helps to determine whom you need to interview and when you need to interview them. For some breaking stories you may not have time to wait for a scheduled visit to a source on your beat. Or you may not have had good reason to contact a source previously.

Whichever the case a phone call that lets sources know the urgency of your need to meet may get you some time for a tightly focused interview. You might even conduct your interview over the phone; this usually works best for sources who know you.

Some sources work to be inaccessible. We shall discuss them and other interviewing issues at greater length in Chapter 10.

## Trustworthy

Sources are trustworthy when you believe that they are honest and deserving of your faith in them and what they say.

How do you know if sources are trustworthy? Actually, you must approach all sources with healthy skepticism. That does not mean you are overtly suspicious, constantly casting wary glances at them. It does mean that you are careful, that you do not come off as a naïve bumpkin who can be led easily to write everything and anything sources give you.

While most sources will be straightforward and honest, some will try to use you to forward their own personal agendas. You cannot automatically assume the former. So, ask yourself these questions:

- Are they in positions that deserve trust and respect?
- Are their positions likely to give them accurate information and clear understanding of the topic you are covering?
- Do they have anything to gain by lying, misleading or holding back?
- Just as importantly, do they have anything to gain by telling all they know?
- Might they be giving you information to damage others?

The media today operate on a chain of trust that extends from sources to audiences. Sources trust that journalists will portray accurately who they are, that they will present accurately what they say. Journalists trust that their sources will be honest and complete in what they share. Editors and publishers trust that journalists will work professionally and ethically and that they will serve their bosses and their audiences fairly. Finally, readers trust that journalists have done their jobs well, that they are delivering information that is clear, complete, honest and accurate.

Trust often is a rare commodity today, hard to win and easy to lose. Treat it as precious.

## Credible

Hand in hand with trust is credibility. If sources are credible, they are believable and what they say is believable—to both you and your readers. Of all the attributes you seek in a source, likely the most important is credibility, and their credibility enhances your credibility and the credibility of the medium you serve.

Credibility is supported by knowledge and trustworthiness, two of the other traits. Those sources that you and readers consider knowledgeable and trustworthy also are likely sources you believe.

Standard procedure for all stories beyond the routine and mundane is to find, interview and cite more than a single source. This has many benefits. A single person often does not have answers to all the questions. Just as importantly, multiple sources can corroborate information you get from each of them, thereby bolstering the credibility of all of them.

Those you interview respond to your questions, and you name them in your story as the sources of the information they provide. Readers can review what each says and decide if each source seems trustworthy and credible. They weigh the information against its source.

Ultimately, if readers do not believe your sources, then they will not believe what your sources say either. Without credibility the media have nothing; their journalists have nothing.

### What Sources Expect of You

You want your sources to be knowledgeable, accessible, trustworthy and credible. Conversely, they want the same of you for many of the same reasons just given.

They want you to come to them reasonably knowledgeable of background information for your beat and especially of their office or area. Whenever possible, they expect that you have done your homework and researched what you could about the topic before you interview them.

They want you to be accessible to them when they need coverage. They need phone numbers and e-mail addresses to contact you. They assume you will return their calls. Sources expect you will keep appointments or at least notify them when you cannot.

They want you to be trustworthy and to work to gain their trust as they work to gain and keep yours. That trust does not come without risk—each of you invests faith in the other until either of you has reason to lose it.

Finally, they want you to be credible. They expect you will be honest and straightforward with them.

The journalist-source relationship is complex. It demands each of you respect the other. Essentially, it rests with the Golden Rule: Do unto others as you would have them do unto you.

## For Practice

8-4. Run your beat and build a source book that includes the following:

a) Names and titles/identifications of all available sources.
b) Contact information for each, including mailing address, phone number, fax number and e-mail address.
c) Regular contact schedule.
d) Interesting background information for each source, including age, religion, college degree(s), family, social affiliations and so on.
e) Comments about how cooperative with you each source has been.
f) Submit to your professor.

## Anonymous Sources

Anonymous sources are those who provide key information for stories but who are not identified in the stories. In most cases the journalists covering the stories know who their sources are; they have agreed not to name them. As such, *unnamed sources* might be a more accurate label for them.

Using unnamed sources can be risky. Alicia Shepard cites a survey of editors suggesting that most feel compelled to accept anonymous sources due to media competition "even though 81 percent considered them inherently less believable." The same editors estimated that more than half of the anonymous sources cited in their publications would go on the record if their reporters pushed harder.

The consensus in newsrooms across the country today is that anonymous sources weaken credibility, that precious commodity. Shepard cites Freedom Forum Chairman Allen H. Neuharth, founder of USA Today, who believes that "when hiding beneath the cloak of anonymity, sources sometimes will tell more than they know." Certainly, they may say more than they would if they had to stand behind the information with their names. Some editors have established policies allowing facts to be published from unnamed sources but not opinions.

Recall the earlier story of the unheated residence hall. Say that while you were waiting to interview Housing Director Eleanor Martin, you chat with her secretary about the situation. She seems guarded in her responses. You find that a bit odd and ask her if there is something more to the story with the lack of heat in Leaverton Hall. She is nervous about answering. You ask again. She admits that there is something going on but that she cannot say anything without risking her job.

You have several choices here:

- You can just ignore it, hoping that what she knows is nothing of consequence.
- You can try to discover what it is by asking her boss or others who may know.
- You can agree to use the information but not to use her name or identity in the story.
- You can agree to use the information only if you get it on the record from someone else.
- You can pressure her to tell what she knows for the record because it is the right thing to do.

All of these possibilities are legitimate, but circumstances should dictate which is preferable. Generally, though, the fourth option is often best. Knowing the information and only needing someone to verify it as a named source is a relatively easier task to accomplish.

So, your conversation with the housing director's secretary continues. By all means be sensitive to the secretary's concerns. Downplaying what she considers a real personal risk more likely will encourage her to stonewall you.

"I understand your concern," you say. "How about if I agree not to use the information unless I can get someone else to verify it first?"

"Well, I don't know. . . ."

"Hey, I'll make sure that whatever you tell me won't be traced to you. Don't you want to help me get the word out about this?"

"You promise not to name me? You'll find someone else who will agree to talk with you? There won't be any way for my boss to find out I told you?"

"Promise."

"OK, but I don't want to get into trouble. And I don't want Mrs. Martin to get into trouble either," she says. "It's just that they found out that the problem with the heat in Leaverton Hall was no accident. Somebody vandalized the HVAC unit, and security is trying to keep the lid on it while they investigate."

While she still is nervous, she also seems somewhat relieved to have shared this secret. Rather than spook her by opening your reporter notebook and jotting down what she is saying, you listen intently and concentrate on remembering key details. Once she is finished, you reassure her, thank her and leave. Outside the office you find a quiet spot, whip out your notebook and quickly write all you can recall. Since your source is anonymous, you do not include any names and you tend to avoid using any direct quotes.

Armed with this information, you march over to Campus Security and ask to talk with the director.

"I have learned that the HVAC unit in Leaverton was vandalized. What can you tell me about that?" you ask him.

"How'd you find out about that? Uh, hmmm. I can't talk about an ongoing investigation," he says.

"Well, if you refuse to comment, I'll just have to go with what I have."

"Uh, I'd really rather you wouldn't do that," he says. "Oh, what the heck. Yeah, it appears someone broke into the HVAC control room and ripped some wires out of the breakers and then used a sledgehammer on the control boxes. A real mess. A real expensive mess."

You continue interviewing the director, getting as many of the facts as you can. Now that you have information from the security director *on record*—a source who can be named and quoted within the story—you have kept your promise to the secretary, and you have your story. Yet, it was her tip that enabled you to succeed. And if the security director had not been willing to reveal what he knew, then you would have interviewed other college officials about the vandalism, including the housing director.

If all refused comment, then you would have had to decide whether to go back to the secretary and ask to use the information without her name, citing "an administrative source," or to sit on the story until someone would go on record.

Ultimately, readers feel better about material that comes from named sources whom they can judge for trustworthiness and credibility.

## *Citation Conventions*

Some material in stories you write is common knowledge—details that educated people likely know and that is contained in documents commonly available to the public. It is unnecessary, for example, to tell readers your source for the common dictionary definition of a university, the date for the Japanese attack on Pearl Harbor, the formula to compute the interest they will pay for unpaid balances on their credit cards or how many calories they get when they eat three scrambled eggs. Whether you already know these facts or had to look them up, they fall into the category of common knowledge that does not require citation of sources.

However, most of the information journalists use in their stories comes from the people they interview or the more specialized documents they read. It is imperative that you cite those sources for all the information you use from them in your stories, following particular traditions and rules, or conventions.

Common citation conventions for journalists deal with the following:

- Names.
- Identifications.
- Speech tags.
- Punctuation.

We will cover these points briefly here and in more depth in Chapter 14.

## Names

Use full names of sources or others in your story on first reference. A cardinal rule journalists follow is to ask sources to spell their names, even if the name *seems* commonplace. For example, which of the following is the correct spelling: John E. Smith, Jon E. Smith, John E. Smyth or Jon E. Smyth? Also, does he want to be called John, Johnny, Jack or Jackie? Does he prefer his name with or without the middle initial? Does he use another nickname by which he generally is known? According to AP style, nicknames usually are given with the full names, such as John E. "Jackie" Smith. However, if he is known *only* as Jackie, the better option would be to use it alone with his last name. The way to know for sure is to ask.

Men also may be named after their fathers, such as John E. Smith Jr., or are the third in their family to carry exactly the same names, such as John E. Smith III. Use such distinctions at the request of your sources. Note that neither requires punctuation.

Give only last names on second and additional references within the same story. AP style recommends this for both men and women, but local style for your publication may vary.

## Identifications

Appropriate identifications in addition to exact names are essential to ensure that readers understand who sources are. Those identifications include the following:

- Age.
- Home address, with city if not the city of publication.
- Job title.
- Role within the context of a particular story.

Returning to the example above, more than one John E. Smith may live within the community served by your newspaper. Therefore, telling readers that the one involved in this story is 45 and lives at 1834 Winchester Court clearly distinguishes him from the John E. Smith who is 77 and lives at 119 W. Main St.

Job titles offer additional separation from those with the same names, as well as relevance for this source being cited. If John E. Smith is the university registrar, his job boosts credibility for what he might say about enrollment figures this semester.

A convention involving titles is that short titles should go before names, with longer titles following: *Registrar John E. Smith* versus *John E. Smith, registrar at Western University*. Use your ear to listen and your judgment to decide whether a title is short or long and respond accordingly.

Another title convention reflected above is that formal titles *before* names are capitalized. Generic titles before names and all titles *following* names are lowercase.

Roles of those named in stories can vary significantly. For example, if Smith is being cited in a United Way story as the chair of its campaign at the university, then that title is more relevant than his registrar's job title. Moreover, his age and local address are irrelevant in that context. However, if he is on trial for embezzlement of college funds, both his age and college title should be included, along with his particular role in that story, defendant.

Be accurate, but also be flexible. Identify sources and others named in your stories so that readers can understand who they are and how they relate to particular stories.

## Speech Tags

You connect sources to what they say in your stories by using speech tags. These include the name of the speaker and an appropriate verb, such as *John E. Smith said*, *Smith said* or *he said* when it is clear from context who is talking.

Four common rules will aid you in effective use of speech tags.

### Prefer *said* in the vast majority of instances.

While many verbs can be used for speech tags, the best is *said* or another tense of the verb *to say*. This is true because *said* is neutral in its meaning and becomes almost invisible to readers. For those limited instances where your source actually is asking a question or adding a comment to something just said, you might use *asked* or *added*, as appropriate.

### Give the speaker and then the speech tag verb, with a few exceptions.

Writing *Andrews said* versus *said Andrews* is preferred because it follows the natural order of subject-verb. An exception is when you follow the name with a long title, such as *said Amos Andrews, vice president for academic affairs at Western University*.

### Place the tag after what was said in most cases.

What people say typically is considered more important than who said it. The exception to this would be when you are moving from one source to another in a story. Then, put the tag first to avoid possibly confusing readers as to the source.

### Use only one tag per paragraph.

Inexperienced writers tend to tag every sentence. Such overkill clutters writing and slows reading. Stick with no more than one tag for each paragraph.

## Punctuation

Proper punctuation of citations can be troublesome for some journalists. The preferred mark is the comma. Use it to separate all tags that *follow* what was said. For tags that precede what was said, use commas only for direct quotes. No mark is needed for tags that precede paraphrases. Commas also are required for long titles that follow names, as in *said Amos Andrews, vice president for academic affairs*. When long titles follow names in tags that precede what was said, use a pair of commas: *Amos Andrews, vice president for academic affairs at Western University, said that . . .*

For additional guidance in these and other conventions, consult Chapter 14.

## *Crafting and Drafting*

We will examine closely your use of information from human sources in Exercise 8-5. When you have completed your rough draft but *before* peer review, do the following:

- Print out a copy of the story draft.
- First, use a highlighter to mark every direct quote.
- Then, read each carefully and decide if it is quoteworthy. If not, paraphrase it.
- Next, use a highlighter to mark every speech tag.
- Are all speech tag verbs neutral?
- For those that are not, are they justified, or do they betray subjectivity or bias?
- Do most speech tags come *after* the quoted material? For those that do not, is their placement appropriate?
- Is each speech tag properly punctuated?
- Is each source properly identified?

## For Practice

8-5. Run your regular beat and locate a story you can primarily develop with your human sources. Then, do the following:

a) Interview appropriate sources and take careful notes.

b) Listen carefully for quoteworthy comments the sources make, and write those down exactly.

c) Draft a story with a lead that effectively opens and best fits the story.

d) Follow citation conventions carefully.

e) Swap stories with a peer review partner or group and give written reader feedback. Submit the draft and peer feedback to your teacher.

f) After your teacher has reviewed your draft and peer feedback and has offered additional suggestions, revise as required.

g) Submit a final draft.

## Chapter 8 Bibliography

"Follow Your Curiosity to Find Better Stories." *Workbench: The Bulletin of the National Writers' Workshop,* Vol. 4. <http://poynteronline.org/content/content_view.asp?id=5369>.

Hafner, Ray. "Smith to Deliver State of the University." *The Daily Cougar.* 16 October 2002. <http://www.stp.uh.edu/vol68/37/news/news2.html>.

Scott, Sir Walter. *Lay of the Last Minstrel. Canto ii. Stanza 22. Columbia Encyclopedia.* <http://www.bartleby.com/100/338.5.html>.

Shepard, Alicia C. "Anonymous Sources." *American Journalism Review.* December 1994.

Song, Gil. "Neighborhood Defeated in Zoning Battle." *The Daily Texan.* 13 November 2003. <http://www.dailytexanonline.com/news/556578.html>.

Stooksbury, Danny. "Name Change Legislation Filed Again." *The Griffon News.* 9 December 2003. <www.mwsc.edu/griffonnews/oldpages/archive/03-12-09.pdf>.

# Chapter 9
# Evidence: Online, Document, Digital

*Knowledge is of two kinds.*
*We know a subject ourselves,*
*or we know where we can find*
*information upon it.*

—Samuel Johnson

## Chapter Contents

## *QuickView*

We continue examining research, moving from human sources in Chapter 8 to online, document and digital sources in this chapter. Certainly, some of the recommendations that apply to researching human sources also apply here, but the major benefit is that documents are fixed sources, not likely to change.

We will review standard procedures for identifying and narrowing topics and organizing and documenting evidence. We will examine effective practices for researching online, especially use of digital searching. In addition, we will discuss news releases, or handouts, and the best use that journalists make of those documents.

We will finish the chapter with tips for using a newspaper morgue and an overview of library research.

---

Audiences need some kind of payback for spending time with stories. Whether audiences are informed, educated or entertained, stories should offer clear rewards. It is the responsibility of storytellers to make sure their audiences are not disappointed.

The plot of a story is essential for audiences to make meaning of what they see, hear or read; yet, the details make this happen. Whether realistic, as in fictional tales, or real, as in news stories, details make stories come alive. Good storytellers use these details to reach out to audiences with tales that grab attention, have purpose and support claims. In other words storytellers provide evidence.

Evidence from human sources, as we learned last chapter, offers powerful proof for claims that storyteller-journalists make in their stories. The interaction between human sources and journalists is key to this success. Knowledgeable, accessible, trustworthy and credible human sources make the task of gathering information easier and more effective.

Equally valuable are fixed sources, which include online, document and digital sources. These are fixed sources because they tend not to change. While they do not offer the dynamic interaction of human sources, they are quite effective for their reliability: They do not change their minds or claim they did not say something.

## *Research*

You should conduct research of fixed sources to gather evidence for stories in the same ways that you conduct research for academic assignments. Your goal in both instances is the same: You want evidence—facts, figures and information—first to discover and then to support claims you will make in your writing.

In the course of your research keep these three questions always before you: What story is here? What do I need to know to tell my story? What do I need to share of it with my readers?

Consider the following steps to conduct your research:

- Identify the topic.
- Hunt generally to frame the topic.
- Narrow the topic.
- Hunt specifically to fill in the details.
- Take plenty of notes.
- Organize the evidence.
- Document the evidence.

### Identifying the Topic

First, ask yourself, "What do I want to know about?" In other words, identify your topic. Say, for example, that you have been assigned coverage of a proposed revenue bond issue that the university will use to build a new residence hall. The story will deal with both topics, the revenue bonds and the residence hall.

While you can gather and present the particulars about this revenue bond issue from human sources and locally produced university documents, many of your readers may be unfamiliar with revenue bonds as a *method* of funding. If you already know quite a bit about revenue bonds, then you can provide the details to help readers understand what they are and how they are used. Your acquired knowledge will allow you to explain without researching or citing other sources.

However, *you* may not know much about revenue bonds either. Your limited understanding of this topic prevents you from explaining it to readers. Unfortunately, some reporters would ignore the need to explain what a revenue bond is and how it is used. They would decide merely to present details of the amount of the bonds and perhaps when they will be sold, an easier and quicker task. Such a decision for modern journalists, though, is a disservice to readers—a missed opportunity to inform and educate them.

Therefore, use revenue bonds as the topic for your research.

## Hunting Generally

Your next step is to hunt generally to frame the topic. This can be a quick step. Seldom do you want to know *everything* about a topic. You want to learn enough to gauge the size and scope of the topic and allow you to decide how you can narrow it for your story.

For example, your initial research on the topic *bonds* might tell you that they are a promise to repay money borrowed for capital improvements at a certain rate of interest or return to the lender. The federal government, states, cities, corporations and other types of institutions issue bonds. Four types of bonds are common: U.S. government bonds, municipal bonds, corporate bonds and zero coupon bonds.

With this basic understanding you can narrow the topic of your additional research.

## Narrowing the Topic

The larger the topic with which you begin, the more you will need to narrow your topic to one that serves the focus of your research. The process of narrowing a topic usually involves adding words, or limiters, to the general topic.

In our example narrowing the topic is relatively simple:

- Bonds.
- Municipal bonds.
- Municipal revenue bonds.
- Revenue bonds issued by a public university.
- Revenue bonds issued by a public university in Missouri.

As you add limiters to your topic, the resulting phrase becomes longer and the topic narrower. Thus, you are seeking details only about revenue bonds that can be issued, or sold, by a public university in Missouri.

## Hunting Specifically

With a narrowed topic you can concentrate time and effort by focusing your research on only a portion of the general topic, the evidence that will have direct bearing on your story's claim.

The narrowed topic in our example, therefore, allows you to hunt for information concerning only revenue bonds that can be issued, or sold, by a public university in Missouri. You can ignore material about other revenue bonds that might be issued by a municipality as well as revenue bonds issued by public universities in states other than Missouri.

## Taking Notes

Your notetaking at this point can be tightly focused, but it still may not be brief. How much you write in your notes, of course, is based on how big of a topic remains and how much evidence you need to share with readers to make clear your explanation.

For narrowed topics in some stories, the amount of information still may be substantial. This is especially true when the researched material is primary material as opposed to background in your story.

Essentially, take notes in the same way as you take notes from interviews with human sources. Summarize most material, paraphrase some material, target key data and capture exact wording for quoteworthy passages. The basic rule of notetaking applies here: Take more notes than you think you will need.

In our example your goal is to explain to readers what the revenue bond is and how the university is using it. In other words, you are giving helpful, necessary background as opposed to providing essential primary evidence. As a result, the researched material that makes it to your story will comprise no more than a few sentences to a few paragraphs.

Thus, your notes eventually include the following: "Revenue bonds are a type of municipal bond where principal and interest are secured by revenues such as charges or rents paid by users of the facility built with the proceeds of the bond issue. Projects financed by revenue bonds include highways, airports, and not-for-profit health care and other facilities. The state of Missouri allows state educational institutions broad authority to issue revenue bonds for various purposes that benefit their students."

## Organizing Evidence

Once you have completed your notetaking, you should organize your evidence. This makes using it in your story easier and more effective. If you have a substantial amount of material, you might consider preparing a scratch outline of the narrowed topic and keying it to your notes. This organizes your notes, especially when you have gathered them from more than one fixed source, and simplifies their retrieval and use in the story.

The borrowed material might look something like this in the final revenue bond story:

The Western University board of regents voted Tuesday to build a new residence hall that would house an additional 156 students.

The price tag for the hall is estimated to be $6.8 million, with 60 percent coming from state and private sources.

The remaining $2.7 million would be funded through revenue bonds issued by the university.

Revenue bonds are authorized by Missouri statutes and usually are sold to banks and other financial institutions. The principal and interest on the bonds would be repaid through the housing charges on students living in the hall.

Officials estimate that the bonds could be retired within 10 years of completion of the project, now set for July of 2005.

The new hall is needed . . .

Notice that the story dictates how the research material is used. Original order gives way to how it better fits the context into which it is placed.

## Documenting Evidence

Begin your notetaking for each fixed source with identifying details:

- Full name of the author, if available.
- Full title of the book, magazine, journal, Web site or CD-ROM.
- Name of the publisher or sponsoring organization.
- Date/year of publication.
- A library book's call number or a Web site's URL, or online address, in case you need to locate it again.

This information makes it easier to cite these fixed sources when you write your story.

The more specialized the borrowed material, the greater the need to document it in your stories. This can be as simple as naming and identifying the author and title of books or author and/or sponsoring organization of Web sites. Incorporate this within the passages that include the borrowed material. At times, you may provide the URL of Web sites so that readers can judge for themselves the validity of the source and material and, if they wish, go to the site. Remember that citations also lend credibility to story content.

At times, no citation to fixed source is given in a story. This is acceptable practice among media, so long as the topic is of general nature and the borrowed material is not quoted exactly from the original sources.

## *Online*

Most of you cannot recall a time when the Internet was not available to you. Yet, the Internet and the World Wide Web actually are quite young. First labeled ARPANET and intended as a decentralized data transfer system for the U.S. military, four university sites were linked in 1968, according to Dave Kristula. Ray Tomlinson developed the first e-mail program four years later. In 1974 came the first use of the term *Internet*, by Vint Cerf and Bob Kahn in their paper on "Transmission Control Protocol," and the World Wide Web was established in 1992.

The Internet has become one of the most important research tools of the modern journalist for several reasons.

First, the amount and variety of information available online continues to grow exponentially, with registered domain names numbering more than 36 million in early 2002. You can find online sources for just about any topic. It is rare that material published in traditional media does not have an online counterpart—although the latter often is an abridged or abbreviated form of the former or is available only to paid subscribers.

Second, it is readily accessible at almost any time and from almost anywhere. This is of considerable benefit for many journalists, who work long after libraries are closed for the day.

Third, authors of online information are increasingly trustworthy, since more of them have established strong reputations for reliability, both online and elsewhere. In fact, authors and organizations today typically publish in both traditional and online media.

Fourth, because of improved trustworthiness, the credibility of online information is greater than ever. Much of this is due to the same measures being applied to online content that have been applied to traditional media, where gatekeepers and longstanding evaluation methods have maintained high quality. Moreover, the larger the audience for a Web site, the more scrutiny it undergoes and the more likely that its content is passing muster.

It is no accident that the criteria we apply here to online sources are the same as those applied to human sources in Chapter 8. In fact, you should apply these criteria to all the research you do, as appropriate. Additionally, you must exercise care in evaluating material you find online, since many sites do not have the same level of trustworthiness and credibility as traditional sources of information. We will discuss this more at length later.

The last point you should know and already may understand about Web sites is that they come and they go. Because many have limited expense invested in their development and operation and others have limited resources to support them, sites shut down on a daily basis. However, seldom is that a serious problem for you. It just becomes a matter of locating and using another similar site.

## Researching Online

The first step in researching online is to analyze your topic so that you can decide how and where to begin. Does your topic have a distinctive word or phrase? When possible prefer a phrase to a single word, since the phrase focuses the search more specifically. Recall our earlier example with revenue bonds where the final search phrase was "Revenue bonds issued by a public university in Missouri." A search for that phrase would generate more results that *suit your needs* than the single term "bonds."

The second step is to pick the best approach and tool to locate the desired information. The vast content of the Internet is of limited value if you cannot find sites where your target material is located. The following three tools provide the best access to information you seek:

- Search engines.
- Metasearch sites.
- Reference sites and subject directories.

**Search Engines**

Search engines likely are the most popular means of locating sites with information you may be seeking. However, do not assume that search engines will turn up *all* appropriate online sites. Studies have found that search engines index only about 16 percent of the total content of the Web, and the engines tend to be biased toward well-known information.

Among the more popular Web search engines are these:

- Alta Vista <www.altavista.com>.
- Excite <www.excite.com>.
- Go <www.go.com>.
- Google <www.google.com>.
- Hotbot <hotbot.lycos.com>.
- Lycos <www.lycos.com>.
- Northern Light <www.northernlight.com>.
- Web Crawler <www.webcrawler.com>.
- Yahoo <www.yahoo.com>.

Several techniques will enhance your success using search engines. If initial search terms are not successful, try synonyms that may generate better results.

Surrounding a search phrase with double quotation marks causes the engine to seek the entire phrase in its original order rather than only individual words within the phrase. Also, capitalizing the initial letters in a phrase will cause the search to respond only to that phrase. This is especially useful with proper names and names of organizations.

Using Boolean searches is another option. This method, available with most search engines, uses connectors such as *and*, *and not* and *or* to join particular search terms. The connector *and* is used to join terms so that only sites containing both will come back in the search. The connector *and not* specifically excludes sites that contain the term(s) following the connector. Finally, the connector *or* will provide hits for sites that include prominent use of each term exclusive of the others.

**Metasearch Sites**

Metasearch sites, also called metacrawlers, send queries to many engines simultaneously and display results from all of them. They are good starting points to see if any information on a subject is located online. They should be limited to simple searches, since many of the engines do not utilize advanced search techniques such as phrase or Boolean searches. The techniques recommended above for search engines also apply here.

The most popular and useful metasearch sites are the following:

- Ask Jeeves <www.askjeeves.com>.
- Dogpile <www.dogpile.com>.
- Ixquick <www.ixquick.com>.
- Mamma.com <www.mamma.com>.
- ProFusion <www.profusion.com>.

- Query Server Federal Government Search <www.queryserver.com/government. htm>.
- Query Server General Search <www.queryserver.com/web.htm>.
- Query Server Health and Medicine Search <www.queryserver.com/health.htm>.
- RedeSearch <www.redesearch.com>.
- Vivisimo <www.vivisimo.com>.

For additional and recent metasearch sites go to a search engine and type "meta-search sites" into the search field.

### Reference Sites and Subject Directories

The third tool is reference sites and subject directories. These organize a wide and often varied range of known sites into categories that allow users to access information easily and quickly.

Among the most popular are the following:

- Academic Info <www.academicinfo.net>.
- Ask ERIC <ericir.syr.edu/Eric/>.
- Encyclopedia Britannica <www.britannica.com>.
- InfoMine <infomine.ucr.edu>.
- Online Books Page <onlinebooks.library.upenn.edu>.
- RefDesk <www.refdesk.com>.
- Subject Directories for Reporters <www.jlmc.iastate.edu/facilities/reading/sub-rep.html>.
- Subject Directories that Identify Quality Web Sites <www.accd.edu/sac/lrc/john/sudirect.htm>.
- Ted Slater's Search Engine Collection <www.ijot.com/ted/tools.html>.
- The Invisible Web <www.invisibleweb.com>.
- The Journalist's Toolbox <www.journaliststoolbox.com>.
- The Poynter Institute for Media Studies <www.poynter.org>.
- Webster's Dictionary <http://www.m-w.com/home.htm>.
- What you need to know about <home.about.com>.
- WWW Virtual Library <www.vlib.org>.

As with metasearch sites you can locate additional subject directories by searching for them with search engines.

In addition to these are numerous content-specific Web sites that provide information about stock prices, weather, countries or states, maps, churches, the bible, music, movies, businesses, people, books, authors, legislation, elected officials and software.

When one of these online tools does not yield desired results, consider sending an e-mail directly to authors, experts or sponsors listed at the site. You also might locate an appropriate newsgroup or listserv of professionals or experts and send a query to its members.

## Evaluating Online Material

Anyone can put up a site that says anything. In many ways the Internet is as free-wheeling and free as the Old West, with limited restrictions or safeguards. While this offers tremendous advantages in giving voice to all, it also means that content can range from great to gruesome.

As a storyteller-journalist you have primary responsibility for the information you include in your stories. Merely citing it to sources is not enough. You also must ensure that your sources and their information are reasonably trustworthy and credible. Your own credibility and that of your newspaper are at stake.

Consider these questions in your evaluation:

### Source of Material

- Who is the author?
- What credentials does he or she have?
- Is there also a sponsoring organization? Does it stand behind the content of the site?
- How reputable are the author and/or organization?

### Accuracy and Completeness of Material

- How well researched is the material?
- Does documentation name the source of the information?
- Are a bibliography or links to other sites included?
- Does the site have a comparable print version?
- How current is information? When was it revised last? Knowing these dates gives you some idea of how well established and maintained the site may be.

### Purposes and Goals of Material

- Are goals of the site clear?
- Is site content popular or scholarly? Is it authoritative?
- Is the site moderated? That is, does it have a "gatekeeper" who evaluates material before it is posted online?
- Is its purpose to provide information, to advertise or to persuade?
- Who seems to be the intended audience?
- Ignoring the need to evaluate the online material that you use is inviting. It is not wise. Evaluating the material is part of your job. It ensures that your story is supported by sound content and that your audience can trust what they read.

## For Practice

9-1. Select a term or phrase for which you want to locate information for a story you are doing. Then, do the following:

a) Go online to a search engine or metasearch site.

b) Type your term or phrase into the search box.

c) Review the Web sites and locate at least *three* that provide relevant information for your story.

d) Print out appropriate pages, making sure you include the URL.

e) Submit to your teacher.

9-2. Select a term or phrase for which you want to locate information for a story you are doing. Then, do the following:

a) Go online to a subject directory site.

b) Click on one of the sites.

c) Type your term or phrase into the search box.

d) Print out the relevant pages, making sure you include the URL for each.

e) Repeat steps b through d for two more sites listed at the directory.

f) Submit all results to your teacher, indicating which subject directory you used in your search.

9-3. Select one of the sites from which you gathered information in Exercise 9-1 or 9-2 and evaluate the site by answering all the questions above concerning the source of material, the accuracy and completeness of material and the purposes and goals of material. Submit your answers to your teacher, including the URL and material you printed from the site.

---

# Handouts

Among the most common fixed sources with which journalists work are news releases, also called press releases or handouts. These are a rich source of material for current and future stories.

Handouts come from every source imaginable—individuals, groups, offices, agencies, businesses, companies, corporations and government entities at all levels—and cover every topic imaginable. Legions of public relations professionals and information specialists spend much of their working days writing handouts.

They have a single goal: to get stories published by the media about the targeted people, businesses, events, items or ideas.

## Picking Up Handouts

Picking up handouts is easy. In fact, most of them will come to you. Many arrive at the newsroom printed on paper via the mail. However, this method is becoming less desirable. Given the high volume of mail that newspapers receive, chances are reduced that handouts will draw enough attention to be considered for publication or coverage. Therefore, public relations professionals seek methods that are more effective.

Frequently, handouts are faxed to media outlets, typically to specific reporters, which increases the speed, cuts the cost of delivery and improves the chances of coverage.

Others are hand delivered to the newsroom and to a reporter by public relations professionals and information specialists. They use this personal touch to provide extra encouragement for coverage. Of course, it also gives reporters an opportunity to ask questions and begin gathering additional material.

Some handouts are distributed at news conferences, meetings or other events to which journalists are invited.

Finally, reporters often will pick up handouts while running their beats. This approach gets basic information into the hands of reporters who are more likely to carry through with coverage.

Increasingly, handouts are delivered digitally. This offers considerable advantages. For one, there is no cost for printing, paper or postage. Second, delivery is nearly instantaneous. Third and most importantly, they can be delivered directly to a reporter's computer as an e-mail attachment. In this form reporters can use particular material by copying and pasting into a new story—saving the time and effort of having to retype. Also, filing handouts for reference or for future coverage is easy. The greatest value, though, is getting handouts to reporters who more likely will use them.

Another digital source for handouts is the Internet, where those producing handouts can make them available either as html or .doc files or both. Html files can be read at the online site, while .doc files can be downloaded easily as word processing files to a reporter's computer. Some online handout resources are even searchable, easing the task of locating information on specific topics. Locate and gather material from them using the same research techniques mentioned previously.

## Using Handouts

Handouts usually look just like the news stories written by journalists, with journalistic leads and structures. In that form they are familiar and understandable to journalists.

In fact, they could be published as presented, and they often are at smaller newspapers with limited staff. At larger papers they might be used to fill holes on deadline. However, most newspapers do not use them as presented because staff journalists are paid to write stories, not merely pass through the stories written by non-staff sources. In these instances, handouts are the trigger for journalists to write their own stories.

In either case, handouts serve their purpose by getting the desired coverage.

Even when handouts are not used right away, wise reporters learn to file them for reference and for future coverage.

If you are working for your campus newspaper or, eventually, at a commercial medium, resist the urge to pass through and publish handouts. Instead, pull from the handout essential details and passages. Then, contact and interview the sources named in the handout, as well as others, paying close attention to quoteworthy comments that you will want to use as direct quotes, while summarizing and paraphrasing other relevant material.

Treat material from handouts as though you were the one interviewing sources named there. Although citing a handout itself in a story you write may not be required, you would be wise to do so, using tags such as "according to a company statement" or "in a university release."

Handouts can be the genesis of fine stories, so long as you understand that they are only a means to that end. Use them as helpful fixed sources, retaining content and creative control of the final story.

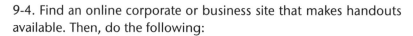

## *For Practice*

9-4. Find an online corporate or business site that makes handouts available. Then, do the following:

a) Scan the handouts and select three that are somewhat closely related, at least in some of the details they include.
b) Print the handouts.
c) Highlight the related material in each handout.
d) On a separate page tell how you would incorporate the related materials in a story you might write.
e) Submit the handouts and your explanation to your teacher.

9-5. Go to an off-campus corporate office, business or agency that produces handouts. Then, do the following:

a) Pick up copies of three handouts that were released at *least* two weeks earlier.
b) Go to local and area newspapers to see if any provided coverage on the focuses of the handouts.
c) If you find stories that used part or all of the handouts, photocopy the published stories.
d) Highlight in the published stories the content that came from the handouts.
e) If you do *not* find any stories that used part or all of the handouts, write a paragraph for each handout in which you offer some reasons why.
f) Submit the handouts and highlighted stories *or* your explanations to your teacher.

## *Newspaper Morgue*

Another valuable fixed-source option is the newspaper morgue. This is a vital part of an in-house library maintained by the newspaper. It includes the contents of previous issues of the newspaper.

The primary purpose of the newspaper morgue is to give reporters access to background information on stories they write. As we learned in Chapter 8, backgrounding provides context for the current story—what happened before that led to what is new.

The traditional newspaper morgue was nothing more than a repository for previous issues of the newspaper, often maintained on microfilm. Microfilm captures the image of full newspaper pages on photographic film. Stored in boxed rolls, it must be threaded and run through a microfilm reader that enlarges and projects the image onto a screen.

The advantages of microfilm are that it takes up less space than the original newspapers, is easier to organize for reference and tends to have a longer shelf life than newsprint—the inexpensive paper used to print newspapers.

Microfilm also has a number of disadvantages. The first is that the image is a negative of the original; in other words, the tones are reversed, with light elements showing up dark and dark showing up light or clear. Readability, therefore, can be difficult.

Second, using microfilm is time consuming. Issues of the paper are shot sequentially—first page to last and chronologically issue to issue. Therefore, you must scroll through much of a roll to find information you are seeking.

Third, heavy use of microfilm tends to damage the film, which becomes brittle over time.

Finally, and most importantly, success at locating information on microfilm is directly related to whether it is indexed and how detailed and accurately the indexing was done. An index is a listing of all keywords from articles that gives issue dates and page numbers where the words are found. The more keywords accurately indexed, the easier the retrieval of information.

Most newspapers today, though, maintain digital morgues. Stored on computer hard drives or CD-ROM, these may include either the text only of published stories or the actual digital versions of newspaper pages.

This offers considerable benefits. For one, storage is simple, with shelf life nearly unlimited. Also, copying and pasting target material into a journalist's computer saves considerable time and effort. Most importantly, locating information is quick, easy and effective using search functions comparable to those for online sites.

Other resources often available in a newspaper's in-house library include a wide variety of standard reference materials in paper or digital form.

## *Library*

Regardless of all the benefits mentioned above concerning online and in-house publications, the standard university or public library remains the most varied, important and trusted resource available to journalists. Modern libraries continue to rely primarily on paper versions of books, magazines and journals of all types. While they may seem old fashioned and time consuming, libraries are indispensable.

One of their chief benefits is that most materials in their collections are more reliable than those you gather online or from handouts. As noted earlier, anyone can put almost anything online. Most Web sites have no "gatekeeper"—someone with expertise and authority to objectively verify the quality of the material. Also, since handouts come from those with stakes in getting media coverage, their objectivity always is open to scrutiny. Libraries, on the other hand, build their holdings using a vast array of long-established gatekeeper, review and selection procedures. For the most part, therefore, you can trust the majority of the material you acquire at libraries.

Your use of the library for news stories is nearly identical to your use of it for research papers you do in your other classes. The approaches you have learned in your English and composition classes, as well as discipline-specific classes, should serve you well in journalistic research. Just remember to keep your research narrowly focused on the specific information you need to support your stories.

## Doing Grocery Bag Research

To gather material from the library, you might do what we term "grocery bag research." When you go to the grocery store, you select food and other products that you plan to use later, often stocking up for several meals at a time. After all, few people want to shop for groceries every day, and fewer still would think of eating their purchases at the store. The goal of grocery bag research is to pick up a large amount of potentially useful information in a short time and then take it with you to use later, either in the newsroom, in your dormitory room or at home.

If your research involves books that you can check out, locate titles and call numbers in the card catalog, which we will cover next. Then, take a paper or plastic bag with you to the stacks and pull all the selected titles from the shelves. Briefly review each book. A quick scan of the table of contents and the book's index, if it has one, should allow you to decide whether or not to drop it in the bag to check out for further review.

With grocery bag research you rarely read an entire book. Instead, you locate pages and passages that you scan for relevance to your research. If the material seems appropriate, go ahead and take notes following the suggestions earlier.

If your research involves periodicals—newspapers, magazines and professional journals—you can modify your grocery bag research to get the most information with the least time and effort.

Working with a paper index, which we will discuss in depth later in this section, first find the article and publication titles, dates of publication and page numbers. After locating the bound or microfilmed articles, scan the pages for relevant material and then photocopy each. Again, based on your subject, your own knowledge of the subject and the particular needs of the story you are writing, you do not necessarily read entire articles—unless it is best to do so in order to have a full understanding of the subject matter. Using your photocopied materials, take notes that you may use in your story.

Searching electronic indexes, which we also will cover later, can simplify your grocery bag research even further, especially if the index is linked to the target articles. In those cases you can pull up the articles on your computer screen, scan them for relevance and then print out pages you want. For electronic indexes that are not linked to articles, follow the same steps as above for paper indexes.

Ultimately, you want to spend quality time *searching* for material and devote more time to *using* the researched material in your stories.

## Using a Card Catalog

The card catalog, whether paper or digital, is the primary means for locating both circulating and reference books in the library's collection. Indexing books by title, subject and author, the card catalog will direct you to appropriate resources. While digital data search engines can review the content of texts for specific keywords and phrases, subject searches of card catalogs are limited to a fixed vocabulary set.

If searching for books using the subject index, you should use terms that are more general and their synonyms. Select all books that are even close to your target subject, and jot down their titles and call numbers—the particular numbers by which they are filed in the library's cataloging system.

## Using Library Indexes

An index is a reference resource that tells users which articles in newspapers, magazines or journals cover a specific topic or are written by a specific author. Indexes provide at least basic citation information for an article; that is, author, article title, publication title, date of publication and page references. Some indexes give abstracts, or summaries, while certain electronic indexes also include the full text of the article. Some full-text selections offer only the text, and others give exact versions of the original in Adobe PDF format.

Indexes are available in paper or electronic formats, sometimes both.

Paper indexes have several advantages. They cover articles prior to 1980, are the only or best option for some subjects and are not troubled by technological problems. Disadvantages of print indexes are that they are updated only monthly or annually, must be searched year by year and must be searched using a fixed vocabulary set.

Electronic indexes have the advantage of being updated daily or weekly, allowing keyword search of the entire range of the collection and including in some indexes the full text of articles. Several disadvantages of electronic indexes are that they are dependent upon technology, their cost tends to prohibit many libraries from maintaining them for all subjects and their coverage rarely runs earlier than 1980.

Indexes are either general or subject.

General indexes cover articles written on a variety of subjects, especially popular subjects of interest to a wide audience. A popular general index in paper format is Reader's Guide to Periodical Literature. Two popular general indexes in electronic format are Academic Search Elite and MasterFile Elite.

Subject indexes, which tend to cover journals rather than magazines, deal with articles focused on more narrow or specialized topics, disciplines or fields of study. A few of the common subject indexes in paper format are Social Sciences Index, MLA Bibliography, Education Index and General Science Index. Examples of subject indexes in electronic format are ERIC, an education subject index; PsycINFO, a psychology subject index; and CINAHL, a nursing subject index.

## Using Other Library Resources

Most libraries maintain vertical files, a collection of fixed documents of local, state and special-topic interest. These documents may range from brochures and pamphlets to booklets and other printed materials.

Audio-visual materials are another common part of library holdings and include records, tapes, videotapes, videodiscs, CDs and DVDs. Most libraries do not maintain a full range of popular titles; instead, they tend to be limited to select areas of local interest. A-V collections at college and university libraries, for example, tend to be based on support for the instructional needs of faculty and classes.

Both vertical file and A-V materials are likely to be accessed through the library's card catalog.

Another resource common to libraries is microfilm and microfiche collections. Many libraries keep current microfilm versions of newspapers and magazines, while microfiche is used for books and academic papers. Major advantages of microfilm and microfiche are in reduced space for storage, lower costs and historical or archival significance. Both print and electronic indexes may be available to locate materials in these collections. Retrieval, as noted earlier, may be somewhat cumbersome, since the microfilm or microfiche must be placed into a reader and searched manually. However, many readers are attached to photocopiers, allowing paper copies of selected material to be gathered and taken from the library.

## For Practice

9-6. Select a term or phrase for which you want to locate information for a story you are doing. Then, do the following:

a) Go to your college or local public library.
b) Search the *card catalog* for the term or phrase.
c) Go to the stacks and find at least one book that offers you relevant supporting information.
d) Take notes, including citation information.
e) On a separate sheet indicate how you would incorporate the borrowed material appropriately into your story.
f) Submit your notes, with citation, and the explanation to your teacher.

9-7. Select a term or phrase for which you want to locate information for a story you are doing. Then, do the following:

a) Go to your college or local public library.
b) Search a *general or subject index* for the term or phrase.
c) Locate at least one article that offers you relevant supporting information.
d) Take notes, including citation information.
e) On a separate sheet indicate how you would incorporate the borrowed material appropriately into your story.
f) Submit your notes, with citation, and the explanation to your teacher

## Crafting and Drafting

When some writers work with documents, they use terms that are not familiar to all their readers. As you read your peer review partner's rough draft, do the following:

• Circle every word that you suspect some readers will not understand *if it were standing alone.*
• If the circled word is a technical term, check to see if the writer has followed it with clear explanation, definition and/or example. If not, suggest some.

- If the circled word is not a technical term, perhaps a more familiar synonym would be appropriate. Suggest one.

## For Practice

9-8. Choose a story topic that you have used in one of the exercises above, or run your regular beat and locate a topic for which you can do a story. Then, do the following:

a) Interview appropriate sources and take careful notes.
b) Listen carefully for quoteworthy comments the sources make, and write those down exactly.
c) Draft a story with a lead that effectively opens and best fits the story.
d) Incorporate into the story the borrowed material from at least one of the exercises above.
e) Swap stories with a peer review partner or group and give written reader feedback.
f) Submit the draft and peer feedback to your teacher.
g) After your teacher has reviewed your draft and peer feedback and has offered additional suggestions, revise as required.
h) Submit a final draft to your teacher.

## Chapter 9 Bibliography

Johnson, Samuel. *Life of Johnson* (Boswell, 1775). John Bartlett, comp. *Familiar Quotations,* 10th ed., rev. and enl. by Nathan Haskell Dole. Boston: Little, Brown, 1919. <http://www.bartleby.com/100/249.77.html>.

Kristula, Dave. "The History of the Internet." *Dave's Site.* August 2001. <http://www.davesite.com/webstation/net-history.shtml>.

# Chapter 10
# Interviewing

*Reading maketh a full man,*
*conference a ready man, and*
*writing an exact man.*

—Francis Bacon

## Chapter Contents

## QuickView

  Beats and interviews likely will be your most important tools for gathering story information. With both you engage other people in carefully orchestrated dialogue

  This chapter will give you advice and tips to help you cover your beat effectively, emphasizing especially how to get started on a new beat. In addition, we will review how to work your beat once you are familiar with it and the people who populate it.

  We will investigate how you might locate and develop story sources, building on material in Chapter 8. Of particular concern in this chapter, though, are difficult and inaccessible sources, especially those who would try to stonewall your efforts to tell stories.

The remainder of the chapter will cover interviewing and offer effective methods for preparing to interview, especially how to draft both closed-ended and open-ended questions that will allow you to get the target material for the story you hope to write.

---

Storytellers love a good story, one that meets three essential criteria:

- It makes a worthwhile point.
- It offers interesting content.
- It appeals to their audiences.

Much of the grist for storytellers' mills comes from imagination, the creative invention of content designed to support these criteria.

However, the best story material is gleaned from life itself. Life experiences already have a key component that enhances good points, interesting content and audience appeal: They are real. We know that many great novelists and short story writers were avid observers of life around them. Most kept daily journals, wherein they recounted what they read, saw and heard. When they turned to the stories they were creating, they often pulled relevant material from their journals and worked it in. As such, their fiction was spawned by the life experiences around them, which supported their fictional accounts even as the accounts reflected life.

Such a classic marriage has been good for both storytellers and their audiences. By drawing from the real experiences of real characters, the demand on invention is reduced and the sense of realism increased.

Storyteller-journalists must meet the same criteria for a good story concerning point, content and appeal. Moreover, they too must be creative in their selection and presentation of material. Storyteller-journalists, though, have a definite edge over storytellers who craft fictionalized accounts. *All* of the content of journalistic stories is drawn from life.

## Working the Beat

As you recall from Chapter 4, a beat is a standard area of coverage, either geographical or topical. It gives reporters a particular focus for their stories; it also helps ensure that a community is thoroughly covered. Your beat is where you will locate most of the sources and information for your stories.

Whether geographical or topical, the beat should be like your childhood neighborhood: A place you knew intimately, along with the people who populated it. Like the Muhlenbachers' swimming pool, where you spent happy, hot summer days; or the Galbraiths' vacant lot, which was just large enough for your sandlot ball games; or Donnie Davis's garage, the scene of the first fire you ever witnessed. No one had to teach you your neighborhood. You learned it by living in it, playing in it, experiencing it.

However, if you were the new kid on the block, it certainly did not hurt to find a friend who could take you around and help you to settle into the neighborhood more quickly and easily. Someone who could show you the ropes.

When you are the "new kid" on a beat, access to the reporter who previously covered it is valuable. If available, that person is a powerful resource who can share much of what he or she already knows about the beat, the background of the key people and the main activities of the beat.

Even with such tutoring, though, the best way to learn your beat is to spend time on it, visiting, observing, being curious, getting to know people and letting them get to know you.

## Learning Your Beat

A new beat probably will be unfamiliar to you. As a student you may know where it is located, but until you begin relating to it as a journalist, you do not know all you need to know to tell the best stories and tell them well.

Consider the following steps in getting to know your beat:

- Locate and review previous stories from your beat.
- Identify and get essential information on sources.
- Arrange get-acquainted visits to your beat.
- Begin a regular schedule of beat coverage.

A good first step is to review the clip files or newspaper morgue to become familiar with the coverage previous reporters have given your beat. Besides providing you a wealth of knowledge about what has been important enough to cover in the past and which sources have been cited regularly, such research will help you to avoid writing on the same old "hot topics" that may have been published by each reporter who once worked the beat.

Second, find out who the movers and shakers are on your beat, those responsible for management and decision making. Your campus telephone or personnel directory should list most of these potential contacts. Write down their names—double-checking spelling for accuracy—and include their official titles, office locations, phone numbers and e-mail addresses.

Every beat has a certain pecking order, ranging from those with most authority and decision making to those with least. While you may be tempted to concentrate your beat development on the supervisors, bosses and others in charge—also called the gatekeepers—you would be foolhardy not to spend nearly as much time cultivating good relationships with the rank and file there—the assistants, secretaries, clerks, janitors, cooks and dishwashers, to name a few. These are people who spend their whole days on your beat. They see what goes on around them. They hear the scuttlebutt in the coffee room. Some of your best stories will begin with tips from them, enough information to send you off asking questions of primary sources.

Third, arrange for get-acquainted visits with the people on your beat. Use that opportunity to learn more about sources and what they do. As appropriate, set up a regular meeting time with key people, which will give you necessary and convenient access. Make sure this fits your deadlines for stories you must complete. Of course, leave your name and contact information with them—encouraging them to let you know of potential stories and opening the door to two-way communication.

Finally, begin your cycle of beat coverage, hitting each office or source on some kind of regular basis. Although you may spend most of your time with a selected group of sources, do not miss the chance on occasion to meet and touch base with nearly everyone on your beat.

Remember a cardinal rule in learning your beat and developing stories there: It is okay to show your ignorance to editors, fellow reporters and even beat sources in order to avoid showing your ignorance to readers of your stories.

## Getting the Most from Your Beat

John Sweeney of the News Journal in Wilmington, Del., offers additional guidelines for covering beats effectively. He recommends maintaining accurate calendars of both official and unofficial activities and events on your beat. You also should keep a tickler file, with folders for daily story ideas this month, folders for upcoming months and even a folder for next year. This is a great resource where you can store clips, notes, questions and ideas that you review and update regularly.

You must understand the policies and procedures that guide the offices and people on your beat. What can they do? What can they not do? What constraints are in place? Where does their funding come from? What limits may be on spending those funds? Especially with the latter, Sweeney recommends "following the money" to find out who is being served by whom.

Find the wise men and women on your beat. Sweeney advises, "These are the 'go to' people who command respect, wield power and dispense advice. Sometimes they hold a title of power, sometimes they don't."

Finally, Sweeney urges that you must know how meetings work—particularly those of government bodies. Where are meeting notices posted? How much in advance is an agenda available? Who is the best person to ask ahead of meeting time for clarification of agenda items?

Although many campus-based meetings are not as formal and accessible as off-campus government meetings, your ability to understand and cover them adds a strong, new dimension to your storytelling.

## Mining Your Beat for Material

Swap business cards with *everyone* you meet—whether on your beat or not—and keep them organized for quick reference. Collect copies of organizational charts and phonebooks. Jot down e-mail addresses, noting whether the recipient checks messages daily, weekly or not at all. Fill your bookshelves with directories of every sort. Ask for annual reports, media kits, brochures and fliers, policy and procedures manuals, ordinances, bylaws and similar publications. Whenever you can, get materials in electronic format, which you can word-search for key terms.

While e-mail messages and telephone calls are indispensable to modern journalists, you must get out of the newsroom. Go to your sources, wherever they are. Showing up regularly at their offices and workplaces is more personal and reveals much more about what is happening there than you can learn from disembodied words on a computer screen or in a telephone receiver.

Once you have established rapport with responsive sources, you should cultivate these professional, often symbiotic relationships, realizing that each of you has something valuable to gain with cooperation. Stay in regular contact with all of them, even if it is just a friendly phone call, a "stop by" or an e-mail message. You never know when some cordial chitchat might generate a super story or important background. Besides, you want your sources to be familiar with you. You want them to feel comfortable contacting you when they are seeking coverage. You want them to consider you their "in" with the campus media.

## Sharing Story Topic Decisions

Give your sources a stake in your storytelling. Find out what they are interested in. How? Ask them. Also, know when to shut up. Listen when sources want to talk about a topic you had not come to cover. Even when the topic may not be newsworthy, show them respect and show them interest.

While many of your questions will deal with work-related issues, do not limit your focus only to those. After all, people are more than just their jobs; learning their range of interests is invaluable. Their knowing that you want to know about them enhances your rapport. Do not forget to ask sources if they are reading you. Your goal is not to seek praise or criticism; you want to see if they are paying attention to what you write. If you get a story tip about their area from someone else, tactfully ask your sources why they did not share it with you first. They may say that they did not think it was newsworthy or that you were interested. Let them know that it was and you are.

Give your readers a stake in your storytelling, too. While you will spend the majority of your time on your beat talking to sources, take some time to visit with readers.

Sweeney says you must know who your readers are. To avoid writing too much to your sources, a real risk for beat reporters, stay mindful of readers' N-I-C—needs, interests and curiosity. Whether it be at the dining hall, in your algebra class, after worship service or waiting for an elevator, ask your readers what interests them and what they are reading about. Such pulse taking keeps you connected and keeps them connected.

## For Practice

10-1. Plan to attend a meeting of a campus group, one that usually is open to visitors or that will give you permission to attend. If possible, select a meeting that already is on your beat. This might be student government, a student organization, an administrative unit or an academic department. Gather the following information for a written report to submit to your teacher:

a) Name of the group.
b) Main role and responsibilities of the group.
c) Copy of the agenda (if one is prepared), to whom it is sent, how it is distributed and when it is available.

d) Frequency of meetings of the group.

e) Who usually attends.

f) Customary length of meetings.

g) Your notes on what was presented and discussed at the meeting.

h) Your notes on answers to questions you asked during or following the meeting.

10-2. Run your beat. Then, do the following:

a) Ask each of your sources what topics or coverage is of interest to them.

b) Ask if they are reading your articles, if some have been published in media to which they have access.

c) Ask a sample of 10 readers—students, faculty and staff on your campus—what topics or coverage are of interest to them.

d) Prepare a written report for your teacher that names all sources and members of your reader sample and tells what each said. Include a section wherein you recommend how you or other student journalists might respond to the information.

## *Finding and Developing Sources*

Regardless of what newspaper beat you cover, you need as many well-placed sources as you can develop, since you cannot anticipate fully the wide range of topics that will confront you.

Many of the stories you tell have ready-made sources. They contacted you to get coverage, or they are the obvious and one-and-only sources for particular topics, also interested in getting their stories told. These knowledgeable, accessible and willing sources make your job easier, and they can be a pleasure to work with. Working with them is the easy part of the job.

### Locating Sources

What do you do when you do not have willing, available sources?

You hunt. You dig. You ask questions of anyone who might provide information or steer you to someone else who might. You become a detective. Like Sherlock Holmes or Joe Friday, use your curiosity and your powers of observation. Your critical thinking skills must be sharp. Examine the evidence you already have to see what it tells you. This is a problem you are trying to solve, so what questions do you need to ask and who likely can answer them?

You also might locate sources by scanning campus directories. Search your campus Web site to link your topic to content and people listed there. Check the Web sites of other colleges and universities. Phone or send an e-mail to the newsroom of nearby college and university campuses.

Venture into your local community when necessary. Begin with off-campus city directories and yellow pages. The chamber of commerce and your local convention and visitors bureau are excellent resources. Contact community groups who may be knowledgeable or can direct you to those who are.

If you become stumped, ask fellow reporters for advice. Your alerting them to a story you are having trouble developing gives them a chance to suggest possible sources. Brainstorming with them may help you to come up with sources or an angle you had not considered.

Still coming up empty handed? Check with your editor or adviser for suggestions. In these situations you must be willing to try harder to locate sources and information.

## Building a Relationship with Sources

Working with sources, just like working with others in your life, benefits from practicing the Golden Rule: Treat them as you would have them treat you. Courtesy and respect are paramount virtues to practice, along with friendliness and empathy. It usually takes time to establish a good working relationship, but the benefits are well worth the effort.

An interview is an interactive experience: Each of you brings something to it and takes something from it. In the process you each respond to the other. While you are assessing your sources, your sources are assessing you. While you may be leery of their motivations, they may be leery of yours. While you are wondering if you can trust what they say, they are wondering if they can trust what you write.

Establishing rapport, as we know, is a key first step to resolving such mutual concerns. This does not mean you and your source are best buddies. Nor does it suggest that you share with each other your life histories. It means that you and the source have mutual respect for one another and trust that the other will be fully honest and reasonably helpful.

This begins by bringing human, personal elements into the interview; in other words, it need not be severely formal and altogether business from the outset. Instead, startup small talk can help to break the ice, especially for your first interview with a source. Your appropriate comments about some personal item in the office or a recent ball game or major event are an opportunity for your source to begin talking about something altogether non-threatening.

Many of your campus sources are in positions of authority—even direct authority over you and other students. While it may be daunting to interview them, especially concerning negative or touchy topics, your responsibility as a journalist requires that you forge ahead. Be respectful of their positions, but do not kowtow to any demands that you spin a story a certain way.

Administrators in the highest levels likely are already practiced at working with journalists and understand the value of doing so. However, mid- and lower-level administrators and staff may not have had such exposure and may be heavy handed working with student journalists. In such instances you both may be learning how to work with one another. Feel your way carefully. Be on the defense about being pushed around, but do so without being defensive.

Steve Buttry, a writing coach at the Omaha World-Herald, says in "Developing and Cultivating Your Sources" that you must be honest with sources: "Never mislead a source. Be honest about the direction a story is taking. If it's going to be a 'negative' story, don't bill it as something else. If you're not going to write a story about a tip, don't indicate that you will. This doesn't mean you have to offend sources needlessly."

On the other hand, cover story ideas that sources and readers suggest whenever you can. Do so and they will suggest more.

You also must be careful that you do not get too close to your sources; this is particularly problematic on beats, where you spend a good deal of time with the same people, getting to know them along with their getting to know you. This does not mean you must be cold and distant with your regular sources. Friendships inevitably spring from working closely with others. But, if you allow personal feelings to cloud your relationships to sources, you may make decisions that are not in the best interest of your newspaper or your readers.

Like other professionals—police officers, judges, teachers and doctors—your sense of ethics must outweigh your friendships.

## Maintaining Healthy Skepticism

When you begin working with new sources, you must be careful. You may not have had time to gauge whether you can trust them. Maintain your guard with those who seem *too anxious* to be interviewed—especially if what they have to say might bring them personal, political or financial gains.

In other words be skeptical—at least initially—if sources work too hard to have their stories told. It is healthy, ethical and wise to question their motivations, even directly. Questions such as "Why is it you are coming forward now to provide this information?" are necessary and appropriate. Of course, it is essential to couch questions of motive as tactfully as you can. You usually will find that their motives are honorable and their intentions above reproach.

If their motives are suspect, however, then you must be especially wary of information they give you. It becomes imperative that you corroborate what they say with other human sources and with document sources, which we discussed at length in the last chapter. In fact, some media have clear policy requiring multiple sources for all stories of consequence, involving sensitive or controversial topics.

In the end your goal with multiple sources is to protect the credibility of your newspaper and to keep your readers accurately informed.

## Handling Difficult Sources

Sources always are open to your covering good news. Most will go out of their way to assist you in developing the best story possible. Life is good and stories are grand in such instances. However, those same smiling, helpful sources may clam up and refuse to comment when the news is negative. They even may attack you for considering its coverage.

Sometimes sources may try to dodge you and your questions. Rather than telling you directly that they do not wish to be interviewed, particularly on a certain topic—and have to deal with the possibility that you will publish a story in which you write that they "refused to comment on the matter"—they practice avoidance techniques such as these:

- They are never available when you phone.
- They do not return your calls.

- Their schedules are booked solid for two weeks—or whatever time it takes to get past your deadline for a certain story.

When this happens, you have limited recourse. Sure, you can write a story that says the source was unavailable for comment, but that does little to help you in your quest for information. Alternatively, you may need to show up unexpectedly and just try to catch your source getting out of a car or returning from the restroom.

These techniques tend to be confrontational and may not get you responses you want—you may only get a direct "no comment" to print, but you finally might get your source pinned down long enough to answer some questions.

## Dealing with Stonewalling

When sources will not comment or are not available, they often assume that, if they do not provide you with information, you will be unable to tell the story. They can *stonewall* your efforts. When this happens, you are facing one of the major challenges of the profession, and you must become even more resourceful.

At these times, you may try to appeal to your sources to do what is best for readers: Inform them openly and handle the crisis or criticism professionally. This "doing-what-is-right" approach usually is more effective, in most cases, than issuing ultimatums or allowing your frustration or anger to surface.

What do you do when you are stonewalled? First, question the source's colleagues and subordinates. Secretaries are excellent alternate sources, and occasionally you may need to promise not to reveal their names in the story. Second, dig deeper into documents that may reveal relevant information that makes you more knowledgeable of your topic and better able to work around the inaccessible human source. Finally, locate and question likely professional, political or business opponents of the stubborn source. Use what they tell you with care, since they may benefit from negative coverage of competitors.

Your goal here is not necessarily to use this second- and third-level material *instead of* your primary source. Rather, you want to be able to appeal to that source with enough information to encourage him or her to answer questions. This is especially effective if the source realizes you will be able to write a legitimate story even without his or her cooperation. You do not want to *have* to do that, you tell your source. You do not want to *have* to print in the story that your source refused to comment. Such statements suggest to readers that the source has something to hide. You would prefer to include his or her side of the issue to have coverage that is more complete and to assure readers that the source is cooperative and has a clear conscience.

Occasionally, some topics you will not be able to cover by attempting such end runs. Aside from the newspaper using the editorial page to comment on the stonewalling of coverage and the lack of cooperation to help inform the public, you have little recourse. Bide your time and move on to other stories.

Remember that no one *has* to give information to a journalist. No law demands such. The First Amendment guarantees the *right* to speak, not the *requirement* to speak.

## *For Practice*

10-3. If you have had to deal already with lack of ready sources, difficult sources or stonewalling, write a report wherein you recount the specifics of the experience, how you handled it, how successful you believe you were in getting past it and what you would do in the future to overcome it.

## *Interviewing*

We shall consider interviewing from two perspectives. The first is the planned interview, where you make appointments with sources from whom you are seeking information for a particular story.

The second is the unplanned or cold interview. You will have regular occasion to do these, for which little preparation is possible, because they come up in the course of running your beat or covering a breaking news story.

### Planned Interviews

Armed with a story idea, the temptation for some storytellers is to go immediately to human sources for information. Curiosity and observation probably have generated questions that demand to be answered. This hunger for information is appropriate and beneficial. It drives many storytellers to work hard to feed the need, yet it must be tempered. Experienced storyteller-journalists know that before they can begin interviewing, it is best to prepare questions that will generate the bulk of the human-source material they need to write an effective story.

Preparation ensures journalists of three things:

- They will have a clear understanding of what details they want to gather from each source.
- They will be able to maintain better control of the interview dynamics.
- They will take notes that are more complete and usable.

As a result of their preparation, they will not waste time and opportunity for themselves or their sources, and their stories will serve sources and readers alike.

### Drafting a Pre-lead

Preparation demands patience, even when curiosity and deadline pressures may urge action. As you prepare for an interview, take time to do your background research, gathering material from the newspaper morgue, the library, the World Wide Web and other document resources.

Next, scan the background you have assembled. Make a scratch outline to get some sense of organization of that material. Then, importantly, jot down a single sentence—which we might call a *pre-lead*—that expresses what *may be* the focus for the new story you want to tell. This sentence forces you to make an early assessment of the story's potential.

It is similar to a scientific hypothesis, a specific statement of prediction that describes in concrete terms what a scientist expects will happen in a study. And like the scientist's hypothesis, this sentence should be the focus or summary idea of the story you think you will be able to tell. Like the hypothesis, though, it is only an educated guess at the possible outcome of the details you gather. It remains flexible rather than firm and fixed.

In fact, like the scientific hypothesis, it may change—even drastically—by the time you finish gathering material and begin writing your story.

## Preparing Standard Questions

With your pre-lead written, you should be able to write appropriate questions that target what is new and its consequences to your audience. Use as a foundation for this list the traditional journalist's questions: who, what, when, where, why, how and so what. Make your questions a blend of somewhat general and quite specific, of closed ended and open ended, but with a definite preference for specific and open ended. And, when necessary, prepare zinger questions.

Importantly, your questions should be short. Long questions tend to cover too much territory, and studies have shown that sources seldom answer long questions completely. Instead, they answer only *parts* of the question—either parts they can recall or parts they prefer. Short questions keep the interview better focused.

You want a few of your questions to be general, to give an overview of the situation, to provide some context for what is new. General questions should help you to weave in elements of the background you already have. Specific questions, though, zoom in on concrete details and examine much smaller aspects of the topic. These are vital if you are to help readers understand what your story should mean to them.

Closed-ended questions are those that seek a particular answer.

- What is the cost of the new football stadium? The answer is a dollar amount.
- Who was elected student government president? The answer is a student's name.
- What is a revenue bond? The answer is a limited definition that your audience can understand.
- Do you favor the development of a master's degree in botany? The answer is yes or no (or perhaps unsure or maybe).

Obviously, you need the information that closed-ended questions deliver, so they are essential for effective interviews. However, they come with an obvious limitation; they often are answered quickly and succinctly, and as soon as they are, you must ask another question. Too many closed-ended questions make an interview seem more like a tennis match—with the ball slamming back and forth from player to player—rather than a discussion where you encourage your source to do most of the talking.

Open-ended questions target no particular answers; instead, they encourage a source to talk, sometimes at length, about a certain aspect of the topic.

- What are the benefits of a new football stadium? The answer is the source's opinions and claims, perhaps supported by some facts and numbers.
- Why did voters elect this student as their president? The answer is an assessment, largely comprised of opinions.

- Why is a revenue bond a good option to fund the new residence halls? The answer is a judgment of the benefits of this funding approach, perhaps contrasted with others.
- What impact will the new master's degree in botany have on the School of Science? The answer is somewhat subjective but enhanced by factual claims.

The major benefit of open-ended questions is that they provide a rich resource of material from your sources. Those people usually are movers and shakers, leaders and followers, decision makers and decision takers, winners and losers, proponents and opponents. They are people in positions of power and authority, those with expertise and experience, those pushing for change and improvements.

They also are people at the opposite end—those most impacted by others' decisions—the recipients, the beneficiaries, the victims. You want the observations, opinions, comments and claims of these people, too, and your stories will provide the kind of depth and balance that best benefit readers.

## Must-Ask Questions

Most interview questions seek particular answers to topics about which you are curious. Include in your repertoire the following questions that you must ask during every interview:

- How do you know that? How did you learn that?
- What does that mean?
- Can you give me an example of that?
- Has that happened before? How often does that happen?

In fact, many of these are questions you may ask repeatedly during a single interview, as appropriate.

## Preparing Zinger Questions

Zinger questions are a type you should prepare for interviews dealing with controversial or negative topics. These questions target the heart of a problem.

Say, for example, that you cover the police beat on campus. A fellow student tells you that her friend was sexually assaulted and raped at a recent fraternity party. The student says that the fraternity brothers involved deny the allegations and that the university has investigated but has taken no action. She insists the university is trying to keep the incident quiet. Since you have not read anything about a rape in the daily incident logs at the security office, her claim may have some substance. You get what details you can from the student and prepare your questions.

The zinger questions, in this instance, might be as follow:

- Why was there no entry for this allegation in the daily incident logs?
- What is the university doing to investigate this matter?
- What do you say to the claim that the university is trying to cover this up?

## Controlling the Interview

When you walk into an interview, you are on a mission. Your target is material for your story—facts, figures, explanations, comments and choice quotes. If you hope to be effective and efficient, you must maintain control of the interview.

We know from our earlier discussions that this involves establishing rapport with your source and guiding the discussion to answers for your prepared questions.

Be sensitive to time. While establishing some rapport early in an interview is valuable, you must learn to gauge how much time to spend on these amenities. For new sources you need to spend time to establish rapport, perhaps five minutes or more before you each feel comfortable. For regular sources you may need only to spend a minute or so re-establishing your connections.

Body language can be an effective clue in this regard. Look for increasingly rushed answers, more frequent glances at a clock or watch or anxious body movements. These may be suggesting that you are overdoing the small talk and should move on to business.

To transition into the interview, consider using a bridge comment, such as, "That was an exciting game, but your time is important. You know that I came here this morning to visit with you about the proposed residence halls." Get out your list of questions, grab your pen, open your notebook and ask your first question.

While you want your interview to *feel* comfortable like a discussion between two associates, you need your source to do the lion's share of the talking. You do so by guiding the conversation first with your basic written questions and then with follow-up, fill-in questions. Even well-written short questions may not get you the answers you need. Sources can digress and their answers can be incomplete—either intentionally or not. If the answer you get is not sufficient, follow up with another question that goes directly to the missing material.

Some follow-up questions seek explanation of concepts or terms with which you are unfamiliar. There is no shame in pleading ignorance of these, especially for new or complex topics. Better that your source knows you are not fully knowledgeable about something than for you to try to write the story without basic understanding of the material. If you do not understand it, you cannot explain it to readers. Ultimately, you do a disservice to them and to your source if you do not fill in such gaps.

Other follow-up questions may pursue information about a fully unexpected comment from your source about the topic at hand. Let your curiosity spawn new questions so long as they expand and enrich your understanding of the target material.

While using prepared questions is essential for good interviews, you need to be flexible. Do not hold firmly to either the specific questions or the order in which you listed them. Remember that an interview is an interactive experience, and it is impossible to predict how it will develop. So long as you gather what you came for, let the interview evolve.

## Asking Zinger Questions

Zinger questions can be difficult for you to ask and your sources to answer. Your efforts to establish and maintain rapport with sources typically keep your relationship positive, friendly and cooperative. However, when you must cover stories that could make sources or the university look bad, it is hard for most sources to remain friendly and cooperative when you ask potentially damaging questions. They may feel betrayed; they certainly may be defensive. They even may stop the interview and ask you to leave.

You, too, probably will feel ill at ease, yet you must remember that your primary allegiance is to your readers, your newspaper and your profession.

Several suggestions may help you to deal with this situation more effectively:

**Hold zinger questions for the end of your interview, whenever possible.**

You want to be able to come away from every interview with as much material as possible. Asking other, less-sensitive questions first should give you many of the details you seek.

**Be courteously persistent in getting answers.**

Reason with sources, suggesting that information coming directly from them will enable them to get the facts straight and to explain the problem in terms that work for them. You also might mention that their refusal to answer will not make the problem go away.

**Be empathetic to your sources.**

This does not mean that you wring your hands, so to speak, and *sympathize* with sources. Instead, you let them know that you understand the difficulty of the situation—that it may be embarrassing or damaging to them or the university, that there may be extenuating circumstances. You explain that your intent is not to judge the situation but rather to present the facts.

## Taking Effective Notes

If you come away from an interview with notes that are clear and complete, your story writing is bound to be easier and the results more effective. Notetaking is not an art; it is a skill you can acquire. Of course, an excellent place to practice is in your college classes. There you have opportunity to focus your listening and write notes on key content.

Focused listening, selective notes and personal shorthand are three tools that can make notetaking in any situation more comfortable and more effective. You may want to review the suggestions from Chapter 2, which can assist you in these tasks.

While many inexperienced reporters are tempted to rely on tape recorders rather than pen and paper, you would be wiser to concentrate instead on effective notetaking. It may be more demanding and difficult, but it also is more reliable. Consider following these notetaking tips:

**Always ask sources to spell unfamiliar terms and proper names.**

Then, repeat the spelling to the source to make sure you wrote it correctly. Rather than a sign of ignorance, clarifying spelling of terms and names is a mark of professionalism.

Look for major themes and central ideas in what your source says.

Make your notes reflect these patterns, marking the material with asterisks or underscoring as a visual guide to the territory you have covered.

Be alert to key words that cue content.

Going into the interview, you should be sensitive to particular terms or phrases attached to significant aspects of your topic. Moreover, most speakers use standard words that signal certain types of content.

Anticipate direction of comments.

Knowing where your source is going with comments can help you cast your notes more efficiently and prepare for additional questions.

Consider how facts support ideas.

Most speakers tend to announce larger concepts and follow with illustration, explanation and details.

Summarize and repackage material into key words and phrases.

Do not lock yourself into the source's exact words and order of material—unless the comment is "quoteworthy," so well put that you want to capture it exactly and authentically.

Listen between the lines to tone and voice.

In addition to the actual ideas, most speakers send additional messages in the *way* they present material. Be sensitive to such subjective and emotional signals. When appropriate, ask about them and include them in the story.

Put to good use the lag between speed of speech and speed of thought.

All people can think much faster than they can talk—or write. When your source pauses to collect thoughts or to consider an answer, keep writing, especially if you are still capturing the last few ideas.

Develop some throwaway questions.

These are designed to keep the source talking while you catch up in writing down the last few ideas. Such questions are not useless and irrelevant. In fact, they should relate to something that the source just said. However, they are questions that generate material you may not actually need to write down.

Ask your source at times to repeat material, especially "quoteworthy" statements.

Again, this may be a catch-up technique, but it also allows you to ensure that your notes accurately capture well-spoken comments.

Position yourself in the interview so that your notebook is not fully visible to your source.

Your goal is not to be secretive. Rather, the actual notes you are taking at any given moment may not always match exactly what your source is saying, and your source may find that disconcerting or disturbing.

**Pregnant pauses are okay.**

Do not be overly concerned by a few quiet moments. They benefit sources by giving them some time to gather their thoughts or to recall specific details. They also benefit you. Some sources speak so quickly that even lags between speed of speech and thought and throwaway questions will not give you enough time to write notes on key material. Silence during an interview can be deafening, especially for inexperienced journalists. At times, ask the source to give you a moment to catch up.

**Ask your source to explain material you do not understand or to repeat well-spoken ideas.**

Too many inexperienced journalists are afraid to admit they do not understand something and, therefore, fail to ask for explanation. Remember that if you do not understand a concept or a term, you likely cannot explain it to readers. Also, requesting a repeat of something important and noteworthy is a compliment to the source—and insurance that you get it right in your notes.

**Ignore distractions.**

Regardless of what is going on around you, focus your listening and writing on the interview.

Your notes are *not* intended to be a transcript of your interview—any more than your geography notes are a transcript of your professor's lecture. Notes should be a combination of facts and numbers, key ideas and terms, and carefully chosen exact quotes.

## Going Off the Record

At times sources will want to give you information "off the record." This means different things to different journalists. For our purposes when some sources ask to go off the record, they are saying they will give you information that you cannot use.

First, you must understand that, like agreeing not to name a source, taking information off the record is a personal pact you make with your sources. Never go off the record if you cannot keep secrets. Agreeing to do so, you are ethically bound *not* to use the material. When faced with the prospect of going off the record, you have two obvious options: You agree or you do not.

If you agree, then you might do so with the stipulation that if you can get the information corroborated by another source, you will use it. Essentially, this lets the initial source off the hook. One of the problems, though, with taking information off the record—especially if you often do so—is keeping track of which details fall into this category. After all, you typically do not take notes for material given off the record, and you can rely on your memory only to a certain degree.

If you do not agree, then sources need not tell you anything. However, in many cases your refusal to take information off the record may not stop sources from going ahead and telling you anyway.

So, why should a source want to go off the record, and why should you agree to do so? Sources go off the record for several reasons. They want to tip you a story. They may have genuine concern about the situation and want coverage that may bring it to light. However, they do not want to risk being identified as the source, even an unnamed source. Alternatively, some sources may hope that giving you information off the record actually may stonewall you. In this instance, they have the appearance of being helpful, of doing the right thing, but their goal is to muzzle you.

Taking information off the record also is tempting—you are a "member of an inner circle," a limited few who share certain secrets. You may be privy to secrets, but you are honor bound to keep them to yourself. In the end you may find your secret knowledge hobbles you, preventing you from doing your job of telling stories, especially stories that should be told.

On rare occasions you might agree to go off the record with sources, but only after you have given the option careful consideration. It may be worthwhile to get the information off the record as deep background—material that is revealing and helpful in understanding a much larger issue.

As a professional, though, you would be wise to establish a personal policy that you never take information off the record, and you should share that policy with sources when they suggest doing so.

## Closing the Interview

Once you have gathered the information you sought, close the interview. Let us revisit several tips from Chapter 2 that apply here.

Ask if the source has anything to add.

If you have done a good job controlling the interview, your source should have been busy answering your questions. There may not have been opportunity for the source to volunteer information outside the scope of the questions. By inviting additional information, you open the door to important, relevant material your source knows and is willing to share.

Ask if you may contact the source if you have additional questions.

This may seem unnecessary, but under the pressure of asking questions, taking notes and keeping the interview moving, you inadvertently may miss holes in material or forget to ask spellings of a term or name. Also, this helps assure sources that you are willing to clarify details that may have been unclear or incomplete.

Ask if the source can recommend others whom you might interview on this topic.

This is a must in closing every interview. On one hand, it helps you to expand your list of appropriate sources, an invaluable opportunity you cannot afford to miss. On the other hand, telling the new source that the first source recommended you contact him or her usually increases your chances of success in gathering more usable material.

Thank your source.

This common courtesy is another mark of the professional that you should acquire early.

---

## *For Practice*

10-4. For a planned interview for coverage of a substantial story with one or more of the sources on your beat, do the following:

a) Complete necessary background research.
b) Write an appropriate pre-lead.
c) Prepare interview questions that cover both the big picture and the specifics of the situation and that are comprised of both closed-ended and open-ended questions, with the emphasis on the latter.
d) If appropriate, prepare several zinger questions.
e) Conduct the interview(s).
f) Submit to your teacher copies of the background research, your planned questions, names and titles of the source(s) you interviewed and the notes you wrote.

---

### Cold Interviews

Planned interviews are demanding, but preparation can make the task easier and more productive.

Cold interviews, on the other hand, increase the tension ante since you are unable to have much time, if any, to gather background and draft interview questions. Instead, cold interviews require that you plan as you go.

As you run your beat, for example, one of your sources may alert you to a story idea that demands you conduct interviews immediately, rather than waiting to schedule them. The story idea might be one that your previous beat runs missed. It could be that its source was not available previously. Or it might be the result of breaking news—an unanticipated event or happening. Whatever the reason, you may have to go with cold interviewing to get the story fresh and to get the story first.

Success at cold interviewing requires you to be extra sharp. As with planned interviews, start with the journalist's questions. You can trust these to draw out basic story information. Then, with your curiosity on high alert, dig deep for additional questions that satisfy what you need to know and what your readers will need to know. If necessary, jot down the new questions so that you are sure to ask them.

Because you are winging it, be more willing to *think aloud* with your sources, repeating key ideas you are hearing and *wondering aloud* how best to explain them to readers.

Most of the earlier recommendations for planned interviewing still apply to cold interviewing, but especially these three:

• Asking sources if they have anything to add.
• Asking to be able to call back if you have more questions.
• Asking if they can recommend others for you to interview.

Cold interviewing is tougher than planned interviewing. It puts more pressure on you to be curious and to think quickly. Yet, putting yourself to the test, especially observing and interviewing for a breaking story, can be one of your most exciting experiences as a journalist.

## Crafting and Drafting

We have discussed the writing process at length in "Storycrafting." We often have discussed the process as three steps—gathering, drafting and revising. However, we also know that the process is recursive, looping back and forth among those steps rather than moving in a linear, direct route. For the story in Exercise 10-5, consider the following tips from Steve Buttry, who encourages recursiveness:

- Begin writing early, even if it is just a paragraph focusing on your story idea or a scratch outline of the plan for your story.
- Write as soon as possible following each interview, shaping the new material you have gathered and blending it into the part of the story it likely will fit.
- Draft the lead early, using it to challenge what you know and need to know about the story.
- Begin looking for holes in your story that you need to fill with material in your notebook, additional sources or callbacks to earlier sources.
- Each time you revisit your draft, read all that you have written, tweaking and tinkering as appropriate to polish.
- Look for surprises, especially if the story focus shifts as you continue gathering material. If that happens, revise the lead and other parts of the story to accommodate the new focus.

## For Practice

10-5. Take the results of Exercise 10-1 or Exercise 10-4 and do the following:

a) Return to your beat to take care of any recommendations your teacher has given you.
b) Draft a story with a lead that effectively opens and best fits the story.
c) Swap stories with a peer review partner or group and give written reader feedback.
d) Submit the draft and peer feedback to your teacher.
e) After your teacher has reviewed your draft and peer feedback and has offered additional suggestions, revise as required.
f) Submit a final draft.

## *Chapter 10 Bibliography*

Bacon, Francis. *Of Studies. Columbia Encyclopedia.* 1996. <http://www.bartleby.com/100/139.35.html>.

Buttry, Steve. "Becoming a Storyteller, Not Just a Reporter." *No Train, No Gain: Training for Newspaper Journalists.* <http://www.notrain-nogain.org/Train/Res/WriteARC/teller.asp>.

Buttry, Steve. "Developing and Cultivating Sources." *ACES* [American Copy Editors Society]. February 2001. <http://www.copydesk.org/words/sources.htm>.

# Chapter 11
# Types of Leads

*If an idiot were to tell you the same
story every day for a year, you would
end by believing it.*

—Horace Mann

## Chapter Contents

## *QuickView*

Because leads are so important, this chapter is one of the most valuable in "Storycrafting." We will build on previous discussions of leads here and in Chapter 12 to give you full understanding of and appreciation for leads.

We will find that not just any lead—regardless of how clever and creative—will do for any story. A lead must be carefully chosen for the story that follows it.

This chapter is rich with examples of the various summary, narrative and other creative leads at your command. Review each carefully, and let your imagination borrow from what you read to apply it in your own storytelling.

## *The Right Lead for the Right Story*

"Leads are the keynotes, the overtures, the tee shots of newswriting," says the late NBC news anchor John Chancellor, writing with Walter R. Mears. "Properly crafted, the lead answers questions before they are asked and promises more answers to follow. The lead sets the theme and points the way."

It is difficult to make too many generalizations about leads, since they are best when they match the stories for which they are crafted, and that is precisely the point you need to grasp here. Your understanding of story content and your creativity in presenting it to readers determine your approach. Fortunately, you have a wealth of choices.

As you likely are aware, summary leads traditionally have opened stories, while current style seems to encourage narrative or other creative approaches.

Paula LaRocque of the Dallas Morning News comments on this tension: "This bandwagon tootling on the 'best' way to begin a story is so much hot air. Neither the summary nor the narrative lead is better. We need both, and more. We need whatever there is."

Instead of focusing on a few types, LaRocque believes writers need to be able to draw from a wide variety of leads. She explains, "That's because compelling leads are as individual as writing—and writing, in turn, is as individual as thinking. More than technique, we need intelligence and understanding, inventiveness and imagination. We need to connect, extend, associate, allude."

In our coverage of leads, here and in Chapter 12, you will acquire a greater familiarity with lead options. Matching each story to a lead that fits best is more art than science. The task will test your creative and critical-thinking skills as you carefully craft effective stories.

## Summary Leads

Summary leads use most, if not all, of the news elements—who, what, when, where, why, how and so what—to open the story in one or more paragraphs. Regardless of the draw of creative approaches, you must respect the value of the summary lead. It can work for *any* news story, and it is clearly the best choice for some.

Those include but are not limited to short news accounts and straightforward news stories.

Short news accounts usually do not demand special treatment. You present the news elements, expand upon the information of the lead and you are done.

The following news brief from The Daily at the University of Washington totals 73 words, with 27 of those given to the summary lead. The story delivers the message quickly and without fanfare. Can you imagine opening this with a narrative or other creative lead?

> The UW voicemail system shut down yesterday for about six hours because of defective hardware, blocking faculty and staff from accessing the roughly 12,000 campus voicemail accounts.
>
> The problem started about 6 a.m. when the system went into a "non-operational state," according to Tammy Stockton, an assistant director for Communication Technologies. Attempts to fix the system were unsuccessful until the faulty hardware was replaced, she said. The system was back online at noon.
>
> —Alex Sundby

Likewise, straightforward news stories expect an objective, writer-neutral presentation. You let the facts speak for themselves in clean, neat fashion.

The writer of the following lead from The Towerlight at Towson University takes no sides in what appears to be a divisive issue. Instead, the first paragraph states that the two sides disagree over the project's scope and who will cover the costs.

> Plans for a proposed stairway from University Village to Millennium Hall hit a standstill when owners of the apartment complex and University officials could not agree on the scope of the project—and who will foot the bill.
>
> The planned staircase would extend from the parking lot in the northeast corner of the property to the drive in front of Millennium Hall, replacing a dirt path now used by students as a shortcut to campus.
>
> Cailin McGough

Sometimes, of course, even major stories of consequence work best with a summary lead.

Some writers of the following lead might be tempted to dramatize the incident. However, instead of a narrative lead the student journalist at the Cornell Daily Sun chose a summary lead using all seven news elements. This is tight writing, with a considerable amount of information presented in the first two paragraphs that totals 40 words.

> Kristen Osborne '04, a student in the School of Hotel Administration, died Monday night after sustaining serious head injuries following a fall at her College-town residence.
>
> Osborne's death is the third student death at Cornell in the last two weeks.
>
> Word of Osborne's sudden death circulated quickly yesterday morning and by midday, shocked and visibly shaken Hotel students had gathered outside of Statler Hall. Many sobbed, hugging and speaking quietly with classmates.
>
> —Marc Zawel

Do not assume that writing such summary leads is merely following a formula, that it involves no real imagination or skill. Matching lead to story in and of itself is skillful. Moreover, as you already may have discovered, crafting even summary leads effectively demands the finesse of a wordsmith, both in their careful organization and tight focus.

## *Organizing the Summary*

Much of the effective organization of a summary lead boils down to exactly which news element you choose to begin it. That choice, in fact, largely determines your handling of the remaining elements and the words and sentences you might use to do so.

Your choice of opening element should not be forced but rather should seem the obvious option, given the possibilities available.

Of the seven news elements, the most common opener is the *what*. As you may recall from Chapter 2, all of the remaining news elements revolve around and relate in particular ways to the *what* you emphasize. This concern is heightened by the fact that many stories allow you to pick from more than one *what*.

The *what* lead that follows is from Collegiate Times at Virginia Tech. The rest of the story uses information from local librarians and The Associated Press to explain the ruling and its local impact.

> Web sites about abortion, gay rights and other research topics may soon be inaccessible to the more than 14 million people who rely on libraries for their Internet access.
>
> The Supreme Court ruled June 23 that libraries were required to install pornography filters for the Internet or be subject to losing federal funding.
>
> —Tiffany Hoffman

Second most common among news elements that open summary leads is the *who*. As we discussed in Chapter 2, the choice of *who* more often is actually a matter of *who did what* or *to whom what was done*. These capitalize on the natural tendency and built-in benefits of focusing on the human elements in stories, whenever possible.

Remember that the *who* are the characters in your stories, the ones who do the acting and with whom the plot unfolds—matters involving elements of storytelling, which we will discuss further in Chapter 13. We relate most easily to people, the things they do, the decisions they make, the things that happen to them and the events with which they are involved. Like the viewer's eye that scans a photograph for and is drawn to the human element, readers seek out and connect to the people in stories.

The lead for the following cheating story, from The Badger Herald at the University of Wisconsin, is a classic *who did what*.

> Several students have confessed to cheating on an accounting take-home test that was due April 3, according to Accounting Department Chair John Eichenseher.
>
> The professor allowed her students to bring the test home so they could attend a lecture by Enron scandal whistle-blower Sherry Watkins, who spoke on campus April 2.
>
> She instructed the students to work independently, but the test problems were clearly solved in groups, according to business school external-relations spokesperson Pam Benjamin.
>
> —Michelle Orris

Two elements, the why and how, compete closely for third among most common openers. Selecting either of these is appropriate when it is compelling enough to edge out the what or the who of the story.

Since the news elements relate uniquely to what in news stories, your concern is why the what happened or how the what happened.

The Oberlin Review at Oberlin College ran the following lead. It illustrates effective use of the why to begin a lead.

Citing aesthetic differences, the College and the Shell gas station on East Lorain and North Main St. will part ways in June. The property, which has been owned by the College since 1986, has been leased to United Refining Company—now TrueNorth Energy, LLC—since 1978. The College has declined to renew their lease, which expires this year.

—Cat Richert

The *how* opener in the following lead, published in The Northwest Missourian at Northwest Missouri State University, emphasizes how a student protested the university's plans to merge with the University of Missouri system. The story gave additional campus reaction to the proposal.

With sheets of notebook paper, green paint and a third-floor South Complex window as his canvas, Rob Pangburn expressed to Northwest his feelings regarding the University's possible merger with the University of Missouri System.
UMm NO!
Pangburn was among a number of students at Northwest who have responded, both positively and negatively, to the proposed merger which could change Northwest's name to the University of Missouri-Maryville. Other suggested changes include the University of Missouri-Northwest.

—Abby Simons

*Where* and *when* leads are used more rarely. Exercise care with their use, since they must be compelling enough to capture attention. Yet, the following examples show that each has its place in launching some news stories.

The *where* lead, from The Daily Pennsylvanian at the University of Pennsylvania, subtly establishes the setting for the story. Although the lead is nearly twice as long as average, it reads easily because of effective flow.

In a small, unairconditioned house decorated with French anarchist posters, the Books Through Bars Collective hosts "packing cafes" every Tuesday and every other Saturday at its West Philadelphia base, boxing a collection of titles ranging from a dated-looking edition of The Yachtsman's Emergency Handbook to John Grisham's The Rainmaker for prison inmates across the country.

—Marie Forgeard

The following *when* lead is a fine example of how that element can effectively open certain leads. Its use in this story from The Daily Iowan at the University of Iowa adds punch to how soon this law will go into effect.

When the clock strikes midnight today, bars all over Iowa City will be required to ban those younger than 19 from their premises, if they haven't already done so—unless they have an exemption from the city.

—Kent Nguyen

The remaining news element—*so what*—is much less likely to open summary leads. It almost never has the substance necessary to compete successfully with the other elements.

---

## For Practice

11-1. Select a news story *with a summary lead* that you submitted for a grade. Then, do the following:

a) Open the story file on a computer.
b) Under your original story draft a *new summary lead* that opens with a different news element than your original.
c) Revise as much of the top of the story as necessary to lead into the original body.
d) Repeat b and c, opening with another news element you had not used.
e) Under these new leads, write three to four sentences *for each lead* wherein you name the opening news element and explain its benefits and drawbacks in relation to the rest of the lead and the body of the story.
f) Print out the entire file, with the two new leads and your explanations.
g) Share your story and its three leads with your peer group, and get their feedback on your leads and assessments.
g) Submit to your teacher.

---

## Narrative Leads

Storytelling is your primary task. Therefore, it should be no surprise that narrative leads should be among the choices you might favor to open your stories.

While the summary lead opens with the most important news element followed by most, if not all, of the remaining news elements, the narrative lead typically relies on an excerpt or dynamic passage from an experience.

The simplest narrative format begins at the beginning of an event—the "once upon a time" approach of traditional fairy tales. While this may work for some narrative leads, your approach usually should be more sophisticated. Like short story and novel writers, who begin their narratives at some telling moment in the chronology of the event, you need to find an appropriate and effective telling moment to launch your own narrative lead.

### The Telling Moment

A telling moment is one pulled or fashioned from the event that has the power to do most or all of the following:

- Capture readers' attention.
- Introduce one or more key characters.
- Establish a sense of setting.
- Initiate the chain of cause and effect that comprises the plot.
- Lure readers into the rest of the story.

That may seem a tall order, but actually, it is no more demanding than expectations we also have of strong summary leads.

The value of the narrative lead, of course, is that it quickly and comfortably pulls readers into stories. Done well, the narrative lead can be as interesting and enjoyable as the beginning of a first-rate novel. Done poorly, it can send readers scurrying to the next story.

The length of a narrative lead is arbitrary, perhaps even more so than that of the summary lead. Some flow seamlessly into the body of the story, leaving little evidence marking where they end and the body begins. Others clearly end at the nut graf, which we will discuss next.

The narrative lead is as long as it needs to be to accomplish the goals just listed. Look at the following "Boom City" example to see how one writer handles this.

## The Nut Graf

One of the keys to the effectiveness of the narrative and other non-summary leads for news stories is the nut graf.

As noted earlier, the nut graf is a paragraph presented early in the story that targets exactly what the story is about. In fact, it is nearly identical to the summary lead in its function of showcasing key news elements.

Nut grafs tend to be relatively short, often no longer than a single paragraph. In addition, they do not repeat details already presented in the narrative lead. Finally, they need to blend well with the material immediately preceding and following.

Positioned either within or immediately following the narrative lead, the nut graf clarifies for readers the central focus of the story. When placed at the end of the narrative lead, it also serves as a subtle and convenient bridge, or transition, from the lead into the body of the story.

The narrative lead example that follows is an effective combination of description, action and quoteworthy comments. Published in The Daily at the University of Washington, the narrative runs nine paragraphs before blending through the nut graf.

> Going north on Interstate 5 (I-5) the strip malls packed with brand-name outlet stores are the only barriers between pavement and trees. Past the outlets, clearly visible from the freeway, is the flickering-bright Tulalip Casino, located on the Tulalip Indian Reservation in Marysville, Wash., about 30 miles north of Seattle.
>
> But the casino is not just a signal to turn off the freeway and head for the game tables—beneath the waterfalls and ornate wooden carvings of the elaborate casino sign, "Boom City" is stenciled in green paint on a piece of whitewashed wood.
>
> Below the lettering, an orange arrow vaguely resembling a missile points the way. The road that unfolds between the casino and the fireworks stands is thickly dotted with homemade signs proclaiming the name, number and slogan of the stand hammered into the ground with wooden stakes.
>
> The sight of these signs resembles the campaign signs that crop up in the roadside near Election Day, and indeed fireworks vendors seem to be jockeying for the potential customer's favor.
>
> "It can get competitive," said fireworks-seller Lisa Enick, "but can also be a lot of fun."

A recent UW graduate and Tulalip tribal member, Debbie Parker, has sold fireworks since she was 16. She stands behind an orange stand emblazoned with painted suns.

"I grew up doing this. I used the money I made to help pay my tuition," she said. Parker has a degree in sociology and American ethnic-studies and was able to get a job with the Tulalip Health and Safety Network.

"[My job] is to help the community grow in a healthy way," she said.

As she spoke, the unmistakable screeching of a rocket zooming into the sky shuddered the stand, followed by a sharp boom as the firework detonated. "It's a free show, and it's great," she said, hardly fazed.

Boom City has been booming for more than 30 years. What began as four stands has blossomed to about 194 stands. But beneath the literally smoke-charged atmosphere of the brightly painted stands is a friendly atmosphere that is cultivated by the Tulalip people.

—Blythe Lawrence

Most readers have a clear sense from the nut graf, the last in the previous excerpt, of where the story goes from here—friendly Native Americans are operating a successful fireworks business.

## For Practice

11-2. Check issues of your campus newspaper to locate two news stories that use narrative leads. Then, do the following:

a) Clip or photocopy the two stories.
b) Clearly identify for each story the material that comprises the narrative lead and the nut graf.
c) On separate paper critique each narrative lead and determine if it meets the following expectations:
   • It captures readers' attention.
   • It introduces one or more key characters.
   • It establishes a sense of setting.
   • It initiates the chain of cause and effect that comprises the plot.
   • It lures readers into the rest of the story.
d) Finally, critique each nut graf and decide if it meets the following guidelines:
   • It is relatively short, no longer than a single paragraph.
   • It does not repeat details already presented in the narrative lead.
   • It blends well with the material immediately preceding and following.
e) Submit your clips or photocopies and your critiques to your teacher.

## Other Creative Leads

Alternatives to the summary lead often are lumped into a single category termed "narrative." However, it is useful to review several specialized formats popular enough among storyteller-journalists to deserve their own labels.

What is noteworthy is that they, like the narrative lead, are approaches first employed successfully by fiction writers. As a matter of fact, it should be clear by now that storyteller-journalists increasingly use in their news stories most of the tools and techniques of short story and novel writers.

What we already have covered concerning narrative leads generally applies to these alternatives. In addition, remember that occasional, appropriate use of each of these should be rewarding. However, using any one of them too often will cheapen its value and reduce its power.

Creative alternatives, including explanations and examples, are the following six:

- Anecdotal leads.
- Scene-setter leads.
- Descriptive leads.
- Direct address leads.
- Question leads.
- Direct quote leads.

## Anecdotal Leads

An anecdote is a relatively brief, often humorous and sometimes poignant story told with a particular point or purpose in mind.

A well-chosen anecdote can captivate readers and add a powerful creative spark to what otherwise might be a routine opening. An anecdote should be chosen for its close relationship to the topic of the news story. The anecdote also should match the tone of the news event.

Follow the anecdote with the nut graf, which completes the task of presenting the key news elements and central idea; however, it has the additional responsibility of firming up any connections between the anecdote and the news event

The following story, covering a Gem and Mineral Show, opens with an anecdote about the Colorado wilderness honeymoon of a woman, Vicki Schuler, and her husband. It is followed by the nut graf, beginning "She displayed some of her findings Saturday and Sunday . . ." See how the nut graf uses Ms. Schuler to connect effectively the anecdote and the news event and then finishes with the key news elements of the story.

Vicki Schuler spent her honeymoon in the Colorado wilderness. One morning, she sent her husband to wash dishes in a nearby stream, and he didn't come back for several hours.

Afraid a bear might have attacked him, she went looking for her husband. What she saw surprised her.

A frying pan in hand, her husband was searching for gold in the stream.

"My husband has been a rock hound," Schuler said. "A rock hound is someone who looks for rocks—like the hound dog."

Schuler, too, became a rock hound and now is a gem and mineral dealer in League City. She has been stuck in the mud and trapped in a car hanging half-way from a bridge. She has dug up dinosaur bones and dragged a log of petrified wood across marshy plains. But she won't stop—it's addictive, she said.

She displayed some of her findings Saturday and Sunday at the University Center Bluebonnet Ballroom. The exhibit was part of The Gem and Mineral Show, sponsored by the Arlington Gem and Mineral Club.

—Kateryna Ivanova

## Scene-Setter Leads

Imagine you are director of a play and working with the stage manager to prepare the stage. Your goal is to establish a realistic and appropriate setting, complete with backdrop, furnishings, sound effects and props—to which the actors bring their lines and their performances. Everything in place on opening night, the curtain rises and the actors bring the characters and experiences of the play to life.

A scene-setter lead puts you into a similar role of director: You establish the necessary setting, background and props. Then, you bring in the characters and reveal the story to readers.

The Daily Titan at California State University, Fullerton published an excellent example of a scene-setter lead, in which the student journalist/director sets the stage for a fascinating story.

> Somewhere between Orange County and Las Vegas, an ordinary exit sign sits on Interstate 15 and has been turning heads for years.
>
> The standard, green board with white lettering wouldn't be much to see if it wasn't for its "Twilight Zone"-like name posted so plainly in the middle of nowhere. "Zzyzx Road" leads to more than the double takes it elicits from passers-by; it leads to an oasis of teaching and research, the CSU Desert Studies Center.
>
> The paved route quickly ends after exiting Zzyzx—pronounced Zye-Zix—Road and becomes four miles of gravel twists and turns, which William Presch, director of the Desert Studies Center, said are specifically left rough to keep unwanted traffic out.
>
> Set at the extreme western edge of the Mojave National Preserve, the center encompasses 1,200 acres at Soda Springs, next to the Soda Dry Lake.
>
> Presch said about 2,000 people use the facility every year from all over the world, who stay anywhere from one to 10 days. Visitors can stay at the site or use the center as base camp to explore the desert.
>
> —Christine Zwaagstra

## Descriptive Leads

Similar to scene-setter leads, descriptive leads use ample specific details to capture reader interest by appealing to their senses. However, more than establishing a realistic, physical place, descriptive leads can either paint word pictures or venture into the abstract, creating an atmosphere or an emotional space.

The following lead from The Daily Nebraskan at the University of Nebraska opens with description of a skater's legs. A few brief quotes later and readers find the nut graf and the story focus—the USA Roller Sports National Indoor Speed and Figure Skating Championships.

> Joey Mantia's legs are a thing of beauty.
>
> The quadriceps muscle bulges forth, almost hanging over the kneecap, skin tighter than your girlfriend's bar-hopping getup. The phrase sculpted doesn't do them justice, each strain so powerfully defined, Mantia could moonlight as a model for an anatomy class's chapter on the muscle system.
>
> Ahhnold would be proud.

"I don't work out," Joey explains, massaging each thigh, readying them for his 500-meter national championship speed skate 45 minutes away.

"I just skate."

That goes for almost anyone in Mantia's field, skating is life. A pro-elite (top-level) speed skater, Mantia is one of approximately 3,000 athletes who will converge on Lincoln for the USA Roller Sports National Indoor Speed and Figure Skating Championships, which run through Aug. 5.

—David Diehl

## Direct Address Leads

Direct address, as you know, is the writer speaking directly to readers. Crafted for the right story, the upside is that direct address leads can provide just the right tone and approach to make your lead memorable. The downside is that some writers become enamored of these leads, using them too carelessly and too often.

The writer of the following lead, from the Kansas State Collegian, uses the direct address lead deftly, with a friendly, informal tone of voice and altogether fitting word choices. Notice, though, that the direct address is dropped during the fifth paragraph, accompanied by a shift in voice and word choices to those appropriate for a nut graf transitioning into a story on job searching.

Graduation is just around the corner, and you get nervous every time your parents' number pops up on caller ID. Why? Because you know what they're going to ask.

"Have you found a job yet?"

It's one of the scariest questions asked of a young graduate of the class of 2003. Especially since the economy has people second-guessing the decisions that might determine their entire careers.

But don't freak out.

Collect yourself and get busy. Kristy Morgan, assistant director of Career and Employment Services, said it isn't uncommon for students to find themselves at the end of the college road with no clear plan as to where to go next.

"We have students come in who have chosen not to deal with the job search until graduation, or it will sneak up on them," she said. "They probably need to work quickly and get a resume together. They need to get serious about the job search because it's time to make that a priority."

—J. J. Duncan

## Question Leads

Question leads seem simple enough. Deceptively simple. Just begin with a question or two that the rest of the story will answer. However, carelessly written question leads are among the most boring and tiresome that inexperienced storyteller-journalists can use to open stories.

To be successful, these leads must do more than just ask questions that the story answers. The questions themselves must demand readers' attention. They must intrigue readers. They must challenge readers to find answers. Whether shocked, surprised or curious, readers must engage the questions.

Certainly, readers of The Daily Campus at Southern Methodist University were at least curious, if not shocked and surprised, at the following lead. Here the second paragraph answers the questions, serves as the nut graf to focus the story and provides transition into the body.

> What is more competitive at SMU: academics or the walk to class? Why do kids here get dressed up everyday and carry book bags worth hundreds of dollars? What are they competing for, given that the Gucci bags and $70,000 Mercedes do not buy grades? What does this materialistic drive earn students, and why does SMU seem to be more extreme than other schools?
>
> The reason, according to many SMU students, is quite simple: The campus culture encourages conspicuous consumption.
>
> —Julie Derham

### Direct Quote Leads

Direct quote leads have fallen out of vogue in recent years, but they still have their place among options you might consider.

The most important guideline to follow in their use is that the direct quote or quotes used in the lead must bear the burden of both grabbing readers' attention and relating clearly to the particular story focus in the nut graf that should follow.

The following lead for a job-hunting story from The Michigan Daily at the University of Michigan handles these demands well.

> "One of my best friends has applied for 120 jobs, and he's still looking," recent LSA graduate David Levin said.
>
> "It's pretty difficult in this economy. It is easier than I anticipated, but still very competitive," said current job hunter and recent LSA graduate Jenny Chou, adding that she did not expect to graduate with a job.
>
> Many graduates are quickly discovering that hunting for a job is very competitive. While the general economic trend has been downward, the job market has remained relatively stable since last year.
>
> —David Weinberg

## For Practice

11-3. Select a news story that you submitted for a grade. Then, do the following:

a) Open the story file on a computer.
b) Review the narrative and six other creative leads and pick one to use for your story (different from the original).
c) Under the original story draft the new lead along with a nut graf, making sure you revise enough of the story to make the new material transition into the original body.
d) Below the new material write three to four sentences each on the benefits and drawbacks of your original and of the new leads.

e) Print out a copy of your story with its two leads and explanations.
f) Share your story and its two leads with your peer group, and get their feedback on your lead and assessments.
g) Submit the materials to your teacher.

## Crafting and Drafting

The following questions are based on a handout from John Wicklein, writing, reporting and editing coach in Gaithersburg, Md. Answer them during your peer review to catch possible holes in your partner's story.

- Fairness: Is the story fair to all concerned? Did the reporter get the other side (or *all sides*)?
- Context: What does this story mean? How does this fit into the broader development or issue? What is its history?
- Impact: Who or what is affected? Who benefits? Who is hurt? How will this story affect readers?
- Future: What will this news lead to? What are the consequences of this?
- Rationale: What is the person's (group's or entity's) reason for taking this action?
- Responsibility: Who or what is behind this?
- Cause: Why did this happen?
- Believability: Does this story make sense? Has someone hoodwinked the reporter?

## For Practice

11-4. Run your regular beat and locate a topic for which you can do a story. Then, do the following:

a) Interview appropriate sources and take careful notes.
b) Listen carefully for quoteworthy comments your sources make, and write those down exactly.
c) Draft a story with a lead that effectively opens and best fits the story. If you opt for a summary lead, give careful consideration to which news element will open it most effectively. If a narrative or other creative lead, make sure that it and the nut graf follow the recommendations laid out earlier.
d) Swap stories with a peer review partner or group and give written reader feedback.
e) Submit the draft and peer feedback to your teacher.
f) After your teacher has reviewed your draft and peer feedback and has offered additional suggestions, revise as required.
g) Submit a final draft to your teacher.

## *Chapter 11 Bibliography*

Chancellor, John, and Walter R. Mears. *The News Business*. New York: Harper and Row, 1983.

Derham, Julie. "A Fendi on Every Shoulder, a Gucci on Every Foot: From Audi to Prada, Brand Names Carry Currency on Campus." *SMU Daily Campus*. 22 April 2003. <http://www.smudailycampus .com/vnews/display.v/ART/2003/04/22/3ea4cc0e67c30?in_archive=1>.

Diehl, David. "Speed Limits Don't Apply in This Sport." *The Daily Nebraskan*. 20 July 2003. <http://www.dailynebraskan.com/vnews/display.v/ART/2003/07/20/3f1b46b9d79e8>.

Duncan, J. J. "Job Search Stressful, Worthwhile Experience: Graduation Guide 2003." *Kansas State Collegian*. 9 May 2003. <http://www.kstatecollegian.com/stories/050903/new_gradjob.shtml>.

Forgeard, Marie. "Local Group Delivers Books through Bars." *The Daily Pennsylvanian*. 31 July 2003. <http://www.dailypennsylvanian.com/vnews/display.v/ART/2003/07/31/3f28a8a4b7200>.

Hoffman, Tiffany. "Filters Approved for Use on Library Computers: The Supreme Court Ruled June 23 That Libraries Were Required to Install Pornography Filters for the Internet or Be Subject to Losing Federal Funding." *Collegiate Times*. 7 July 2003. <http://www.collegiatetimes.com/index.php?ID=1587>.

Ivanova, Kateryna. "All That Glitters: The 46th Gem and Mineral Show Features Jewelry with Precious Stones and More." *The Shorthorn*. 5 August 2003. <http://www.theshorthorn.com/archive/2003/summer/03-aug-05/n080503-05.html>.

LaRocque, Paula. "Hooking the Reader Depends on Variety of Well-Written Leads." *Quill 83: 6* (July/August 1995).

Lawrence, Blythe. "Little Town, Big Boom." *The Daily*. 1 July 2003. <http://www.thedaily. washington.edu/past_all.lasso?-database=DailyWeb.fp5&-layout=List&-response=news_old.lasso&-recordID=33134&-search&-Token.Date=07/01/2003>.

Mann, Horace. Michael Moncur, *The Quotations Page*. <http://www.quotationspage.com/>.

McGough, Cailin. "UV Staircase Project at a Standstill: Project Halted as Complex Owners and Towson Officials Try to Reach Agreement." *The Towerlight*. 12 May 2003. <http://www.thetowerlight. com/vnews/display.v/ART/2003/05/12/3ebf1daecf09c>.

Nguyen, Kent. "19-Only to Miss Billiards Club." *The Daily Iowan*. <http://www.dailyiowan.com/news/449062.html>.

Richert, Cat. "College Refuses to Renew Lease for Shell Station." *The Oberlin Review*. <http://www.oberlin-review.org/news/article8.htm>.

Simons, Abby. "Students' Reactions Mixed Over Change." *The Northwest Missourian*. 17 April 2003. <http://www.missourianonline.com/Archives/archive.php?week=2002_2003/0417>.

Orris, Michelle. "Accounting Students Reportedly Admit to Cheating." *Badger Herald*. 25 April 2003. <http://www.badgerherald.com/vnews/display.v/ART/2003/04/25/3ea8af32aae0a?in_arc>.hive=1.

Sundby, Alex. "Defective Hardware Shuts Down Campus Voicemail." *The Daily*. 6 August 2003. <http://thedaily.washington.edu/news.lasso?-database=DailyWeb.fp5&-layout=List&-response=newspage.lasso&-recordID=33251&-search&-Token.Count=63>.

Weinberg, David. "Graduates Struggle in Current Job Market." *The Michigan Daily*. 12 May 2003. <http://www.michigandaily.com/vnews/display.v/ART/2003/05/12/3ebf24bccfc72?in_archive=1>.

Wicklein, John. "Finding the Holes." *No Train, No Gain: Training for Newspaper Journalists*. http://www.notrain-nogain.org/train/res/edit/jw.asp

Zawel, Marc. "3rd Death in Two Weeks Hits C.U. Campus: Osborne '04 Died Monday Night; Visitor to Cornell Remains Hospitalized After a Nearly Fatal Jump the Same Evening." *Cornell Daily Sun*. <http://www.cornellsun.com/articles/8468/>.

Zwaagstra, Christine. "Zzyzx: A Road to Nowhere?" *Daily Titan*. 7 May 2003. <http://dailytitan.fullerton .edu/issues/Spring%202003/May.7/stories/zzyzx.html>.

# Chapter 12
# Drafting the Lead and Conclusion

*If any man wish to write in a clear style,*
*let him be first clear in his thoughts;*
*and if any would write in a noble style,*
*let him first possess a noble soul.*

—Johann Wolfgang von Goethe

## Chapter Contents

## QuickView

We continue in this chapter with our review of leads, particularly advice to improve your drafting of leads. We also will find effective examples of leads that you could be proud to call your own.

We will see how leads that are interesting, provocative, telling and inviting can capture attention and prepare readers to move into the body of the story.

The easiest way to keep leads simple is to keep them short. Well-chosen words, sentences and paragraphs that tell the story well *and* are short make leads memorable.

Finally, we will discuss conclusions—when they are not appropriate and when they are.

# Capturing Readers' Attention

Of all the tasks you must accomplish as a storyteller, the most important is capturing the attention of your audience and encouraging them to read your story.

The stories you already have written may have succeeded in doing this. Or not. Our concern in this chapter is to examine how you might incorporate into your own storycrafting the strengths of leads we considered in the last chapter.

Too many writers assume that their stories will be read just because they are published. However, people today tend to be selective about what they spend time reading. Studies tell us several things about newspaper readers:

- The majority is older.
- Most do not read their newspapers completely from front to back.
- They skim headlines and leads, delving further into those stories they find appealing.
- They read until their curiosity is satisfied.

Your campus audience is even less likely to read newspapers, but when they do, they also choose stories that satisfy their interests and curiosity.

So, how do you improve the chances that what you write will have a willing audience?

The key is your lead.

Regardless of the particular approach you take to begin your story, the lead should be interesting, provocative, telling and inviting. If it is not, then all the effort you put into the rest of the story may be for naught. It simply will not be read.

## Interesting Leads

Leads are interesting if they appeal to the needs and desires of readers. You should first consider what interests your readers. What draws their attention? What is important to them, especially right here and right now? What causes them to stop what they are doing to look?

The demand is not only to compete for readers' time among the many things they may choose to do in addition to reading newspapers but also to compete for readers' interest among the many stories published in each issue.

Consider this lead from the University of Florida Alligator. What do you find interesting about it? How does it capture your attention?

> The first thing students will notice about UF's new $20 million bookstore and "front door" project probably won't be the fact it's opening a month late.
>
> They'll notice the aquarium.
>
> In the 700-gallon tank, hundreds of both orange and blue fish, all Florida-grown, teem amid aquatic plants also raised in the Sunshine State.

The new 50,000-square foot facility opened Monday, even as plaster dust clung stubbornly to the orange and blue tile in the main stairwell.

—Warren Kagarise

The storyteller of this lead intrigues readers by saying first what they will *not* notice about the bookstore opening. Then, he heightens the intrigue and interest by saying what students will notice, and it is *not* the bookstore.

## Provocative Leads

Leads should have grabber quality, like carnival barkers who can pull yokels in from the midway to the freak shows.

Once your lead has interested readers, it must hold their attention and pull them into the story. Readers who have paused expect a payoff. In other words how will the story make it worth their time to continue reading?

The following lead was published in The Daily Northwestern at Northwestern University. What makes this lead provocative, able to pull readers into the story?

Decked out in a dark suit, dress shoes and red tie, Weinberg freshman Prajwal Ciryam resembled the quintessential politician.

But he insisted he wasn't nearly as confident as he looked.

"I'm honestly scared to death," he said 15 minutes before election polls closed Thursday night. "Your hopes really get up once you make it to the runoff. Losing to no confidence would be a much greater shame than losing to a good candidate."

Ciryam had no reason to worry. The academic vice presidential candidate emerged victorious in Thursday's runoff election.

—Laurel Jorgensen

The storyteller launches her piece with description of the "quintessential politician," who is not as "quintessential" as he appears. Because she has the benefit of knowing the outcome of the election when she writes the story, the writer is able to play the candidate's pre-count jitters against the clear victory he won.

Provocative leads often involve some kind of emotional appeal. Introducing key characters early helps to cement this connection. Readers can relate more easily to people than they can to facts, and they tend to recall compelling feelings and people long after they have forgotten specific numbers and concepts.

## Telling Leads

Leads should be telling. They should have "aboutness"—a clear focus on a particular message for readers, which we discussed in Chapter 2.

Certainly, well-written summary leads achieve this goal. Yet, even the most creative lead must contain a kernel of the story's focus. Full focus then may be delayed until the nut graf, the vital packet of material high in the story that targets exact content.

Speech leads can be dreadfully ho-hum, with some writers drafting leads like the following: "A nature writer and adventurer spoke to 20 people Monday afternoon in Fisk Hall." Fortunately, the writer of the following lead, also from The Daily Northwestern, gives readers a key point of the speaker's address, a strong option for speech leads. The direct quote in the second paragraph lends power to that point.

> Nature writer and adventurer Gretel Ehrlich doesn't believe in learning about cultural traditions through history books. Instead, she makes a point of going straight to the source.
>
> "The pen never preceded the moment," Ehrlich told a crowd of 20 people Monday afternoon in Fisk Hall as part of the Literature of Fact lecture series.
>
> Ehrlich, the author of eight books and a contributor to The New Yorker, Time and National Geographic, spoke candidly to the audience about her most recent work. The non-fiction story "This Cold Heaven" discusses the lives and history of the Inuit people who have lived in Greenland for almost 5,000 years. Ehrlich spent parts of seven years in the Arctic Circle to gain perspective on the reality of life in a country "isolated by ice."
>
> \* \* \* \* \* \* \* \* \* \*
>
> —Courtney Barnes

## Inviting Leads

Readers should be comfortable with leads, which should invite them to continue reading in the much same way as an appealing entryway welcomes and encourages guests to come into a home.

Your readers should not feel they have been tricked or trapped into reading stories. They should feel that stories are written just for them, tailored for their interests and designed to fit like well-worn shoes.

The student journalist of the next lead, from the Minnesota Daily at the University of Minnesota, invites readers into the story as comfortably as taking them by the hand for a pleasant walk. Examine carefully the playful word choices. How are they inviting to readers?

> It only takes a quick stroll along the Washington Avenue Bridge to realize something odd is afoot on the West Bank. Outside Anderson Hall, nestled next to the bridge, a mysterious tree stands, branches hung low by its strange fruit: pairs of shoes by the dozens.
>
> For most passers-by, the shoe tree is a familiar, yet puzzling sight that never stops sparking curiosity.
>
> "I've been trying to figure out where it came from for three years now," said Kate Nelson, a junior sociology student, as she walked on the bridge.
>
> Getting to the root of the tree's origins proves difficult. There seems to be as many ideas about how it started as there are shoes slung about its limbs. Still, most people do not even know the stories.
>
> —Lee Billings

Therefore, you should eschew formulas. What worked yesterday or last week may not work now. Instead, write for the moment and for the story. Craft leads to match particular content. This approach improves chances that leads will be fresh, fitting and, of course, inviting.

## *Keeping Leads Simple*

The simpler your lead, the more likely it will be effective. Simplicity, you must understand, has nothing to do with the ideas presented. The grandest, most complex ideas can be presented simply, just as routine, simple ideas can be presented in complex, convoluted ways.

Rather, simple leads typically benefit from a single concept: short.

Short applies to both the particular words as well as the total number of words that comprise the lead, and good storytellers know that short is better than long.

This emphasis on short probably is the opposite of what you previously have practiced as a writer in three distinct ways:

- Your continuing growth as a reader and writer has exposed you to an expanding vocabulary, often involving words that have been less common, more specialized and usually longer.
- As you have grappled with increasingly sophisticated concepts in your classes, your sentences often grew and their structures became more complex.
- Academic writing—that which you complete for your classes—tends to emphasize longer, more complex sentences, and longer paragraphs, which traditionally are structured with topic sentence plus supporting details.

Ultimately, your success as a writer has come from longer words, longer sentences and longer paragraphs comprising longer writing assignments.

Until now. You need to change direction. Why? Because well-chosen shorter words packaged in shorter sentences and shorter paragraphs are faster and easier to read, and when it comes to modern news stories, particularly news leads, readers expect faster and easier.

Finally, it is important that you understand that your writing will benefit from *varying* lengths of words, sentences and paragraphs. Using some longer elements is necessary to provide relief from the emphasis on shorter. In addition, a limited number of longer words, sentences and paragraphs will help to make short elements seem even shorter, by way of comparison.

### Emphasizing Short Words

Shorter words and shorter sentences are more readable by a larger audience with differing backgrounds and reading abilities. Most reading formulas use these criteria as the basis for their indexing of reading difficulty.

So, how short is short? Of course, the answer to that question is relative and variable.

With words, for example, generally pick the shortest when you can choose among several words of comparable meaning. If a longer word is the only one available or better fits the context, use it.

Look at the following lead from The Daily Kent Stater as an example. If you ignore proper nouns, all but four words of the 67 in the two paragraphs are only one or two syllables.

"Parry four! Extend! Lunge!" The man dressed head-to-toe in white shouted commands while rubber-tipped swords swung and jabbed across the room.

Usually, the man styles himself Tim Radden, a high school art teacher from Akron and chairman of the Northeast Ohio Division of the United States Fencing Association. But for eight weeks during the summer, he becomes Mr. Tim, fencing instructor for the Kent for Kids program.

—Matthew Schomer

## Structuring Sentences

Next, you should rely primarily on simple, declarative sentences—single subject-plus-verb packages written in active voice. Active voice, we might explain briefly, has the subject doing the action of the verb, versus passive voice, where the subject receives the action of the verb. Active voice is both more natural and shorter than passive.

The Auburn Plainsman ran the following story, which uses primarily simple, declarative sentences written mostly in active voice.

Xing Ping Hu is not a typical Auburn professor. She doesn't teach any classes. Hu spends much of her time in her Funchess Hall laboratory observing termites.

"I always knew that I wanted to work in the bug world," Hu said.

Hu's interest in termites began while she was working at Louisiana State University. The federal government sponsored termite research, and Hu was enticed by it.

Hu is an assistant professor at Auburn. She has what she calls a dual appointment—she does research in her lab and goes out into the community to discover particular termite problems.

—Sonya Nave

Shy away from using more than a few compound sentences, where you present two or more subject-plus-verb packages joined by coordinating conjunctions—and, or, nor, but, for, yet, so.

Also, tend to avoid complex sentences, with two or more subject-plus-verb packages joined by subordinating conjunctions. The list of subordinating conjunctions is lengthy and includes the following: after, although, as, as if, as long as, as though, because, before, even if, even though, if, if only, in order that, now that, once, rather than, since, so that, than, that, though, till, unless, until, when, whenever, where, whereas, wherever, while.

However, some complex sentences can be short and quite effective, as is the case with the complex sentence in the first paragraph of this lead from The Collegian at Penn State University.

The Nittany Lion's roar will be a mere whimper this week as he nurses a bludgeoning injury to the head.

About 75 percent of the Nittany Lion's right ear at the Lion Shrine is missing. The glue and some stone from the last time the ear was repaired is visible at the open wound.

—Jocelyn Brick-Turin

## Deciding Paragraph Length

With paragraphs, especially summary lead paragraphs, anything longer than 30 words may be too much, with average summary lead paragraphs running closer to 20 words. The best test is to read the sentences aloud and listen for flow and readability.

In addition, shorter paragraphs tend to be more *visually* inviting to readers. This is especially true when news stories are formatted in standard newspaper columns, whose width is about a third of that for material printed on an 8½ × 11 inch sheet of paper or about half of that for material printed on a typical textbook page. Therefore, identical paragraphs *appear* much longer when formatted for newspapers than they do when formatted for a classroom assignment printed on typing paper.

An easy way to remember this emphasis on short is that most sentences are best if they follow the "one-subject rule"—one subject per sentence and one subject per paragraph.

Paragraphs of two to four sentences are commonplace for news writers, and even paragraphs of a single short sentence are useful for emphasis and variety.

## *For Practice*

Select five stories *with summary leads* that you previously wrote and submitted for grades. Then, complete exercise 12-1 *or* 12-2.

12-1. If you have access to word processing software that provides readability statistics (such as the Spelling and Grammar checker in Microsoft Word), then open the disk files of each of your six stories with summary leads and do the following:

a) Highlight *only* the lead.
b) Run the readability statistics analysis.
c) Make note of the following data:
  • Word count.
  • Average characters per word.
  • Average words per sentence.
  • Average sentences per paragraph.
  • Percentage of passive sentences.
  • Flesch-Kincaid Grade Level.
d) Submit printouts of the leads and data above.

## *For Practice*

12-2. Alternatively, if you do not have access to word processing software that provides readability statistics, do the following:

a) Name the news element that opens each lead.
b) Count the number of words in each lead.
c) If any leads are longer than 20 words, revise them in effective ways
  to trim the total to 20.

d) Revise leads to eliminate the following:
- Too many unnecessary long words or long sentences.
- Passive voice.
- Compound or complex sentences.

e) Submit both original stories and revised leads.

## Drafting the Lead

As you draft your lead—whether it be a summary, narrative or other creative lead, pay attention to exactly how you begin it.

If a summary lead, which element do you use to open it? You first should decide what kind of summary lead the story needs—a *what* lead, a *who* lead or so on. Such awareness relates closely to understanding what you are doing with the material you have. And if you understand what you are doing, you more likely will do a better job of it.

If a narrative or other creative lead, exactly what words are privileged enough to deserve the opening spot? You have only a few seconds to grab readers' attention and stop them from moving on to another story. Do not waste them with less than your best up front. You likely will not get a second chance.

Read carefully and listen closely to the one or more paragraphs that comprise your lead. Is it interesting, provocative, telling and inviting?

If not, do not delete your original. Instead, draft a second or even third lead below the first that opens with another news element; captures the central idea with different verbs, different nouns or both; or puts a more powerful word into the opening spot.

Then, take a few moments to compare the leads and pick the one that works best.

A final bit of advice concerning drafting your lead: Staring at a blank computer screen or sheet of paper can be daunting. If "the perfect lead" does not come to you quickly or easily, you are in good company. Your best material often comes during revision, so consider drafting the body of the story and writing the lead later.

We will discuss revision more fully in Chapter 15.

## Conclusions

Whether you should write stories with conclusions is an issue that today continues to be debated. The growing popularity of narrative frames, which we will review in Chapter 13, is evidence that more journalists—and their editors—recognize the value of conclusions. Yet, even as their use increases, conclusions are not appropriate or necessary for every story.

And remember that a conclusion is not merely the *end* of a story; it is a carefully fashioned story element and, when used, is second in importance to the lead.

### The Argument against Conclusions

Historically, few news stories, especially in newspapers, were structured in ways that invited or even allowed conclusions. Several reasons supported this approach:

- Use of the inverted pyramid.
- Typesetting and printing methods.
- Time pressures.

The inverted pyramid, with its summary lead and most-to-least-important ordering of material, did not need a conclusion. Journalists wrote until they said what they needed to say or ran out of material or time. Readers learned that the most important material came first and that they could stop reading at any point that their interest was satisfied.

Typesetting and printing methods also encouraged stories without conclusions. Until the advent of computerized composition and layout of newspaper pages, employees outside the newsroom handled the task of typesetting and actual composing. Simple line-counting formulas gave reporters and editors a general idea of how long stories would run, but until they were set in type, that measure was only an educated guess.

Moreover, the actual fitting of stories onto pages was accomplished by lopping the bottom of the story. Because most stories used inverted pyramid, this seldom caused any problems; whatever was cut was never as important as what remained.

Finally, time pressures on everyone involved with the newspaper publishing process made stories with conclusions troublesome. They would slow writers, who would not be able to write until they ran out of time or material. It also would delay editors and composing room workers, who would have had to exercise much more care in what they could cut in order to fit stories onto pages that had been designed using pencil and paper sketches.

However, modern typesetting and printing methods no longer require this labor- and time-intensive process. Writers know exactly what lengths their stories will be. Editors can quickly and easily drop each story piece of the page puzzle into place on computer screens. Then, at the punch of a key, they can send full pages directly from screen to printing plate.

Yet, at many newspapers the inverted pyramid continues to dominate. The form makes it quick and easy for most journalists to write, editors to compose and readers to read. The following story, from The Sentinel at North Idaho College, opens with an inviting descriptive lead but then moves into inverted pyramid for the body. It has no conclusion, ending with information about where the students' work can be viewed.

The sound of the lathe machine matched the beating of his heart as he carefully concentrated on the work before him. Jared Gill was nervous. Very nervous.

Recalling his recent participation in the Skills USA competition brought a smile to the young man's face.

"I kind of screwed up on the first part," said Gill, a machine technology student who hails from Lewiston. "But then everything just came together."

Gill is just one of 16 students enrolled in the Trades and Industry Division at NIC that took part in the competition, April 4-6, at Boise State University. Six of the students, including Gill, took top honors, enabling them to advance to national competition in Kansas City in June.

Skills USA is part of the Vocational Industrial Clubs of America (VICA), an organization of trade, industrial and technical students.

Each student must compete at the local level before advancing to state or even national competition. The local competitions took place in NIC's machining shops.

"It's completely voluntary," said Jim Straub, machine technology instructor. "The state has to be willing for its school to participate, and then each school gets to decide from there.

"It's good national exposure," Straub said.

A second machine technology instructor, Victor Gillika, added that participating in such events can only lead to great accomplishments for the students themselves.

"It's the challenge to get there that makes them do it," he said.

The machining students focused on operating equipment such as lathes and milling machines to produce objects made of metal that the judges set before them. Each phase of the competition was timed. Drafting students produced architectural layouts, while diesel and collision repair students focused on the intricacies of their craft, such a fixing a problematic car.

However, technical skills were not the only portions of the competition. "The students could also participate in what they call the professional part," Straub said, "which would be something like giving opening and closing speeches and going through job interviews."

The job interviewing process becomes very critical to second-year students like Gill. According to Straub and Gillika, at the Skills USA competition companies will send out representatives to gatherings such as these, offering prospective employees chances at lucrative careers.

"Most people don't know about that side of things—about what we do here," Straub said. "These aren't dirty blacksmith occupations. Everything is very clean and controlled. It's an excellent option to train and get good paying jobs. We prepare students to hit the ground running."

"They work very hard," Gillika added.

Those who placed in the competition were drafting students Paul Marx and Greg Mass, diesel students Kevin Moudy and Casey Streeter, collision repair student Les Berg and Gill. Also participating were drafting students Ashley Wisniewski, Brooke Wright, T.J. Eixenberger and Ben Larsen, machining students Bob Bybee and Devin Byers, diesel student Franklin Krier and collision repair students Michael Hopkins, Robert Burton, and Paul Prety.

Samples of the students' work can be found in a display case near the lakeside entrance of the Hedlund Building.

—Marie Strong

## The Argument for Conclusions

Reliance on the inverted pyramid is shifting in favor of narrative and creative forms that more effectively present the story and engage the reader.

Stories with narrative or other non-summary leads allow journalists to craft powerful conclusions to their stories. Yet, good conclusions do not just happen. They are not incidental appendages following the body of the story. Time, effort and planning are essential if conclusions are to be effective.

First, be selective about drafting stories with conclusions. As noted earlier, straight-news stories with summary leads and inverted-pyramid development should *not* have conclusions. They do not belong.

For stories that will benefit from them, craft your conclusions with the following points in mind.

### Try to develop some sense of the kind of conclusion you might write as early as you can in the writing process.

Conclusions are integral elements of the structure of stories where they are used. Your conclusion helps determine what material you use and how you organize it. Prepare your story and your readers for your conclusion.

### Shorter usually is better.

Dragging out a conclusion likely will cause it to lose its punch. Like the melodramatic and often poorly acted deaths in some movies where the character takes forever to die, too-long conclusions can make some readers wish *they* had.

### Consider a conclusion that drives home a point.

This point should flow naturally and logically from the previous material in the story. The "hook," discussed in Chapter 13, is such a conclusion.

### Avoid a conclusion that does little more than summarize the story.

Writers sometimes try to force a summarizing conclusion because they cannot imagine any other. That approach was dull for your composition class essay, and it is dull for news stories. Let the lead or nut graf handle the job of summarizing the story.

### A story with *no* conclusion tends to be better than a story with a *weak* conclusion.

The following story exemplifies a powerful conclusion that hooks back to the lead to provide a comfortable and satisfying finish. Published in The Digital Missourian at the University of Missouri, the story makes strong use of narration and description.

It was a family event Saturday at the Sixth Annual Freeze-Off in Fayette as children and their parents enjoyed homemade ice cream under the towering trees at the historic courthouse square. But for Kim and Dale Wayland, the term "family event" takes on a whole different meaning.

"I beat him again," Kim Wayland said of her husband, Dale Wayland.

Kim Wayland won the Best in Show award, a new award this year, and $300 for her homemade chocolate fudge sundae. Dale Wayland had entered the contest with his peanut butter cup ice cream. There were 17 entries for homemade ice cream, with Kim and Dale Wayland entering three.

The couple enters the contest every year, and Kim Wayland thought this would be the year her husband would bring home the grand prize. In previous years, Kim Wayland has won the contest four times, twice for first place and twice for second.

Dale Wayland won second place in the exotic round while Kim Wayland took home the grand prize and a second place award in the classic division for her strawberry concoction.

"We practice all year," Kim Wayland said. "I'm an ice cream guru. I'm sort of the Martha Stewart of ice cream."

While there are those who make the ice cream, there must also be those who judge it—a job most people would willingly accept.

James Mauser has been an ice cream judge in the Freeze-Off for three years and said he has tasted some of the best ice cream ever at this event.

"This is just a real wonderful hometown experience," Mauser said. "You can't get this in a big city. It's just like a movie."

The historic courthouse square in the heart of Fayette held hundreds of onlookers. They sat in their lawn chairs and listened to gospel and folk music while children blew enormous bubbles and ate ice cream in the August afternoon.

"It is a real nice place to get together," presiding commissioner of Fayette, Lowell Eaton, said. "It is a lot of hard work and volunteering, but people love it."

The Freeze-Off wasn't just about ice cream, however. The festival included a fiddler's competition, an art show, a children's treasure hunt, face painting and various bands.

After the ice cream judging, people were still waiting for their own taste of ice cream in a line that stretched to the end of the town square while the winning couple stood with prizes in hand.

Kim and Dale Wayland walked away from the show with $400. They said the money will be well spent when they travel to Jamaica for vacation next weekend.

"Four hundred isn't bad for a weekend," Kim Wayland said as she looked at her trophy and husband with pride.

—Taylor Mueller

## For Practice

12-3. Select a previously submitted news story without a conclusion that would benefit from one. Then, do the following:

a) Open the story file on a computer, and print a copy.
b) Find an appropriate angle to use for a conclusion.
c) Under the original story write the conclusion.
d) Then, moving up from the conclusion, revise enough of the story to fit the new material onto the original body.
e) Below the new material write three to four sentences each on the benefits and drawbacks of the original story and of the story with a conclusion.
f) Print out the story with a conclusion and your explanations.
g) Share both stories and explanations with your peer group, and get their feedback on your conclusion and assessments.
h) Submit to your teacher.

## Crafting and Drafting

   We consider some additional concerns here, based on a hand-out from John Wicklein, writing, reporting and editing coach in Gaithersburg, Md. Cover each during your peer review to locate any missing details in the story you are reading.

- Answers to any questions raised by the reporter and not answered in copy.
- Nuts and bolts: Include addresses, titles, age, place; identification, as in "a former professor from the University of Missouri-Columbia."
- Facts that could make details clear.
- Numbers that need to be checked to make sure they add up to the total.
- Comparative figures, as in "an increase of $25,000 over last year's budget." What was last year's figure? "The second-biggest budget." What was the biggest?
- Nut graf following a creative lead.
- Follow-ups to an idea introduced in the lead.
- Background graf on a continuing story.
- Explanation of words, phrases and processes that readers might not understand.
- Attributions: Who said that?
- Locator paragraphs (or locator maps): Where is this?

## For Practice

12-4. Run your regular beat and locate a topic for which you can do a story. Then, do the following:

a) Interview appropriate sources and take careful notes.
b) Listen carefully for quoteworthy comments your sources make, and write those down exactly.
c) Draft a story with a lead that effectively opens and best fits the story.
d) If appropriate, also draft a conclusion.
e) Swap stories with a peer review partner or group and give written reader feedback.
f) Submit the draft and peer feedback to your teacher.
g) After your teacher has reviewed your draft and peer feedback and has offered additional suggestions, revise as required.
h) Submit a final draft to your teacher.

## Chapter 12 Bibliography

Barnes, Courtney. "Author Gives Voice to Inuit People Isolated by Ice: National Geographic Contributor Says Cultural Immersion Enriches Reporting." *The Daily Northwestern*. 4 March 2003. <http://www .dailynorthwestern.com/vnews/display.v/ART/2003/03/04/3e64aec6b5d4e?in_archive=1>.
Billings, Lee. "U Students Unclear About Origins of Shoe Tree." *The Minnesota Daily*. 21 April 2003. <http://www.mndaily.com/articles/2003/04/21/5692>.

Brick-Turin, Jocelyn. "Nittany Lion Shrine Loses Part of Ear." *The Daily Collegian*. 30 July 2003. <http://www.collegian.psu.edu/archive/2003/07/07-30-03tdc/07-30-03dnews-05.asp>.

Jorgensen, Laurel. "'Scared to Death' Ciryam Wins Comfortably for AVP: Votes for Freshman Easily Dominate Over No Confidence Option in Runoff." *The Daily Northwestern*. 18 April 2003. <http://www.dailynorthwestern.com/vnews/display.v/ART/2003/04/18/3ea005127050e?in_archive=1>.

Kagarise, Warren. "New Facility Has Aquarium, Bookstore." *The Independent Florida Alligator*. 5 August 2003. <http://www.alligator.org/edit/news/issues/stories/030805bookstore.html>.

Mueller, Taylor. "A Family Affair: Nothing Makes a Hot August Day a Little More Bearable Like Friends, Family and the Fayette Freeze-Off." *The Missourian*. 3 August 2003. <http://digmo.org/news/story.php?ID=3042>.

Nave, Sonya. "Auburn's Termite Expert Unveiled." *The Auburn Plainsman*. 20 March 2003. <http://www.theplainsman.com/vnews/display.v/ART/2003/03/20/3e79f41ab758b?in_archive=1>.

Schomer, Matthew. "Grab Your Epée and Go." *The Daily Kent Stater*. 30 July 2003. <http://www.stater.kent.edu/today/073003/grabyour.htm>.

Strong, Marie. "Technical Program Competes: Six Earn Top Honors at Statewide Level." *The Sentinel*. 6 May 2003. <http://www.nic.edu/sentinel/archives/vol56/issue10/news/09news.html>.

von Goethe, Johann Wolfgang. Michael Moncur, *The Quotations Page*. <http://www.quotationspage.com/>.

Wicklein, John. "Finding the Holes." *No Train, No Gain: Training for Newspaper Journalists*. http://www.notrain-nogain.org/train/res/edit/jw.asp.

# Chapter 13
# Story Structure

*Your manuscript is both good and
original, but the part that is good is
not original and the part that is
original is not good.*

—Samuel Johnson

## Chapter Contents

## *QuickView*

Structuring your stories moves in two directions in this chapter: pure narrative and frames. This will cover a lot of ground.

The first direction involves working with elements of storytelling and pure narrative in writing your news stories. The result is exciting storycrafting that will allow you to expand your options and your creativity.

Next, we will examine the 13 most popular frames—patterns used to organize news stories. Also, we will offer you guidance on how to pick a frame to suit your lead and then how to structure content for that frame.

Finally, we will cover connections you use to organize your stories: transitions, repetition of key words and phrases, use of pronoun references, use of parallel structure, dingbats and subheads.

Try not to let the amount of new material here overwhelm you. Pick up what you can on first reading; then, return to this chapter and re-examine the material you did not quite grasp the first time.

---

". . . [S]torytelling is an essential part of what makes us human." So writes Jack Lule in his "Daily News, Eternal Stories: The Mythological Role of Journalism." He continues: "We understand our lives and our world through story. Perhaps stories are so much a part of us because human life itself has the structure of story. Each of us has a central character. Each of us knows, better than we know anything, that life has a beginning, middle, and end. We *need* stories because we *are* stories. Stories will stop, it is clear, only when humanity stops."

While good storytellers relish opportunities to create enticing and crisp story beginnings, they often devote more of their efforts to presenting the rest of their stories in interesting, appropriate ways. As we know from Chapter 11, the lead not only opens a story but also directs how the rest of the story should be developed.

Storyteller-journalists today realize that it is one thing to hook readers with a provocative lead. It is quite another to hold on to them until the end of the story.

Alice M. Klement and Carolyn B. Matalene say recent studies suggest "readers want the most surprising or mind-bending or hunch-confirming information packaged so that it can be read easily—the biggest bang for the smallest buck." Importantly, they claim, "Gathering a bunch of facts and stuffing them into tired forms gets yawns." What has worked for decades, many journalists are finding, is not working today. Thus, our concern in this chapter is fashioning story content following the lead with a structure that works—for both the material and readers.

## Structuring the Story

By now you have had a number of opportunities to practice writing news stories. Some stories may have come more easily than others. Count yourself fortunate because "easy" is not a term that describes writing most of the time for most writers.

Some of your stories also may have been more effective than others. Whether or not they came easily, effective stories are those that succeed in a vital way: They present material clearly, completely, appropriately and interestingly to a particular audience.

As we discussed in Chapter 11, the first step in writing your draft usually is to craft the lead—the point of the story. Well-written leads focus readers' attention on what they can expect from the story; they also focus writers' attention on how to structure the story. Therefore, we take up here where Chapter 11 and Chapter 12 finished off.

With the lead in front of you, perhaps you sense that narrative will serve well to structure the story. The advantage of narrative is that it embodies the essential qualities of storytelling in its ability to capture reader interest in powerful, creative ways.

As we have discussed previously, though, you should not consider narrative for every news story. Some should be told using traditional journalistic formats. You have available a variety of options in frames, one of which should best suit both material and readers.

# Applying Elements of Storytelling to News

Storytellers deal with both fiction and nonfiction. Storyteller-journalists, though, must confine their attention *only* to nonfiction, that which is real, factual and relatively objective. While the source of material for storyteller-journalists may be different than that for storytellers of fiction, they share common tools in what we call the elements of storytelling.

These elements help form the foundation for our discussion on writing narrative, particularly pure narrative.

Certainly, drawing upon elements of storytelling does not mean journalists may abandon truth. Rather, the goal is to empower storytelling. Lule defends the relationship well: "Does embracing storytelling mean finally forsaking all attempts at accuracy and, much worse, accepting some fiction, some liberties with the facts for the sake of story? Not at all. Although storytelling is a subjective, creative exercise, news is not fiction and news is not false. News does not fail from a lack of objectivity. News fails from a lack of good storytelling."

It is no accident that memorable news stories may sound like excellent short stories or novels. Janet Burroway says, "Fiction tries to reproduce the emotional impact of experience." So do many news stories. She explains that the necessary features of good stories are conflict, crisis and resolution. Likewise, these features often comprise well-told news stories. Let us review each feature.

Most professionals agree that one or more of the following the conflicts comprise stories:

- Man against man.
- Man against nature.
- Man against machine.
- Man against God.
- Man against himself.

Understand, though, that this list is descriptive as opposed to prescriptive: It describes what stories do rather than what they *should* do. The experience of the story itself should determine the conflict at work.

Crisis follows conflict, Burroway says, at the point when the outcome is inevitable. Resolution finishes story action, with what she calls "walking away from the fight."

## Elements of Storytelling

The following are what most professionals consider the standard elements of storytelling:

- Character.
- Setting.
- Plot.
- Point of view.
- Dialogue.
- Theme.
- Style.

We can gain additional insight into storytelling if we relate these standard elements to their counterparts in journalism, namely, the five Ws, H and SW.

*Character* involves those who populate a story and take part in the action in some way. The protagonist is the main character, the one who primarily generates the plot of the story, with the opponent labeled the antagonist. In journalistic stories character relates to the *who*.

*Setting* is the story's time and place. Yet, location alone seldom is sufficient to determine setting. All those concrete details that comprise the reality of a story contribute to our understanding of setting. Setting is further influenced by background that provides a context for the story; knowing what else was happening just outside the story can help readers better understand the impact and meaning of what is happening inside the story. Most of this connects to the journalistic *when* and *where*.

*Plot* relates to the various events and situations that comprise the story, giving it meaning. While narrative is a series of events in chronological order, plot traces the chain of cause-effect of those events. Dynamic stories grow out of conflict, particularly conflict involving the protagonist. *What* is the main journalistic element that corresponds to plot; however, *why* and *how* are other journalists' questions that provide details of plot in storytelling. Hard news relies more on plot than does soft news, which often stresses character development.

*Point of view* in storytelling is determined by who the narrator is, who tells the story—the perspective from which the story is presented. It answers "who is standing where to share what with whom."

*Dialogue* reveals character and advances the plot. Hearing characters speak, whether in a novel or a news story, offers insight into who they are and how they relate to what is happening in the story.

*Theme* can be more difficult to determine in storytelling, since it seldom is specifically named. It is the pattern of meaning or concept we are left with once we are done reading. In fact, it answers the question, "What did I get out of this?" We can relate this to the *so what* of journalists' questions.

*Style* is the use of language in a story—all those conventions storytellers have at their disposal to make their telling personal, unique and effective. The short list of these includes sentence structure, phrasing, dialogue and word choice. Together they establish the voice of the story, who the narrator sounds like and what the narrator's attitude to the story seems to be. We will cover style in Chapter 14.

## Tracing Elements in a News Story

Remember that elements of storytelling are not unique to fiction, that they have place in news stories as well. Let us read the following excerpt of a character-based news story from Kentucky and then examine it for elements of storytelling.

### Running the show

By Paul Leightty

She throws a mean fastball. She's a competitive long-distance runner. She's been on the UK Dean's List since 1999, and she's active in community service throughout Lexington.

Now this year's homecoming queen is Student Government president, and she's ready to make something of her brief term in the office.

She is Mary Katherine Thompson, a corporate communication and political science senior from Owensboro. She was sworn in as SG president Feb. 26, after Tim Robinson resigned.

Her friends and family say she's active—almost too active.

"The one thing she needs to do more is chill out," said older brother Blake Thompson, an accounting senior at UK.

Thompson was elected vice president alongside Robinson and succeeded him by the rules of the SG constitution. Robinson resigned after dropping his classes and pleading guilty in court to interfering with voter registration.

"As far as student representation goes, Mary Katherine is the ideal president because she knows the most eclectic group of people," said Joe Ruschell, who replaced Thompson as vice president and was previously SG Senate chairman.

"She doesn't always have to have her hair done or make-up on. She's not afraid to get up and do a speech after she's run 15 miles.... She's totally down to earth," said biology senior Jordan Kathman, who is Thompson's second cousin and friend.

With five brothers and a large extended family, Thompson said she places high value on her family. Two brothers are also UK students, and three younger brothers back home in Owensboro.

Andrew Thompson, a biology freshman and next-youngest in the family, said his sister has consistently been there to watch out for him.

"When I first came into high school, it was her senior year and I wasn't very outgoing and she introduced me to everybody," he said. "By the second or third week of school, I had all the seniors saying 'hi' to me."

He said his sister was much the same when he started at UK.

Blake Thompson said it's always been difficult to live up to the standards that his sister has set—both on the baseball field and off.

"She does so well at most of the things she puts her hands on, it's hard being her brother, because parents expect the same out of everybody," he said.

He said he remembers once playing baseball with his sister and some of his friends, and his sister's pitching turned out to be too much of a challenge for the other players.

"A couple of them quit because they said she threw too hard," he said.

Mary Katherine Thompson, whose first role in SG was as at-large senator before becoming vice president, has worked in a variety of occupations.

She interned in the office of U.S. Sen. Jim Bunning last summer and was the College of Communication Ambassador in the 2001-02 school year. Last year she volunteered at Lansdowne Elementary, setting up a peer-mediation program and was a substitute teacher for Fayette County Schools.

As student leader at the Catholic Newman Center from 1999 to 2002, she headed a mission trip to Jamaica and was assistant Sunday School teacher. She has run in numerous marathons, including twice in the Chicago Marathon (26.2 miles), and placed first in her division in the Kentucky Derby Festival Mini-Marathon (13.1 miles).

"She called me after running the Chicago marathon and she was just crying because she was so excited and proud of herself," said Sarah Baltzley, a friend of Thompson's and agricultural biotechnology senior.

The Kentucky Kernel
The University of Kentucky

### Character

The protagonist is Mary Katherine Thompson, who is the new Student Government president following the resignation of another character, SG President Tim Robinson. Thompson is a "round" character, in that a wealth of details about her makes her quite identifiable; she has depth. The storyteller tells us up front a great deal about Thompson: She plays baseball, is a long-distance runner, has been on the Dean's List since 1999, provides community service, was homecoming queen this year and is a corporate communication and political science senior from Owensboro, Ky.

Other characters in this story are "flat," since we know little about any of them. These are news sources for the storyteller, people who know Thompson and whose comments provide insight into who she is. They are Blake Thompson, her brother; Joe Ruschell, the new SG vice president; Jordan Kathman, Thompson's cousin; Andrew Thompson, another of her brothers; and Sarah Baltzley, a friend of Thompson.

### Setting

The story takes place in Lexington, Ky., at the University of Kentucky during spring 2003. The context for the story, which further establishes setting, is that Mary Katherine Thompson became Student Government president with the resignation of SG President Tim Robinson who had dropped his classes after pleading guilty in court to interfering with voter registration.

### Plot

The plot is thin in this story because most conflict exists outside and prior to this story. It revolves around a vice president replacing a president, who has resigned. The new president is a senior with only a few months left to serve before graduation. The writer refers to the earlier conflict but does not develop it. However, some sibling tension seems apparent in the relationship between Thompson and her brother Blake.

### Point of View

The point of view is third person, though not altogether as objective, neutral and sterile as many news stories. The storyteller's choice of sources and the positive details shared from them reflects a narrator with a tone that is friendly, even supportive. This is typical of character-based, soft-news stories and personality profiles.

### Dialogue

The quotations in this story are exceptionally revealing, portraying a hardworking and hard-playing young woman.

### Theme

What does one get out of this? In other words what is the pattern of meaning in the story? What is the *so what*? We might say that the theme is one of winning. Thompson is accustomed to doing well, usually winning at all she does. She did not seek the office of Student Government president, but she did not shirk the responsibility, and even in the short time she will hold office, she is busy working for improvements.

### Style

This story tends to follow closely AP style and is otherwise informal, friendly and upbeat. The storyteller's voice is consistent with the point of view.

## Using Elements of Storytelling

Finding such parallels between storytelling and well-written news stories is valuable. It reveals that many effective journalists sense the roots common to the two genres. They capitalize on the elements of storytelling to make their news stories more powerful and compelling.

You can consider the elements as a way of *looking at* your material rather than a *specific arrangement* of it. They allow you to engage your material differently, and for those of you who already are familiar with writing fiction, this engagement can be liberating.

For example, you might employ these elements by selecting one and allowing it to dominate the story. A sensitivity to the element character in "Running the Show" is rewarded with material that portrays the nobleness of the young woman and the dynamic, even heroic, qualities she possesses.

However, were you to select the element setting, your concern would be with details that effectively and powerfully fixed the place—the *where* of the five Ws. That does not mean you ignore other details, but rather that you allow setting to control content. Everything else spins from it.

Likewise, emphasizing plot is equivalent to stressing the *what* of the story over the other choices available. Had "Running the show" emphasized plot, the storyteller would have relied more on details surrounding the former president, particularly events that forced him from office. Content would have zeroed in more on *what* happened and the *why* and *how* in the transition of power to the former vice president. Although the story certainly would have included key points about character, setting and theme, those would have been downplayed in favor of plot.

Finally, elements of storytelling may help you craft a variety of frames, which we will discuss later.

## *Writing Narrative*

Creative writers, as you know, employ elements of storytelling in short stories and novels, both of which are strong narrative forms. Likewise, you might consider using pure narrative, with the majority of your material following chronological or time order.

If you are uncomfortable with or unsure about writing pure narrative, a good place to start is using narrative in only parts of your stories—typically the several paragraphs that trace the account of some event in an action story, such as a dramatic rescue from a burning residence hall or a three-car pileup in front of the campus entrance. This kind of narrative often is termed narrative in the service of exposition—with its purpose to illustrate or explain a major point in the story.

Pure narrative, on the other hand, is the form that literary journalists and others have used successfully as a dominant organizing pattern, especially in magazine writing. Increasingly, newspaper journalists are following suit. Consider pure narrative when you cannot tell the story in a better way.

How do you go about writing pure narrative? First, the earlier you decide to write narrative—preferably in the material-gathering and interviewing stage—the better. This is vital because you must gather the right details and ask the right questions in order to present effective narrative. The material must flow smoothly and completely, detail by detail, usually in the order that it happened. Narrative is unforgiving of any holes in the action—details you do not have because you did not ask for them.

Next, forget the inverted pyramid. Do not write an article or a report. Tell a *story*.

Chip Scanlan of the Poynter Institute for Media Studies, a leading advocate for narrative journalism, writes, "Now articles have their place, but late at night your kid will never say, 'I can't sleep. Tell me an article.' No, they beg to be lulled into slumber or diverted from the terrors or boredom of the day's end by the story with its suspense and setting, its theme, that core of meaning that drives everything: its characters, its plot, its complications, its suspense and climax."

The following steps should move you in the right direction:

- Begin the story at the beginning is good advice, at least for your first draft.
- Concentrate on *showing*, not just *telling about*.
- Establish early the setting, the real place and the real context of the experience, but let action, reaction and interaction dominate most of the time.
- Introduce your characters, both the good guys and the bad guys, but not all at once. Do it naturally, bringing them onto your story's stage at the right moments. Describe them and show them in action, relating to one another.
- Let the conflict(s) unfold, revealing the friction that heats emotions and brings characters into confrontations with the experience and with one another.
- Take readers through the crisis, but do not overdo this moment. If the story is worth telling, let it tell itself here.
- If the experience has a resolution, present it. It is the end of the experience. It may be the end of your story, too.
- Once you have told the story, convert your lead to a nut graf and find a spot to drop it in. Better higher than lower in your story, but try not to interrupt the narrative flow too much.

During revision, which we will discuss in Chapter 15, you may wish to consider a new beginning. Pull to the top of the story a powerful moment or image to which you return at the end of the story. This "hook" is an effective device that helps to pull readers through the middle of the story and gives them a real sense of pleasure when they discover it again. The trick in making it work is to use effective transitions to connect the hook.

Alternatively, you may let readers meet your protagonist and then move naturally into the action, setting and conflict.

Flashbacks are another device to consider. Essentially, you insert an earlier moment into your narrative, allowing readers to see something that has bearing on the current experience. You must exercise care in transitioning into and out of the flashback.

One point bears repeating: While storytelling fiction and storytelling news share many common features, you must base the content of your news stories only on facts, not fiction.

## For Practice

13-1. Find five interesting news stories. Then, do the following:

a) Identify in each story the following elements of storytelling:
- Character.
- Setting.
- Plot.
- Point of view.
- Theme.
- Style.

b) Submit to your teacher photocopies of the stories and your answers.

## Frames

As you recall from Chapter 6, frames describe how writers package content in news stories. They are the alternatives to pure narrative that you should consider for story development.

Frames are no magic bullet for taking care of tough choices you face as a storyteller. All writers struggle, at least at times, with how they will organize their material for best results. And just knowing about these structures and seeing how others use them will not automatically make your writing stronger.

The following are the most commonly used frames identified in "Framing the News: The Triggers, Frames, and Messages in Newspaper Coverage," a recent Project for Excellence in Journalism study. It is not vital that you commit all these to memory. Rather, get a sense of the frames your professional colleagues are using for their stories. See how sample leads set the stage for development of each frame.

### Straight News Account

Primarily presents the five Ws and H.

### Arizona cities wait for OK on firework displays

By Sandy Yang

With wildfires burning across Arizona and drought conditions persisting, some cities are waiting until the last minute to decide whether to light the fuse on Fourth of July fireworks.

ASU Web Devil
Arizona State University

## Conflict Story

Stresses conflict that is inherent to the situation or is growing among participants.

### Guilford house debate heats up

**Head of Guilford Association will file suit against TU if events are held without resident**

By Mike Morris

An injunction will be issued to stop Towson University officials if they follow through with plans to entertain at Towson's $2 million Guilford mansion before a new president resides there, Guilford Association President Howard Friedel said Saturday.

The Towerlight Online
Towson University

## Consensus Story

Focuses primarily on the points of agreement in an issue or event.

### College Party offered prizes for votes

By Amber Brozek

"It's free" is a phrase many students tune their ears to, and when it came to the student elections last week, political campaigns held this motto high.

The Daily Nebraskan
University of Nebraska-Lincoln

## Conjecture Story

Concentrates on conjecture or speculation of what is to come.

### Perlman announces Phase II of budget cuts

By Ashley Cooper

When facing a lose-lose battle, one can skulk away in cowardice and pessimism. Or, one can fight with dignity and cognizance as University of Nebraska-Lincoln Chancellor Harvey Perlman has done to attack the university's budget shortfall.

Under much scrutiny for the initial budget reduction proposals he handed down March 10, Perlman initiated an "Unofficial Faculty Opinion Vote" on May 5 to gauge faculty support for his administration and its leadership during this climactic period. On May 15, Lancaster County Election Commissioner David J. Shively, announced an 89-percent vote in Perlman's favor.

Tuesday Perlman announced his second round of budget cut proposals, in what he said he hoped would be his last reductions meeting with the media.

The Daily Nebraskan
The University of Nebraska-Lincoln

## Process Story

Develops how to do something, how something is done or how something works.

### ODU personalizes student Web site access

By Ta'china Roig

Old Dominion is putting together a portal program to enhance communication throughout the campus.

A portal is a Web site that provides all the services its users might need in one convenient place. Any interaction that a member of the university community might have with the university can be handled entirely within the context of the portal. The university portal will be a single point of access to information and services for all with a legitimate need.

The portal is personalized to the specific needs and characteristics of the person visiting the site, using information from university databases and other sources.

Mace and Crown Online
Old Dominion University

## Historical Outlook

Places current event or situation into historical perspective.

### English classes show off writing skills

#### 850 students participate in annual event

By Ebony Caldwell

English 121 students transformed their English papers into visual aids at the 5th annual Celebration of Student Writing in the McKenny Union Ballroom yesterday.

More than 850 students created projects based on research work in their English 121 classes. Projects also came from English papers written earlier in the semester.

Eastern Echo Online
Eastern Michigan University

## Horse Race

Tells who is winning and who is losing.

### Election results upheld; McConnell reaffirmed president

By Brooklyn Noel

Jonathan McConnell was officially announced as the 2003–2004 SGA president after the SGA Board of Elections found that the contests brought by SGA Sen. Michael Joffrion and junior Adam White did not provide enough evidence to overturn the election.

The Auburn Plainsman
Auburn University

## Trend Story

Explains how the current news item fits an ongoing trend.

### Good nutrition lacking at EMU

#### Busy lifestyles make eating right hard

By Erin Medell

An incoherent grunt leaves your mouth as you stretch your dilapidated, cold sweat drenched body on the faded couch. Your stomach rumbles as you survey the beer-can littered floor for the nearest item of food, which happens to be a candy bar. The colorfully wrapped chocolate delight melts as it graces your tongue, yet your stomach feels sour.

Busy schedules, lots of pressure, and financial worries can leave college students feeling burnt-out, irritable, or just downright sleepy. Getting enough rest is a major part of feeling good, as most of us know, but another aspect many students overlook is that you are what you eat.

Eastern Echo Online
Eastern Michigan University

## Policy Explored

Presents policy and its impact.

### USUAA changes constitution, bylaws

#### Student government tackles problems

By Rosey Robards

Student government at the University of Alaska Anchorage is cleaning house in an effort to become more efficient. They recently approved several changes to their Constitution, including the addition of an activities committee.

The Northern Light
The University of Alaska-Anchorage

## Reaction Story

Stresses the reaction or response from one or more key figures.

### Called up

**N.C. State student Conrad Hayter had less than a week to prepare to go**

By Thushan Amarasiriwardena

Soon after finishing up his forestry class last Monday, N.C. State student Conrad Hayter received a call. It was his commander—Hayter was told to prepare to head overseas before the next week was out. And before he could let the emotions flood over him he had to start a series of actions that would allow him to leave his country, life and peace of mind behind while jumping into a world of uncertainty.

Technician
North Carolina State University

## Reality Check

Examines closely the truthfulness of a statement or information.

### Not all officers meet goals

By Rebekah Kleinman

ASUA members realize campaign promises can be difficult to keep
Last Thursday a new group of ASUA officers were inaugurated, bringing a fresh set of plans and ideas to the student government. But some incoming officers will be forced to pick up where their predecessors left off.

A year ago, as with every year, the Associated Students of the University of Arizona senators ran for office, each with campaigns offering promises to UA students, faculty and staff members.

Since last March, some of those promises have materialized, but others were left on the campaign platform.

The Arizona Daily Wildcat
The University of Arizona

## Wrongdoing Exposed

Uncovers injustice or criminal acts.

### Promise unfulfilled

By Mike Morris

Towson University President Dr. Mark L. Perkins resigned Friday after only 282 days on the job when the University System of Maryland Board of Regents issued him an ultimatum.

Regents told Perkins he had the option to either resign or they would seek his dismissal at a meeting this Friday, according to Perkins' letter to the campus community, distributed via e-mail to all faculty and students Monday morning.

The Board confronted Perkins during an emergency executive session Friday with findings of a recent audit showing $860,000 spent on renovations to his $850,000 Guilford mansion, bringing the total to more than $1.7 million.

The Towerlight Online
Towson University

## Personality Profile

Profiles a key news figure.

### In e-mail era, one professor sticks to letters and phone calls

**Professor Jonathan Strong bucks convention, relies on more old-fashioned methods**

By Julia Lifschultz

With the proliferation of electronic communication, what began as a quick way to communicate has become a way of life. However, there are the few and the proud who remain detached from the world of the Internet, content with—and longing for—the days when all communication was face-to-face.

The Tufts Daily
Tufts University

# Using Frames

Now that you have a range of options for development, reread your lead and try to determine where it wants to go, what it seems to want to do for readers. If you have done a good job drafting the lead, it should suggest how you might draft the body.

Like models for other creative activities—Hai Ku poetry, impressionist paintings, jazz saxophone pieces and even Michael Jordan jump shots—frames offer you models, none of which is as firmly structured as templates but all of which are clear enough to use as basic guides.

Ask the questions of your lead in the next section, and read carefully the advice on structuring the body of the story.

Next, review your interviewing notes and *listen* to what they tell you. Do they fulfill the promise of your lead, especially as you respond to questions? If they do, then you are in business. Proceed with drafting the rest of the story following the pattern suggested.

If your notes do *not* support your response to the following questions, then you may need to revise the lead or return to gathering material that will fit the lead's purpose.

## Matching a Frame to Your Lead

The following questions direct your attention to the lead and are followed by patterns you may consider to develop the body of the story.

*Did you settle comfortably with a summary lead that includes the most important of the five Ws, H and SW?*

You may be working with a *straight-news story*. Develop the body with remaining news elements, followed by supporting and expanding details and quoteworthy comments presented most to least important.

*Is the lead a paragraph or two clearly focused on a compelling conflict?*

You might wish to organize material as a *conflict story*. Move from the lead with explanation of the conflict. Develop all sides of the argument, often with one responding to comments of the other but with reasonably balanced evidence.

*Did you write a lead that suggests mostly widespread agreement on an important issue?*

A *consensus story* may be an appropriate structure. Full explanation of the issue being addressed might provide transition into the body. Follow with sufficient comments from sources who have a stake in the issue to make clear the dominant view, including a healthy number of quoteworthy comments.

*Is the lead particularly concerned with speculation about the outcome of some upcoming event or situation?*

A *conjecture story* might satisfy the goal of organizing your material. Summarize the issue to which the claim or speculation is addressed. Then, develop the rest of the story relying on comments from key source(s) that expand upon the claim and justify the position with evidence.

*Does your lead summarize key points about how to do something or how something is done?*

A good choice might be to present a *process story*. Early in the body explain key concepts or terms that might be unfamiliar to readers. Follow with step-by-step presentation of the points of the process, including explanations for how and why. Do not forget quoteworthy comments from stakeholders in the process.

*Did you write a lead that positions a current news event in relation to previous, similar or repeating events?*

Consider the *historical outlook story*. First, bridge the current event to the history of the event or similar events. Then, give expanded historical elements with reference to the current event at regular points or following.

*Is your lead focused on the winners and losers of a contest or election?*

Choosing to pattern your material as a *horse race story* may work well. Offer circumstances surrounding the status of each contender. Use supporting and explanatory material that covers first the victor, followed by the opponent(s). Quoteworthy comments from all parties, interspersed at appropriate points, are particularly important.

*Does your lead stress a current situation or event that reflects a trend?*

Not surprisingly, a *trend story* could be the answer to how to develop the story. Transitional material connects the current news item to the trend it fits. Finish the story with full details on the trend, which you then compare and contrast with additional details of the current event.

*Is a concern with policy—either current or proposed—the heart of your lead?*

You may find a *policy explored story* is the best format for your story. Expand the policy details, particularly considering new versus old, if applicable.

Next, expand the impact details, offering quoteworthy responses from both policy makers and those affected.

*Did you incorporate a provocative quote from the key source that you tagged to the circumstances surrounding a situation?*

You may wish to draft a *reaction story*. Complete details on the situation or event that has spawned the reaction can provide transition into the body. Additional reactions should allow the source(s) to do as much of the telling as possible with quoteworthy comments.

*Does your lead suggest to readers that the story will review a statement or information to see if it holds up under scrutiny?*

Your best option may be a *reality check story*. Consider following the lead with claim(s) made about the information or statement, particularly those contrary to the expected, relying as much as possible on quoteworthy comments. Include evidence supporting the claim(s).

*Is your lead concerned with revealing wrongdoing?*

A *wrongdoing exposed story* might allow you to develop effectively the supporting material. Early in the body present comments from the particulars in the case, especially the person alleged to have committed the injustice or criminal act. Follow those with additional supporting details concerning the wrongdoing and/or its consequences. Include other quoteworthy reactions from the public.

*Does your lead offer readers an appealing glimpse of an individual?*

You may find that *personality profile* is your method for structuring the story. Draft a nut graf, if necessary, that justifies the selection of this person for a profile. Follow that with generous, appropriate description of the person and comments by or about the person.

---

## For Practice

13-2. Review the front pages of four issues of your campus newspaper and do the following:

a) Read each story on the front pages.
b) Identify the frame used for *each*.
c) Select a single story of consequence, outline its content and identify what triggered the coverage.
d) Submit to your teacher photocopies of the front pages and your answers.

---

## *Making Connections*

When we write, our ideas typically are clear to *us*. We understand what we mean even if we do not present ideas well or connect them clearly. However, readers do not have the luxury of knowing all that we know in the same ways we know it.

It is important, therefore, that we help them by providing cues to show logical relationships between one idea and another, between one paragraph and another, even between one part of the story and another.

### Transitions

The most common cues are called transitions—words and phrases that serve as bridges between ideas. They alert readers to how they should handle information we give them. While transitions cannot cure poor organization of material, they certainly can make it easier for readers to relate the parts of a well-organized story.

As you use these, remember that overdoing transitions is almost as much a problem as ignoring them. Like a candy addict in a chocolate factory, you may be tempted to stick transitions everywhere. The solution is to use them *where you need them*. Pick a handful that seem comfortable and make sense to you. Use them where they seem to fit well in your writing. Then, try a few more until you provide enough connections to make relationships clear. It is not necessary to memorize this list, but you might refer to it regularly when you need just the right term to help make sense of your ideas.

The following are frequently used transitions, categorized according to the meaning or relationship they give to your writing.

- Addition: and, again, and then, besides, equally important, finally, first (second, etc.), further, furthermore, in addition, lastly, moreover, next, nor, too, what's more.
- Comparison/contrast: after all, although, but, by comparison, compared to, conversely, however, in spite of, meanwhile, nevertheless, nonetheless, notwithstanding, on the contrary, on the other hand, still, where, whereas, yet.
- Concession: granted, naturally, of course.
- Emphasis: absolutely, definitely, extremely, in any case, in fact, indeed, positively, naturally, surprisingly, always, certainly, emphatically, forever, never, obviously, undeniably, unquestionably, without a doubt, without reservation.
- Example: as an illustration, for example, for instance, in this case, in another case, on this occasion, to demonstrate, to illustrate.
- Exception: despite, however, in spite of, nevertheless, of course, once in a while, sometimes, still, yet.

- Proof: because, besides, evidently, for, for the same reason, furthermore, in addition, in any case, in fact, indeed, moreover, obviously, since, that is.
- Summary: accordingly, as a result, as I have said, as I have shown, consequently, hence, in brief, in conclusion, on the whole, therefore, thus, summing up, to conclude.
- Time: and then, finally, formerly, immediately, later, next, previously, soon, then, thereafter.
- Time sequence: after a while, afterward, again, also, and then, as long as, at last, at length, at that time, before, besides, earlier, eventually, finally, formerly, further, furthermore, in addition, in the first place, in the past, last, lately, meanwhile, moreover, next, now, presently, shortly, simultaneously, since, so far, soon, still, subsequently, then, thereafter, too, until, until now, when.

## Other Organizing Devices

Other devices for connecting ideas, paragraphs and sections include the following:

- Repeating key words and phrases.
- Using pronoun references.
- Using parallel structure.

The first, repeating key words and phrases, takes deft handling for it to work well and to avoid making your writing sound like first-grade sentence practice. Moreover, many of you have been urged to avoid redundancy in your writing. However, effective repetition is not redundant. So long as you do not overdo the repeated words or phrases, they can aid coherence by serving as clear and logical connections between sentences and paragraphs. For example, in the previous section on transitions, that word is used five times after the heading. Moreover, synonyms for transitions in that section include *cues*, *words and phrases*, *connections* and *term*.

Next, pronoun references work not only as a relief valve for feared over-repetition of key words and phrases but also as a legitimate alternative. The only caution is that you must be sure that readers can understand exactly what each pronoun refers to. For example, in the previous paragraph the two pronouns *it* and *they* are pronoun references that refer clearly to nouns that precede them, *repeating key words and phrases* and *repeated words or phrases*.

Third, the use of parallel structure is probably the trickiest of the three. This device depends upon your being able to identify related passages of material and then craft them in the same grammatical constructions. For example, in the bulleted list just shown, each of the items is a device for connecting material. The grammatical structure used to help signal this is the gerund phrase.

## Subheads and Dingbats

Two final options for making connections include the somewhat more mechanical and visual use of subheads and dingbats.

Subheads signal readers about the main ideas to be covered in the sections that follow them. They usually are reserved for longer stories, where they aid readers in understanding the major topics that comprise the piece. As a design feature they help to provide visual relief to blocks of gray text.

Subheads should be relatively short, are usually written in parallel structure and try to encompass equal chunks of material.

Dingbats are icons that often emphasize elements in lists. The most common is the bullet, preferred for most publications for its simplicity and efficiency at drawing attention—but not *too much* attention. Others include checkmarks, pointing hands, diamonds, blocks and arrows. Desktop publishing, in particular, has made available a mind-boggling array of dingbats, with entire font packages devoted to them. Nevertheless, the exact choice of dingbat is one usually reserved for editors and publishers, not individual writers. You would be wise, therefore, to stick with word processing bullets whenever you need to break out elements in lists.

An important concern when using dingbats is presentation of the material in the list. Write elements tightly and in parallel structure. In addition, consider presenting the full bulleted list first, followed by amplification of each item in the list.

---

## For Practice

13-3. Select three stories from your campus newspaper, clip them out or photocopy them. Then, do the following:

a) Underline each use of transitional words, repeated key words and phrases, pronoun references and parallel structure.
b) Number each underlined item.
c) On a separate sheet of paper write the numbers, list the underlined items and identify the kind of organizing device being used.
d) Submit the stories and sheets to your teacher.

---

## Crafting and Drafting

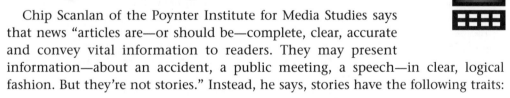

Chip Scanlan of the Poynter Institute for Media Studies says that news "articles are—or should be—complete, clear, accurate and convey vital information to readers. They may present information—about an accident, a public meeting, a speech—in clear, logical fashion. But they're not stories." Instead, he says, stories have the following traits:

- Feature characters rather than sources.
- Communicate experience through the five senses and a few others: a sense of people, sense of place, sense of time and, most important, sense of drama.
- Have a beginning that grabs a reader's attention.
- Have a middle that keeps the reader engaged.
- Have an ending that lingers in the reader's mind like the reverberations of a gong.

As you draft your story for Exercise 13-4, follow Scanlan's suggestions as closely as you can, blending those with recommendations from earlier in the chapter.

During peer review look for Scanlan's attributes in the stories you read and offer suggestions to writers on how they might include or improve each attribute.

---

## For Practice

13-4. Run your regular beat and find a topic for a story that you can develop as a narrative. Then, do the following:

a) Interview appropriate sources and take careful notes.
b) Listen carefully for quoteworthy comments the sources make, and write those down exactly.
c) Draft a story using a creative lead, nut graf and narrative development.
d) Swap stories with a peer review partner or group and give written reader feedback.
e) Submit the draft and peer feedback to your teacher.
f) After your teacher has reviewed your draft and peer feedback and has offered additional suggestions, revise as required.
g) Submit a final draft to your teacher.

---

## Chapter 13 Bibliography

Amarasiriwardena, Thushan. "Called Up: N.C. State Student Conrad Hayter Had Less than a Week to Prepare to Go." *The Technician*. 15 April 2003. <http://technicianonline.com/read/tol/news/007427.html>.

Brozek, Amber. "College Party Offered Prizes for Votes." *The Daily Nebraskan*. 14 March 2003. <http://www.dailynebraskan.com/vnews/display.v/ART/2003/03/14/3e716037dfd5b?in_archive=1>.

Burroway, Janet. *Writing Fiction: A Guide to Narrative Craft*. Boston: Little, Brown and Co., 1987.

Caldwell, Ebony. "English Classes Show Off Writing Skills: 850 Students Participate in Annual Event." *Eastern Echo*. 11 April 2003. <http://www.easternecho.com/archives/archives/2003_winter/2003_04/20030411/news/20030411/20030411_english.html>.

Cooper, Ashley. "Perlman Announces Phase II of Budget Cuts." *The Daily Nebraskan*. 22 June 2003. <http://www.dailynebraskan.com/vnews/display.v/ART/2003/06/22/3ef6467feac7a>.

"Framing the News: The Triggers, Frames, and Messages in Newspaper Coverage." Project for Excellence in Journalism. *Journalism.org*. <http://www.journalism.org/resources/research/reports/framing/frame.asp>.

Johnson, Samuel. Michael Moncur, *The Quotations Page*. <http://www.quotationspage.com/>.

Kleinman, Rebekah. "Not All Officers Meet Goals." *The Arizona Daily Wildcat*. 7 May 2003. <http://wildcat.arizona.edu/papers/96/149/01_1.html>.

Klement, Alice M., and Carolyn B. Matalene, eds. *Telling Stories: Taking Risks*. Belmont, Calif.: Wadsworth Publishing Co., 1998.

Leightty, Paul. "Running the Show." *The Kentucky Kernel*. 14 March 2003. <http://www.kykernel.com/dynakernel/story.php?id=384>.

Lifschultz, Julia. "In E-mail Era, One Professor Sticks to Letters and Phone Calls: Professor Jonathan Strong Bucks Convention, Relies on More Old-Fashioned Methods." *The Tufts Daily*. 18 May 2003. <http://www.tuftsdaily.com/articleDisplay.jsp?a_id=2109>.

Lule, Jack. *Daily News, Eternal Stories: The Mythological Role of Journalism*. New York: Guilford Press, 2001.

Medell, Erin. "Good Nutrition Lacking at EMU: Busy Lifestyles Make Eating Right Hard." *Eastern Echo*. 24 June 2003. <http://www.easternecho.com/news/20030624/20030624_junk.html>.

Morris, Mike. "Guilford House Debate Heats Up: Head of Guilford Association Will File Suit against TU if Events Are Held without Resident." *The Towerlight.* 9 September 2002. <http://www.thetowerlight. com/vnews/display.v/ART/2002/09/09/3d7be1c486e15>.

Morris, Mike. "Promise Unfulfilled." *The Towerlight.* 8 April 2002. <http://www.thetowerlight.com/vnews/ display.v/ART/2002/04/08/3cb1aa263015d>.

Noel, Brooklyn. "Election Results Upheld; McConnell Reaffirmed President." *The Auburn Plainsman.* 13 March 2003. <http://www.theplainsman.com/vnews/display.v/ART/2003/03/13/3e702d3e9b402?in_ archive=1>.

Robards, Rosey. "USUAA Changes Constitution, Bylaws: Student Government Tackles Problems." *The Northern Light.* 25 February 2003. <http://www.uaa.alaska.edu/light/news/news1(Feb25).html>.

Roig, Ta'china. "ODU Personalizes Student Web Site Access." *Mace and Crown.* 22 April 2003. <http://www.maceandcrown.com/php/story/article.phtml?story=969&section=n>.

Scanlan, Chip. "Narrative Journalism: Ride the River, Scan the Banks." *Poynteronline.* 11 December 2000. <http://www.poynter.org/content/content_view.asp?id=3746>.

Scanlan, Chip. "What Is 'Narrative,' Anyway? Part III: How We Tell Stories." *Poynteronline.* 15 October 2003. <http://www.poynter.org/content/content_view.asp?id=50255>.

Yang, Sandy. "Arizona Cities Wait for OK on Firework Displays." *ASU Web Devil.* 21 July 2003. <http://www.statepress.com/news/445650.html>.

# Chapter 14
# Story Style

*Say all you have to say in the fewest possible words, or your reader will be sure to skip them; and in the plainest possible words or he will certainly misunderstand them.*

—John Ruskin

## Chapter Contents

## *QuickView*

Style is a particular way that we do something. It is a powerful personal expression of who we are, tempered by our talents and creative energies. Our concern in this chapter, of course, is writing style.

We shall examine the following news writing styles: conventional, contemporary, AP, local newspaper and personal. These components of news style guide *how* you tell your stories. Given its scope and unfamiliarity for many inexperienced journalists, AP style probably is among the more challenging of the lot. Yet, using AP style is no more difficult than checking a dictionary or English handbook. You must remember to check it.

Even though much of journalistic style is restrictive, your choices as a writer still give you considerable creative control of your storytelling.

---

Style is an important matter in the 21st century lives of many people. Whether the style involves hair, music or writing, it is a distinctive reflection of individuals within larger communities.

Hairstyle, for example, often is categorized according to hair length, as well as color and curl. Many celebrities' hairstyles are their trademarks—the individual look they give their hair. For example, Gwyneth Paltrow is known for her long, sleek and smooth locks, while Halle Berry sports a short, spiky cut. Your own hairstyle says a good deal about who you are.

Much of what distinguishes the music of one rock group from another is their style, the sound they give their music. The British rock band The Yardbirds is a good example of innovative rock style. Many believe they redefined the role of the guitar in rock music, adding a bolder, heavier and more amplified electric bass; establishing the supremacy of the guitar; and creating a sound that was unique to classic rock of the 1960s. Similarly, the style of music you prefer reflects characteristics of who you are.

Writing style, like music, tends to be rather complex, categorized by types, or genres. Story content determines the specific message we deliver, and story structure shapes the organization of that message. Style, though, works with writing as a filter—like the proverbial rose-colored glasses—through which content and structure are presented. It shapes both, resulting in an exactness of what the writer believes and means.

Whether hair, music or writing, style involves our personal preferences. At times, we are willing to match the style of others—because of our respect for their status or because it suits our taste. At other times, we seek to establish our own look, sound or voice.

This chapter will encourage you to bring together in your own storytelling appropriate traditional, popular contemporary and personalized individual elements of style.

## Style Choices

As you begin working as a journalist today, you have more style options available in your storytelling than ever before. That is exciting. It also is a bit daunting.

The excitement is born of the myriad of choices, enabling you to choose style filters that best mold your story for its audience. However, having more choices can daunt some writers, making them unsure of exactly which filters might be most appropriate. This dilemma may be likened to your preference for a buffet menu for dinner versus eating just what Mom sets on the table in front of you.

If you find yourself in the latter group, take heart in knowing that practice and experience will reduce your anxiety, even though it will not eliminate it. Recall that even the best writers often wring their hands over exactly how to cast their messages.

Some styles are conventional, developed over time in the tradition of the genre. Others are contemporary, relatively new styles that meet the current needs of the genre and interests of particular audiences. And still other styles are the creative contributions of individual storytellers.

Style choices you make ultimately must fit the topic about which you are writing, the publication for which you are writing and the audience to whom you are writing.

# Conventional News Style

Throughout much of its history, the news story has been filtered by a style that tends to be conservative, straightforward and regimented. This conventional journalistic style emphasizes content that is objective and tightly focused on the basic news elements and that is structured using the summary lead and inverted pyramid.

## Objective Content and the Basic News Elements

The goal of objectivity is writer-neutral content; that is, content about which the writer takes no sides and reflects no personal feelings. Filtering content so that the journalist remains somewhat distanced from the people, events or issues involved is like the emergency room doctor who must remain detached from the drama as she struggles to save the life of a severely injured 3-year-old child. In both instances human nature may draw each to become emotionally involved, but professionalism demands that both retain an objective stance.

Many journalists believe that this lends greater credibility to the media role as watchdog.

Yet, you may find that objectivity is difficult. In fact, most journalists do. At those times, consider the following advice:

- When your human nature urges you to respond, take a moment to clearly identify your opinions and feelings, for once identified, they are easier to control.
- Present evidence and comments from all sides of controversial issues in an effort to maintain balance. Sometimes balance is as close as you may come to objectivity.
- Examine carefully your language to make sure that it is not "loaded" and does not convey an underlying bias. Word choices usually convey this, like the difference between *said* and *mumbled* or *police officer* and *pig*. Each of the pairs of words may carry the same denotation, or intended meaning, but each has quite different connotation, or associated feelings.

Conventional style also calls for content based on facts, especially facts supporting the basic news elements—who, what, when, where, why, how and so what. Material beyond the range of these elements may be irrelevant. This emphasis allows journalists to retain a carefully targeted focus. While it offers limited flexibility, it encourages faster reporting and easier writing, obvious benefits for journalists on deadline.

## Summary Lead and Inverted Pyramid Format

Structure shaped to fit the summary lead and inverted pyramid format is another attribute of conventional style. You should recall from Chapter 11 that the summary lead presents most, if not all, of the basic news elements at the top of the story, within the first paragraph or several. The most important of those elements opens the lead, with the others following in a comfortable and effective package.

The inverted pyramid, which we have covered in several chapters, organizes supporting details from most important to least. This style demands less of the creative impulse and more of judgment in weighing importance and using it to organize material.

This simple, well-defined structural style reduces the demand on writers to pick from a number of options, thereby speeding the process of writing the story. Readers also gain by engaging stories that follow familiar formats.

## Contemporary News Style

Contemporary journalistic style is largely the product of three movements spawned during the latter half of the 20$^{th}$ century—each of which is a reaction to what some believed were limitations of conventional news style.

Those movements were new journalism, literary journalism and public journalism.

New journalism, which began in the 1960s, capitalizes on the power of the narrative to deliver the news message. Its practitioners—Tom Wolfe, Hunter Thompson, Norman Mailer and Truman Capote, to name a few of the better known—tend to reject traditional news style in favor of a more literary presentation, one that offers a wider view of the world and our place in it.

This involves factual reporting using the sensory details, narrative structure and specialized insight of the novel. Particular tools these writers used were sound, plot, setting, feelings, direct quotations and imagery.

The movement away from traditional journalism continued with the advent of literary journalism in the 1970s. Literary journalism seeks to legitimize and expand the efforts of new journalism. According to Mark Kramer in the foreword to "Literary Journalism," practitioners "immerse themselves in subjects' worlds and in background research." They prefer writing about routine events in special ways that offer fresh insights. Style tends to be plain and spare, with literary journalists writing from disengaged positions. Their stories, Kramer writes, "mix primary narrative with tales and digressions to amplify and reframe events."

During the early 1990s media began experimenting with what came to be known as *public journalism.* This movement builds on the dynamics of new journalism and literary journalism but encourages media to do more than mirror the problems of their communities. Instead of reporting and then stepping back, media are encouraged to participate actively with citizens and community leaders in finding and implementing solutions to benefit all stakeholders in the community.

We will discuss public journalism more fully in Chapter 19.

The impact of these movements, of course, has been to reduce the supremacy of conventional style, what previously was touted as "the only way" to report and write news. Contemporary style respects objective content but encourages involvement, interpretation and creativity. Structure tends to be more open, with freedom to choose either summary or creative leads and inverted pyramid or narrative development.

As a result of these attempts to redefine and to expand the role of journalism, much of the storytelling that journalists do today is a blend of conventional and contemporary styles. This gives journalists a wider range of options to tailor stories for particular content and specific audiences.

## Responsive Content

Content shaped by contemporary news style is interactive and proactive. Journalists are much more concerned with what interests their readers, they are more involved with the world around them and they are more sensitive to the human condition that comprises the stories they report.

As a result, content tends to be multi-faceted. Factual reporting is important, but the writer-neutral stance of conventional journalism is replaced by a writer-responsive stance. More than ever, the various stakeholders of the community—including but no longer limited to the journalist—shape content.

Content includes traditional news elements. It also includes more of the human element, both in how journalists engage their sources and in what they tell their readers. This layer of material, which gives literary dimension to contemporary storytelling, is supported by the elements of storytelling we discussed in Chapter 13.

Contemporary style, therefore, shapes stories that are better rounded, that tend to have greater depth and that appeal to the preferences of many modern readers.

## Content-Specific Structures

Given the flexibility that journalists have in determining content for their stories, it should be no surprise that contemporary leads and structure necessarily are tied to it. The summary lead shares the stage with creative leads, while story structure is more a matter of what works best to deliver the message.

Content is the force that drives lead choices today, as we learned in Chapter 11. While the summary lead is still popular and appropriate for many stories, it increasingly gives way to creative leads.

Our discussion of frames in Chapter 13 showed that journalists today take full advantage of their newfound freedom, with a recent study of newspaper front pages identifying 13 frames comprising the lion's share of story approaches.

A close examination of those frames reveals that content also is the chief factor in structural choices that journalists make. With the study revealing that only one in six stories today uses the straight news frame—with its emphasis on summary lead and inverted pyramid, its dominance has diminished considerably.

## *Other Style Matters*

Common to both conventional and contemporary styles are a number of other matters, including the following:

- Short words, sentences and paragraphs.
- Simple, declarative sentences.
- Powerful verbs.
- Active voice.

We know from Chapter 12 that news style privileges short words, sentences and paragraphs. This tradition of the genre stresses economy in word usage and sentence structure that might best be described as terse, crisp, direct and focused. Short words, sentences and paragraphs are considered vital for speed and ease of reading.

Do not confuse this emphasis on short with abrupt, telegraphic or abbreviated. The goal is using the fewest words and the simplest structures to deliver the message effectively and efficiently and to make the point clear.

Simple, declarative sentences also support this preference for short. More importantly, they do a good job presenting ideas clearly because writers tend to do a better job maintaining sentence control. Too often, sentences that are complex muddle the point we try to make. Readers are primary beneficiaries of simple, declarative sentences, which allow them to comprehend meaning more quickly and easily.

Inexperienced writers try to rely on nouns and a flurry of adjectives and adverbs to enliven their writing. While these are necessary to complete meaning, use only those you need. The real power in sentences should rest in their verbs. Verbs are the muscles of language, and they are crucial to excellent writing.

Finally, prefer active voice to passive, serving both an economy of wording and a more natural order of presenting ideas.

## *Overview of Associated Press Style*

Published style guides, the most popular of which is the The Associated Press Stylebook and Briefing on Media Law, are the next component of the journalistic style you should use in your writing. These guides standardize how journalists make writing decisions about everything from abbreviations and capitalization to spelling and punctuation.

While some term the AP Stylebook the journalist's bible, it might better be compared with a usage handbook or specialized dictionary. And that is the best way to use it. With more than 5,000 entries, few journalists know all that the stylebook contains.

The secret to using AP style is knowing when and how to refer to it. The following axiom will help you in this regard: If something in your writing might be presented in more than one way, do not guess. Check the stylebook. The most common reason that journalists make AP style errors is that they prefer to guess rather than check.

How you should use it is rather simple. Of the eight major sections of the stylebook, you will deal primarily with only the first, the "Stylebook" section. Under it are the following seven headings:

- Key.
- An A to Z listing of guides to capitalization, abbreviation, spelling, numerals and usage.
- Internet guidelines.
- Sports guidelines and style.
- Business guidelines and style.
- A Guide to Punctuation.
- Bibliography.

The Key explains how to interpret the entries. This is handy reading for first-time stylebook users.

Once you are acquainted with that, the most frequent section you will use is the A to Z listing. The stylebook's Guide to Punctuation is excellent, making it a close second in frequency of use. Next likely would be the Internet guidelines.

You will use the sports and business sections only if your story deals with one of those topics.

The following sections present some of the more common AP style guidelines that you will use covering your campus community. For convenience these are organized by category versus the alphabetical format in the stylebook. For complete listings, of course, refer to the AP Stylebook.

## Abbreviations

academic degrees: Do not abbreviate. Instead, write as bachelor's degree, master's degree, doctorate, and include the discipline of the degree, if appropriate: *master's in psychology, doctorate in English.*

addresses: Abbreviate Ave., Blvd. and St. only with numbered addresses. Spell out all other similar words. Abbreviate compass points only with numbered addresses: *4 Winchester Court, 2618 N. Main St.* but *North Main Street.*

months: Abbreviate months with six or more letters when they are used with a specific date: *Aug. 10* and *Aug. 10, 2003* or *June 10* and *June 10, 2003.*

organizations: Abbreviate only after the full name has been used in the story: *grade point average* and *GPA* on second reference. Exceptions may be those abbreviations and acronyms by which organizations are better known: *CIA, FBI, YMCA.*

state names: Abbreviate using upper- and lowercase and set off with commas when used with a city, town or village all but the following eight state names: Alaska, Hawaii, Idaho, Iowa, Maine, Ohio, Texas and Utah. Use the following forms, about half of which vary from ZIP code abbreviations: *Ala., Ariz., Ark., Calif., Colo., Conn., Del., Fla., Ga., Ill., Ind., Kan., Ky., La., Md., Mass., Mich., Minn., Miss., Mo., Mont., Neb., Nev., N.C., N.H., N.J., N.M., N.Y., N.D., Okla., Ore., Pa., R.I., S.C., S.D., Tenn., Vt., Va., Wash., W.Va., Wis., Wyo.*

titles: Abbreviate the following when used before full names, except in direct quotations: *Dr., Gov., Lt. Gov., Mr., Mrs., Rep., the Rev., Sen.*

United States: Write out as a noun but lowercase with periods and no space as an adjective: *She enjoyed her visit to the United States. He is an avid collector of U.S. coins.*

## Capitalization

Congress: Capitalize *U.S. Congress* and *Congress* when referring to that body.

Constitution: Capitalize with or without the *U.S.* in all references to the *U.S. Constitution.* Capitalize only with the name of a state or nation in all other uses. Lowercase in all uses *constitutional.*

department: Lowercase names of academic departments, except for proper nouns and adjectives: *history department, department of history, English department, department of English.* Capitalize the formal names of government departments, including those where the title is flopped and the *of* is dropped: Department *of Agriculture, Agriculture Department.* Lowercase when used as a modifier for academic titles: *department Chairman Matthew Gilmour.*

directions, regions: Lowercase compass directions: *north, south, east, west, southern Missouri, eastern Idaho.* Capitalize specific geographic regions: *The North defeated the South in the Civil War. Flannery O'Connor is a Southern writer. He spent time in the Midwest before traveling south. Courageous pioneers settled the West. The wind was blowing west across South St. Paul.*

historical periods and events: Capitalize names of accepted epochs in archaeology, geology and history: *the Bronze Age, the Dark Ages, the Middle Ages.* Also capitalize popular periods and events: *the Exodus* (referring to the Jewish departure from Egypt), *the Renaissance, the Boston Tea Party, Prohibition, the Great Depression.* Lowercase century: *the 21$^{st}$ century.*

french fries.

ice age: Lowercase because it does not refer to a single period.

Indians: Preferred term for those in the United States is *American Indian*, but try to specify the name of the tribe: *Her father is a Cherokee chief.*

Internet.

legislature: Capitalize when preceded by a state name. Retain capitalization when the reference is to a particular state legislature: *The Missouri Legislature overrode the governor's veto.* Lowercase generic and plural uses.

plurals: In all plural uses lowercase common noun elements: *Democratic and Republican parties, Massachusetts and Pennsylvania avenues, the departments of Labor and Justice.*

political parties: Capitalize both the name and the word *party* when commonly used as part of the organization's name: *the Democratic Party, the Republican Party.* Capitalize the following, and similar, when they refer to a specific party or its members: *Communist, Conservative, Democrat, Liberal, Republican, Socialist.* Lowercase political philosophies, such as *communism, communist, fascism, fascist.*

room: Capitalize when used with the number of the room: *Room 222, Popplewell Hall.*

seasons: Lowercase fall, winter, spring and summer unless part of a formal name: *Winter Olympics.*

Web, Web site, Web page, but webcast and webmaster.

## Numerals

General guidelines: Write out numbers less than 10, but use figures with the following common exceptions:

- addresses: *4 Winchester Court.*
- ages of people, places and things: *His son will be 8 next month. The 4-year-old building was destroyed. My shoes were only 9 years old.*
- cents: *6 cents.*
- dollars: *$2.*
- dates: *Aug. 7.*
- dimensions: *5 feet tall, 5-by-7 photograph.*
- highways: *U.S. Route 1.*
- percentages: *2 percent, 8.4 percent.*
- proportions: *1 part water and 6 parts dye.*
- scores: *The Royals beat the Yankees 9-6. Arnold Palmer shot a 4 on the first hole.*

- speed: *3 miles per hour.*
- temperature: *8 degrees.*
- times: *6 a.m.*

Write out numbers at the beginning of a sentence, except for years: *Two hundred dollars was the average price for those shoes. 1963 was the year President John F. Kennedy was assassinated.*

fractions: Spell out amounts less than 1, and use hyphens between the words: *one-half, seven-eighths.*

millions, billions: Generally use figures and the terms *million* or *billion* and decimals rather than writing out all figures in large numbers: *1 million, 3.7 billion.*

## Punctuation

The Guide to Punctuation is clearly written and offers helpful examples. The following entries deal primarily with those matters that relate to AP style as opposed to standard usage. For additional guidance check the entry for each type of punctuation in the stylebook. Remember the earlier advice: Most errors occur because the writer did not check the stylebook.

### Apostrophe

decades: Do *not* use an apostrophe for decades: *She was in her 30s. The Great Depression spanned much of the 1930s.*

descriptive phrases: Do not use the apostrophe for words ending in *s* if the meaning is primarily descriptive: *citizens band radio, Kansas City Royals catcher, a writers handbook.* The stylebook offers a memory aid for this kind of usage: If you can recast the phrase and it makes sense using *for* or *by*, it qualifies: *a radio band for citizens, the catcher for the Kansas City Royals, a handbook for writers.*

omitted figures: *The winning football team of '03, the '60s, the Spirit of '76.*

plural of single letters: *His report card had all A's. He has trouble pronouncing his r's.*

rock 'n' roll: Uses two apostrophes.

special expressions: These are exceptions to the general rule for words ending in *s* and followed by a word beginning with *s*: *for appearance' sake, for conscience' sake, for goodness' sake.*

### Colon

Use a colon to introduce lists, texts and so on only if the material before the colon is a complete sentence: *Go to the store and get the following: bananas, eggs and milk. Go to the store and get bananas, eggs and milk.*

Capitalize the word following a colon only if it is a proper noun or the beginning of a complete sentence: *Remember the earlier advice: Most errors occur because the writer did not check the stylebook. Do not forget what to check to avoid errors: the stylebook.*

### Comma

For elements in a series do *not* use a comma before the conjunctions *and* and *or*: *He was pouting, she was upset and neither was satisfied. The recipe called for two eggs, a cup of milk and one-half cup of flour.*

Use a comma to separate adjectives equal in rank if the comma could be replaced by *and* without changing the original meaning: *It was a dark, stormy night. Her long, flowing hair spilled across the pillow.*

Use commas to set off the short form of political party affiliations as follows: *Sen. Kit Bond, R-Mo., was governor of Missouri before being elected to the Senate.*

Use commas to set off the state when it follows a city, town or village: *St. Joseph, Mo., is the home of the Pony Express.*

junior, senior: Abbreviate following a name but do not set off with commas: *John Smith Jr.*

incorporated: Abbreviate following a company name but do not set off with a comma: *Acme Widgets Inc.*

### Hyphen

Use figures and a hyphen for betting odds: *His chances of passing the class were 1000-1. She bet on the horse despite the 25-1 odds.*

### Parentheses

The stylebook discourages use of parentheses. Use commas or dashes instead. Parentheses, however, are acceptable when inserting material in a proper name: *St. Joseph (Mo.) News-Press.*

## Titles

Composition titles: Apply the following guidelines to titles of books, computer games, lectures and speeches, movies, operas, plays, poems, songs, television programs and works of art:

- Capitalize main words, including prepositions and conjunctions of four or more letters: *"The Sound and the Fury," "Doom," "The Gettysburg Address," "To Kill a Mockingbird," "The Marriage of Figaro," "This Property Is Condemned," "The Raven," "America the Beautiful," "Gunsmoke," "Perseverance."*
- Capitalize articles *a, an* and *the* as well as words of fewer than four letters when they are first or last words of a title.
- Use quotation marks around titles listed previously except for the Bible and books that are primarily catalogs of reference material, including almanacs, directories, dictionaries, encyclopedias, gazetteers and handbooks: *The Farmers Almanac, Webster's New World College Dictionary, World Book Encyclopedia.*

courtesy titles: Do not use courtesy titles *(Mr., Mrs., Ms., Miss)* except in direct quotations or where they are needed on second reference to distinguish between a man and woman with the same last names. However, remember that alternate local publication style may prevail.

formal titles: Capitalize before a full name on first reference but lowercase and set off with commas following a name. Preference is for long titles to follow names: *college President James Scanlan* or *James Scanlan, president of Missouri Western State College.*

generic or occupational titles: Most are not capitalized even if used before names, but consult the stylebook for particular examples: *attorney William French, music teacher Janet Thompson, store manager Cynthia Blake.*

military titles: Capitalize military ranks used as formal titles before full names on first reference. On second reference use last name only. The stylebook entry gives an extensive listing of preferred abbreviations for military ranks. Also, follow this style for firefighters and police officers, preceding the rank with lowercased *police* or *fire*, if needed for clarity.

names: On first reference use a person's full name, including the middle initial. On second reference use only the last name.

religious titles: On first reference precede the full name with *the Rev.* Use last name only on second reference.

## Usage

annual: Do not describe an event as annual until it has been held at least two successive years. Instead of first annual, write that organizers plan to hold the event annually.

boy: applicable until the 18th birthday, after which *young man* or *man* is used.

contractions: The stylebook seems to discourage their use. However, it also says that a number of contractions are included in the Webster's New World College Dictionary, and anything in the dictionary is generally acceptable.

daylong, weeklong, yearlong, lifelong: All of these and similar are one word.

dictionary: Use the most recent edition of Webster's New World College Dictionary for spelling, style and usage questions not answered by the stylebook.

differ from, differ with: It is *differ from* if you mean to be *unlike*. It is *differ with* if you mean to *disagree.*

drunk, drunken: The adjective *drunk* is used after a form of the verb *to be: She certainly was drunk last night.* The adjective *drunken* is used before nouns: *drunken driving, drunken slumber.*

e-mail, Web site: The term *e-mail*, with a lowercase *e* and a hyphen, and *Web site*, as two words, are exceptions to Webster's.

entitled, titled: *Entitled* means one has the right to do or have something: *He was entitled to receive a refund when he withdrew from classes.* Use *titled* to refer to a composition title: *My favorite book is titled "To Kill a Mockingbird."*

fewer, less: Use *fewer* for individual items and *less* for bulk or quantity: *She had fewer than 50 pairs of shoes. She had less than $10 in her purse.*

getaway.

get-together.

girl: Preferred until the 18th birthday, after which *young woman* or *woman* is used.

headlong.

head-on: Use for both noun and adjective forms.

holidays and holy days: Capitalize these.

homemade.

home page: Two words.

hometown.

hooky.

hopefully: Means in a hopeful manner. Do not use to mean it is hoped, let us hope or we hope.

host: Do not use as a verb.

identification: Identify every person in your stories with at least three elements: full name, including middle initial; age; and home address. Profession or occupation also is a valuable identifier.

irregardless: Term is a double negative. Use *regardless*.

jeep, Jeep: Lowercase the military vehicle, but capitalize the civilian reference.

Jell-O: The generic *gelatin* is preferred unless context calls for the trademarked name.

Jet Ski: The generic *personal watercraft* is preferred unless context calls for the trade-marked name.

judgment: Not *judgement*.

kids: The term *children* is preferred.

Kleenex: The generic *facial tissue* is preferred unless context calls for the trade-marked name.

Kmart: No hyphen and no space.

lady: Do not use as synonym for *woman*.

Medal of Honor: The nation's highest military honor awarded by Congress. There is no Congressional Medal of Honor.

more than, over: Use *over* for spatial relationships: *The balloon floated over the crowd.* However, *more than* usually is preferred for number references: *I spent more than $50 on that dinner.*

nicknames: Use a person's nickname instead of the given name if the person prefers: *former President Jimmy Carter.* Otherwise, insert the name surrounded by quotation marks: *William A. "Crazy Legs" Johnson.*

OK, OK'd, OK'ing, OKs: Do not use the term *okay* or its derivatives.

percent: One word.

professor: Lowercase in front of a name. Do not abbreviate.

Time references: While common sense and clarity are the chief guides, the style-book provides a sizable number of entries dealing with time:

- Use *today, this afternoon, tonight* and so on in stories for afternoon publications.
- Use *today* when an exact day is not intended: *Americans today are more overweight than ever.*
- Use the day of the week for references one week before or after the date of publication. For dates beyond that range use only the month and a figure. Never give both day and date.
- Use figures for times, a colon to separate hours from minutes with *a.m.* or *p.m.*, as appropriate: *8:30 a.m., 5 p.m.* The only exceptions are noon and midnight, which are preferred for clarity. Never use *:00* for the top of an hour. Because they are redundant, avoid references such as *11 a.m. this morning* or *tonight at 7 p.m.*
- Do not use *next* or *last;* instead, the past or future verb tense will indicate which day or month is intended: *She was arrested on Monday. He will run for mayor in April.*
- Generally, position time elements near the main verb, but the best test is to listen to your sentence and move the time element where it is clear and sounds best.

TV: Use capitalized without periods or space as an adjective, as in *TV program guide* or with standard constructions, such as *cable TV*. Otherwise, use *television*.

## For Practice

14-1. Pick a story you previously wrote and submitted for a grade. Then, using a pencil, do the following:

a) Print a new copy of the story.
b) Examine the story carefully for its adherence to AP style, and circle each style error.
c) In the space above the circled error, write the correction.
d) In the right margin write the page number from the stylebook where you found the answer.
e) Submit to your teacher.

14-2. Find a copy of your campus newspaper that you can mark and do the following:

a) Scan every story carefully to locate any style errors.
b) Underline and number each.
c) On separate paper write the number of the error, the error, the correction and the page number from the stylebook where you found the answer.
d) Submit to your teacher the marked newspaper and your correction sheet.

## Quotation Style

The material you gather from your sources comprises much of your storytelling. This borrowed material, whether quoted directly or indirectly, requires speech tags for attribution, punctuation and appropriate structures.

We first reviewed quotations in Chapter 3 and Chapter 8. We will take a few moments here to reconsider each of these.

### Using Speech Tags

Speech tags give the source and an appropriate verb for information you use from human, print, online and other sources—whether you quote the material directly or indirectly.

First, make clear to readers from whom or what the information comes. Usually, of course, that involves giving the full name of the source, especially on first reference. After that, you might mix use of the last name with clear pronoun references and generic nouns to avoid tedious repetition. Note this usage in the following example:

> "Angela Robertson will make a fantastic student government president," sophomore Willy Gruder said.
>
> She is best qualified, has worked hardest and has the best ideas of any candidate, he added.
>
> The political science major said that Robertson knows what she is talking about and deserves a chance to prove it.

Second, pick your speech tag verb with care. While hundreds may be available, you are wiser to use a form of the verb *to say*. *Said* and its various tense formats are short, clear and neutral. Readers tend not to notice its use even when repeated. Occasionally, if context allows, you might use other verbs, yet take care that those verbs do not reflect biases you may have about the speaker or the message content. See the following illustration:

> Gruder ballyhooed Robertson's previous contributions to student government.

The verb *to ballyhoo* means to promote an issue in a boisterous way. While that verb is colorful, it also is subjective and carries negative connotation. Replace it with a neutral alternative, such as *pointed to* or *stressed*.

Third, prefer speaker-plus-verb order, as in the examples earlier. It is natural and, consequently, clearer to readers than the verb followed by the speaker.

Fourth, use no more than one tag per paragraph. Any more is superfluous.

Fifth, prefer presenting the quotation first, followed by the speech tag. An exception to this is when you are shifting from one speaker to another. Open the material from the second speaker with a tag to avoid any confusion that the source is the first speaker.

Finally, always begin a new paragraph for a different speaker.

## Punctuating Quotations

Quotation marks for direct quotations, commas and occasionally colons are the three punctuation marks you will use.

Open and close direct quotations with quotation marks. The only tricky part here is where to position other punctuation with the closing quotation mark. The rule is that commas and periods *always* go inside closing quotation marks. Dashes, colons, semicolons, question marks and exclamation points go inside when they belong to or apply only to the quoted matter; otherwise, they go outside closing quotation marks.

Commas are used to connect speech tags to direct quotations. For paraphrases use commas only when speech tags follow the paraphrased material. No punctuation is used when tags precede paraphrases. Finally, you may use a colon to join a speech tag that introduces a long direct quotation. The following examples show these rules at work:

> Another Robertson supporter, Kae Enright, said, "I have known Angela for the past three years, and nobody is a better choice for president."
>
> Robertson is a member of her sorority and both are biology majors, Enright said. They first met when Phi Mu Sorority held a get-acquainted party during the fall of their freshman year.
>
> She believes a majority of students will agree that Robertson will be responsive to their needs.
>
> However, not everyone agrees with Gruder and Enright. Bob Berger, a member of Lambda Chi Alpha, is one.
>
> "She would ruin everything!" the junior accounting major said. His claim is based on Robertson's campaign platform in which she proposes to change rules for student government financial support of campus events.
>
> Getting funding for longtime events sponsored by student organizations will become next to impossible, Berger said.
>
> "If she is elected, I can't begin to imagine the damage she will do," he said.

## Structuring Quotations

You have three patterns for structuring both direct and indirect quotations: Tag last, tag first and tag middle.

Prefer the tag-last format in most instances, as noted earlier. This puts the quoted material into first position, where it properly receives most emphasis.

Use the tag-first format when shifting to a new speaker or source. Moreover, it has value in providing some occasional variety to the tag-last format. Also, it may simply sound better for some indirect quotations.

The tag-middle format works well with multi-sentence paragraphs of quoted material. There, it still privileges the beginning quoted material but also serves as transition to the remaining quoted material. Tag-middle also is acceptable for a single-sentence passage, but you must insert the tag carefully to avoid awkward phrasing, as in the following example of weak structure:

"Clubs and organizations," Berger said, "can't afford to elect Robertson."

See how each of the following variations reflect these patterns. While these examples are direct quotations, paraphrases follow the same patterns.

"Clubs and organizations can't afford to elect Robertson," Berger said.

Berger said, "Clubs and organizations can't afford to elect Robertson." "Clubs and organizations can't afford to elect Robertson," Berger said. "It is already tough just breaking even when sponsoring events. Her proposal will kill campus events."

## For Practice

14-3. Pick a story you wrote and submitted for a grade (though not the one you used in Exercise 14-1). Then, do the following:

a) Print out a new copy of the story.
b) Review carefully your quoted material and check each passage for speech tag usage, quotation punctuation and quotation structure.
c) In the space above each passage of weak, awkward or incorrect quotation style, write an improved or corrected version.
d) If the changes become too cumbersome to pencil in to your hard copy, underline each and then open the word processing file and keyboard the changes there.
e) Submit to your teacher the original story and, if applicable, the improved/corrected version.

## Local Publication Style

Most mass media follow AP style, yet many also have a local style that overrides AP style or goes beyond it.

This is certainly true of commercial newspapers. Some local newspapers have developed and maintain extensive local stylebooks. The San Antonio (Texas) Express-News has its Cyber-Stylebook online at <http://www.mysa.com/extras/style/>.

According to the newspaper's Web site, the Cyber-Stylebook is designed for both its staff and its readers: "Although most newspaper stylebooks confine themselves to the use of words in certain contexts, the Express-News book goes beyond this. In addition to serving as a guide for reporters and editors to use during the production of each day's Express-News, it's written to quickly educate newcomers to San Antonio on some of the baffling array of places and terms they encounter. For long-time residents and Alamo City natives, it's full of handy reminders."

Other newspapers depart from AP style on only a few obvious items. For example, AP style over the years has dropped the use of the courtesy titles Mr., Mrs., and Ms. for news stories. However, some local newspapers, like the St. Joseph (Mo.) News-Press, have adopted the opposite approach—using all of these courtesy titles on second reference, as appropriate. Other newspapers still use these courtesy titles in obituaries. The campus press increasingly are establishing local style and producing their own stylebooks. Many are combined with staff policy and training materials.

The bottom line is that style is a matter of preference. If local newspapers disagree with the style that the Associated Press has established, they have the prerogative to change it to meet their preferences.

## Personal Style

As we have learned in this chapter, journalistic style is extensive and can be demanding.

Conventional news style calls you to craft objective, fact-based content that develops the five Ws, H and SW using summary leads and inverted pyramid. Contemporary news style pushes you to be reader focused and writer responsive. Content shapes the structure of your stories, allowing you the choice of either summary or creative leads and whatever development works best.

Your writing should use short words, sentences and paragraphs; simple, declarative sentences; powerful verbs; and active voice.

Moreover, you have the burden of AP style, quotation style and local style to follow. You may wonder if there is any room for *you* among all those rules and requirements.

Fortunately, you still control what your stories say and how they say it. Outside of these guidelines, word choices are abundant. Sentence, paragraph and story structure leaves you with the opportunity to write stories that reflect the unique person you are. And content choices are boundless.

All creative endeavors begin with common tools and a range of limitations. It is left for the individual artist to work with those tools and under the same restrictions in order to create.

Practice your craft. Polish your results. Leave your mark.

---

## Crafting and Drafting

You should examine closely your style for the story in Exercise 14-4. Keep a detailed style log of each time you make a decision in your story concerning style that we have reviewed in this chapter, particularly the following:

- Word, sentence and paragraph length.
- Simple, declarative sentences.
- Powerful verbs.
- Active voice.
- Associated Press style.
- Quotation style.
- Local publication style.

## For Practice

14-4. Run your regular beat and find the best topic for a story. Then, do the following:

a) Interview appropriate sources and take careful notes.
b) Listen carefully for quoteworthy comments the sources make, and write those down exactly.
c) Draft a story using the lead and development that best suits the topic and audience.
d) Swap stories and *style logs* with a peer review partner or group and give written reader feedback
e) Submit the draft, style log and peer feedback to your teacher.
f) After your teacher has reviewed your draft and peer feedback and has offered additional suggestions, revise as required—especially any additional style concerns that your teacher has noted.
g) Submit a final draft to your teacher.

## Chapter 14 Bibliography

"Cyber-Stylebook: 2003 Edition." *San Antonio Express-News*. <http://www.mysa.com/extras/style/>.

Kramer, Mark. "Breakable Rules for Literary Journalists." Foreword to *Literary Journalism: A New Collection of the Best American Nonfiction*. New York: Ballantine Books, 1995.
<http://www.bu.edu/mkramer/litjourn.html>.

Ruskin, John. Michael Moncur, *The Quotations Page*. <http://www.quotationspage.com/>.

# Chapter 15
# Revision: Editing and Proofreading

*Editor: a person employed by a newspaper, whose business it is to separate the wheat from the chaff, and to see that the chaff is printed.*

—Elbert Hubbard

## Chapter Contents

## *QuickView*

This is a "beefy" chapter, covering the most common concerns with revision.

Revision deals with editing and proofreading, each targeting different kinds of problems you may encounter in your writing. Our review will use series of questions that spotlight common weaknesses and errors, followed by advice for correcting them. Examples amply illustrate the errors and corrections.

Do not expect quick fixes to the errors addressed in this chapter. Initially, you should work your way through and familiarize yourself with the material. Then, return to the chapter and follow its recommendations as you revise your own stories.

Most of you will best understand what we cover here only when you can connect it to your own writing.

---

Writing for many inexperienced storytellers is like holding up a bank: Get in, get the loot and get out as quickly as possible.

Certainly, as a storyteller-journalist you often must work quickly on deadline. Yet, you must remember that your first shot at telling a story usually is your only shot. A story poorly told cannot be retold better the next day or the next week.

It is important that you write effectively, with a message that is complete, correct, clear and compelling.

An audience listening to a polished piano concerto delights in its quality of sound, its beauty of melody, its ease of flow and its apparently effortless delivery. They do not hear the hours upon hours of misplayed notes, inexact tempo or repeated measures that the musician put into practice before the performance.

What is particularly deceptive about listening to a finished piece of music is understanding how much effort went into its preparation.

So it is with excellent writing.

We earlier covered aspects of revision in Chapter 1 and Chapter 5. The important lesson you must learn from this chapter and apply to the storytelling you do hereafter is that drafting is only the first step in achieving success. The vital component of excellent storytelling is revision. For our purposes revision involves editing and proofreading. This chapter will take you through aspects of both activities.

## *Reader-Focused Revision*

Writing is an individual, personal and mental activity. It is something you necessarily do on your own.

Writing begins with an internal focus. You listen to your writer's voice—whether silent or audible—as you consider your text. What are you saying, and how are you saying it? You answer as a reader of your own writing. The problem is that, as reader of your own text, you know more about the message than the text says. As reader you bring to the reading all the interviews, notes, research and background that you as writer brought to the writing. Other readers do not have access to all of that. They have only your finished text.

Learn this important point: You may draft by yourself, but you must revise for your readers. That is, you must see with your readers' eyes and hear with your readers' ears.

## Revision Steps

You may recall from Chapter 1 that some writers draft quickly, seeking to capture and shape content from beginning to end before they revise. Other writers, though, write a bit and then reread and revise before moving on to write more. Thus, revision is not a matter of *if* but *when*. Use whichever drafting method works for you, but serious and final revision must wait until a first draft is complete. Only then can you have a reasonable sense of what your story might say and how it might say it. Only then can you shift to reader-focused revision.

From our discussion in Chapter 5 you may recall the following editing concerns:

- Lead.
- Content.
- Structure.
- Clarity.
- Style.

Proofreading, or line editing, deals with these issues:

- Spelling.
- Grammar.
- Punctuation.

Because this sequence moves primarily from most-to-least important revision, we will use the same order in this chapter. Questions, explanations and examples will assist you in your revision. If a different order works better for you, follow it. What is important is not the order but the activities themselves. Do all of them all of the time if you hope to be an effective storyteller.

To make revision more productive, recall this advice from Chapter 5:

- Print a hard copy of the story and work from that.
- Consider only one aspect of revision at a time.
- Read aloud and read the material slowly.

## Weak and Missing Content

Most of you work diligently to draft strong content, with effective leads and complete details. Certainly, that is your goal.

Yet, stories may be weak in one or both areas, and you must address these weaknesses during revision. Readers may forgive a few surface errors in spelling, punctuation or grammar. They even may overlook some structural and style errors, and they may wade through some long passages.

However, the same cannot be said of weak or missing content. Readers are inclined to ignore stories that do not have strong, inviting leads, and they may be confused or misled by stories with weak content.

## Story Leads

A strong lead is essential. Without it the rest of your efforts may go for naught. Therefore, spend sufficient time and effort considering your lead, keeping in mind that you are revising for readers who do not know all that you know about the story.

Review the following lead:

> The Western University Student Senate met Thursday to discuss raising student fees by $50 a year. Following heated debate, the issue passed 11-9.

Does the opening element have impact? Is it provocative? Is the most important point of the story given top billing? Does the lead grab attention? Does the lead invite readers to move into the rest of the story? The answers: No. No. No. No. And no.

The lead opens with *who did what*. However, it is a weak *who did what*, stressing that "they met to discuss"—a dull, deadweight lead focus if ever there was one. The second sentence tries unsuccessfully to redeem the lead with reference to "heated debate" and finally gives students the news: They will be paying $50 more a year in fees. The lead paragraph length is good at 23 words.

Look at this revision:

> Two votes will cost Western University students an extra 50 bucks a year.
> That was the margin by which the Student Senate passed the student fees bill Thursday.
> The 11-9 vote followed debate that erupted more than a dozen times into shouting matches and name calling that were reminiscent of a Saturday night wrestling match at Civic Arena.

The revised lead keys on the two-vote margin and tells readers in the first sentence the impact of the vote. The second paragraph clarifies that *what* and adds color to the "heated debate" reference in the original lead. The 13-word first paragraph of the lead is balanced against a 15-word second paragraph and a 30-word third paragraph.

Consider the following questions as you revise your own leads.

*Does the lead grab attention? Does it invite readers to move past it into the body of the story?*

The first word, at least the first sentence, needs to be precisely crafted for attention and impact. Do not be satisfied with what you drafted. Do not settle for OK. Rewrite it. Reach for your best.

Consider opening with a stronger word or coming at the lead from a different angle. Review the frame options in Chapter 13. Perhaps you have a provocative quotation or dynamic description lower in your story or still in your notebook. Use it to open the lead. Then, rework the rest of the lead to blend with the new opener and to provide effective transition into the body.

If a summary lead lacks impact, consider replacing it with a creative lead. Rework the summary as your nut graf. If a creative lead does not seem appropriate for the topic, write a summary. Tweak the lead. Massage it. Once it captures readers, you should be able to hold them, at least for the top of the story and probably beyond.

*Does the lead include news elements that provide the main point of the story, whether in a summary format or nut graf?*

If your lead is a summary, make sure it opens with the most important news element. Follow it with the remaining elements packaged for clear flow and easy reading. The end of the summary should provide transition into the body of the story.

If your lead is creative, locate and put brackets around your nut graf. Make sure it summarizes the story's main idea. It should fit comfortably within the lead or at its end, where it should aid transition into the body of the story. If you are dissatisfied with its placement, move it around, adjusting the nut graf to fit the new location.

*Does the lead drag, running too long—or at least seem as though it does?*

Count the words in your lead. If too long, cut it. Make it as tight as you can without losing key material. Examine carefully each word in the lead to make sure it carries its weight. If you have attribution in the lead, try to drop the name lower.

## Telling Details

Within the lead and beyond, telling details solidify stories. These details begin with the basic news elements and extend through their supporting material. They should be concrete and vivid. They should name real people and real things. They should evoke mental pictures.

Draw from your interview notes and recollection of the event or people you covered. Use the following questions to review details.

*Is each basic news element presented with the most appropriate, specific term?*

Underline the basic news elements in your lead. Each should be a telling detail. If any is not, consider what it will take to make it so while keeping your writing tight.

*Is each element developed with telling details in the body of the story?*

Using a separate sheet of paper, track the material you use to expand and explain the basic news elements in the body of the story. Try the following steps to assist you.

- First, turn the paper so that it is wider than it is tall.
- Second, write each element across the top and draw lines to make columns under the elements.
- Third, list in each column the details from the body of the story that support each element.
- Fourth, examine your lists to make sure each element has supporting detail. Add to those that need expansion and explanation.
- Finally, and most importantly, make sure that the supporting material is comprised of telling details.

# Weak Structure

As you draft, it is difficult to remain aware of how each sentence and paragraph fits the whole story. Revision gives you the chance to inspect the assembled pieces of the story. Weak structure of sentences and paragraphs can slow reading and obscure meaning. Examine each sentence and then each paragraph to understand how it relates to the others

## Sentences

Listen for flow and connections as you read each sentence aloud. Pay particular attention to the first and last words of sentences—prime spots for powerful words readers remember. Consider the following questions in your review.

*Are most sentences simple and declarative?*

Here you are looking for sentences that are a single subject-verb-object package, as in the following example:

> The $50 fee increase will boost Senate Activity Board coffers to fund programming and organizations by $1 million annually.

This order eases both reading and comprehension. Do not rely exclusively on these, however. You are free to use a compound or complex sentence occasionally to join related ideas, to avoid unnecessary repetition and to add variety.

*Is active voice used for most sentences?*

With active voice the subject is the *doer* of the action of the verb rather than its *receiver*, as in passive voice. See how this sentence slows with passive voice in the following version:

> Senate Activity Board coffers to fund programming and organizations will be boosted by $1 million annually with the $50 fee increase.

The majority of your sentences should be active, but occasionally, passive is appropriate and even necessary—either when you want to emphasize the receiver of the action or when the doer of the action is unknown.

*Are sufficient transitional devices used to connect sentences?*

Simply trailing one sentence after another may not reveal clear relationships between ideas. Common devices to show these connections are appropriate transitions, effectively repeated words, clear pronoun references and parallel structure. If necessary, return to Chapter 13 to revisit these.

## Paragraphs

Once you have checked sentence structure, examine paragraph structure. Your concerns here are length, order and connections. The following questions will help you to address these.

*Are most of your paragraphs relatively short, running one to four sentences?*

As with sentences short paragraphs are preferred but should not be used exclusively. The variety that comes from occasional short or longer paragraphs enhances interest. Reserve short paragraphs for either emphasis or transition, and use longer paragraphs for extended development of key ideas.

*Are paragraphs presented in logical order?*

Appropriate order is essential for clear and easy understanding of ideas. Certainly, use of inverted pyramid demands that you organize paragraphs most to least important, while narrative calls for time order. Yet, even within those patterns paragraph order should be logical. For example, related ideas should be grouped, and sequential material should follow the order in which it occurred.

*Are sufficient transitional devices used to connect paragraphs?*

Similar to sentences, paragraphs may need additional help to show readers relationships between each, using the same devices as used with sentences.

# *Poor Word Choice*

A news story with the potential for reader interest and impact will be crippled by poor word choices.

Weaknesses here may be traced to use of abstract words rather than concrete or to over-reliance on nouns and modifiers rather than verbs in your writing. Effective revision demands a critical, nitpicky perspective.

## Abstract versus Concrete

As you may know, abstract is the intangible, the general, the generic or the group. Concrete, on the other hand, is the tangible, the real, the specific or the single thing.

Both the abstract and the concrete comprise your lives, your experiences and your ideas. Both kinds of material should appear in your writing. Concrete is not always the best choice, nor is abstract always the poorest choice. Concrete may be preferred, but abstract is useful and necessary at times. Use the following questions to guide your revision.

*Are effective abstract terms used for passages that provide summary or overview, where the development pattern calls for general to specific?*

By necessity the content of summary leads and nut grafs is more abstract or general than the material that expands and explains them. The goal is to use a level of abstraction general enough to be short and to introduce details that follow but specific enough to avoid vagueness. For example, a story on problems facing student government might use one of the following leads:

Problems continue to plague student government.

Financial woes are hampering student government activity.

A shortfall in the student government budget has forced cutbacks of annual events sponsored by campus organizations.

A $19,000 student government deficit has forced cancellation this year of the weekly Filmfests and Bowlathons and matching funding for events sponsored by campus organization.

Notice how the level of abstraction evolves in each lead from general and vague to more concrete and specific.

In addition, within the body of the story you may find transitional and summary paragraphs or sentences that benefit from the same kind of appropriate abstraction. Such selective abstraction guides readers and aids organization.

*Are concrete nouns and modifiers used where the story should show particular moments, places, things or people?*

Most of the words in your story should be concrete, particularly when they are in passages that follow the summaries, overviews and introductions mentioned earlier. Readers are better able to understand and to relate to the concrete, which provides precise answers to questions they may have.

With adjectives, for example, rather than say something is *expensive*, give the actual cost. Rather than *old*, tell the exact age. Instead of writing *many*, note how many.

Vague nouns also should be replaced by specific. Do not call something a *tool* if you can use its specific name, such as a *bench grinder*. It might be a *little house*, but readers would visualize a better word picture from a *five-room bungalow*.

Writers may rely on general terms because they tend to come easily or because the writers forgot to get the specific details from interviews or research. You must capture concrete terms while newsgathering if you hope to put them into your story.

## Verbs versus Nouns and Modifiers

Inexperienced writers rely too much on nouns and modifiers—adjectives and adverbs—to carry the meaning of the sentence. Yet, the power words in sentences, as we noted in Chapter 14, are the verbs. Verbs carry the main meaning of the sentence. Action verbs make sentences come alive. At the same time, no one would suggest you ignore nouns and modifiers; use as many as necessary to make your point, and make most concrete.

The following questions should help to guide your revision.

*Are most sentences built around strong verbs?*

Underline the verbs in your sentences. Then, examine each for its effectiveness. Rather than *looked*, try *scanned*, *inspected*, *stared* or *squinted*. Of course, do not pick a stronger verb just because it sounds better. Make sure it also is appropriate for the context, and be careful that none insert your own biases into the sentence.

*Do sentences use some form of* to be *as main verb?*

Be wary of sentences with main verbs using forms of *to be*, like *was*, *is*, *will be* or *have been*. Besides relying on weak verbs, those sentences may carry extra noun and modifier baggage. Revise them with a stronger verb, especially if it allows you to cut unnecessary nouns or modifiers. For example, rather than say *He was manager of the store*, say *He managed the store*.

Of course, some sentences benefit from a form of *to be*. Rather than *President Kennedy was located in Dallas when Lee Harvey Oswald shot him*, write *President Kennedy was in Dallas when Lee Harvey Oswald shot him*. Instead of *The funeral will be held Thursday at 9 a.m.*, say *The funeral will be Thursday at 9 a.m.*

## Tight Writing

Tight writing is essential for storytellers. In this revision category are the following flaws:

- Unnecessary adverbs.
- Unnecessary prepositional phrases.
- Circumlocutions.
- Redundancies.
- Nominalizations.

Eliminating these should pare your writing of most remaining excess baggage.

### Unnecessary Adverbs

Most revision guidelines recommend cutting as many adverbs as possible. These modifiers—which describe, qualify or limit verbs, adjectives and other adverbs—are prime wordiness culprits. While you need not be ruthless in their removal, you should be picky about any you keep.

One of the common adverb targets is *very*. So convinced of its lack of value, Mark Twain suggested inserting *damn* wherever writers used *very*. This would ensure that editors would cut the offending term, leaving the writing as it should be.

Consider the following questions in your review of adverbs.

*Does your story use any of these adverbs:* basically, hopefully, just, mostly, often, practically, really, so or very?

Read your story, underline the adverbs listed and consider cutting them *unless* you are convinced of their need. Alternatively, locate each adverb with the search feature of your word processing software. Read each usage, and begrudge any you keep.

Occasionally, you may need the weight of a qualifier like *very*; however, consider revising with more effective word choices. For example, replace *very angry* with *livid* to add the kind of punch you seek.

*Can other adverbs in your story be cut?*

A more global method of locating adverbs is to search for those words with *–ly* endings. If you wish, use the Find command in your word processing program. Access the command from the pulldown menu, and type *ly* into the search box. This will not catch all adverbs, but it will locate most of them. As earlier, your goal is careful reading and then elimination of unnecessary adverbs.

## Unnecessary Prepositional Phrases

Writing needs prepositions and the phrases they introduce. At least most of time. Therefore, eliminating any is not just a matter of locating and cutting. Some may not be needed; others might be replaced with tighter forms.

Most you will keep. Good judgment will help you in this decision-making.

Let us review some examples of unnecessary prepositional phrases. The following is typical: *The student with ambition will prevail.* Replace it with *The ambitious student will prevail.* Look for puffed-up prepositional passages where you are trying to make something sound more important than it is. For example, rather than *Sources must be treated in an ethical way*, use *Sources must be treated ethically*. You replace a wordy prepositional phrase with a useful and shorter adverb.

Check the following list for additional unnecessary prepositional phrases and appropriate replacements.

- *He left at an early hour.* Replace with *He left early.*
- *The accident victim remained in a confused state.* Replace with *The accident victim remained confused.*
- *The turkey was large in size.* Replace with *The turkey was large.*
- *He heard a strange type of sound.* Replace with *He heard a strange sound.*
- *The UFO was round in shape.* Replace with *The UFO was round.*

## Circumlocutions

Circumlocutions are wordy, roundabout ways of saying something. They wheedle their way into our writing because we think the passage sounds more important. Instead, circumlocutions tend to be pompous language. Always replace them with shorter equivalents.

The following list is not exhaustive, but it should clue you to common circumlocutions you may find. Recommended replacements follow each.

- A large number: many.
- As regards: about.
- At a rapid rate: rapidly.
- Aware of the fact that: know.
- Cannot be avoided: must, should.
- Come to the conclusion: conclude.
- Concerning the matter of: about.
- Conduct an inspection of: inspect.
- Considering the fact that: because, since, why.
- Due to the fact that: because.
- For the reason that: because, since, why.
- Give a summary of: summarize.
- Give instruction to: instruct.
- Has the ability to: can.
- Has the capacity for: can.
- Has the opportunity to: can.

- In a situation in which: when.
- In light of the fact that: because, since, why.
- In reference to: about.
- Is able to: can.
- Is in conflict with: conflicts.
- It could happen that: could, may, might.
- It is crucial that: must, should.
- It is important that: must, should.
- It is necessary that: must, should.
- It is possible that: could, may, might.
- Make a decision: decide.
- Make an assumption: assume.
- On the grounds that: because, since, why.
- On the occasion of: when.
- Owing [due] to the fact that: because, since, why.
- Prior to: before.
- Readily apparent: obvious.
- So long as: if.
- Take action: act.
- The majority of: most.
- The possibility exists for: could, may, might.
- The reason for: because, since, why.
- There is a chance that: could, may, might.
- There is a need [necessity] for: must, should.
- This is why: because, since, why.
- Under circumstances in which: when.
- With regard to: about.

## Redundant Pairs

Redundant pairs are unnecessary repetition where both terms mean the same thing or one term already includes the other in its definition. Many are so common that they are clichéd. None should be retained in your writing.

The following list offers a glimpse of common redundant pairs, along with recommended revisions.

- Basic fundamentals: basics *or* fundamentals.
- Each individual: each.
- End result: end *or* result.
- Final outcome: outcome.
- Free gift: gift.
- Future plans: plans.
- Important essentials: essentials.
- Past history: past *or* history.
- Past memories: memories.
- Sudden crisis: crisis.
- Terrible tragedy: tragedy.

- True facts: facts.
- Unexpected surprise: surprise.
- Various differences: differences.
- Very unique: unique.

## Nominalizations

Another problem, nominalization, is a weak noun form of a verb.

For example, rather than *The discovery of the budget shortfall was made by the treasurer*, write *The treasurer discovered the budget shortfall*, or rather than *The budget deficit was a result of a drop in collection of student fees*, write *The budget deficit resulted from uncollected student fees*. In both examples the weak noun has been returned to its verb form, and the number of words has been cut. In addition, the revised first example replaces passive voice with active.

---

## *For Practice*

15-1. Pick a story you previously wrote and submitted for a grade (but not any used for other exercises in this chapter). Then, do the following:

a) Print a copy of the story from your computer file.
b) Check for the following errors, one category at a time, and underline those you find:
  - Unnecessary adverbs.
  - Unnecessary prepositional phrases.
  - Circumlocutions.
  - Redundant pairs.
  - Nominalizations.
c) On separate paper write each heading and below it list the errors from your story and their corrections.
d) Submit the marked story and the separate listings to your teacher.

---

## *Style Errors*

We know from Chapter 14 that writing style is the personal and professional preferences for how to say something. It is the filter through which we present our ideas.

During revision you should review your writing for compliance with the following styles:

- News style.
- AP style.
- Quotation style.
- Local publication style.

### News Style

In addition to matters we addressed earlier in this chapter, examine your story for objectivity, where necessary and appropriate. Remember that news stories are neutral on all issues, not only those considered controversial. An exception to this is news coverage developed according to public journalism principles and practices. We shall discuss those at length in Chapter 19.

Otherwise, use the following questions as starting points in your review.

*Have you attributed to sources all opinions and all claims?*

The distinction between opinion and fact is difficult for some writers to grasp. In our personal experiences we believe and say things that are fixed and unchanging. Even though we may give them the power and authority of facts, they still are our opinions. For example, we can say *The United States is a representative democracy. Elected officials who follow a constitution and a system of laws govern it. The United States has 50 states.* All these are facts.

Suppose we say *The United States is the freest country in the world.* Even though we might support this with a dozen convincing reasons—including facts—that does not make the original statement a fact. It is an opinion, a claim we make.

So long as what they claim is something with which most or all of their readers agree, some writers think they can present it unattributed. They think wrong. Neither popularity nor widespread acceptance opens the way for you to include your own or unattributed opinions in news stories.

Therefore, comb your story carefully for opinions, and cut them or make sure each has clear attribution to an outside source.

*Does your story rely on subjective terms rather than neutral? Does it include "loaded words"—that is, words that carry inappropriate connotations, or feelings?*

Subjective or abstract terms can get writers into trouble. For example, say you write *The student government candidate spent a small fortune in his re-election bid.* While *small fortune* seems factual, it is subjective. An acceptable alternative is *The student government candidate spent $8,500 in his re-election bid.* The actual figure is precise and may well encourage many readers to respond, "Golly, that is a small fortune!" The result is the same, but it comes legitimately.

Loaded words also are a problem. Speech tag verbs are sometimes the culprits. You may believe that a speaker whimpered when she said something; even most listeners might agree. Yet, you are wiser to use a content-neutral verb, such as *said*.

You also might find loaded adverbs in your story: *The professor brutally criticized the student for being late to class again.* Cut *brutally*. It is loaded and unacceptable—unless attributed to a source.

## AP Style

If you are seeking a simple solution to editing your story for AP style, you will not find one here.

The only reliable way to ensure that your story complies is to check every abbreviation, every capitalization, every punctuation mark, every title and every usage. That is a tall order, but it gets easier. As you become familiar with AP style, you will have fewer items to look up in the stylebook, reducing the time and effort involved.

Until then, remember the advice from Chapter 14: If something in your writing might be presented in more than one way, do not guess. Check the stylebook.

## Quotation Style

Quotations are the stuff of which news stories are made. Whether presented as paraphrase or direct quotations, the ideas, observations and opinions of your sources comprise most of the content of news stories.

As you edit, use the following questions dealing with these aspects of quotations: form, speech tags, punctuation and structure.

*Do summary and paraphrase comprise the majority of the quotation forms?*

In Chapter 3, you were advised to limit the number of direct quotations. Novice journalists use direct quotations as crutches to avoid having to write what sources meant rather than what they said. Ideally, the fewer direct quotations, the better.

Be selective. Directly quote only the most quoteworthy of what sources tell you. Summarize some. Paraphrase the rest.

*Are indirect quotations effective and true paraphrases, or are they direct quotations with the quotation marks dropped?*

There is work involved in paraphrasing borrowed material. It is easier to use the original wording; however, it is not better. Crafting indirect quotations is similar to translating text from English to French; the meaning is retained even as the form changes. The distinct advantage, especially for readers, is that most paraphrases tend to be clearer and shorter.

Some of you may assume that direct quotations speak for themselves; they require no "translation." You would assume wrong. Even interesting or clever-sounding quotations may be muddled, incomplete or misleading. Your task as storyteller-journalist is to avoid all of those. Clean up such direct quotes with well-cast paraphrases.

Also, presenting a source's actual words without quotation marks is deceptive and unethical. Readers rely on quotation marks as signals that these are sources' exact words. They understand that paraphrases are the writer's reasonable "translation" of the exact words. Do not cheat your sources and your readers by dropping the marks.

*Are most speech tags presented in subject-verb order?*

Quotation style prefers subject-verb order for speech tags because it follows the natural order of ideas. You may depart from this order only for tag-last quotations where a long title or identifying phrase follows the speaker:

"Damn the torpedoes!" said John Smith, executive officer of the U.S.S. Dolphin.

*Do most speech tags use content-neutral verbs?*

As noted earlier, avoid loaded words for speech tag verbs. The most reliable, content-neutral choice is the verb *to say*.

*Are speech tags joined to tag-first paraphrases without punctuation?*

The only speech tags joined to their messages without punctuation are tag-first paraphrases:

The college president said student tuition would increase 10 percent.

*Are speech tags joined to all direct quotations and tag-middle or tag-last paraphrases with commas?*

Commas are used to join speech tags to all remaining quotations of both types.

*Are most quotations presented in tag-last order?*

The preference for tag-last order lends emphasis to the message of the quotation over its source. Follow this pattern in most cases. Occasionally, when a VIP such as the president is speaking, you may opt for tag-first order. Also, tag-first quotations are useful when you shift to a new speaker.

## Local Publication Style

Because local publication style pertains to limited areas and has the potential to cover almost any departure from AP style, it is impractical to say much about it here. The only advice worth mentioning is to handle local style in the same way you handle AP style: Check everything.

# *Spelling Errors*

Spelling errors are the bane of many writers, both novice and veteran. Because even casual readers might spot these errors, they tend to be more disconcerting. Readers who find misspelled words may wonder what other errors in the story are less obvious. Writers are embarrassed, certainly, when spelling errors slip into publications, but they suffer more with the loss of reader credibility.

Most misspelling can be attributed to a single cause: Writers guess instead of check.

## Spellcheckers

What makes misspellings more unforgivable is the availability of spellcheckers—a common feature today with all but the most rudimentary word processing software.

Some applications allow users to set spellcheck to operate during composing, so that you know immediately that something may be awry with the spelling of a word. Others require that you initiate the command to check spelling, typically after you have finished your story draft. Most word processing software can suggest alternative spellings.

Writers have no excuses to avoid using this powerful digital tool to catch most misspellings.

Be advised, though, of two caveats. First, the effectiveness of a spellchecker is based on how large its resident dictionary is. If the word processor does not find a word in its files, it will flag it as misspelled—even if it is not. For those limited cases consult a paper or online dictionary. Second, follow suggested spellings with care. Because the software does not know the context in which the word is used, it might recommend a correctly spelled but altogether wrong word.

Just do not make the mistake of guessing.

## Proper Names

Spellcheckers are of limited help with proper names—that is, the capitalized formal names of people, places, events and things. The software's dictionary is too limited to include more than the most popular, such as names of presidents, states, major cities, countries and so on.

Therefore, when spellcheckers encounter most proper names, they flag a possible misspelling. This is good, especially for beginning journalists.

When you realize that a flagged word is a proper noun, you may be tempted to ignore it and move on. Resist the urge. A cardinal rule among professional journalists is to check the spelling of all names, not once but twice. Follow this double-checking practice while interviewing and researching. Follow it again while proofreading. Readers, especially those named in your story, will appreciate your attention to detail.

## *For Practice*

15-2. Pick a story you previously wrote and submitted for a grade (but not any used for other exercises in this chapter). Then, do the following:

a) Print a copy of the story from your computer file.
b) Underline all quotations and paraphrases.
c) Use the quotation style questions to review all quotations.
d) On separate paper write each quotation that has problems along with your revision.
e) Submit the marked story and the revisions sheet to your teacher.

15-3. Pick a story you previously wrote and submitted for a grade (but not any used for other exercises in this chapter). Then, do the following:

a) Open the computer file of the story with a word processor that has a spellchecker.
b) Run the spellchecker, noting on a separate sheet any misspelled words and their corrections.
c) Be sure you also check proper nouns and note any revisions you make for those.
d) Print out the revised story.
e) Submit the revised story and the revisions sheet to your teacher.

## *Punctuation Errors*

The second proofreading task focuses on punctuation. Because punctuation provides clues for readers to know how words and passages relate to one another, it is worth your time to review.

Some writers struggle with punctuation, especially commas. They are unsure what marks are required where because they do not know the rules that apply. Instead, they punctuate their stories by habit.

If the habits are good and follow rules, this works fine. However, habits that do not follow rules will litter your writing with mistakes. Readers may overlook occasional minor punctuation errors, but professional writers know that they must eliminate even those if they hope to polish and perfect their craft.

## Grammar Checkers: Punctuation

Leading word processing software features grammar checkers. Similar to spellcheckers, grammar checkers can be set for automatic review or accessed by command.

Microsoft Word, like other software, includes a punctuation component in its grammar checker. According to Word's Help window, punctuation checked includes commas, colons, end-of-sentence punctuation, punctuation in quotations or semicolons used in place of commas or colons.

When using the checker, though, review each recommendation carefully. Checkers are fallible and can give incorrect recommendations for the context.

## Commas

Commas are hobgoblins that haunt writers. Experience has led them to believe that many commas are "discretionary." Sadly for them, the opposite is true. Most comma placement follows clear, consistent rules. Discretionary commas are rare.

One maxim you should follow is using commas only when required by rule, structuring your writing, if necessary, to reduce the need for them. Why? Even correctly used, commas slow reading. The following questions will help you with the most frequent comma rules.

*Are commas used to separate more than two elements in a series, with no comma before the coordinating conjunction?*

Whether series elements are single words, phrases or sentences, commas are needed. AP style, though, drops the comma before the conjunction, as in the following examples:

Students need to come to class with textbooks, notebooks, pencils and pens.

Proper preparation makes their classes less frustrating, less embarrassing, more effective and more enjoyable.

Lifting weights every Monday, jogging a 5K every Wednesday and swimming 20 laps every Friday kept the professor in decent shape.

Good diet and exercise help people to stay sharp, they help them to stay healthy and they help them to enjoy life.

*Does a comma set off introductory elements from the rest of the sentence, including transitions, verbal phrases, adverb clauses and long prepositional phrases?*

This category of comma rules is not difficult to follow if you can identify the parts of sentences involved.

Transitions are words and phrases that show how material that follows links to that preceding. You may wish to check the list of common transitions in Chapter 13 to refresh your memory.

Students seldom are anxious to return to classes following vacation. However, they have few alternatives.

Verbal phrases include infinitive phrases, gerund phrases and participial phrases.

To be the best you can be, you must set and follow goals.

Running across campus, the student made it to class with only a minute to spare.

Fatigued by the all nighter, the football player fell asleep in the dining hall.

Adverb clauses, also called subordinate or dependent clauses, are complete ideas with subject and predicate. They cannot stand alone, though, because subordinate conjunctions introduce them.

If your roommate likes to stay up late listening to loud music, you may find it hard to sleep.

Long prepositional phrases that introduce sentences need commas following so that readers can distinguish between the subjects of the sentences and supporting material. On the other hand, short introductory prepositional phrases do not need commas. By the way, many writers consider prepositional phrases of more than five words long.

For the benefit of the rest of the students in class, you should not snore when you sleep.

In class sleeping students can be distracting.

*Are commas used to join compound sentences?*

Compound sentences are two complete sentences joined with a comma and one of the coordinating conjunctions: and, or, nor, but, for, yet, so.

Andy was the captain of the football team, and his girlfriend, Megan, was a cheerleader.

*Do commas set off parenthetical elements?*

Parenthetical elements, which are qualifying or explanatory, include interior transitions and interior clauses and phrases.

Loud music in student dorm rooms, unfortunately, can make life difficult.

Success in the classroom, as most of you already are aware, is seldom a matter of luck.

The volleyball coach, delighted at the success of her team, congratulated each player for her contribution.

The student, tired and hungry, struggled through the snow to the cafeteria.

*Are commas used to set off the year when used with the month and day?*

Nearly everyone places a comma between day and year in date phrases; however, AP style also requires a comma follow a year in such constructions.

The assassination of President John F. Kennedy on Nov. 22, 1963, brought the nation together in grief.

*Are commas used to set off nonessential elements from the rest of the sentence?*

The AP Stylebook has an excellent section on the punctuation of essential and nonessential elements. The key to this rule is understanding what nonessential means. We will start, though, with the meaning of essential elements: a word or group of words that is vital to the intended meaning of the passage. Do not use commas with essential elements, as in the following examples.

My brother Steve owns a diesel truck repair shop. [This is essential when there is more than one brother.]
Clark Gable and Vivien Leigh starred in the movie "Gone with the Wind." ["Gone with the Wind" is an essential appositive, naming which movie.]

Nonessential elements are informative only; if they were omitted, the intended meaning of the passage would not be lost. Use commas to set off nonessential elements.
The most common nonessential elements are appositives, which rename or describe a noun preceding, and relative clauses, which are introduced by who, whom, which and that.

The professor's wife, Marian, came from the same small town in Iowa where Johnny Carson was raised. [The professor has only one wife; therefore, her name is nonessential.]

Students learned that "Gone with the Wind," the most popular film of 1939, portrayed a romanticized view of slavery in The South. [That "Gone with the Wind" was the most popular film of 1939 is informational. Only one film fits that description.]

Phi Sigma Kappa, which was the oldest fraternity on campus, usually took "most active organization" honors. [That the fraternity is oldest on campus is only informational. It already has been named.]

*Do commas set off a series of adjectives equal in importance?*

Called coordinate adjectives, these line up in front of nouns to equally qualify and modify their meaning. A test of whether or not adjectives are coordinate is if you can use *and* between each and the meaning remains the same.

The big, fuzzy, pink slippers are her favorite.

Do not use a comma if the adjective immediately preceding the noun is more important than the others.

The long, hot summer months stretched out interminably.

## Other Common Punctuation Errors

The remaining most common punctuation errors include the following:

- Comma splices, where commas are used alone to join two complete sentences.
- Missing commas to set off nonessential elements.
- Unnecessary commas between subjects and verbs.
- Unnecessary commas after *although*, *and*, *but* and *such as*.
- Unnecessary colons between verbs and their objects and between prepositions and their objects.
- Using *it's* or *its'* for *its*, where the first is a contraction for *it is*, the third is a possessive pronoun and the second is just plain wrong.
- Unnecessary apostrophes for nouns that are only plural, not possessive.
- Semicolons between subordinate clauses and main clauses.

A good proofreading practice is to circle every punctuation mark. Then, review each to make sure it is used correctly.

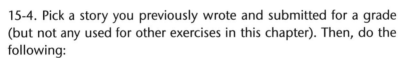

## *For Practice*

15-4. Pick a story you previously wrote and submitted for a grade (but not any used for other exercises in this chapter). Then, do the following:

a) Print a copy of the story from your computer file.
b) Circle all punctuation.
c) Use the punctuation questions to review all punctuation.
d) On separate paper write each sentence with punctuation problems along with your revisions.
e) Submit the marked story and the revisions sheet to your teacher.

15-5. Pick a story you previously wrote and submitted for a grade (but not any used for other exercises in this chapter). Then, do the following:

a) Open the computer file of the story with a word processor that has a punctuation checker.
b) Run the punctuation checker, noting on a separate sheet any punctuation errors and their corrections.
c) Print out the revised story.
d) Submit the revised story and the revisions sheet to your teacher.

# *Grammar Errors*

Grammar covers quite a bit of territory. As a result, grammar decisions are similar to punctuation decisions—we make many by habit rather than by rule.

While perhaps less common than punctuation errors for aspiring writers, grammar errors occur. When they do, they can be jarring to readers.

## Grammar Checkers: Grammar

As noted earlier, many word processing programs have grammar checkers. The grammar checker in Microsoft Word, for example, addresses the following: capitalization, commonly confused words, hyphenated and compound words, misused words, negation, numbers, passive sentences, possessives and plurals, relative clauses, subject-verb agreement and verb and noun phrases.

Word's grammar checker also covers style options, including clichés, colloquialisms, contractions, gender-specific words, jargon, sentence length, split infinitives, successive nouns, successive prepositional phrases, unclear phrasing and wordiness.

While grammar checkers can be quite helpful, they are not as reliable as spellcheckers because of the greater complexity of grammar rules. Therefore, using them will demand that you carefully review recommendations. When in doubt, consult an English usage handbook.

## Common Grammar Errors

Those grammar errors most likely to appear in your writing include fragments, run-ons, shifts in tense, subject-verb or pronoun agreement and use of who, whom, that and which. The grammar checker should alert you to most of these mistakes. Use the following questions as starting points in your grammar proofreading:

*Have you checked sentences to make sure each has a subject and appropriate main verb?*

Fragments tend to be less an error with structure and more an error with punctuation. That is, writers set off a fragmented passage with a period rather than correctly join it to a sentence preceding or following.

Students cheered at the football team's championship win. The first in school history.

This needs a comma following *win* instead of a period. Change to *Students cheered at the football team's championship win, the first in school history.*

*Are there any instances where two complete sentences are joined without coordinating or subordinating conjunctions and necessary punctuation?*

Run-ons are two complete sentences run together without required conjunctions and/or punctuation. This problem also tends to be rooted in faulty punctuation.

An English degree can equip students for many exciting careers they include advertising, graduate school, marketing, publishing, sales, teaching and technical writing.

The run-on here can be corrected in one of four ways. After the word *careers* you could do one of the following:

- Insert a period.
- Insert a semicolon.
- Insert a comma and coordinating conjunction, such as *and*.
- Insert a comma and replace *they include* with *including*.

*Is the verb tense logical and consistent?*

The most common verb tense in news stories for finished events is past. If the coverage is for something ongoing, then present, present perfect and the "historical present" are logical. If the event is yet to come, future tense should be used. A shift in tense from one of these within the same story must be logical and justified. When it is not, you have a tense shift error.

Look at the following coverage of an ongoing event to see an example of this mistake:

> Student senators are meeting this week to review irregularities in recent student government elections.
> Charges included faulty ballots at some polling places, early closing of some polling places and electioneering by several presidential candidates.
> Senate President Andrea Eckdahl believed that some of the charges had merit and hoped to settle the controversy quickly.

See how the following example corrects the tense shift errors, which are underlined, and makes present tense consistent throughout:

> Student senators are meeting this week to review irregularities in recent student government elections.
> Charges <u>include</u> faulty ballots at some polling places, early closing of some polling places and electioneering by several presidential candidates.
> Senate President Andrea Eckdahl <u>believes</u> that some of the charges <u>have</u> merit and <u>hopes</u> to settle the controversy quickly.

*Does the number of the subject agree with the number of the verb?*

Sentence subjects are singular or plural. The related verbs must match the subject's number. When they do not, they are errors in subject-verb agreement. The problem usually can be traced to prepositional phrases or to relative clauses that follow the subject. The following examples illustrate how a prepositional phrase and a prepositional phrase with a relative clause can lead to the problem:

The beginning of classes are a stressful time for most students.

He is one of those students who is always late to class.

In the first example the writer matches the verb number to *classes*. However, *classes* is the object of the preposition *of*; the subject of the sentence is *beginning*. In the second the writer matches the number of the verb *is* in the relative clause to *one*, but the clause modifies and must agree with *students*, the noun to which the relative clause refers.

Check "one of those" constructions by turning them around to read *Of those students who are always late to class, he is one.* Of course, it is not required that you use that order in your stories, only that you use it to check for correct agreement.

Therefore, the sentences should read as follows:

The beginning of classes is a stressful time for most students.

He is one of those students who are always late to class.

*Does pronoun number match the number of its noun antecedent?*

Pronoun agreement, like subject-verb agreement, requires that pronouns match the number of their antecedents, the nouns to which the pronouns refer. The following illustrates the error:

If a student is late to class, their teacher may think they are disrespectful.

The problem here is with *their* and *they*. The antecedent of these plural pronouns is *student*, which is singular. The error usually is the result of writers trying to be politically correct in avoiding what used to be the standard, the "generic he," or the equally troublesome "he/she." The best way to correct such pronoun agreement errors, when context allows, is to make the antecedent plural:

If students are late to class, their teacher may think they are disrespectful.

*Are* who, whom, that *and* which correct *in each usage?*

Let us discuss *who* and *whom* first. *Who* is subjective while *whom* is objective. In other words, *who* is subject of a clause, and *whom* is object of a clause. A simple test will help determine which to use. Where you are using *who* or *whom*, replace it with a personal pronoun, such as *he* or *him*. If *he* fits the context, use *who* in the clause. If *him* fits, use *whom*.

She was picky about who she chose as a boyfriend.

Police are seeking the one whom is responsible for vandalizing the auditorium.

Therefore, applying the test to the first sentence, we get *she chose him*. The clause should read *She was picky about <u>whom</u> she chose as a boyfriend.*

Applying the test to the second sentence will give us *he is responsible*. The clause should read *Police are seeking the one <u>who</u> is responsible for vandalizing the auditorium.* Moreover, because writers may drop that or who if the result remains clear, an alternative would be *Police are seeking the one responsible for vandalizing the auditorium.*

Now, let us review *who*, *that* and *which*. People require *who*, and things require *that*. In addition, essential clauses use *that*, and nonessential clauses use *which*.

*The students that gave blood were excused from their PE classes.* This should read *The students* <u>who</u> *gave blood were excused from their PE classes.*

*The movie which was lost has been found.* This should read *The movie* <u>that</u> *was lost has been found.*

## For Practice

15-6. Pick a story you previously wrote and submitted for a grade (but not any used for other exercises in this chapter). Then, do the following:

a) Print a copy of the story from your computer file.
b) Use the grammar questions to review all grammar.
c) On separate paper write each sentence with grammar problems along with your revisions.
d) Submit the marked story and the revisions sheet to your teacher.

15-7. Pick a story you previously wrote and submitted for a grade (but not any used for other exercises in this chapter). Then, do the following:

a) Open the computer file of the story with a word processor that has a grammar checker.
b) Run the grammar checker, noting on a separate sheet any grammar errors and their corrections.
c) Print out the revised story.
d) Submit the revised story and the revisions sheet to your teacher.

## Crafting and Drafting

Chip Scanlan of the Poynter Institute for Media Studies credits Jacqui Banaszynski with the following story approaches, all of which he says can be applied to any subject of substance. For example, each of the approaches could deal with anorexia.

- Profile: Tell who the people behind the story are. Cover the central character of an event, issue, trend or development. Profiles also can reveal a place, a building or an event.
- Explanatory piece: Called "one of the most overlooked genres in American journalism," explanatory pieces tend to develop how and why of subjects.
- Issues and trend stories: Explore a social issue or trend. Consider the broader implications of local events and issues.
- Investigative piece: The timeworn adage "Follow the money" is operant here. What system or situation demands inspection, close up and incisive?
- Narrative: Central character, plot and core tension comprise the story.
- Descriptive/Day in the Life: Sometimes it is better to consider a slice of a larger narrative, which allows you to narrow your view and tighten your writing.

## For Practice

15-8. Run your regular beat and find a topic for which you can do a story following one of Banaszynski's six approaches. Then, do the following:

a. Interview appropriate sources and take careful notes.
b. Listen carefully for quoteworthy comments the sources make, and write those down exactly.
c. Draft a story using the best approach of the six that fits your topic and your audience.
d. Swap stories with a peer review partner or group and give written reader feedback
e. Submit the draft and peer feedback to your teacher.
f. After your teacher has reviewed your draft and peer feedback and has offered additional suggestions, begin revising. As much as possible, use the questions in this chapter to guide your revision, and give yourself enough time to do your best.
g. Submit a final draft to your teacher.

## Chapter 15 Bibliography

Hubbard, Elbert. Michael Moncur, *The Quotations Page*. <http://www.quotationspage.com/>.
Scanlan, Chip. "Jacqui Banaszynski's Six Paths to Story." *Poynteronline*. 11 December 2002. <http://poynteronline.org/column.asp?id=52&aid=11738>.

# Chapter 16
# Online Publishing

*The difference between the almost right word and the right word is really a large matter—'tis the difference between the lightning-bug and the lightning.*

—Mark Twain

## Chapter Contents

## *QuickView*

The first time someone on campus stops you in the hall and says he or she enjoyed your story, you will understand the thrill of being published. That is why this chapter is exciting—it provides you and your peers the basic know-how to publish your work online.

We will review both barebones links pages and enhanced index pages as primary formats for your online publication. Also, we will see what kinds of content, in addition to your stories, that you should consider for your site. You also will learn which software you need to prepare and package that content.

Finally, we will examine basic Web design principles that will help to make your site worth a visit.

---

The most enjoyable part of storytelling is being able to actually share your story. While your peer group and teacher are regular readers of your stories, increasing the size of your audience is a valuable goal of both storytellers and journalists.

That is what this chapter is about. If you and your class do not have regular access to publishing in a printed newspaper, publishing your stories online is an excellent and inexpensive alternative. In fact, as we shall see, an online publication offers many benefits over a print publication.

This chapter is targeted at novice Web page authors. It will cover a variety of online publication options, including basic concepts, recommended software, design suggestions and preparation guidelines.

## Online News Publications

The Internet is a popular venue for many people today, particularly college students like you. Online sites are accessible from anywhere in the world; all one needs is a computer, an online connection and the Web address, or URL. Putting news online is fast and easy—once you know the basics—and it usually is cheap.

We will explore two options you and your class might consider for your online news publication: barebones links pages and enhanced index pages.

Each of these offers variations with advantages and disadvantages, but both should be within your grasp. Base your choice on what form you want to present your stories to readers and how much time and work you are willing and able to put into developing and maintaining the online site.

### Barebones Links Pages

As the name suggests, barebones links pages are little more than a Web page with clickable links that allow users to read the posted files. These are your fastest and easiest route online; they also can be humdrum, with no visual appeal to site visitors. However, if your main concern is to make your stories available to readers, this will do the job.

Three files that you might consider linking from barebones pages are as follows:

- Word processed .doc files.
- Web-based .html files.
- Fully designed newspaper page files formatted as .pdfs.

The fastest and simplest links page is the first. It offers an identifying heading and a list of links to word processing files, such as those produced with Microsoft Word. Users click on a link, and depending on the computer platform and its default settings, the file that opens will be identical to the word processing file you prepared and posted. Its disadvantage is that it gives readers nothing more than the words of the story, with no design elements to enhance presentation.

Another option is linking to .html files. The difference between these and .doc files is that .doc files need word processing software to be viewed outside the Web browser while .html files are read with the browser software. This requires that you convert your word processing file to .html, a simple procedure. In the process you even might consider doing some simple formatting, such as adding subheads to your stories. The drawback is the same as that for pages with word processing files: It is not much to look at.

A third possibility is linking to .pdf files, which are created with Adobe Acrobat Distiller. These .pdfs can display replicas of print newspaper pages—replete with headlines and photographs to accompany stories—designed with software such as Adobe PageMaker, Adobe InDesign or Quark Xpress. The drawback is the time and effort required to produce the newspaper pages in the first place. However, once you create those and convert them to .pdf, posting them is as simple as the first two.

The benefit of the barebones links page is that you publish your stories and make them available to readers with moderate time and effort.

See an online example of the barebones links page at the "Storycrafting" Web site, the URL for which is listed in "Using This Textbook" at the front of this book.

## Enhanced Index Pages

With enhanced index pages you prepare your story files in the same way as for barebones links pages. The only thing you change is the Web page that visitors will see online. This online news publication lets you enhance the look and appeal of the Web page that presents the links.

You might consider one or all of the following options for improving the Web page's appearance:

- Color elements.
- Backgrounds.
- Appropriate icons.
- Images.
- Story summaries or lead-ins.

Each of these is intended to make your site more interesting and inviting to readers and encourage them to click-through to your stories.

The drawbacks are minimal but worth noting. First, while you might write the .html coding yourself to make these elements work, your easier choice is to design the page using wysiwyg software. As you may know, wysiwyg (pronounced "wizzy-wig") is an acronym for "what you see is what you get." This software simplifies writing the .html coding by allowing you to use pulldown commands and shortcuts to give you formatting on the screen that looks like what you want. Hence, the acronym. It is readily available with a component of Netscape Navigator, called Netscape Composer, or with software like Microsoft Front Page, Adobe PageMill or many other less-sophisticated programs.

Step-by-step guides for basic .html coding and use of Netscape Composer or Microsoft Front Page are available online in the "Instructor's Resource Manual" at the "Storycrafting" Web site.

Second, you must locate Web sites that provide backgrounds and icons. Many of these are readily available online, and most offer free files. Go to an online search engine and keyboard "free Web backgrounds" or "free Web icons." Of course, you also could design and digitize your own icons.

Finally, for story-related images—appealing additions to your site—you need to produce the digitized files yourself or have someone else do so.

See an online example of the enhanced index page at the "Storycrafting" Web site.

### Online Newspapers

The most sophisticated, but also most demanding, online news publication is an online newspaper. Your campus newspaper already may design and maintain one. If not, you can see plenty of examples by going to one of the following:

- <http://postrockcountry.com/NewsJunkie/col.htm>.
- <http://www.journalismjobs.com/collegepapers.cfm>.

You can locate other listings of online college newspapers by keyboarding that phrase into a search engine.

Most are similar to enhanced index pages and include features, sports, opinion and specialized columns in addition to news. While a full online newspaper may be in your long-range plans, preparing one is beyond the scope of this chapter.

## *Story File Preparation*

The first step in producing your online news publication is preparing your story files.

Preparation of these can be simple. Because your choice of online news publication will determine which to use, it is important that you decide that first. Otherwise, you will do more work than necessary, or you will have to redo file preparation so it matches demands for the site.

Certainly, you might opt early on for the barebones links page just to get things rolling and then move up to one of the variations of the enhanced index page as you and your colleagues become more confident in handling the task.

### Preparing .doc Files

Getting .doc files ready is almost a no-brainer. This is the same format you get from your standard word processing software, such as Microsoft Word. It works well for either barebones or enhanced pages. Also, newspaper pages created with page-design software and converted to .pdf can import .doc files.

Consider these tips using your word processing software to prepare your files before posting:

- Add a newspaper-style headline versus a title. The first reflects the essence of the lead; the second just announces the subject.
- Add a byline.

- Include an e-mail address for the writer, which encourages interactivity with readers. By the way, Microsoft Word automatically makes e-mail addresses clickable links.
- Keep the filename short and simple, but clear. Avoid using slash marks (/). Remember that the *exact* filename is required for posting and linking.
- If you are using a Macintosh computer, add the extension—the period and the "doc." Without it the Web browser will not know what kind of file it is.

## Preparing .html Files

Getting .html files ready is just about as simple. Follow the five preparation tips suggested for .doc files, but use the .html extension instead.

To see the .html coding for the sample pages listed earlier, open one in a Web browser and pull down under View to Source in Internet Explorer or under View to Page Source in Netscape Navigator.

## Story Revision

If you have done an effective job writing your story for print, no revision is needed for barebones pages, since they will not be read online as part of the Web page. However, limited revision may be beneficial for .html or .pdf files posted to enhanced index pages.

A study of users by Jakob Nielsen suggested that a considerable majority of the people in the sample, 79 percent, always scanned new Web pages, with only 16 percent reading word by word. Therefore, he recommends the following for Web writing, including several points that spill over into Web page design, which we will discuss later.

Highlight keywords.

This includes hypertext links, typeface variations and color. However, resist putting links within your story. Instead, place links to related material at the end, where they will not disrupt reading.

Use meaningful subheads.

While few of you would use these in your original stories, they are excellent additions to online text, breaking up gray blocks and cluing readers to content. Use the same type size as for body text, but make subheads bold and set them off in separate lines.

Use bulleted lists.

These are a must for online text. They help readers to quickly grasp key points.

Stick to one idea per paragraph.

This is standard for journalistic writing and a must for Web pages.

# *Images*

Standard online images, also called art and graphics, include photographs, line art, maps, charts, tables and icons. The addition of appropriate images can make online publications inviting. Few printed newspapers, for example, can afford the cost of running all full-color photographs, front to back. Yet, once processed, color is no more expensive to publish online than black and white.

A key word in the last paragraph is *appropriate*. Just because you *can* include all the art and graphics you want does not mean that you *should*. Do not use images just because they are available. Images should be chosen for the following reasons:

- To support content.
- To enhance design.
- To draw readers to certain parts of the page.

## Online Image Formats

The two most common online image formats are gifs and jpegs.

Gifs respond better to sizing up than jpegs. That is, gifs usually look better when enlarged beyond their original size. Images with lettering always should be formatted as gifs in order to keep letters sharp and readable. A minor drawback for gifs is that they tend to be larger file sizes than jpegs at the same dimensions. Remember, too, that color-image file sizes are larger than black and white. File size is a concern mainly because a larger file size takes longer to load into the browser page.

The optimum resolution for online images, represented by dpi or dots per inch, is 72 dpi. Higher resolutions increase file sizes but offer no benefits in how images appear on Web pages.

Using software like Adobe Photoshop, you can manipulate images—enhance them; resize them; add, change or remove color; combine images; add or remove parts of the images; or change their format.

Macintosh users should add the appropriate extensions to image files—.gif for gifs and .jpg for jpegs.

## Clip Art

Clip art covers a wide range of line drawings of every subject imaginable with a multitude of styles, both black and white, single color and full color.

The term comes from earlier days of offset publishing when designers purchased large books of prepared art from which they selected pieces and then clipped, or cut, the items from their pages. When these were photographed for pages, they were sized up or down to fit.

Most clip art today is digitized already, cutting out the need to photograph or scan it for reproduction. Sizing for page designs is as simple as clicking on an image and dragging one of the corners in or out to make it fit. A tip for novice designers is to make sure and hold down the shift key as they drag in order to keep consistent the proportions of the images.

As suggested earlier, use a search engine to find art you need. You can locate clips of a particular subject using a keyword search and enclosing the descriptive string in quotation marks. For example, if you want a line drawing of a motorcycle, type the following phrase into the search engine, including the quotation marks (but not the period): "free motorcycle clip art" or "free Harley clip art."

Once you find the art you need online, save the image to disk.

## Icons

This category of art includes images typically used as a symbol for something. Most designers use icons to emphasize material and to help readers spot standard links

Generic icons include those classified as "bullets" and used for emphasizing passages of text. One caution in the use of word processing or font-based bullets: Not all of them transfer online as the image you are seeking. You will need to test each to make sure that it looks right on the Web page.

You can locate specialized icons at online art sites. The benefit of these, because they are image based rather than font or software based, is that they will always appear as you intend.

The following are a few tips for using icons:

- Pick icons that are obvious in what they symbolize.
- Use icons in consistent ways with which readers can become familiar.
- Do not use *too many* icons; any emphasis device loses its punch when overused.
- Size them to match the text with which they are placed—large enough to be readable but small enough to avoid drawing too much attention.

## Backgrounds

Whether or not you notice them, all Web sites have backgrounds. Many are white. However, backgrounds can be any color and can include textures and images.

Backgrounds are like the painted or wallpapered walls in your home. You do not want them to be so obvious and loud that they overwhelm the art and other furnishings. That is often the reason many homeowners choose white or neutral wall paints. They want them to complement the room and its contents, to lend a particular mood to the room.

Likewise, the secret to effective use of backgrounds is that most readers do not consciously notice them. Rather, they may "sense" them initially and only be aware of them upon closer inspection. The background should not compete with the contents of a Web page. It should complement it.

You can set a solid-color background with .html coding or with wysiwyg software, or you can locate textured or image backgrounds at online sites. You even can load your own images to serve as backgrounds, again by using the correct .html coding.

Remember the following background guidelines:

- Keep backgrounds simple to avoid distraction.
- Keep them muted to avoid problems with readability.
- Keep them appropriate so that they complement the page content.

## Photographs

Of all the images you may consider using for your Web page, none is more powerful than excellent photographs, appropriately chosen and sized.

Excellent photographs follow six basic criteria:

- They are sharply focused.
- They are free from dust, scratches and other detracting blemishes.
- They make immediately clear who or what the subject of the photograph is supposed to be.
- They present the subject at an appropriate size for "reading."
- They present the subject in a context that is neutral or complementary rather than busy and distracting.
- Probably most importantly, they tell a story.

Soft-focused or "fuzzy" photographs should not be used. They force readers to examine their glasses or to strain their eyes, checking whether it is they or the image that is to blame. The problem may be traced to the shooting or the preparation of the photo. Either it was not sharply focused when it was captured on film or on disk, or it was not sharply focused when scanned from negatives, slides or prints.

While Photoshop and other image-manipulation software can improve slightly the sharpness of photos, proper use of both camera and scanner is the best bet to eliminate the frustration of fuzzy photos.

Seldom will photos shot with digital cameras have problems with dust or scratches, unless the lens is dirty. These problems are more common with film-based cameras and can be traced to sloppy processing or careless handling of film, slides or prints. A dirty scanner also may be the culprit. Clean equipment and proper handling should minimize these problems.

After they are digitized, fortunately, you can use Photoshop and other software to remove most blemishes.

The intended subject of a photo is emphasized in two ways: It tends to be the largest element in the photo, and natural lines, contrasting tones or color and other elements help to lead the reader's eyes into it.

Size of the subject *in the photo*—versus the size of the photo itself—is another critical aspect of excellence. Inexperienced photographers too often err by shooting too far from their subjects. Move close to shoot. Alternatively, if the original photo was shot too far away, enlarge and crop the image—that is, cut out unwanted or distracting portions of the original image—during processing, either in the darkroom, on the scanner or with software like Photoshop.

Size of the photo on the Web page is the next criterion. Not all photos should be presented large in the design, but all should be large enough to make out necessary detail to understand the photo. Select one photo to be dominant on a page—that is, at least twice the size of any other images.

Photos should be shot in contexts, or backgrounds, where other things in the scene do not compete with or distract reader's eyes from the intended subject. Many photos can be improved by cropping tightly to eliminate competition and distraction.

Above all, excellent photos tell a story. This does not mean a caption, or cutline, is unnecessary, but it expects that what is happening in the shot should be interesting, powerful and straightforward for readers.

## Scanning Images

Vital to any Web-publishing operation is a scanner that can accommodate both film or slides and printed images. The cost of these varies widely, generally based on how fine a resolution they can produce and how quickly they can scan images. If most of the scanned images you need will be seen *only* online, as opposed to being printed on paper, a lower-resolution, slower scanner is sufficient and is more economical.

You would be wise to scan at a higher resolution, such as 300 dpi for a fixed file and then reduce the resolution of the file after manipulation to the Web optimum of 72 dpi for the online file.

Because it would be impractical to try to explain here how to use a particular scanner, you should read carefully the manual that comes with the unit. Moreover, you may be able to locate Web sites that provide additional explanation, usage tips and answers to questions or problems you may have.

## Manipulating Images

As should already be clear, image-manipulation software, like Adobe Photoshop, is another vital tool for Web publishing. Fortunately, many scanners come bundled with "light" versions of Photoshop or similar programs, so cost need not be a factor in your having access to them.

Photoshop is not as "user friendly" as some other types of software with which you already may be familiar. Its learning curve tends to be longer, meaning it takes more time for users to become proficient with it. Yet, time invested in learning Photoshop basics is worth it.

As a minimum you should know how to do the following with image-manipulation software:

- Adjust gray tones or colors to improve image appearance.
- Change image format to either .gif or .jpeg.
- Change image resolution.
- Touch up images—particularly by removing blemishes, improving contrast or color tones or improving brightness.
- Crop and resize images for most effective presentation.

As with scanners you should review the manual that accompanies your image-manipulation software. In addition, you can find dozens of excellent Web sites that explain use of Photoshop by providing step-by-step procedures for the common manipulations listed.

# *Web Design Basics*

We cannot cover here all the fine points concerning Web page design; hefty books and semester-long classes are more appropriate to that task. However, we will review the basics that will help to get you started designing effective pages.

The guiding principle of design is this: Keep it simple.

Realize that simple does not mean boring. Simple design is easy for you to package and easy for readers to follow—two distinct benefits.

Wysiwyg software today makes it possible to add lots of bells and whistles to your site. As we have stressed previously, though, just because you *can* do something does not mean you *should*. The chief purpose of your site probably is not to wow visitors with all of its features. You want them to read your stories. Design decisions, therefore, you should be based on how each serves that goal.

Follow these general design guidelines:

- Avoid using Web page frames.
- Avoid animations or marquees that run constantly.
- Keep image file sizes small enough to load in 10 seconds, but certainly no longer than 30.
- Group and then split elements into related, logical sections.
- Establish and maintain a consistent look, or theme.
- Minimize how much scrolling a user must do. The usual rule is to design pages no more than two screens deep.
- Do not allow any material to be more than three clicks away from the homepage.
- Include an e-mail contact link and most recent update line on at least your homepage.
- Troubleshoot your pages *online* after each update to make sure they look as planned and links are working properly.

As you become more proficient in design, go online to explore other well-designed Web sites that you find appealing. Decide what makes them so, and begin learning how to replicate those design features on your site. In addition, you can acquire a wealth of more advanced techniques by locating Web sites that feature such advice or by checking out from a library or buying from a bookstore one or more "how-to" books dedicated to effective design.

## Text Width

When you type stories with word processing software, most likely you format them to run the full width of an $8\frac{1}{2} \times 11$ page, six inches of text with side margins at 1.25 inches each. However, such wide-column presentation is not necessarily best for Web design.

Most designers believe that readers of publications—as opposed to word processed text—prefer narrower columns than the full width of either typing paper or Web pages. Moving their eyes across a wider expanse tends to be more tiring.

This matter of text width is more important than it may seem. While it affects readability, text width is one of the more powerful influences on design, largely determining the overall look of Web pages.

You have many options available in establishing your page columns, ranging from narrower one-column formats up to three columns. One possibility to consider is a single-column text block that occupies 40 percent of the page space (left or right), with the remaining space set aside as a column for supporting images and navigation elements. Or you might center a text block that occupies 50 percent of the page space, with columns left and right given to images and navigation. Somewhat generous margins left and right usually enhance the look of the design and improve readability.

When you locate a design that appeals to you, stick with it as a standard for most of your pages. Occasionally, for specific content or for variety, use another format—either from wysiwyg software templates, templates you can find at various Web sites or templates of your own creation.

See online examples of various text widths at the "Storycrafting" Web site.

## Color

Online color opportunities are limitless. Or nearly so. You can use colors, in addition to black, for display type, body text, boxed text, image borders, horizontal rules, icons and other graphics. Of course, your page background also can be color.

However, do not use color on the same page for *all* of those—or even for more than one or two. Careful and selective use of color is essential.

The simplest and most common background color is white, just as the simplest and most common text color is black. While you may think this combination dull, its chief advantage is readability. It is this maximum contrast between black and white that makes text more readable.

If you decide to use a background color other than white, make it light toned, such as a light gray, ivory or blue. Make text color black or a complementary dark tone. Keep contrast between background and text high.

Another tip for using color is to establish some consistency, on the same page and from page to page. In that way readers become familiar with your site's "look."

Finally, try to make sitewide color choices complementary so that they do not clash with one another.

## Display Type

Display type includes all type elements larger than body text. Headings and headlines are the most common display type, but lead-ins or teasers for stories also might be classified as display.

Your choice of font for display should follow some clear plan, which reflects consistency and which complements the font of your body text. Sans serif fonts have consistent thickness and lack embellishments called serifs, the short crosslines or ticks at the ends of the letter strokes. They usually are good choices for display. They are clean and more readily match body text fonts. Arial is a common sans serif font on PC-based platforms, while Helvetica is an equally common sans serif on Macintosh.

Size of display type is contingent upon how it looks on the page, especially when compared to other type there. If your body text is 12–14 points, then display type at 24–48 points is large enough to stand out.

## Body Text

Body text will comprise the bulk of type on any page. Studies have suggested that serif types are more readable, with thick-thin lines and the small embellishments that help to move the eye along. Stick with a standard serif font, such as Times Roman. Because it is found on every computer, you can trust that your body text will display the same on each.

As noted earlier, the size of your body text probably should be 12–14 points. Smaller than that decreases readability. Larger than that and the text appears too large, competes too much with display type and will eat up too much space.

## Images

Keep the following tips in mind when choosing images:

- Use supporting images that are appropriate.
- Use enough to help tell the story, but not too many.
- Size some large, but do not size any too small.

So, which images are appropriate? Those that visually report the story beyond your words. For example, you could share the shock and grief that students on your campus felt following the 9-11 disaster using thousands of words. Yet, one photograph might tell more powerfully the emotional impact.

How many images should you use? You *can* have too much of a good thing. Rather than run four or five photos, even if they are excellent, consider using the best two, with the stronger shot dominant—at least twice the size of the second. Running the best of the best maintains high quality, and the contrast in size makes the large photo seem even larger.

How large should images be? Size, of course, is relative. Web page readers relate image size first to how it compares to their computer screen size or the Web page size. Next, they relate image size to how it compares to other elements on the page, especially to other images but also to blocks of text and boxed items. Therefore, make one image on the screen dominant. Also, do not run images too small to be "read." Forcing readers to strain and wonder what an image portrays is frustrating, a waste of a good image and a waste of page space.

While photos likely are the strongest images you might use, do not discount the value of good clip art. Use of these should follow the same advice as earlier, particularly in their appropriateness.

## *Designing Barebones Links Pages*

Barebones pages are the most practical and utilitarian of those we are discussing. In and of themselves, they are not appealing. Their purpose is to provide a means for readers to locate and click through to your stories. A single Web page should be able to handle this task.

As a minimum you should design your page with the following elements:

- Main heading. This should be the title of your online publication.
- Publication logo. Consider designing this image as a visual signature for your publication.

- Weekly publication dates.
- Links to stories or newspaper posted each week.
- E-mail contact link.
- Current update line.

The next step is to decide what file format you want to provide readers: .doc files, .html files or .pdfs of fully designed newspaper pages. The first format is ready to go. The second will have you save the word processed story as .html, a task made easy with Microsoft Word using a menu command. The third, as we discussed earlier, demands you first design and package a print newspaper and then save it as a .pdf. In each case you will link to these files on your barebones page.

Coding files for barebones pages is easy and a good way to begin learning how to code .html. Nevertheless, if you are technologically challenged, then you may wish to use wysiwyg software.

Wysiwyg programs, like Front Page, are nearly as easy to use as word processing software. In addition, Front Page provides a handful of attractive templates that make creating professional-looking pages simple. Probably the best reason for knowing .html is that it allows you to check and troubleshoot pages prepared with wysiwyg software.

Once designed, maintaining this page should be quick and easy. Examples are located online at the "Storycrafting" Web site.

## Designing Enhanced Index Pages

While quite similar to barebones pages, enhanced pages are an important step up. They can provide an inviting design in addition to aiding readers in locating and clicking through to stories. This site should have a homepage that links to separate weekly publication pages.

As a minimum you should design your homepage with the following elements:

- Main heading.
- Publication logo.
- Links to weekly publications, along with related dominant images.
- E-mail contact link.
- Current update line.

The weekly publication pages should include the following:

- Main heading.
- Publication logo.
- Date of publication.
- Lead story link with a dominant image.
- Remaining links to weekly stories, categorized to content.

At this point you have several options available. Whether you choose .doc or .html as your story file format, you need not do anything beyond creating links and posting stories.

Ideally, though, you might design each story page with the following:

- Display type for headlines and, perhaps, story lead-ins. Story lead-ins are more than second-level headlines. They serve as transitions from the headline to the beginning of the story and often are written as full sentences.
- Reduced text widths for the stories.
- Appropriate photos or clip art, with one sized dominant.
- Related charts or graphs.

To create the enhanced index pages, you can do the .html coding yourself or use wysiwyg software. The latter is the simpler approach, of course.

If you choose .pdf as your format, you can treat their indexing the same as .doc files, with whatever additional enhancements you may want for the site's homepage. As mentioned earlier, most of the work involved in preparing .pdfs is in designing the original print pages. Posting them is simple.

While enhanced pages are somewhat more demanding, their benefits make them well worth it. You can find examples of enhanced pages at the "Storycrafting" Web site.

## *Online Publication Siting*

While preparing your Web site, you need to find a server with space to store your files and Internet access for you to upload materials and for readers to view them.

The ideal server will give you sufficient space to upload all your story and image files for the semester's news publication. It also should allow one or more members of your class ready access to upload files and maintain the site. Finally, high-speed connections will ensure that access is not too slow.

You have at least three server options:

- Campus server.
- Free-space server.
- Local Internet service provider.

The first and most logical option is your campus server. It is possible that space already is allocated to classroom activities. Thus, it should be a simple matter for your teacher to make arrangements.

One possible drawback is that your campus likely has site guidelines that may limit access or restrict content.

Locating a Web site that offers free Web space is a second alternative. Most likely, you will have ready access to the site with high-speed connections. Also, few such sites have restrictions that would limit the content you and your colleagues likely will put on your page. For example, you can get 15 MB of space at Yahoo! GeoCities. Go to <http://geocities.yahoo.com/ps/learn2/HowItWorks4_Free.html> to learn more.

That is just the beginning. A listing of 58 sites offering free Web page space of more than 20 MB is at <http://www.freewebspace.net/>. Most of these offer online tools to assist your Web design and many have free help desks.

However, these free-space servers usually have one drawback: They use either frames or pop-ups to present advertising to your page's visitors.

A third possibility is a local Internet service provider. As a public service to your college and to the local community, a local ISP might be willing to allocate sufficient space for your online news publication. Like the free-space servers, your local ISP likely would not restrict access or content and probably provides high-speed connections.

While the local ISP probably would not run advertising on your pages, your providing a sponsorship line at the bottom of your homepage would be a worthwhile gesture.

## Uploading Files

With files and server ready, your next step is to upload files. File transfer protocol programs are used to upload files to or delete files from the server. A handful is available free, including WS_FTP Pro or LeapFTP for PC-based platforms and Fetch for Macintosh platforms. A site listing free FTP and other software for Windows is <http://www.free-software-downloads.org/>. You can download Fetch at <http://fetchsoftworks.com/>.

Beyond the software, all you need to upload and delete files is the *exact* server URL; the *exact* access code, if any; and the *exact* filenames of pages and stories. We cannot stress enough the requirement for exactness here. Any variation in capitalization, spacing or lettering may cause problems.

After uploading files, open the Web page with your browser to make sure that they display properly. Click every link to make sure it opens the correct file. You do not want to find out from potential readers that your page looks odd or your links are not working.

## Online Publication Access and Promotion

When you are satisfied that your new Web site is in order, you should decide who you want to visit it and how you will promote, or market, your site.

Three likely audiences include class members only, campus readers and off-campus/worldwide.

Handling access and marketing for your class should be easy. In-class announcements that give the site's URL should do the trick. Making the site available to campus readers is only slightly tougher. They need to know of the site's existence and the site's Web address. You might publicize this information in the campus newspaper, in fliers posted around campus, on campuswide e-mail lists and electronic message boards or even on the campus Web site. The advantage of electronic marketing, of course, is that a clickable URL can be included, making it quick and easy for visitors to go to your site.

Promoting your site for an off-campus and worldwide audience is a bit more challenging. Remember that the only way for someone to visit your site is to know it is there and to have the URL to connect to it. Search engines are your best resource for this.

Visit online search engines and complete forms available to ask that they list your site. For example, Yahoo!'s site submission page is <http://docs.yahoo.com/info/suggest/>, Google's site submission page is <http://www.google.com/addurl.html> and MSN's site submission page is <http://free.submit-it.com/msnsubmit.htm>. Follow the steps at each to request your site be included.

Another option is to find a free URL submission site that will submit your information to multiple sites. For additional sites go to a search engine and type "free URL submission sites." You should have plenty to work with.

## Timely News

With your online news publication operational, you now have a commitment to readers, the same responsibility of any recurring publication. You should make it available by a fixed deadline every week, every two weeks or every month. Once that is established, work backwards with initial and intermediate deadlines that will allow your class to complete tasks in an efficient sequence. Minimum deadlines should cover the following, in the order indicated:

- Stories.
- Story file preparation.
- Art and graphics preparation.
- Web page design.
- Page production and uploading.

If your class plans to use page-design software to produce print-style newspaper pages that you convert to .pdf, you will need to add at least two more deadlines between the art and graphics preparation and the Web page design:

- Newspaper page design.
- Newspaper page production.

Regardless of which options you choose, class members should be assigned to teams handling the particular duties in each area. Then, *one person*, responsible for assigning tasks and meeting deadlines, should be in charge of each team.

Regular visitors will come to expect new stories on schedule. Miss a few deadlines, though, and visitors will lose confidence in your site.

As we will discuss in Chapter 19, convergence takes full advantage of multiple media to get news to readers in the quickest and most effective way. One of the real benefits of your online news publications is the immediacy with which you can post new information and new stories. If unexpected events happen or if new information on a previous story becomes available, you can write a story and make it available right away. There is something especially exciting about running an "extra" or staying on top of a breaking story. Consider doing so and enjoying the rush.

Finally, although your current "issue" is constantly before you and demanding most of your attention, make sure that previous issues and stories remain accessible to readers. For the most part this means that you do not delete previous pages, links and stories. In fact, as you work your way through the semester, you may even link back to previous stories when you write a new story on the same or a related topic. This adds depth and history to your coverage and benefits readers who may not have read the previous stories.

Archiving of news is a valuable service that newspapers, magazines and journals can provide over their broadcasting counterparts.

## Crafting and Drafting

Working with your teacher and based on the size of your class, you might organize two staffs, with one staff working every other issue. Whether your class opts for .doc, .html or .pdf files and bare-bones or enhanced pages will determine how many teams will comprise each staff. As made clear in the chapter, the more sophisticated the final publication, the more teams and time are necessary.

## For Practice

16-1. Your task is to produce a new online news publication or to enhance an existing one.

## Chapter 16 Bibliography

Nielsen, Jakob. "How Users Read on the Web: They Don't." *Alertbox*. 1 October 1997.
    <http://www.useit.com>.
Twain, Mark. George Bainton. *The Art of Authorship* (1890). *Respectfully Quoted: A Dictionary of Quotations Requested from the Congressional Research Service*. Washington D.C.: Library of Congress, 1989.
    <http://www.bartleby.com/73/540.html>.

# Part 3
# The Profession

# Chapter 17
# Journalistic Conduct

*True glory consists in doing what deserves to be written; in writing what deserves to be read; and in so living as to make the world happier and better for our living in it.*

—Pliny the Elder

## Chapter Contents

## *QuickView*

Tradition expects journalists to act appropriately in a public forum, where they guard the public good to earn the public trust. Therefore, your professional conduct, how you behave as a journalist, is not a private matter.

It is that professional and public behavior we will explore here. We will begin with a review of the foundation of journalistic conduct as influenced by morals, ethics and law, with ethics as the key factor.

From there we will cover the other characteristics of proper journalistic conduct, including objectivity, truth, accuracy, balance and fairness, respect and courtesy, integrity and honesty, independence, accountability and taste.

In the process you should be able to establish a firmer foundation for your professional conduct.

---

When they roamed the countryside and villages long ago, storytellers told tales, both tall and small. Many were fanciful, while others may have carried at least a few grains of truth. A handful was reasonably accurate reports of events they witnessed or about which they heard. No one—not the storytellers nor their peers nor their audiences—held these minstrels to standards beyond the demand that their stories interest and entertain.

Over the centuries, though, the expectations of audiences and storytellers themselves grew. They no longer were satisfied with news accounts that may have been as much fiction as fact. As they further defined their discipline, journalists embraced higher standards that clarified how they would ply their trade and that eventually gave them status as a profession.

These standards of practice evolved into a widely accepted code of conduct that directs how journalists should work and behave. On the surface this might seem rather simple. It is not. Because the code continues to be shaped by practice, social interaction and laws, many issues of conduct are not straightforward, clear cut or settled.

This complexity of meeting the demands of our profession should become clearer as we move through this chapter and learn the basics of ethics and journalistic professionalism.

## *Role of Journalism*

The Project for Excellence in Journalism cites the role of journalism as "helping define community, creating common language and common knowledge, identifying a community's goals, heroes and villains, and pushing people beyond complacency." Journalists fulfill their role following what PEJ terms the nine core principles:

1. Journalism's first obligation is to the truth.
2. Its first loyalty is to citizens.
3. Its essence is a discipline of verification.
4. Its practitioners must maintain an independence from those they cover.
5. It must serve as an independent monitor of power.
6. It must provide a forum for public criticism and compromise.
7. It must strive to make the significant interesting and relevant.
8. It must keep the news comprehensive and proportional.
9. Its practitioners must be allowed to exercise their personal conscience.

These core principles permeate all aspects of journalistic conduct and are reflected in the ethics and professional expectations discussed in this chapter and throughout this book.

# Foundation of Journalistic Conduct

Journalistic conduct typically is directed by three widely accepted codes: morals, ethics and law. All are similar to one another in their focus on right and wrong behavior, and some provisions are nearly identical.

Similar provisions have guided humans and our societies for centuries. Basic principles, in fact, tend to transcend religious, cultural and legal boundaries. Yet, none of the codes are fixed, unchanging or universal. Ultimately, each person decides with which provisions he or she will comply.

## Morals and Ethics

A clear notion of ethics is important to our professional practice. Let us first distinguish between morals and ethics. While both define right and wrong conduct, each arrives there using different standards. Interestingly, on many issues the resulting guidelines are identical.

The term *morals* is from the Latin *mos*, meaning "custom." The term *ethics* is from the Greek *ethos*, meaning "character."

A group determines custom over time, while character pertains to personal attributes. Therefore, societies have customs, and people have character. Furthermore, we might say that morals guide how members of a group treat one another while ethics guide how groups relate to other groups. Finally, morals come from authorities, whether they be religious or cultural, and ethics come from personally accepted principles. In practice we typically attribute moral codes to religion or society and ethical codes to organized professions and groups.

Carol Marin is uncomfortable with interchanging *moral* and *ethical*. She writes, "'Conscience' and 'morality' seem to hold a bit too much righteousness and rectitude for what journalists really do when they try to do it, the right thing. 'Ethical' suggests a search for guidance for conduct and decision-making, a process rather than a doctrine."

Whether a particular act is a moral or ethical violation always is open to circumstance, interpretation and contention. For example, at one time in our history slavery was morally and ethically (and legally) accepted—at least across the Old South. Much of the sentiment in the North, however, considered slavery both immoral and unethical even though it was legal in certain states. Therefore, if a Northern abolitionist helped a slave escape, the Southern owner could claim theft of property. Yet, because the abolitionist's moral and ethical view would not allow any person to be considered property, this "theft" would be justifiable, albeit illegal, behavior.

Similar controversial issues—war, abortion, cloning and using animals for scientific research—continue to force debate and division today, caused by fundamental differences in moral and ethical perspectives.

Recent newsroom scandals have spotlighted a clear disregard for even the most fundamental journalistic ethics, have focused on concerns that the profession has become soft in its ethical expectations and have further eroded the fragile credibility that journalists need from their audiences.

## Codes of Ethics

A number of journalistic organizations give members voice in shaping the professional conduct they expect of themselves. The results are organized in what most organizations call their code of ethics, the most popular of which belongs to the Society of Professional Journalists. The code, which is online at <http://spj.org/ethics_code.asp>, reflects the positive behavior expected of journalists. It serves as a comprehensive and clear guide for how journalists should act. The four major admonitions in the code are the following:

- Seek truth and report it.
- Minimize harm.
- Act independently.
- Be accountable.

If we are to prosper as a profession, we must stabilize and embrace such professional ethical codes and practice them in our professional lives. Actually, many of our concerns about ethics and professional behavior would be minimized if we worried less about whether we *can* do something and more about whether we *should* do something.

## Law

The third powerful influence on journalistic practice is law. It, too, shares common concerns with morals and ethics—particularly in distinguishing between right and wrong behavior.

Examining law and ethics, Paul S. Voakes cites the most frequent differences between the two systems: People consider law obligatory and ethics aspirational, "a system of conduct we emulate only when we feel inclined to. The law, however, often implies a requirement."

Other people believe law is rigorous, logical and objective while ethics are intuitive and subjective.

Violations of the law draw sanctions from external forces, such as the penal system. Violations of ethics, though, result in pangs of conscience or, at the most, social and group disapproval.

The demands of law are not necessarily identical to the demands of ethics. Voakes says, "Law and ethics can propel two persons in the same situation into two different actions. Some actions can be perfectly legal, yet most people would consider them unethical."

These contrasts clarify the relationship between law and ethics and suggest the longstanding conundrum journalists face in meeting ethical expectations. Specific points will be addressed in the review of ethical values later.

In much of their practice journalists are not compelled by law to act in certain ways. No law, for example, requires that they be objective, accurate, honest or independent in their storytelling. That is the province of ethics.

On the other hand, with First Amendment principles as a basis, laws enacted by the states restrict media and protect the public. Although complete books and full classes of study are devoted to media law, we will cover in Chapter 18 a few of the essential provisions of law.

# *Objectivity*

Of all the ethical and professional demands you face as a journalist, none is more insistent than the charge to be objective. The concept of objectivity has been part of journalism since the beginning of the 20th century.

Walter Lippmann and Charles Merz, both associated with the New York World, argued that scientific method offered a purer approach to newsgathering and reporting. Science, with its emphasis on gathering evidence and weighing it impartially and dispassionately, would remove the flawed human element, the journalist. At least, that was the intent.

## Objectivity as the Ideal

As one of journalism's longest standing principles, objectivity seeks to give readers facts, not feelings. The following is the ideal:

- Objective reporting is true.
- It is accurate.
- It is balanced and fair.
- It is unbiased.

However, objectivity does not always live up to its high standards.

A recent credibility study, conducted by the American Society of Newspaper Editors, suggests that news coverage is not as objective as it needs to be. A majority of the public believes journalistic points of view and biases help determine what stories are covered and how they are covered. Readers claim journalists write for editors, not for them.

For what it is worth, the study found the public sees television as more biased than newspapers.

Many today would argue that journalistic objectivity is a myth. In gathering material and writing their stories, reporters are subjective in whom they interview, what questions they ask, what information they use and what angle they take. In order to limit the impact of these subjective elements, proponents of objectivity argue that journalists must be vigilant that their stories are true, accurate, balanced and fair.

Howard A. Myrick reminds us that regardless of what we would like them to be, the media are businesses. He takes to task journalism classes that claim the media exist to provide news and public service. "The abject and uncomfortable truth is that the profit incentive is the force that guides the daily activities of news organizations. The reality of the profit motive and its impact on the character, quality and, especially, objectivity in the news is inescapable—and usually negative," he writes. This situation is particularly troublesome today as difficult economic conditions, media mergers and declining bottom lines challenge media survival.

The ASNE study lends strong support to Myrick's claim. A clear majority of the public responding charged that the main concern of newspapers is making money, not serving the public interest.

In addition, part of the blame for problems with objectivity must go to writing itself. As accurate and authentic as we would wish to make it, writing is not reality. It is a representation of reality. Yet, short of being there to witness everything, audiences must rely on writing.

Purely objective writing is the ideal. According to Myrick, "it is a goal well worth pursuing, for the good of the profession of journalism and, more importantly, the good of the nation."

## Alternatives to Traditional Objectivity

Recognizing the problems associated with traditional objectivity, some journalists encourage alternatives. The first is objectivity of method. Another is a greater focus on fairness.

In criticizing traditional objectivity, Philip Meyer says, "Objectivity, as defined by the knee-jerk, absolutist school of media ethics, means standing so far from the community that you see all events and all viewpoints as equally distant and important—or unimportant." All views and claims get equal weight, resulting in "a laying out of facts in a sterile, noncommittal manner, and then standing back to 'let the reader decide' which view is true."

Meyer calls this "objectivity of result, defining objectivity not by the way we go about our business of gathering and interpreting the news, but by what we put in the paper." The product is measured, with this number of lines for this group and that number of lines for that group. Equal numbers result in objectivity.

One solution, Meyer believes, would go hand-in-hand with public journalism, an approach we shall cover in Chapter 19. That solution is objectivity of method, wherein reporters use data-intensive methods and follow the scientific standard of replicability. He recommends the following approach:

- Reporters inform their investigations with theories of the underlying causes of events.
- They develop operational tests of those theories.
- They document steps in executing their tests with a paper trail that others can follow and come up with the same results.

Hank Glamann proposes the second alternative. In offering solutions to problems with media credibility, he targets bias, which objectivity is intended to dispel. He writes, "In terms of addressing concerns about bias, my advice is this: Redouble your efforts to be fair and abandon your efforts to be objective."

While this recommendation may seem rather harsh, Glamann is not alone. An increasing number of working journalists and journalism educators agree with him. He argues, "No one can be truly objective. To do so, you would have to be able to see the world through a lens uncolored by your life experiences, and no one can do that."

Moreover, Glamann believes "we do ridiculous and hurtful things in the name of objectivity." For example, a story about black political activism includes comments from a white supremacist for balance. Or a story about domestic-partner benefits for city employees is "balanced" with views from a conservative Christian leader who claims homosexuality can be cured. In search of objectivity news coverage can go awry.

"One who is fair has a mind that is open but discerning, a sensitivity to the rich tapestry of humanity. Striving toward the goal of fairness is a never-ending endeavor," he adds.

Objectivity today clearly is a professional standard under review. Whether you choose traditional objectivity, a greater emphasis on fairness or some other reasonable approach, your goal continues to be giving readers fair and appropriate content they need to understand the message of each story.

## *Truth*

The Code of Ethics of the Society of Professional Journalists lists first "Seek truth and report it." There follows a list of dos and don'ts, all of which are valid and vital to professional practice. The nine core principles from the Project for Excellence in Journalism, presented earlier, also name truth as journalism's first obligation.

Steve Geimann, former president of the Society of Professional Journalists, writes, "Truth is elusive and sometimes can be tortured to make a point. We have a responsibility to get the truth. In an increasingly competitive profession, with the Internet increasingly competing with TV and newspapers, professional journalists have an even greater obligation to be more responsible and accurate."

Above all else, truth must be what journalists strive to deliver. This is noble and necessary; it also can be difficult. A nagging question among the most difficult facing journalists remains unanswered: What exactly is truth?

Most often, the distinction is not between what is true and what is false. It is more a matter of *whose* truth and *which* truth, hairsplitting that can befuddle even the most dedicated and professional journalist.

Commenting on the media maelstrom following the Clinton-Lewinsky scandal, Geimann criticizes the profession: "Instead of seeking truth—the foundation of the SPJ Code of Ethics—newspaper and broadcast journalists were more interested in copying and chasing each other. Instead of identifying anonymous sources, otherwise respected journalists abdicated their responsibilities to other reporters and editors who often seemed to follow a looser set of ethical guidelines."

There certainly are documented cases of journalists writing stories wherein they intentionally presented questionable data, fabricated sources and quotations, distorted information and even boldfaced lies. However, most of the time journalists reach for the truth in their stories. They do not always find it.

Truth can be slippery. Each of us views life from a unique perspective, one that we each privilege as truth, *our* truth. In newsgathering where multiple sources claim different takes on the same experience or issue, we still must try to give readers the truth. How to do so is the challenge.

Probably the wisest solution is to recall that material you gather is evidence. Just as in a courtroom, you must present evidence to make the case to your jury of readers. Consider one of the following approaches in getting at the truth of the experience or issue.

- Present all evidence that seems valid, even if it may be contradictory. This allows readers to decide the truth for themselves.
- Privilege one source's perspective over others due to that person's status or credibility, the person's ability to recall or to interpret or simply the better perspective from which the person saw the event or understands the issue. Explain this to readers. The story also should indicate that other sources offered conflicting evi-

dence. This approach forces you to evaluate sources on behalf of your readers and to give them evidence from the most valid.

Give it your best, and any reasonable attempt to present the truth complies with ethical demands.

## Accuracy

Closely tied to presenting the truth is another ethical and professional axiom—that your story is accurate. Accuracy involves careful reporting that gets the facts right.

Yet, according to a report from the Journalism Values Institute, sponsored by ASNE, "getting the facts right is not the same as getting the 'right facts.' Editors said newspapers must provide the background, context and perspective required to paint a complete picture for people. When it comes to accuracy, the 'right facts' means reflecting the tone, language, experiences and emotions of the public—coverage that 'rings true' to readers."

Accuracy gives readers a sense of thoroughness and coherence. News coverage transcends "accurate" to become "authentic," which the ASNE editors explained, "conveys what people see, hear and experience living in their communities."

### Precise, Authentic Reporting

A baseline expectation of accuracy is insuring that the facts of your story are correct, beginning with the little things. Names are spelled correctly. Dates, times and places are right. Numbers are exact.

This is a goal too often missed in newspapers today. The ASNE credibility study confirms that both the public and journalists believe too many factual, spelling and grammar errors litter our newspapers. Journalists blame deadline pressures. Greater concern for accuracy, over time, will help to reduce these mistakes. Until then, published corrections are an important remedy, one that makes the public feel better about a newspaper's credibility.

Accuracy at this higher level demands precise reporting. You exercise care that no detail is too routine to escape exactness. Errors in basic facts, as we have noted previously, trouble readers and force them to suspect that other material in a story may not be correct. Such skepticism can cascade, resulting in readers who distrust whatever they find printed in their newspapers.

In the end you lose that which is most precious: credibility.

Precise reporting forces you to rely first on sources to support the story. As your storytelling moves beyond basic facts to explanation, you must guard against distortion or manipulation caused by either your sources or yourself. Regardless of the reasons, anything beyond the facts or how the facts might reasonably be interpreted may be a violation of your ethical responsibility.

At the next level the authenticity gained from accuracy is the real prize. Authentic stories have facts that are right and the right facts to make stories "ring true," the ASNE editors observed. Such coverage provides the tone, language, experiences, emotions and range of voices that capture the essence of the story. It includes background that reveals enough about story sources that readers can judge the value of what they say. It reaches past the official perspective "to reflect how a community talks and thinks about an issue" or responds to an event.

Such stories are real, and readers get much more than just the facts. They acquire understanding.

## Verification

The chief means by which you can ensure accuracy in your storytelling is verification, a consistent method by which you check information for accuracy and validity.

Verification does not allow you to guess at anything. It does not permit that you rely on your memory for the facts of a story. It expects, instead, that you take precise notes and follow them when you write. It pushes you to corroborate what a source tells you with evidence from other sources. It requires that you check everything for accuracy. Then, you check again.

The public polled in the ASNE credibility study responded that newspapers should hold stories until they can be double-checked; a majority of journalists agree.

The Project for Excellence in Journalism offers several pointers for verification:

### Do not add anything to your story that was not there.

This includes inventing characters or details or rearranging events. The event, experience and characters must speak for themselves.

### Never deceive your audience.

Avoid embellishing in any way a narrative account, and do not mess with direct quotes beyond correcting grammatical errors.

### Be transparent about your reporting methods and motives.

Transparency means that you allow these to be clearly visible by answering the following in your story: "How do you know what you know? Who are your sources? How direct is their knowledge? What biases might they have? Are there conflicting accounts? What don't we know?"

The Rule of Transparency also extends to your sources. Do not bluff them. Do not mislead them. Do not trick them. Do not lie to them. These and more abuses have been done in the name of truthseeking.

### Do your own reporting.

If media learned anything of value from the Clinton-Lewinsky scandal, it was their need to go back to this axiom. The argument that other media outlets were presenting third-hand reports of anonymous sources swayed too many in the media to violate this rule.

### Keep an open mind.

The point here is that journalists should not think they understand too much. They must remain skeptical about not only what they see and hear but also, the Project for Excellence in Journalism writes, about "their ability to know what it really means. In other words, journalists need to recognize their own fallibility, the limitations of their knowledge."

Verification shuns errors. It disdains vagueness. It also discourages shoddy newsgathering and writing. As a result, it respects readers, enhances objectivity and encourages credibility.

## Accuracy Checklist

Consider using an accuracy checklist to guide review of your stories so that they are accurate. The following 12-point checklist, developed by the Society of Professional Journalists, is a handy resource to keep on your desk as you draft and revise.

1. Do you have a high level of confidence about the facts in your story and the sources that are providing them? If not, can you tell your story in a more accurate manner? If you have any doubts about your sources, can you delete them or replace them and achieve a higher likelihood of reliability?
2. Have you attributed or documented all facts?
3. Have you double-checked the key facts?
4. Can you provide the properly spelled name and accurate telephone number of every source cited?
5. Are you highly confident that all the factual statements in your story reflect the truth?
6. Are you prepared to defend publicly your fact checking and whatever other measures that were taken to verify your story?
7. Are the quotes in your story presented fairly, in context?
8. Are you quoting anonymous sources? Why are you using those? Are you prepared to defend publicly the use of those sources?
9. Are you using any material documents or pictures provided by anonymous sources? Why? What is your level of confidence about the validity of this material? Are you prepared to defend publicly the use of that material?
10. Have you described persons, minority groups, races, cultures, nations or segments of society—e.g. business people, Viet Nam veterans, cheerleaders—using stereotypical adjectives? Are such descriptions accurate and meaningful in the context presented?
11. Have you used potentially objectionable language or pictures in your story? Is there a compelling reason for using such information? Would the story be less accurate if that language or picture were eliminated?
12. Do your headlines (or broadcast promos or teases) accurately present the facts and context of the story to which they are referring?

## *Balance and Fairness*

Companions to objectivity are balance and fairness. Recognizing the difficulty in being fully objective in both gathering and writing, most journalists seek instead to make their stories balanced.

The intent of balance is to avoid slanted or one-sided coverage. It assumes that all stories, indeed, have two sides, let alone *only* two sides. Also, it puts many journalists into positions where they consider coverage balanced if it is equal. That is, as noted earlier, the number of sources, the number of quotes and even the number of lines for each side is the same, or nearly so.

The editors of the Journalism Values Institute, sponsored by ASNE, registered concerns about this notion of balance, which journalists often interpret as giving both sides of a story. They said, "The news coverage that results can become conflict-driven, taking on the feel of sharp dichotomies such as pro and con, right and wrong, winners and losers, either and or."

Alternatively, they recommended giving *all* sides to a story, "an approach that reflects how communities work. The approach recognizes that a range of diverse viewpoints exists; that there are solutions along with problems; that at the same time the unusual occurs, the profoundly ordinary exists; and that there is good with the bad."

Rather than balance, the editors encouraged fairness or wholeness, achieved by following these guidelines for reporters:

- Avoid moving too quickly to extremes, where stories most likely will take on the aura of conflict. Instead, seek to include moderate voices, areas of agreement and points of compromise.
- Open channels to new voices in the community who represent layers beyond the official and usual sources.
- Uncover and understand one's own preconceived notions about a given subject.

Although some editors believe conflict makes for a good story, it should not be the most frequent frame used to focus coverage. When most stories in newspapers deal with conflict, those deserving that frame lose their edge.

Balance is important to the public, so much so that the ASNE study found that most readers believe a story should not be published if only one side can be reached for comment.

## Respect and Courtesy

Too often overlooked in discussions of journalistic conduct are the respect and courtesy with which journalists should treat their sources and their readers. Both of these are driven by the Golden Rule: Do unto others as you would have them do unto you.

Generally, we might say that respect is a frame of mind while courtesy is a way of acting. It is difficult to have one without the other because of their relationship to one another.

Recall that no law compels people to give information to journalists. No one, from president to pauper, has to agree to be a source for a story you write. Sources agree to talk with journalists at their own discretion. There is no denying that your sources are doing you a favor. Consequently, regardless of their status, background or current situation, you must treat them with respect.

In such situations there is little room for your ego. Even when a source offends you in some way, ignore it—if you hope to keep that person as a viable source. It cannot be a matter of who started it or who deserves what. While no one expects you to grovel or to put up with any kind of abuse, you may have to take a bit of guff.

Finally, treat news sources and subjects with compassion, particularly those who are victims of crime or tragedy.

The SPJ Code of Ethics calls for journalists to respect the public. In its "Minimize Harm" section the code expects compassion and sensitivity for all those who must deal with the consequences of news coverage, particularly children, as well as those affected by tragedy and grief.

The ASNE credibility study found that readers believe newspapers are inconsistent in showing respect for and knowledge of their readers and communities, a point with which journalists in the study did not fully agree. Some of this perceived lack of respect might result from readers' belief that journalists are willing to hurt people just to publish a story.

You also must be courteous with sources. This involves treating them in right ways. You address them appropriately. You make appointments and keep them. You apologize for any missteps. You thank them for their information.

Your readers also deserve your respect and courtesy. While you do not typically address readers directly, your demeanor in writing to them and for them should reflect your respect for their intelligence, their perspectives and their value as your readers. Without them you have no audience.

Your respect and courtesy for readers are further supported by efforts you make to know them and to understand them. The resulting image you hold of readers should be authentic and positive, which should stimulate an appropriate tone in your writing.

Courtesy expects that, when you discover errors or they are brought to your attention, you follow up with appropriate published apologies and corrections.

## *Integrity and Honesty*

Integrity is one of those character traits that all of us want—even if we cannot pin down exactly what it is. Simply, integrity is moral soundness, where there are no differences between our conscience and our behavior.

Honesty, often considered almost synonymous to integrity, is a desirable character trait most of us clearly understand. It is the good-faith intent to convey truth as we know it and to avoid misleading or deceptive communication. Three dimensions of honesty are truthfulness, sincerity and candor.

Journalists must embrace these values as sacred.

Violations range from intentional lying or deceptive withholding to fudging on the facts or exaggerating the truth. Unfortunately, well-publicized, high-profile incidents in recent years have given the public reason to suspect that dishonesty and lack of integrity may be all too common in the media.

Among the most common violations of integrity and honesty is plagiarism—using the ideas and words of others without giving them due credit. Because it is stealing, it is immoral. Because it is dishonest, it is unethical. And in some circumstances, at least, it also is illegal.

Bottom line, plagiarism is wrong.

Across disciplines on college and university campuses today plagiarism is growing at an alarming rate. One of the main reasons for this may be the ease with which the Internet has made information readily available. Search engines simplify locating material on any topic imaginable. Saving that material comes at the click of a key.

Once in a file on a computer, it is so inviting to copy and paste all that into another piece of writing.

So, what harm is done? And who will know?

Plagiarism harms your integrity and honesty, those basic traits that define who we are and that weigh what we are worth. Plagiarism harms the publication wherein the material was published, further eroding credibility among readers. Finally, plagiarism also harms the profession by cheapening the value that some journalists give to honesty and to the intellectual products of others. If the material taken and used without credit were yours, you certainly would have a clearer sense of the harm done.

Plagiarism is not worth it, especially when you can avoid the problem by using quotation marks for exact borrowings and giving credit to sources of material that is not common knowledge and not your own.

Your reputation for integrity and honesty is valuable beyond measure. Guard it and treasure it.

## Independence

All the effort put to objectivity, truth, balance and fairness will be of little consequence if journalists do not practice an appropriate measure of independence.

In its report on the nine core principles of journalism, the Project for Excellence said, "Independence of spirit and mind, rather than neutrality, is the principle journalists must keep in focus. While editorialists and commentators are not neutral, the source of their credibility is still their accuracy, intellectual fairness and ability to inform—not their devotion to a certain group or outcome. In our independence, however, we must avoid any tendency to stray into arrogance, elitism, isolation or nihilism."

Independence for journalists cannot be a distant ideal. It must be real and substantive if the media are to meet their vital responsibility as watchdogs of those in power, as well as serve their roles as informers, educators and even entertainers. In their watchdog role journalists speak for those who have no voice and against those who are swayed unduly by power. No other entity in this country—or around the world, for that matter—can give the public the kind of oversight that the media provide.

According to SPJ's Code of Ethics, independence means that journalists should:

- Avoid conflicts of interest.
- Resist associating with people and activities that may threaten integrity or credibility.
- Turn down any perks—gifts, favors, free travel and special treatment—or involvement with other jobs, politics, public office or community service organizations if they threaten integrity.
- Hold accountable those in power.
- Deny to others any special treatment.
- Avoid granting favors or money to sources for information.

Conflicts of interest, payoffs and other favoritism have been the historic bane of some in the profession. The best in the business, though, learn to draw the line that separates them and makes possible the fair coverage of even tough, consuming issues.

Ultimately, any activity, real or perceived, that may compromise your independence may be an ethical violation.

## Accountability

Accountability is a relatively recent addition to the ethical responsibilities of journalists. It reflects a growing concern that the media is unresponsive to the public, more intent on serving its own interests instead of the audience it serves.

The SPJ code expects journalists to be accountable in the following ways. They should:

- Clarify and explain news coverage and invite dialogue with the public over journalistic conduct.
- Encourage the public to voice grievances against the news media.
- Admit mistakes and correct them promptly.
- Expose unethical practices of journalists and the news media.
- Abide by the same high standards to which they hold others.

The clear message that these provisions send to the media is that they are responsible for educating the public about the work they do. When journalists do not work as they should, the public should call them on it, and the media should be up front about admitting and correcting errors and unethical conduct. Journalists and media who abide by this code stand a good chance of helping to repair the media's damaged credibility and lingering disenchantment among citizens about the job media are doing.

## Taste

The final issue of ethics and professional conduct is taste, more specifically good taste. Certainly, taste tends to be quite personal and largely subjective. Nevertheless, well-informed journalists who have realistic notions about their audience—what it likes and what it does not—should understand the limits of good taste and refrain from treading on them.

This is especially true for crime coverage, especially that focusing on victims. How much you *should* report versus how much you *can* report goes right to the heart of good taste. The SPJ code deals with taste under its "Minimize Harm" section, wherein it adds that journalists should "avoid pandering to lurid curiosity."

The claim that journalists thrive on sensationalizing news is not new and continues to be reinforced by public opinion surveys. Rather than responding defensively, media should be more proactive in their ethical responsibility to show good taste.

## Codes of Ethics Online

Go online to read the full texts for the following codes of ethics:

- Society of Professional Journalists Code of Ethics. <http://spj.org/ethics_code.asp>.
- American Society of Newspaper Editors Statement of Purpose. <http://www.asne.org/index.cfm?ID=888>.

- Associated Press Code of Ethics. <http://www.apme.com/about/code_ethics.shtml>.
- Code of Ethics and Professional Conduct of the Radio-Television News Directors Association. <http://www.cychron.com/Adviser/BroadcastProd/rtndaethics.htm>.

## Crafting and Drafting

Accuracy is essential for news stories. Therefore, we pay particular attention to it in your story for Exercise 17-1. After you have written your draft, do the following before peer review:

- First, check the accuracy of your draft by using the SPJ accuracy checklist.
- Also, keep a written log of additions, deletions or other changes you make as a result of the checklist.

## For Practice

17-1. Run your regular beat and find the best topic for a story. Then, do the following:

a) Write a story using lead and development most appropriate for the topic and your audience.
b) Swap stories and your written accuracy log with a peer review partner or group and give written reader feedback
c) Submit the draft, written log and peer feedback to your teacher.
d) After your teacher has reviewed your draft and peer feedback and has offered additional suggestions, revise as required—especially any additional accuracy concerns that your peers and teacher have noted.
e) Submit a final draft to your teacher.

## Chapter 17 Bibliography

"Accuracy Checklist: Society of Professional Journalists." *Journalism.org*. <http://www.journalism.org/resources/tools/reporting/accuracy/spj.asp?from=print>. From the Society of Professional Journalists, 3909 N. Meridian St., Indianapolis, Indiana 46208, www.spj.org. Copyright © 2003 by Society of Professional Journalists. Reprinted by permission.

"Code of Ethics." *Society of Professional Journalists*. <http://spj.org/ethics_code.asp>.

"Developing a Method of Verification." Project for Excellence in Journalism. *Journalism.org*. <http://www.journalism.org/resources/tools/reporting/accuracy/verification.asp?from=print>.

"Examining Our Credibility: The Findings in Brief." *American Society of Newspaper Editors*. 4 August 1999. <http://www.asne.org/kiosk/reports/99reports/1999examiningourcredibility/p5-6_findings.html>.

Geimann, Steve. "Not Our Finest Hour." *Quill 86: 2* (1 March 1998).

Glamann, Hank. "The Credibility Problem." *ACES* [American Copy Editors Society]. <http://www.copydesk.org/credibility.htm>.

"It's Not Just Both Sides—It's All Sides: The Modern Newspaper Needs to Reflect the Many Dimensions of Its Communities." *American Society of Newspaper Editors*. 17 August 1999. <http://www.asne.org/works/jvi/jvibalan.htm>.

"'Just the Facts' Isn't Enough: 'Basic Facts' Must Be Complemented by 'Right Facts' for Coverage to Ring True to Readers." *American Society of Newspaper Editors*. 10 February 1997. <http://www.asne.org/works/jvi/jviaccura.htm>.

Marin, Carol. "Journalists Need Help with Ethical Decisions: In Today's Newsrooms There Are Plenty to Be Made." *Niemann Reports: The Elements of Journalism*. Summer 2001.

Meyer, Philip. "Public Journalism and the Problem of Objectivity." September 1995. <http://www.unc.edu/~pmeyer/ire95pj.htm>.

Myrick, Howard A. "The Search for Objectivity in Journalism." *USA Today Magazine*. November 2002.

Pliny the Elder. *Quotations for Creative Thinking*. <http://creativequotations.com/>.

"A Statement of Shared Purpose." Project for Excellence in Journalism. *Journalism.org*. <http://www.journalism.org/resources/guidelines/principles/purpose.asp>.

Voakes, Paul S. "Rights, Wrongs, and Responsibilities: Law and Ethics in the Newsroom." *Journal of Mass Media Ethics 15: 1* (2000).

# Chapter 18
# The First Amendment, Libel and Privacy

*Were it left to me to decide whether
we should have a government without
newspapers or newspapers without a
government, I should not hesitate a
moment to prefer the latter.*

—Thomas Jefferson

## Chapter Contents

## QuickView

This is a tedious chapter. Discussions of law usually are. The concerns with the First Amendment, libel and privacy are numerous and sometimes complicated. That does not excuse you from working as diligently as you can to avoid what could be damaging and expensive mistakes.

We will cover only the basics of media law here—enough, perhaps, to sensitize you to the seriousness of the topic, to give you basic familiarity with its scope and to alert you to seek professional guidance if you ever are unsure of possible violations.

Storytelling as a journalist holds you to a high level of expectation. It is not enough to tell a story well. You must tell it truthfully, accurately and fairly.

Our discussion of ethics and journalistic conduct in Chapter 17 stressed what you *should* do. Our discussion of libel and privacy in this chapter stresses what you *must* do. This is more than a shade of difference. Unethical behavior and unprofessional conduct can draw anything from a slap on the wrist to the loss of your job. Violations involving libel and privacy can get you and your publication hauled into court, where you face stiff fines.

Your rights, guaranteed by the First Amendment, always must be tempered by your clear understanding of legal limitations determined by state laws covering libel and privacy.

## The First Amendment

The foundation of our freedom of speech, including the broad freedoms enjoyed by the media, is the First Amendment: "Congress shall make no law respecting an establishment of religion, or prohibiting the free exercise thereof; or abridging the freedom of speech, or of the press; or the right of the people peaceably to assemble, and to petition the government for a redress of grievances."

Along with most Americans, you likely have some passing familiarity with the First Amendment, based on popular films, television programs and novels. Applying the First Amendment in practice has been guided largely by the Supreme Court, which according to James C. Goodale, continues to uphold the role of the press as a check on official power. Court rulings over the years have defined more carefully the parameters of the First Amendment.

First, prior restraint can be allowed in only the rarest of cases. That is, government attempts to *prevent* publication of information are severely limited.

Next, public figures must bear a greater burden of proof to win libel cases—proving the medium acted with malice. Moreover, public figures must be thicker skinned than private citizens; parodies, even those considered "outrageous," are protected speech.

The press has wide latitude in publishing truthful information about a matter of public significance that it obtains lawfully, unless the government can show a state interest of the highest order. Particular topics on which the court has applied this principle include publication of confidential judicial misconduct hearings, names of rape victims and names of alleged juvenile offenders.

Importantly, the government cannot tell the press what to print. In *Miami Herald Publishing Co. v. Tornillo* the Supreme Court struck down a Florida law that granted political candidates equal space in replying to a newspaper's criticism and attacks on their records. Its rationale is that the First Amendment bars the government from forcing the press to publish anything that it does not wish to publish. Broadcast media, however, are not afforded the same equal space protection.

Although the First Amendment does not require the government to tell anything to the media, the federal government and many state governments have passed freedom of information and open meeting laws—thereby granting media the right to obtain certain information and the right to observe most government proceedings.

As a result, Goodale believes that "over the course of the 20th century the Supreme Court has breathed life into the text of the First Amendment by upholding the right of the press to pursue its mission, no matter how odious that mission might seem to those in power."

A 2003 survey conducted by the First Amendment Center reveals how the public feels about the First Amendment and the media:

- About 60 percent of those responding support First Amendment freedoms, but 34 percent say the First Amendment goes too far.
- The growing number of media outlets owned by fewer corporations has decreased the number of viewpoints available to the public, according to 52 percent of respondents. Fifty-three percent believe the quality of information also has suffered.
- A whopping 80 percent of Americans think media owners exert substantial influence over their organizations' newsgathering and reporting decisions. A mere 4 percent disagrees with that perception.
- Not surprisingly, a small majority of the public, 54 percent, prefers keeping limits on how many radio, television and newspaper outlets a single company may own, yet half oppose increased regulation.
- Forty-eight percent of those polled say Americans have too little access to information about government efforts to combat terrorism, an increase of 8 percent from 2002.
- Finally, about 55 percent of the public opposes a constitutional amendment to ban flag burning, a slight increase from 51 percent in 2002.

However, realize that the First Amendment, like most of our freedoms, carries with it responsibilities. Violations of those responsibilities, involving libel and privacy, can cost the media dearly.

## Libel

Two aspects of media law powerfully impact your storytelling: libel and privacy. We will review these issues briefly here. For more information check one of numerous books dedicated to media law or consult an attorney.

Do not assume that only professional journalists need to worry about libel. Each year college and university newspapers are sued for libel, and many more are threatened with it. Whether your publication is commercial, nonprofit or academic, print, broadcast or online, you must know what libel is and the consequences of committing it.

First, the key distinction between libel and slander is that libel is print, broadcast or online while slander is spoken, presented outside of mass communication channels. Both are violations of many of the same criteria, but libel is the one with which you should be most concerned.

State statutes set most libel laws, which means that the exact specifications for libel and punishment for violations can vary from state to state. Also, most libel suits are civil, rather than criminal. Therefore, those found guilty of libel are not likely to be jailed. However, they may face severe financial penalties.

The best way to avoid libel is to make sure your stories are both accurate and fair.

## Conditions of Libel

Libel, according to the online First Amendment Handbook, "occurs when a false and defamatory statement about an identifiable person is published to a third party, causing injury to the subject's reputation." To determine if material is libelous, you must understand defamation. The standard definition is communication that "exposes a person to hatred, ridicule or contempt, lowers him in the esteem of his fellows, causes him to be shunned or injures him in his business or calling."

The burden of proof in libel suits is on the plaintiff, the person who claims to have been defamed. For libel suits to be successful, therefore, plaintiffs must prove *all* the following conditions in most states.

- The material is false.
- The material is defamatory, either on its face (*per se*) or indirectly *(per quod).*
- The material is about one or more identifiable persons.
- The material is distributed to someone beyond the offended person.
- The material is made with fault.

Let us review each of these conditions.

### The material is false.

That the material is false is a standard condition. Libel has nothing to do with whether you *knew* something in your story was false. For example, you write a crime report for your college newspaper in which you write the following: "Police arrested Jim Doe, 21, of Kansas City, Mo., on suspicion of raping a 19-year-old female dormitory resident." However, you discover later that you miscopied the name from the police report. The suspect actually was John Doe, Jim's twin. You have libeled Jim Doe.

Ignorance is no defense. Courts have held that journalists are expected to exercise reasonable care in verifying the facts they use. If they do not, their defense is severely weakened.

### The material is defamatory, either on its face (per se) or indirectly (per quod).

The defamation must harm the plaintiff, rather than being merely insulting or offensive. The harm can be to the individual's character or reputation, as well as the person's business, occupation or property. Thus, owners can claim libel on behalf of their businesses or partnerships and boards can claim on behalf of their corporations.

The distinction between libel *per se* and libel *per quod* is worth noting.

According to "Types of Libel," libel *per se* is the more serious of the two, since plaintiffs do not have to prove they have suffered damages or loss. The only requirement is that a reasonable person would understand the libel because it is obvious or evident due to the language used. Thousands of words and phrases in the English language meet this provision. They may involve politics, race, religion, professions or occupations, or they may impugn the plaintiff's honesty, integrity or morals.

The following words are the kind that meet *per se* guidelines: adulterer, ambulance chaser, cheat, crook, conspirator, drunkard, grafter, hypocrite, mistress, phony, quack abortionist, racketeer, shyster, swindler, unchaste, unprincipled and unreliable.

For example, language drew a libel suit and out-of-court settlement at a Florida high school in 2001, according to "Underground Paper Case Settled," a report from the Student Press Law Center. An underground newspaper that parodied a school newspaper identified a black teacher by a racial epithet and called into question her teaching abilities.

Nine students were sued and settled just days before the case came to trial.

In libel *per quod*, the words, phrases or statements may be harmless in themselves, but attached circumstances make them libelous. Defamation by circumstance is much more common, a result of errors or negligence. The list of such defamations includes errors in names, addresses, occupations and so on. The earlier John Doe example fits this condition.

A 1996 Student Press Law Center report tells of a libel suit filed because of an erroneous title given to the plaintiff. In a pulled quote for an article published by a Virginia university newspaper, the school's vice president for student affairs was identified as "director of butt licking."

The mistake resulted from use of "dummy copy" that the staff stored in its computer system for each issue. Even though the staff mailed the official an apology following the incident, she filed suit.

The plaintiff's lawsuit claimed the incorrect title implied the official committed an "a crime involving moral turpitude" and the actions of the paper "injured [the official's] employment, office, and professional standing without justification." However, Dr. Cathy Packer, a media law professor at the University of North Carolina at Chapel Hill, said, "I think it's name-calling and name-calling is not actionable."

## The material is about one or more identifiable persons.

Next, the libelous story must clearly identify the plaintiff. Most often, this identification is with a person's name, but other kinds of identifying details can qualify. On the other hand, you cannot be held for libeling a group of individuals large enough that individual identities are not obvious. The common figure usually is 25. Therefore, you cannot libel the entire faculty at a university.

Also, you cannot libel a dead person.

## The material is distributed to someone beyond the offended person.

This condition means that someone, a third party in addition to the writer and the offended person, has seen the questionable material. Usually, this involves regular publication of the newspaper or magazine or broadcast of the TV or radio program. However, it still may be considered "published" if it is seen or heard by a third party—by students crowded around a computer screen in a newsroom, for instance.

## The material is made with fault.

Material made with fault means that the news organization was somehow at fault in the libel. It most commonly deals with the issue of public versus private individuals, wherein the former have a greater burden of proof in libel cases than the latter.

Private individuals have only to prove two points concerning fault:

- A medium acted negligently in failing to find that a statement was false.
- The statement defamed the private individual.

However, whether one is considered a public official or public figure rather than a private citizen is the chief concern of fault. Generally, public officials are those with *substantial* responsibility for the conduct of government affairs. Not all public employees fall into this category. The Illinois First Amendment Center in "Public versus Private Individuals" identifies public officials as those who "occupy positions of pervasive power and influence" or otherwise private citizens who involve themselves in a public controversy as they help to find a solution.

Three questions have become standard in deciding if a person is a public figure:

- Does the person have access to the media to rebut any accusations?
- What is the extent of the person's voluntary association with the limelight or a particular public controversy?
- Does a genuine "public controversy" already exist or was it created by the publisher/broadcaster?

This public-private label is a critical distinction. On it hinges whether the plaintiff must prove actual malice, a much more difficult argument than simple negligence. This stems from the 1964 U.S. Supreme Court case of *New York Times v. Sullivan*, which raised the bar for public officials. They had to prove that a medium published a defamatory statement knowing it was false and with "reckless disregard for the truth," otherwise termed actual malice.

Court cases since then have established the following three criteria for use in actual-malice decisions:

- Was publication of a story urgent (e.g., rush news item) or was there time for the reporter to check the facts?
- Was the source of a story reliable or suspect?
- Was the story probable on its face or improbable enough to warrant further investigation?

## Defenses to Libel

Even when journalists do everything by the book, an unhappy person still may sue for libel. The number of unhappy people willing to sue rises as even small errors find their way into publications. And the bigger the mistake, the more likely journalists and their media will be slapped with suits.

State libel laws generally recognize the following defenses.

### Truth

The standard rule is that truth is absolute defense to libel. More importantly, the facts in question must be *provably* true in court, where libel cases are settled. Recall that the definition of libel includes falsity. A true statement, no matter how hurtful it may be to one's reputation, cannot be libelous.

However, if a source gives you information "off the record," guidelines require that you make every effort to check that the source is not lying. Claiming you were lied to is no defense. If you are subsequently sued for libel, your source must be willing and able to stand up in court and support the claims. If not, your chances of winning the suit are slim.

Chris Horrie recommends you examine material carefully *before publication* using the following guidelines:

- Separate fact from comment or opinion. Facts are far more valuable—and dangerous—than opinions.
- Double-check all facts with unimpeachable sources.
- Never rely entirely on "off the record" sources. If you have the slightest doubt about a matter of fact, cut it or corroborate it with a second source.
- Rely on official sources whenever possible. Be skeptical about what you are told by unofficial sources.
- Tell stories without malice and in the public interest.
- Write clearly and simply.
- Shoot for 100 percent accuracy, even down to the punctuation. Mean what you say; say what you mean.

## Consent

Those who give consent to publish information about themselves cannot later sue even if the material, accurately reported, damages their reputations. While the best support for consent is a signed statement, such usually is not a standard practice in most interviewing situations. Alternatively, a tape recording, witnesses to the interview or well-written reporter notes become the proof.

One concern you must have involving consent is whether the source was qualified or able to legally give consent. A minor child or a person with mental defect might not qualify in this regard. If unsure, seek additional consent from either parents or guardians.

## Privilege

Privilege is the balancing of the public's need for certain information against the possible harm the information may cause to an individual's reputation. Journalists and the media are protected by qualified privilege in the fair and accurate reporting of governmental activities. These include official records, official statements and official meetings.

While they vary from state to state, state laws protect reporting even false and defamatory material if these conditions are met:

- It must come from one of the protected "official" activities.
- It must be reported fairly and accurately.
- The source of the report must be clearly stated.

Some legal hairsplitting occurs in determining what qualifies as "official." However, as long as the record, statement or meeting is connected to a governmental unit, you likely are on safe ground. On your campus, for example, meetings of a government-appointed board of regents would qualify. However, even the fair and accurate reports of administrative activities at private colleges would not. Privilege also is questionable with reports of student government groups at both public and private schools.

Where journalists often face problems is in their reporting of the information. If their reports include errors or if they stray too far from the specific content or intent of the original material in drawing assumptions, they open themselves to libel.

## Opinion

The courts have given media wide latitude in the publication of opinion. Like privilege, this balances the common good against the rights of the individual.

By definition opinion cannot be libelous since, not being fact, it cannot be proven true or false. However, be aware of a few legal distinctions.

First, material must, indeed, be opinion, not merely facts introduced by "in my opinion" claims. For example, whether you write, "The president is a liar," or "In my opinion the president is a liar," both would be considered statements of fact. On the other hand, if you write, "The president is a weak leader," that is opinion and therefore protected speech. The use of the term *alleged* also does not automatically provide protection.

Second, if statements of opinion are supported by facts, they may be held libelous. Yet, most courts are willing to give protection to things on public display or matters of public interest. These would include reviews and assessments of plays, books, TV programs and other creative endeavors, as well as criticism of the acts of officials and agencies of the government. For example, so-called crusades against dishonest or bungling government or dishonest or other criminal activities usually are safe if the medium acts responsibly.

## Limited Defenses

Many states also recognize limited or partial defenses to libel. While these may not stop judges or juries from finding a journalist or medium guilty of libel, they might reduce potential financial judgments.

"Libel and the Law" offers eight partial defenses against libel:

- Innocent mistake or accident: Defendants can be partially excused if the libelous material was published either unintentionally or without their realizing it was libelous.
- Retraction, apology or correction: Importantly, published with the same prominence as the offending material, these might satisfy an offended person enough to have him or her forgo a lawsuit. Even if they do not, they suggest the publication seeks to act responsibly and could reduce any subsequent judgment.
- Repetition: This involves a libelous story previously printed elsewhere, such as one from a wire service.
- Lack of malice: If the publication can demonstrate good faith and justifiable ends, many judges and juries will not grant punitive awards.
- Self-defense/reply: This can be successful at times if the publication can show the libel was in response to an earlier attack by the plaintiff.
- Uncontradicted rumor: If a publication can show the offending material was a published version of widely circulated rumors that the plaintiff had not tried to deny, damages may be lessened.
- Use of authority: The defense here is that the offending material came from a source reasonably expected to be accurate.

- Prior bad reputation: This defense rests on the premise that the plaintiff already had a poor reputation in the community, which the offending material likely would not harm further.

## Libel Checklist

The following are "A Dozen Tips to Avoid Being Burned by a Hot Story," a checklist offered by the Student Press Law Center for use by student reporters and media.

1. Activate your common sense. While the nitty-gritty details of libel or privacy law can be confusing, the main ideas are straightforward, generally conforming to common sense. For example, libel law in a nutshell: (1) don't publish things that aren't true or that you don't have the evidence to reasonably support and (2) don't be a sloppy reporter. Privacy law: don't publish or gather information that is nobody else's business.

   Common sense also dictates that if you don't understand something or if a story doesn't make sense, ask enough questions of enough people until it does. If you are confused, rest assured that your readers would be as well.

2. Remember your role as a journalist. Your job is to accurately relate the facts of a story to your readers. Go into a story with an open mind and not just looking for information that supports any preconceived version of the story that you might have. Your job is to find and report the facts as they exist. Do not be content with anything less. Good reporting is hard work. Be prepared to invest the time and energy necessary to get the story right. No excuses. If you're not willing or can't do so, leave the story for someone else.

3. Take good notes. The "Golden Oldie" of libel lawyer advice. Record facts and interviews scrupulously, including who said what and when. If you know you are a weak note taker, invest in a tape recorder.

4. Documents, documents, documents. Get it in writing. If your source tells you during an interview that she acquired her information from an internal memo, ask for a copy of the memo. And then read it to make sure that what your source told you jibes with what's in the memo. Also, whenever possible, cite a public record as your source for information. In most cases, doing so will protect you from liability even if it later turns out the information contained in the public record was wrong.

5. Don't overstate the facts. You are a reporter not a salesman. Get rid of the "bigger is better" mentality. Your football coach who can't account for $1,000 of the team's budget does not need to be labeled "corrupt" or the "ring-leader of the largest financial scandal in school history." "Two sources" is not "many sources" or "a number or sources"—it is "two sources." And it is perfectly okay for a problem to just be a "problem" and not a "crisis." You get the idea. Finally, you should generally avoid the temptation to interpret the facts or reach a conclusion or an opinion for your readers. In covering a sensitive story, it is safer to let the facts speak for themselves.

6. Don't overstate the credibility of a source, either to yourself or to your readers. When interviewing a source, ask yourself if you think he's telling the truth. Does he have a reputation as a liar? Does he have any reason to harm the subject? If you are relying on statistical data or some other published report, establish that

source's reliability. If, for example, the manner in which the statistics were compiled has been reasonably questioned, say so in your story. Remember that one exceptionally credible source is worth far more than a dozen semi-credible sources. Finally, anonymous sources should be used sparingly. And at least you should know the identity of your confidential source.

7. Always give the subject of your story an opportunity to present his or her side. Not only does this give a story an essential element of fairness, it also provides you with an opportunity to catch—or at least confirm—parts of a story that may be subject to debate or question.

8. Eliminate the non-essential. Sensitive stories are not the place to show off your literary talents. Leave the flowery prose and melodrama for the features page. Write carefully and purposefully. Edit out sources or subjects that do not contribute to the "core" of a story. They are potential plaintiffs. Delete unnecessary (even though interesting) allegations. Tell what you know and how you know it. No more. No less.

9. Seek the input of others. Prior to publication, ask others to look at your story and offer their criticisms or suggestions. After working endless hours on a story, "fresh eyes" are essential for catching gaps, inconsistencies, confusing phraseology, mistaken attributions and all of the other small traps that are forever hidden to one who has already read the copy twenty times. This is also the time to contact your adviser, an attorney, the Student Press Law Center or someone else well-versed in media law if you have specific questions about the legality of a story. An ounce of prevention sure beats sitting in court.

10. Prior to publication, step back and look at the "Big Picture." Forget the little details upon which you have focused so long and hard. Read the story through one last time. Taken as a whole, are there any obvious questions you failed to ask or glaring sources you didn't contact (for example, a person in a room who witnessed a key—and disputed—meeting)? Look at your story from different points of view. Do you believe each of your subjects and sources would feel they were treated fairly (even if they didn't like the story itself)? What about headlines and subheads—are they fair and accurate? Are the graphics, photos and accompanying captions correct and not misleading? The bottom line: Make sure the story makes sense to you and fairly presents the facts as you know them.

11. After publication, respond to complaints courteously and fairly. Studies have shown that a person who perceives that he or she has been treated rudely or arrogantly by a media organization is far more likely to sue than one who believes that they have been shown the proper respect. Select one person—preferably a "people person"—to whom all complaints should be referred. While that person should not admit fault or provide information about specific news-gathering practices, he or she should listen carefully to the caller's complaints, promise to investigate the matter—and then do so. Where a correction or retraction is appropriate, publish it in a timely fashion.

12. Finally, if you need help—legal or otherwise—don't be afraid to ask for it. As a student, you're not supposed to know it all. And ask for that help sooner rather than later. It's much easier to put out a brush fire than a forest fire.

# *Privacy*

More people know more about you today because of technological advances. Consequently, the personal demand for privacy has grown. The concept of privacy rests on the right to be left alone.

As with libel the right to privacy is more limited for public figures than for private citizens. Public figures, according to the First Amendment Handbook, "are said to have voluntarily exposed themselves to scrutiny and to have waived their right of privacy, at least in matters that might have an impact on their ability to perform their public duties."

Private individuals, on the other hand, increasingly have sought to shield their lives from the media's prying. As a result, the media more frequently are targets of lawsuits. Private individuals can forfeit much of their right to privacy, though, if they thrust themselves into the spotlight. At that point they are considered public figures—at least insofar as the public issue is involved.

You can violate privacy in most states in the following four ways:

- Intrusion.
- Disclosure of private facts.
- False light.
- Misappropriation.

Let us examine each of these violations.

## Intrusion

When you intentionally intrude, physically or otherwise, into a person's solitude, private area or private affairs, you may have invaded privacy. The violation is less concerned with what is reported and more with how journalists gather their material.

The Student Press Law Center report "Invasion of Privacy Law" lists the three common types of intrusion:

- Trespass: You cannot go onto private property without the owner's consent and you cannot harass a person.
- Secret surveillance: You cannot use bugging equipment or hidden cameras. However, anything you see or hear while you are positioned in a public place is acceptable, so long as you do not use any technology to increase your perception.
- Misrepresentation: You cannot lie or in some other way misrepresent yourself beyond reasonable expectations. Undercover reporting, though, is acceptable if the disguise is not used for trespass or activities that would not otherwise be allowed.

## Disclosure of Private Facts

The Student Press Law Center explains that "a private facts claim can arise following the disclosure of truthful information about the private life of a person when the publication would be both highly offensive and embarrassing to a reasonable person and not of legitimate public concern."

This is a ticklish area for journalists, who may find private details at the heart of many stories. Importantly, while libel concerns details that are false, disclosure of private facts involves those that are true.

For example, the truth of a private person's sexual activities, health, economic status or educational records likely is off limits. The SPLC explains in "Invasion of Privacy Law" that private-facts lawsuits have good chances of success if an offended party can prove the following:

- The information is sufficiently private or not already in the public domain.
- The information is sufficiently intimate.
- The information is highly offensive to a *reasonable person.*

Privilege, however, protects the fair and accurate reporting of the contents of public records, including police reports, judicial proceedings and birth certificates. Thus, for example, reports of people seeking or granted divorces are protected. Also, while an arrest for some crime or offense certainly can be embarrassing, courts consider its coverage legitimately newsworthy and protected.

Another defense is newsworthiness. This applies to public figures for almost anything and applies to everyone if the report involves recent criminal behavior.

## False Light

The online First Amendment Handbook says that false light occurs when all of the following circumstances are true:

- Information published about a person is false or places the person in a false light.
- Information is considered highly offensive to a reasonable person
- Information is published "with knowledge or in reckless disregard of whether the information was false or would place the person in a false light."

While false-light invasion of privacy is similar to defamation, the key point that separates it is that the plaintiff does not need to prove injury or damage to reputation.

Plaintiffs may claim false light for either words or photographs. It can be as simple as a cutline for a photograph that mistakenly identifies a bystander as the one being arrested for a crime. Although false light is recognized in about 30 states, recent court decisions in four states have rejected its validity. Some legal scholars, therefore, suggest that false light eventually may lose standing as an invasion of privacy.

## Misappropriation

Unauthorized use of a person's name, photograph, likeness, voice or other endorsement to sell a product or service is misappropriation.

Even if one's entire name is not used, courts may find misappropriation if a reasonable person might identify the plaintiff. However, photographs used for legitimate newsworthy purposes are acceptable, such as news photographs on the cover of a publication.

## Consent as Defense

The best defense to avoid any of these invasion of privacy claims is consent. While not required, written consent always is the safest method.

That consent, of course, must meet the following guidelines:

- The consent must be freely and openly given.
- What is being consented to must be clear.
- The person giving consent must have the legal right to give it.

## Privacy Checklists

Good defenses, of course, ultimately may protect you and your publication from being *successfully* sued for invasion of privacy. However, you are wiser from the outset to take all the reasonable and appropriate steps you can to avoid that likelihood. Consider using one of the following checklists. The first is the Reporter's Privacy Checklist from the First Amendment Handbook.

**A. Consent from the Subject**
   Is the subject an adult?
   If not, do you have parental consent?
   Is the person mentally or emotionally disabled and unable to give consent? Have you obtained valid consent from a guardian or other responsible party?
   Has that consent been revoked?
   Is the subject currently a private or public figure? Has the person's status changed over time?

**B. Method of Obtaining Information**
   Is it a public place?
   If it is a private place, do you have permission to be on the premises and permission to interview or photograph?
   Was the information contained in a public record? A semi-public record?

**C. Content**
   Would publication of the information offend community standards of decency?
   Have the facts been embellished with information of questionable accuracy?
   Is the information outdated and not obviously of current public interest, or has a current event revived its newsworthiness?
   Is the information vital to the story?

The second checklist is "Respecting Privacy Guidelines" and was prepared by Bob Steele of the Poynter Institute for Media Studies.

- What is my journalistic purpose in seeking this information? In reporting it?
- Does the public have a justifiable need to know? Or is this matter just one in which some want to know?
- How much protection does this person deserve? Is this person a public official, public figure or celebrity? Is this person involved in the news event by choice or by chance?
- What is the nature of the harm I might cause by intruding on someone's privacy?
- Can I cause considerable harm to someone just by asking questions, observing activity or obtaining information even if I never actually report the story?

- How can I better understand this person's vulnerability and desire for privacy? Can I make a better decision by talking with this person?
- What alternative approaches can I take in my reporting and my storytelling to minimize the harm of privacy invasion while still fulfilling my journalistic duty to inform the public? For instance, can I leave out some "private" matters while still accurately and fairly reporting the story? Or can I focus more on a system failure issue rather than reporting intensely on one individual?

## Crafting and Drafting

After you have gathered your material, try drafting your story using "focused freewriting." This approach involves your writing as much as you can from what you recall rather than labor over your notebook, pulling material into the story. Only after you have completed a draft should you go to your notes. Then, firm up your direct quotes and paraphrases, add exact figures and facts and polish the details.

The benefit of focused freewriting is that *it frees you to write*. Also, it challenges you to understand *what the story means and explain it to readers* rather than relying too much on sources to tell the story.

## For Practice

18-1. Run your regular beat and find a topic for which you can do a story. Then, do the following:

a) Interview appropriate sources and take careful notes.
b) Be especially attentive to information in your story that may be libelous or invade one's privacy.
c) Draft a story using the best format that fits your topic and your audience.
d) Swap stories with a peer review partner or group and give written reader feedback
e) Submit the draft and peer feedback to your teacher.
f) After your teacher has reviewed your draft and peer feedback and has offered additional suggestions, begin revising.
g) Submit a final draft to your teacher.

## Chapter 18 Bibliography

"'Butt Licking' Mistake Draws $850,000 Suit." *Student Press Law Center Report 17: 3* (1996).

"A Dozen Tips to Avoid Being Burned by a Hot Story." *Student Press Law Center.* 1996. <http://www.splc.org/legalresearch.asp?id=26>.

Goodale, James C. "Issues of Democracy." *USIA Electronic Journal 2: 1* (February 1997). <http://usinfo.state.gov/journals/itdhr/0297/ijde/goodale.htm>.

Horrie, Chris. "Defamation." *Westminster Journalism: Media Law Web.* <http://www.geocities.com/medialawweb/>.

"Invasion of Privacy." *First Amendment Handbook.* <http://www.rcfp.org/handbook/c02p09.html>.

"Invasion of Privacy: False Light." *First Amendment Handbook.* <http://www.rcfp.org/handbook/viewpage.cgi?0204>.

"Invasion of Privacy Law." *The Student Press Law Center.* 2001. <http://www.splc.org/legalresearch.asp?id=29>.

Jefferson, Thomas. "Thomas Jefferson on Politics & Government: Quotations from the Writings of Thomas Jefferson." *Thomas Jefferson Digital Archive.* Ed. John P. Foley. Funk and Wagnalls, 1900. <http://etext.virginia.edu/etcbin/ot2www-jeffquot?specfile=/web/data/jefferson/quotations/www/jeffquot.o2w&act=surround&offset=1143330&tag=51.+Freedom+of+the+Press&query=newspapers>.

"Libel." *First Amendment Handbook.* <http://www.rcfp.org/handbook/viewpage.cgi?0101>.

"Libel and the Law." *Integrated Publishing.* <http://www.tpub.com/journalist/95.htm>.

"Public versus Private Individuals." *Illinois First Amendment Center.* 17 December 2002. <http://www.illinoisfirstamendmentcenter.com/Main.asp?SectionID=29&SubSectionID=29&ArticleID=9>.

"Reporter's Privacy Checklist." *First Amendment Handbook.* <http://www.rcfp.org/handbook/viewpage.cgi?0209>.

"State of the First Amendment Overview." *The First Amendment Center.* 2003. <http://www.firstamendmentcenter.org/Sofa_reports/index.aspx>.

Steele, Bob. "Respecting Privacy Guidelines." *Poynteronline.* 1 July 1999. <http://www.poynter.org/content/content_view.asp?id=4643>.

"Types of Libel." *Integrated Publishing.* <http://www.tpub.com/journalist/94.htm>.

"Underground Paper Case Settled." *Student Press Law Center Report 23: 1* (2001).

# Chapter 19

# Trends: Public Journalism and Convergence

*I have been in the editorial business going on fourteen years, and it is the first time I ever heard of a man's having to know anything in order to edit a newspaper.*

—Mark Twain

## Chapter Contents

## *QuickView*

You are living in exciting times as a storyteller-journalist. The combination of dynamic new technologies plus challenging new trends is energizing the profession like never before.

The two most important trends, public journalism and convergence, are the focus of this chapter. We will find that neither trend can claim complete support among working journalists and journalism educators. Yet, both are influencing the profession, and both will require that you work differently as a journalist.

In addition to reviewing their origins and status, we will examine advantages and disadvantages of public journalism and convergence. Most importantly, we will peer into the future to anticipate how each will relate to the world in which you will tell your stories.

---

As storytellers you enter a profession with a long history, filled with traditional approaches and expectations. You also enter a profession influenced by more recent trends, which help to shape how modern journalists tell their stories.

Embedded in our discussions in "Storycrafting" has been regular reference to a dynamic influence on the work you do—technology, particularly the computer and the Internet. Both have helped to shape the profession in innumerable ways and made the task of storytelling faster, easier and more effective.

Related to and growing from the technological advances are two powerful trends in journalism that should continue to affect the profession and its practitioners for a long time. Those trends are public journalism and convergence. This chapter will investigate what these involve and how they likely will influence you now and in the future.

## Public Journalism

The first trend that has made news coverage more powerful and effective—and more controversial, at least for journalists—has been public journalism. Also termed *civic journalism* and *community journalism,* it is among several shifts in recent years that have responded to reader dissatisfaction with media and media re-evaluation of their contemporary role.

Common practice with traditional journalism has been to provide coverage that may point to problems in the community. After identifying problems, media tend to step back and allow community leaders to move forward and work toward solutions. This approach, most journalists have felt, allows media to perform their watchdog role while maintaining sufficient distance to remain objective.

Public journalism also identifies community problems. The difference is that the media do not step back afterwards. Instead, media engage community leaders and readers and work together to help bring about necessary changes and improvements. Media also are encouraged to be more candid up front in explaining how and why they are tackling certain issues.

Ultimately, public journalism seeks to move beyond what is traditionally labeled news to explore new avenues of participation and new voices of information.

### Origin of Public Journalism

The movement saw its beginnings in the early 1990s in political coverage, particularly elections, where it attempted to reverse the growing apathy of voters and their sense of disenfranchisement. Since then, it has spread and has involved issues that are more varied.

In a 2002 survey of Public Journalism activities, Lewis A. Friedland and Sandy Nichols explain that newspapers began practicing public journalism by focusing on the relationship of the press to democracy, which led to projects involving local elections. Along the way the first practitioners applied techniques that have become public journalism's hallmarks, including citizens' agendas, issue grids and other means of getting new voices into stories.

Encouraged by early successes, they began addressing larger communitywide issues, coupled with citizen solutions.

Friedland and Nichols write, "As the larger community-wide deliberations and problem solving efforts worked, newspapers began to refocus attention on specific issues, particularly about who was included or excluded in the 'civic map' of coverage. This led to attention to how racial and ethnic diversity could be systematically incorporated into coverage, and to attention to the problems of young people and students, among others."

Mike Dillon believes that public journalism returns to the roots of the profession. He writes, "Civic Journalism taps into time-honored values of American journalism that reach back far beyond the Age of Objectivity. The core principle of Civic Journalism—that journalists have a duty to enhance civic discourse and provide reasoned guidance to the public in civic affairs—can be found in the words and deeds of Benjamin Franklin, James Gordon Bennett, Horace Greeley, E. W. Scripps, Joseph Pulitzer, William Allen White, Upton Sinclair and other pioneers of the American press."

He notes that the traditional distancing journalists have maintained actually is a relatively recent shift, adding, "Press pioneers of the 19th and early 20th centuries felt no such ambiguity about the public mission of the press. While they differed in temperament, outlook, ideology and methods, the publishers and editors who shaped journalism after the colonial age would probably have agreed that a good newspaper should be an omnibus of human experience. It should be inquisitive, broad and inclusive, autonomous, and willing to use its tremendous social influence to shape public affairs."

Richard Oppel was editor of the Charlotte (N.C.) Observer in 1992 when it launched "Your Vote," one of the early public journalism projects. He explains of public journalism: "I saw it as returning to the traditional roots of journalism, and away from political journalism of the 1980s: horse-race polls, insider politics and manipulation by candidates and their managers."

## New Avenues, New Voices

The innovative techniques that public journalists brought to bear were not new in themselves, but they were new in their application to journalism. Those techniques include the following:

- Civic mapping: Media began mapping their communities in order to identify better the particular constituencies and their unique needs.
- E-mail access: Media made e-mail addresses of reporters and editors available to the community, encouraging citizens to dialogue with journalists and easing access to letters columns.

- Interactive Internet sites: Media developed interactive tools, such as clickable maps and tax calculators to provide citizens with additional specific information they could use.
- Polls and surveys: Media polled and surveyed citizens in order to learn more about their opinions and interests.
- Focus groups: Media brought together citizen representatives from unique neighborhoods or demographic groups to learn more about their opinions and concerns.

These techniques offer what Dillon calls "a corrective to conventional news narratives that are typically spun out of the words and deeds of 'the usual suspects'—public officials, corporate spokespeople, pundits. At heart, 'newsgathering is normally a matter of the representatives of one bureaucracy picking up prefabricated news items from representatives of another bureaucracy.'"

Under the influence of public journalism, media gave voice to large segments of the community, who helped not only to answer the questions but also to draft them. With traditional journalism, Dillon says, "the public is virtually invisible." Readers are the end of the news production process, but only as consumers, not participants.

Including these new voices of the community is more than patronage or lip service. The new voices acquire status as meaningful stakeholders, and journalists are exercising what Jay Rosen terms "casting decisions" in deciding "whom to cast in what roles in the drama of public life."

Rosen, one of those credited with public journalism's development, believes that positioning people as citizens means to treat them as:

- Making their own contribution to public life.
- Potential participants in public affairs.
- Stakeholders, with a personal interest in public affairs.
- Citizens of the whole, with shared interests.
- A deliberative body—that is, a public with issues to discuss.
- Choosers, decision-makers.
- Learners, with skills to develop.
- Connected to place and responsible for place.

## Goals of Public Journalism

Jan Schaffer, executive director of the Pew Center for Civic Journalism, believes the goals for public journalism include the following:

- To enrich journalism.
- To make it more authentic.
- To build public capital—engaging people in problem solving or deliberation.
- Most importantly, to deliver meaningful connections.

She observes that the advent of the Internet and Web chats offers new forms of connection. These "connections built attachments with audiences, which then built relationships with the news organizations." Connection, she suggests, is replacing convergence in many newsrooms. With connections, the focus for journalists is on their audiences. The first step is to focus on relationships with them, the connections with them; from this follows better journalism.

She believes the effort to build connections is moving into the following:

- Showing as well as telling.
- Delivering knowledge plus news.
- Providing lots of entry points.
- Providing venues for telling your own story.
- And composing your own internal story or narrative.

Oppel says, "Public journalism's goal is to reconnect the press with the reader. It is not traditional stenographic reporting, where 'elites' of the media and politics talk over the heads of readers. It is the press's effort to create an environment where citizens can have a reasoned discussion about community problems."

Additionally, some proponents argue that another goal of public journalism is helping to portray a city's master narrative—the story that frames and underlies the daily life and daily decision making in a community.

Rosen offers additional understanding of a master narrative. "Journalists are storytellers and they are pledged to provide a story that is accurate and fair. But we often overlook a certain aspect of story-telling, and that is the ability to shape a master narrative," he explains.

He defines a master narrative as "the story that produces all the other stories; or, to put it another way, the Big Story that lends coherence and shape to all the little stories journalists tell." Ultimately, a master narrative "is not a particular story journalists write; it is the story they are always writing when they tell the stories they typically tell." An example of a master narrative that Rosen suggests involves election coverage, where the master narrative is winning—who is winning, how they are winning, why they are winning and so on.

Rosen concludes, "Public journalism is about improving the master narrative, so that it produces good stories that simultaneously tell the truth about public life and create more space for citizens."

Steve Smith, executive editor of the Statesman Journal in Salem, Ore., expresses the heart of this developing trend when he writes that "we reflect the life of our community every day in all of its wholeness and complexity." An additional goal is to tell readers "what we know when we know it, and hard news is job one. Civic journalism is hard news. It's hard news as defined by citizens. And that's our first job."

As proclaimed by many other public journalism supporters, Smith says, "We give voice to the voiceless, and we defend the defenseless. We recognize the positive lives led by our community's young people every day." Finally, his newspaper empowers citizens to exercise their citizenship, reflecting the foundations of public journalism.

## Criticism of Public Journalism

Marilyn Greenwald says that public journalism has had a healthy cadre of critics from its arrival in the early 1990s. Its opponents "frequently couched their criticisms in terms commonly applied to religious zealotry or McCarthyism: Evangelical, they said. A cultlike movement, complete with its own jargon, they believed. These opponents also exhibited a certain smugness, secure in their view that this, too, like New Journalism, shall pass as a serious form of reporting."

Proponents of the movement, though, were just as fervent in support of public journalism. Greenwald says they "maintained a beatific air and smiled tolerantly at those who thought declining newspaper circulation, plummeting confidence in the press and an explosion in celebrity journalism were temporary phenomena. Times were changing, they maintained, and conventional ways of reporting and editing were buggy whips in an era of the Model T, like it or not."

What sets the two sides at odds, she believes, is less a matter of method of reporting and editing and more a matter of philosophy. Public journalism may employ some unconventional reporting methods, but its practitioners' way of thinking has sparked most of the debate. "Public journalism, with its emphasis on focus groups, polls and citizen involvement in news selection, challenged long-held notions that reporters remain detached from newsmakers and focus their attention on officials in charge," Greenwald writes.

This goal of detachment, in the guise of objectivity, has been the mainstay of journalism for nearly a century. As we discussed in Chapter 17, objectivity seeks to position journalists to tell stories from a neutral perspective that encourages fairness and completeness over advocacy and selectivity. As a reaction to the political and special-interest press that preceded it, objectivity was a valuable bridge. It enabled journalists to improve their storytelling by distancing themselves as much as possible from subjects, sources and readers.

However, that distance—sought with the noble goal of sanitizing reporter motives and story content—eventually cost the media. Studies and polls in the last 25 years repeatedly have criticized the media for a long list of faults. The following are the three most common: the public's belief that media do not care about what *they* care about, media have their own agenda and media are disconnected from the communities they serve.

Supporters believe that public journalism responds to these concerns in ways that suit our topics and our times. Hodding Carter III, president of the Knight Foundation, argues passionately in support of public journalism: "Forget the critics, who have never seemed to grasp even the most rudimentary of public journalism's basics. This is not the same thing as mindlessly throwing away news judgment to give the people what they say they want. That form of patronizing contempt for the public and the public interest is unforgivable, and journalism, like politicians, already patronizes the public too frequently."

## Future of Public Journalism

While much of the debate concerning public journalism that bubbled in professional journals during the last half of the 1990s has eased, its proponents claim public journalism remains very much alive today.

The 2002 study by Friedland and Nichols says that 322 newspapers—one-fifth of the total in the United States—have practiced some form of public journalism. Schaffer believes public journalism has become part of mainstream journalistic practices. She cites an American Society of Newspaper Editors survey that solidly approved four professional journalistic approaches, which were not labeled as such:

- 96 percent approved or somewhat approved of a newspaper reporting on alternative solutions to community problems, pointing out tradeoffs that may be involved.
- 88 percent approved of newspapers developing enterprise stories, supported with editorials, to focus public attention on a community problem and helping the community move toward a solution.
- 71 percent approved of a newspaper polling the public to determine the most pressing community issues, then trying to get candidates to focus on those issues.
- 68 percent approved of a newspaper conducting town meetings to discover key issues in the community and following up with stories focusing on these issues and some possible solutions.

A number of other studies support Schaffer's claim that a majority of so-called traditional newsrooms have acquired many of the attitudes and practices that shape public journalism. Rosen suggests, "It can't be new forever. . . . It has become a routine part of coverage. A healthy number of newsrooms have learned it, and they do it. It's not a controversy any more."

## Public Journalism on Campus

Your campus is an ideal community for practicing public journalism. Many of the concerns driving commercial media to engage their communities with public journalism techniques are the same concerns campus media face.

Review these 10 tips from Schaffer, written the week after the Sept. 11 attacks. They could easily serve as guideposts for how student journalists might establish public journalism on campus:

1. Let ordinary people see themselves in your stories doing ordinary and extraordinary things: rescuing survivors, searching for the missing, overcoming obstacles, grieving their losses. Let them see the capacity they have to transcend tragedy.
2. Give people space to tell their own stories. They need to share their joy or grief, their despair or triumph.
3. Stay interactive. Create zones of connectivity where people can trade information, chat, vent or ponder. This might include chat rooms, talk-back sections of the paper, e-mail invitations to write for the newspaper, etc.
4. Chronicle history at large; explain, as well as condemn, the terrorists.
5. Toss out old taboos and let your readers and viewers see that journalists are human, too. You are not seeking to profiteer off calamity; rather you share in the suffering.
6. Likewise, let public officials be human—unvarnished in their uncertainty, tentative in their approaches.
7. Ban rubbernecking coverage; citizens want to do more than ogle. Celebrate the capacity of individuals to heal, to rebuild, to make a difference in your community.
8. Rise above petty competition. Set more overarching priorities.
9. Position your news organization to be a good citizen in your community.
10. Create a forum for people to share their ideas, values and aspirations.

## Convergence

Nonmedia industries long ago realized the benefits of convergence. Now, John Morton explains, "We are seeing concentrations of ownership—in telecommunications, cable television, radio, television, oil production, banking and a host of other industries—that would have been unthinkable 20 years ago because of antitrust concerns. The rules have been changed by the globalization of business and, especially for media companies, the rise of the Internet."

Convergence is one of the more intriguing media phenomena in recent years. It involves cooperative efforts of different media outlets in a community—newspaper, television, radio and Internet—which share resources, particularly staff and content. This cooperating multimedia group even may share the same owner, although increasingly competing media are seeking convergence agreements.

While this may not sound all that terrific, such sharing of resources previously would have been unacceptable—even for media under the same owner. Most media are fiercely competitive, always seeking to scoop and upstage other outlets in town.

## Development of Convergence

Discussions of convergence invariably center on one operation that has been around long enough to claim a strong track record: the Tribune Co., with converged facilities in Chicago and Orlando.

The Chicago Tribune, founded in 1847, bought WGN-AM radio in 1924 and WGN-TV in 1948. During their long history under the same ownership, the three outlets maintained strong competition and never cooperated—each doing its job as it did it best. The debut in 1993 of CLTV began changing all that. Alicia C. Shepard writes of that occasion: "The advent of CLTV was accompanied by the arrival of a television camera in the ink-stained newsroom. While not so unusual today, a TV camera in a newsroom in 1993 was like an elephant in a museum. Awkward. Frightening. Distracting. And a nuisance."

From that point on, the Tribune Co. was committed to the Internet as well as expecting its newspapers to work closely with television and cable outlets in those communities where the company owned all three. In 1997 the company joined forces with Time Warner Cable in Orlando to create Central Florida News 13, a cable TV outlet whose news operations were supported by the Orlando Sentinel, another Tribune Co. property. Print reporters began by discussing their stories on the air in "talk-back" segments. Eventually, the 300-person Sentinel staff bolstered the efforts of the cable TV station's 12 reporters, providing coverage unthinkable by traditional TV news operations.

In 2000 the company stepped up its pace with the purchase of the Times Mirror, giving the Tribune Co. newspapers in Los Angeles, Baltimore and New York. Their goal, Shepard believes, "is to re-create in some fashion its multimedia models in Chicago and Orlando, finding multiple uses for content. The long-term approach is to create a network of regional media hubs in Los Angeles, Chicago and New York that will be irresistible to national advertisers."

Media General operates a converged facility in Tampa, where the Tampa Tribune and WFLA-TV have joint quarters in a 121,000-square-foot building completed in

2000. Called The News Center, it features one floor for the Tribune news operations and another for WFLA-TV news operations. Tampa Bay Online is the company's new-media presence. All three share a common assignment desk. Combining newspaper and TV outlets in one building is possible, according to Gil Thelen, because Media General owned both before 1975, when the FCC banned cross ownership in the same market.

Examples of cooperative agreements among media owned by different companies include the following:

- Washington Post, Newsweek, NBC and MSNBC.com share news stories.
- The New York Times and TheStreet.com, an Internet financial news provider, have established a joint newsroom.
- The Wall Street Journal shares content with CNBC, NBC's business channel.
- TheStreet.com has additional agreements with Fox News, Yahoo! and America Online.

In fact, Steve Geimann estimates that 50 media companies had formed partnerships or signed agreements by 2001.

The driving force behind such ventures, Morton says, is the Internet. Kelly Heyboer, reporter for the Newark Star-Ledger, says that more than 1,100 of the nation's 1,500 newspapers are online, including every one of the 100 largest papers. Only a handful has turned a profit yet. So, why are they willing to continue investing in a revenue-draining proposition? The answer is online presence.

Moreover, Shepard believes the Internet's popularity and continuing rapid growth are what compel media outlets to seek cooperative arrangements. "Much of this frenzied wooing is a frantic attempt to prevent even more 'eyeballs' from abandoning traditional media," she says. "Three years ago, just over a quarter of computer users (27 percent) were using the Internet, according to Harris Interactive, a market research firm. Today, 81 percent of computer users go online. In December, individuals spent an average of 514.5 minutes online, according to Media Metrix, which measures Internet traffic. One out of five people say the Internet has decreased the time they spend reading newspapers, according to InterSurvey, a market research firm. Nearly half of the 4,600 questioned said the Net has reduced the amount of time they watch television."

The Internet is the platform that makes it possible for television, cable, print, radio and magazine to join forces in capturing the same audiences and the same advertisers. Shepard cites Bob Ingle, president of Knight Ridder Ventures, who believes that money is not the chief Internet commodity: "It's time. The Internet is moving so fast that people are forced to partner because they just can't flat do it all. You can't hire enough people. You can't learn it all. You wind up partnering to pull together the pieces that you think will make your strategy work. You can either partner or buy it. Buying it can be very expensive."

One impetus behind current convergence trends is the development of broadband, which can move data up to 125 times faster than the standard home modem. Shepard explains, "Broadband means huge chunks of graphic-laden data no longer have to squeeze through a narrow funnel; it means Internet access will come much faster, and will always be available when your computer is on. No more dialing into a modem and getting a busy signal. No longer will one have to grab that magazine while waiting for full-screen, full-motion video to download, and the video will look more like television and less like pictures of Neil Armstrong's walk on the moon."

Newspaper consultant Neil Skene observes that competition in many markets has been overshadowed by partnerships. He writes, "Reluctance is giving way to the recognition that more and more people want their news faster than a next-day newspaper can provide it."

## Advantages and Disadvantages of Convergence

Breaking down walls of competition is not easy, but convergence brings with it the promise of rich rewards.

Shifting their priorities demands media see their role in new ways. The E. W. Scripps Co., according to Skene, has told its newsrooms that they no longer are in "the newspaper business." They are in "the news-gathering and dissemination business." Under this model newspapers do what they have done best: They tell stories. What changes is the means by which those stories are shared with audiences.

Thelen, executive editor of the Tampa (Fla.) Tribune, says that their goal is to satisfy the changing needs of readers and viewers. "Our rationale: Be there with news and information whenever and however our customers need and want us to be. For breaking news, we aim to 'publish' on the first available platform, usually television but sometimes online. On enterprise, we want to extend the work of our journalists across platforms in a natural way."

The benefit of convergence is twofold, according to Diane H. McFarlin, ASNE president and publisher of the Sarasota (Fla.) Herald-Tribune. First is the potential for driving advertising revenues. Second is the economy of being able to tell multimedia stories using fewer managers and support personnel.

What each partner brings to the convergent operation is its "brand"—its name and reputation—which media believe is their most important asset. For example, Shepard writes, "While there's little doubt a Washington Post connection lends MSNBC.com a certain cachet, the Web site in less than four years has built its own desirable brand. Since MSNBC.com's 1996 inception, it has grown rapidly to become the most popular news site on the Web, surpassing arch-rival CNN.com last June in terms of unique users each month."

Even rich rewards do not come without some cost, however.

Shepard suggests that critics of convergence fear that companies, such as The Tribune Co., will try to do too much with their resources, weakening or homogenizing the news product and stretching their employees to the point where journalism is hurt.

Bob Haiman agrees. The president emeritus of the Poynter Institute for Media Studies is a strong critic of media convergence. Haiman told Mike Wendland that he worries that the practice would dilute independent, diverse journalism by merging media and messages. Moreover, some excellent newspaper reporters may suffer because they do not look good on television. "The journalism business is allowing itself to fall in love with some new words that really convey bad ideas," Haiman says. "Convergence may end up being good for the media companies, but I feel it will be bad for journalism." Ultimately, he predicts that convergence—like many of the dot-com startups of the 1990s—will flop.

McFarlin points to another concern: "There's a bigger elephant in the room, though, and that's the fear that convergence is just another excuse for slashing newsroom payrolls."

Breaking down the separation between news and advertising, a long-held newspaper tradition, is a potential drawback as online operations and convergence increase. Further blurred, Skene notes, are distinctions between "content" and "advertising," between promotion and reader service. He writes of journalists, "Generally, people do not lose their sense of ethics by talking to advertising or other business people. But the loss of the artificial barriers means that individuals must be more careful about the ad hoc ethical decisions they may be called upon to make. And managers will need to help staffs, which often have limited experience in traditional newsrooms, prepare for the ethical issues that might arise."

## *Future of Convergence*

Convergence is happening today, and all signs point to its continuing. Of the many things we can expect of it, the most predictable is that it will grow and evolve as technology grows and evolves and as the marketplace demands such changes.

The current platform for delivering converged products is the Internet, most often accessed via computers. Yet, the increased availability of broadband will usher in other advances that are just beginning to take hold, namely wireless portable devices (WPDs).

J. D. Lasica, senior editor of Online Journalism Review, explains advantages of WPDs:

They're push media.

Instead of waiting for users to click to news sites, WPDs will deliver online newspapers wirelessly and automatically several times a day. With the most popular online newspaper, The New York Times, able to claim that average users stop by only 3.6 days a month, WPDs will increase drastically the frequency that readers engage content.

Prospects for advertising are more favorable.

Online publishers now must contend with "a bottomless advertising hole with ads that are noisy, distracting and ignored," according to Lasica. Newspapers on WPDs, however, "can be formatted in a graphical layout that locks in a limited amount of display ad space, commanding premium rates."

For the most part, the Web requires us to be tethered to a PC or laptop.

WPDs, though, will be as mobile as their users.

Vin Crosbie is a managing partner at the consulting firm Digital Deliverance and chairman of Publishmail, an e-mail publishing service provider. He writes about WPDs: "Device manufacturers have realized that most consumers don't want to carry multiple devices that each performs only a single function or medium. The manufacturers also know that selling a multifunction device gives them the broadest market and revenues."

These new tools will wirelessly and automatically deliver to consumers "interactive, intact, and individualized newspaper editions with sophisticated graphic layouts featuring finite amounts of display-quality advertising space," Crosbie predicts. "Each intact edition will appear in tabloid-format print layout (broadsheets shall have to adapt), but with hyperlinked texts and screen-mapped graphics. Click the story about the speech to hear that speech, click the still photo to see the video of that event, all available through the always-on wireless connectivity of these devices."

Another technological breakthrough will come in the form of electronic paper by the end of this decade. E-paper will replace liquid crystal display screens and rigid tablets, increasing the device's flexibility and portability. In addition, Crosbie says that "e-paper uses one hundredth of the electric current that LCDs do, extending battery life one hundred times as long."

As these and other as-yet unnamed technologies impact the marketplace, convergence will continue to benefit media by reducing competition for news and increasing competition for time and revenue. Consumers also should enjoy more varied and extensive access to multimedia news and information.

## Convergence on Campus

Even though development of multimedia operations is gathering steam in the commercial media, college media have been slow to follow. A recent Internet search of online college newspapers that was done for "Storycrafting," for example, turned up little evidence of converged media.

College media historically have been willing to take risks in implementing new-media technology on their campuses. Because research into campus convergence is limited, we can only guess why more campuses have not launched converged operations.

The following may be a few of the more compelling reasons:

- Lack of faculty expertise and impetus.
- Lack of curriculum.
- Cost of hardware, software and facilities.
- Continuing competition between campus media.
- Lack of incentive.

A spring 2002 survey of college journalists attending two national conventions, one in New York and the other in California, may help to explain. Researchers polled students from 359 schools about their use of new-media technology. While the majority, 67 percent, reported their newsrooms had Web sites, the remaining third had no online outlets.

Steven Chappell and Laura Widmer observe, "Perhaps equally disturbing is that even among those student newsrooms with Web sites, and therefore, new-media technology, few are using it in an innovative or convergent fashion. The survey indicates that of those publications with Web sites, 85 percent are simply using their online component as 'shovel-ware,' that is, the reprinting of their traditional content in a Web-based environment. Few are using the Web as a breaking news medium, and even fewer are combining traditional news outlets on campus into a convergent newsroom."

The study suggests that lack of curriculum may be partly to blame. Only 22 percent of the students said that formal training from advisers, faculty members or new-media professionals was available to teach use of new media and the Internet in the newsroom. The numbers are better when asked if informal training were available; then, 62 percent said yes.

Responses concerning media advisers' knowledge of new media also are revealing. Since media advisers at most campuses tend to provide both leadership and training, their multimedia expertise is vital. Of the 195 valid answers in the study, only 15 said their adviser is more knowledgeable than they or other students in the use and training of new-media technology in the newsroom.

Finally, Chappell and Widmer found that of 187 respondents whose campuses had more than one journalistic medium, only two said there was any sharing of newsgathering and dissemination among them.

While the overall picture may be bleak, some campuses are responding to the challenge of introducing convergence technology to their students.

Rod Sandeen, vice president/administration of the Freedom Forum, talks about one such school, Northwestern University. "Most journalism students at the Illinois school are learning to shoot video," Associate dean Richard Roth told Sandeen. "It fits into our philosophy that they all need to know how to do on air and online." Students in newspaper and magazine sequences must take New Media Storytelling, in which they learn to shoot video for online news.

Another university that has converted its curriculum to train students for media convergence is the Annenberg School at the University of Southern California. Beginning fall 2002, says Steve Outing, senior editor at the Poynter Institute for Media Studies, "Those longing for a career in newspapers will be required as part of their academic training to appear on television and radio. Future TV news correspondents will have to write for newspapers. And everyone will learn to create content for the Internet."

Outing believes that the term convergence may conjure an image "of the lone-wolf reporter lugging around notebook and pen, mobile phone, laptop computer, digital camera, audio recorder, and video camera." However, the USC program "aims to impart enough multiple-platform knowledge so that the journalist can be comfortable when asked to do something out of the ordinary—like the print or online reporter being asked to supply a video clip for a Web presentation."

The USC curriculum, Outing says, was built on the work done at the University of Kansas journalism school, the first to take multi-platform education seriously.

Betsey Blakeslee tells of the multimedia curriculum and experiences at Piedmont College, a small, 110-year-old liberal arts college in Northeast Georgia. There, students must take 30 hours of courses in writing; advertising and promotion; production for radio, film, television and the Internet; telecommunications; visual communications; communications law; media and society; and a general survey course. In addition, the school's media are converged, with student reporters working for radio, television, newspaper and Internet outlets.

Another school making some concession in its curriculum to multimedia is the University of Missouri. There, Outing says, photojournalism students are encouraged to take videography. However, the director of the photojournalism sequence, Zoe Smith, told him that an obstacle to requiring multimedia preparation is that journalism majors can take only 25 percent of their total course work in journalism due to accrediting guidelines.

## *Preparing to Be a Multimedia Journalist*

So, what should you do now so that you will be ready to meet the challenges of working as a multimedia journalist?

Most journalism professionals and educators stress that you still should learn the basics of good media writing. You must be able to identify worthwhile, interesting stories; gather appropriate, appealing and informative content; and tell stories effectively with imagination.

The concept of the "one-man band," once suggested by McFarlin, is not the benchmark that most convergent operations are seeking. Instead, in addition to journalism basics, Cynthia Gorney offers five other skills that will make you more marketable in a multimedia world:

### Be able to meet multiple deadlines.

Deadline survival skills likely are part of the traditional regime you will acquire in your basic writing courses. Crank those up a few notches to be able to revise leads and to update stories for different media, especially as new information becomes available.

### Become somewhat adept at dictation.

While you write most of your stories seated comfortably at a computer, situations demand that you also can whip out your cell phone and call in the heart of a story working from material in your notebook.

### Have basic familiarity with television and video.

Mostly, this is as fundamental as being comfortable with sitting in front of a camera and telling about the story you just reported. Take a new-media or beginning video course to ready yourself.

### Develop a knack for imaginative thinking about art and graphics.

This may demand that you occasionally are saddled with a digital camera and told to grab some good supporting shots for the story you are reporting. It more often means that you can discuss with photographers what kind of shots they might capture to accompany your story. Ultimately, it expects that you develop a visual sense that helps you and others tell the story beyond words.

### Understand how to research topics online.

You must be practiced and comfortable with locating pertinent information online. You can firm up this skill now, as you gather information for news stories and as you complete assignments for many of your other classes.

## *Crafting and Drafting*

You should find stories you do for either Exercise 19-1 or Exercise 19-2 to be challenging as well as exciting. In the first you should develop a story with one or more of the public-journalism techniques covered in the chapter. In the second you should use some convergence techniques.

## For Practice

19-1. Run your regular beat and find the best topic for a story. Then, do the following:

a) Try to incorporate into your newsgathering some of the following public journalism techniques mentioned earlier:
   * Ask sources what questions *they* would like answered in your story.
   * Seek sources for your stories that you have not usually interviewed, offering new voices the chance to be heard.
   * Let people tell more of their own stories, either as part of your story or as sidebars to run with your story.
   * Prepare and distribute a survey of students, seeking their responses concerning the topic of your story.
b) Write a story using lead and development most appropriate for the topic and your audience, and be sure to feature your public-journalism materials.
c) Swap stories and your additional public-journalism materials with a peer review partner or group and give written reader feedback
d) Submit the draft, materials and peer feedback to your teacher.
e) After your teacher has reviewed your draft and peer feedback and has offered additional suggestions, revise as required.
f) Submit a final draft to your teacher.

19-2. Run your regular beat and find the best topic for a story. Then, do the following:

a) Write a story using lead and development most appropriate for the topic and your audience.
b) Develop some of the following convergence components mentioned earlier:
   * Put your story online and try to have it linked from other existing sites.
   * Prepare an interactive online component to your story, such as a clickable map, a message board or a live chat with one or more key sources. Include the information and links with your print story. If you have a Web version, provide links there.
   * Either shoot some appropriate supporting video or have someone shoot it for you. Have it edited and digitized, then put it online and link it to your Web story.
   * Audiotape key sources in your story, wherein you capture key comments and explanations. Have it edited and digitized, then put it online and link it to your Web story.
   * If you have broadcast outlets on campus, work with their editors to share your story, perhaps by agreeing to tell about the story in a Q-and-A format with a student who already works there.
c) Swap stories and your additional convergence activities or materials with a peer review partner or group and give written reader feedback
d) Submit the draft, materials and peer feedback to your teacher.

e) After your teacher has reviewed your draft and peer feedback and has offered additional suggestions, revise as required.

f) Submit a final draft to your teacher.

## Chapter 19 Bibliography

Blakeslee, Betsey. "Integrating News Across Radio, Television, Internet and Newspaper." 2002. Paper presented at the *Annual Convention of the Association for Education in Journalism and Mass Communication*, Miami Beach, Fla.

Carter III, Hodding. "On Journalism: Is Civic Journalism an Answer?" *American Society of Newspaper Editors*. 1 December 1998. <http://www.asne.org/index.cfm?id=1320>.

Chappell, Steve, and Laura Widmer. "Enhancing Traditional Student Media with New Media Techniques." 2002. Paper presented at the *Annual Convention of the Association for Education in Journalism and Mass Communication*, Miami Beach, Fla.

Crosbie, Vin. "After the Web: Pervasive Portable Media." *American Press Institute*. 1 February 2002. <http://americanpressinstitute.org/content/p1527_c979.cfm>.

Dillon, Mike. "Present Tense, Past Tense: The Historical and Philosophical Roots of Civic Journalism." <http://www.pewcenter.org/doingcj/speeches/a_dillon.html>.

Friedland, Lewis A., and Sandy Nichols. "Measuring Civic Journalism's Progress: A Report Across a Decade of Activity." *Pew Center for Civic Journalism*. September 2002. <http://www.pewcenter.org/doingcj/research/r_measuringcj.html>.

Geimann, Steve. "Task Force on the Professions in the New Millennium." Columbia, S.C.: Association for Education in Journalism and Mass Communication, 2000.

Gorney, Cynthia. "Superhire 2000." *American Journalism Review*. December 2000. <http://www.ajr.org/article.asp?id=386>.

Greenwald, Marilyn. "Considering 10 Years of Public Journalism." *American Society of Newspaper Editors*. 12 June 2002. <http://www.asne.org/index.cfm?id=3603>.

Heyboer, Kelly. "Going Live." *American Journalism Review*. January/February 2000. <http://www.ajr.org/article.asp?id=408>.

Lasica, J. D. "News on the Go: The Coming Mobile Revolution Will Require Newsrooms to Undergo a Sea Change in Strategic Thinking." *Online Journalism Review*. 3 April 2002. <http://www.ojr.org/ojr/future/1017876499.php>.

McFarlin, Diane H. "What We Mean When We Speak of Convergence." *American Society of Newspaper Editors*. 15 July 2002. <http://www.asne.org/index.cfm?id=3681>.

Morton, John. "The Emergence of Convergence." *American Journalism Review*. January/February 2000. <http://www.ajr.org/article.asp?id=620>.

Oppel, Richard. "On Public Journalism: Three Steps to Improve Public Journalism." *American Society of Newspaper Editors*. 26 May 1999. <http://www.asne.org/kiosk/editor/97.jan-feb/oppel1.htm>.

Outing, Steve. "USC J-School to Teach Convergence to All: It's a Long Overdue Change in Journalism Education." *Editor and Publisher*. 27 March 2002. <http://www.editorandpublisher.com/editorandpublisher/features_columns/article_display.jsp?vnu_content_id=1448331>.

Rosen, Jay. "Theoretical Foundations: Public Journalism as a Democratic Art." *International Media and Democracy Project*. 17 July 2002. <http://www.imdp.org/artman/publish/article_23.shtml#top>.

Sandeen, Rod. "A Look at Media Convergence: How Much Multimedia Should Students Learn?" *American Society of Newspaper Editors*. 6 April 2000. <http://www.asne.org/kiosk/editor/00.march/sandeen1.htm>.

Schaffer, Jan. "Building Zones of Connectivity." 8 August 2002. <http://www.pewcenter.org/doingcj/speeches/s_aejmczones.html>.

Schaffer, Jan. "Civic Journalism: 10 Tips for Rebuilding Frameworks of Society." *American Press Institute*. 19 September 2001. <http://americanpressinstitute.org/content/415.cfm>. (With special thanks to the Pew Center for Civic Journalism, <http://www.pewcenter.org/>.)

Shepard, Alicia C. "Tribune's Big Deal." *American Journalism Review*. May 2000. <http://www.ajr.org/article.asp?id=533>.

Skene, Neil. "The Changing Culture of the Newsroom." *American Society of Newspaper Editors*. 10 March 2000. <http://www.asne.org/index.cfm?id=3268>.

Smith, Steve. "Civic Newsrooms: Building New Reflexes." *Pew Center for Civic Journalism. Civic Catalyst Newsletter*. Summer 2002. <http://www.pewcenter.org/doingcj/civiccat/displayCivcat.php?id=353>.

Thelen, Gil. "Convergence." *American Society of Newspaper Editors*. 18 August 2000. <http://www.asne.org/kiosk/editor/00.july/thelen1.htm>.

Twain, Mark. "How I Edited an Agricultural Newspaper." *Mark Twain: Collected Tales, Sketches, Speeches, & Essays, 1852–1890* (1992). *The Columbia World of Quotations*. Ed. Robert Andrews, Mary Biggs, and Michael Seidel. New York: Columbia University Press, 1996. <http://www.bartleby.com/66/8/62208.html>.

Wendland, Mike. "Convergence: Repurposing Journalism." *Poynteronline*. 18 December 2002. <http://www.poynter.org/content/content_view.asp?id=14558>.

# Index